GOD, MAN
AND
CHURCH GROWTH

Contributors to this volume

Bishop J. Waskom Pickett, of the United Methodist Church, Donald McGavran's colleague of his Indian days, now retired,

Colleagues of the Faculty of the Fuller School of World Mission:
Arthur F. Glasser, Dean and Professor of Theology
Ralph D. Winter, Professor of the Historical Development of the Christian Movement
Alan R. Tippett, Professor of Missionary Anthropology (and Editor of this volume)
Charles H. Kraft, Associate Professor of Missionary Anthropology
C. Peter Wagner, Associate Professor of Latin American Affairs
Roy E. Shearer, Psychologist, Teaching Associate
J. Edwin Orr, Evangelist and Historian, Spring Quarter Lecturer

Visiting Professors and Lecturers who have served at the School of World Mission:
David B. Barrett, Research Secretary, Anglican Consultative Council, Nairobi, Kenya
J.B. Kessler, Netherlands Bible Institute, Doorn
Cal Guy, Professor of Missions, Southwestern Baptist Theological Seminary, Fort Worth
J.T. Seamands, Professor of Missions, Asbury Theological Seminary, Wilmore, Kentucky
J.T. Shepherd, Education Secretary, Christian & Missionary Alliance
William R. Read, Technical Manager, Brazil Project, MARC
Edward Dayton, Director, MARC

Graduates of the School of World Mission:
Lloyd Kwast, Professor of Missions, Biola College, La Mirada
Alan Gates, Conservative Baptist Seminary, Taichung, Taiwan
Tetsunao Yamamori, Professor of Human Relations, Milligan College
Charles Bennett, Director of Research, Missionary Aviation Fellowship
David Liao, Field Director for Taiwan, Overseas Crusades
Edward Murphy, Latin America Area Secretary, Overseas Crusades
Joel Romero, Conservative Baptist Missionary to Argentina
Gunnar Kjaerland, Field Superintendent Norwegian Lutheran Mission in Ethiopia
James Sauder, Mennonite Missionary to Honduras
Stan Shewmaker, Missionary to Zambia, Church of Christ
Erwin Spruth, Missionary to New Guinea, Lutheran Church-Missouri Synod

Edited By
A. R. Tippett

GOD, MAN
AND
CHURCH GROWTH

A FESTSCHRIFT IN HONOR OF DONALD ANDERSON MC GAVRAN

WM. B. EERDMANS
PUBLISHING CO.

255 JEFFERSON AVE. S.E., GRAND RAPIDS, MICH. 49502

PRINTED IN THE UNITED STATES OF AMERICA

CONTENTS

Greeting   vii
Foreword   ix
Preface   xi

PART I: Donald Anderson McGavran: Three Portraits   1

1. Donald A. McGavran: Missionary, Scholar, Ecumenist,
   Evangelist — J. Waskom Pickett   5
2. The Orient Awaits An Optimistic Missiology — David
   C.E. Liao   14
3. Portrait of a Missiologist By His Colleague — Editor   19
4. Bibliography of Donald Anderson McGavran   43

PART II: God's Purpose and Man's Responsibility   49

5. Church Growth and Theology — Arthur F. Glasser   52
6. Continuity and Change in Christian Mission — Jack F.
   Shepherd   70
7. The Role of the Holy Spirit in Church Growth — John
   T. Seamands   95
8. Toward a Christian Ethnotheology — Charles H. Kraft   109
9. Perfection Growth — Alan Gates   128

47417

v

PART III: God's Work in Human Structures   143

10. Pragmatic Strategy for Tomorrow's Mission — C. Peter
    Wagner   146
11. The Psychology of Receptivity and Church Growth —
    Roy E. Shearer   160
12. Cultural Compulsives — Alan R. Tippett   167
13. Church Growth as Modernization — William R. Read   188
14. Home Attitudes, Administrators and Field Reflections —
    Cal Guy   200
15. New Approaches to Mission (Tonga, Zambia) — Stan
    Shewmaker   216
16. Church Planters and Ethnolinguistics — Charles H. Kraft   226

PART IV: God in Human History   253

17. Christian History in Cross-Cultural Perspective — Ralph
    D. Winter   256
18. Evangelical Dynamic and Social Action — J. Edwin Orr   273
19. Digging for the Facts (Latin America) — J.B.A. Kessler   282
20. Ethnohistorical Research in West Cameroon — Lloyd
    Kwast   295

PART V: God and Man in Field Situations   311

21. Psychological Dimensions of Church Growth (Honduras)
    — James Sauder   314
22. The Key Personality in a People Movement (Colombia)
    — Ed Murphy   328
23. Taking Stock of an Ethnic Unit for Church Planting
    (New Guinea) — Erwin Spruth   342
24. Communicating the Gospel to Illiterate Nomads
    (Ethiopia) — Gunnar Kjaerland   356
25. Symbolism and Syncretism (Argentina) — Joel Romero   366

PART VI: Research Techniques for the Work of God   377

26. Applying the Comparative Method to Church Studies
    (Japan) — Tetsunao Yamamori   380
27. The Discipling of Africa in This Generation — David B.
    Barrett   396
28. Disciplined Planning and Data Retrieval — Edward R.
    Dayton   417
29. Aviation and Mission — Charles Bennett   430

CONCLUSION: Where Do We Go From Here? — Editor   441

GREETING

To Dr. Donald Anderson McGavran:

This is a *Festschrift.* We honor you, Donald McGavran, missiologist, on the occasion of your 75th birthday. The contributors to this volume are persons who, at some time or other, have either been your associates (I remember you call them "missionary associates" rather than students) or your professional colleagues. The question of who the contributors were to be was the first problem of the editorial process. Over a hundred case studies and degree theses in missiology have been produced at the School of World Mission at the Fuller Theological Seminary since 1965, and nearly half that number of printed books—all reflecting the influence of your ideas. Many of your colleagues are frequent writers for technological and missiological journals. Here was an embarrassment of riches.

As editor, I had to decide between three options. Were the contributors to produce a scholarly volume which might become a text book for a graduate course in missiology, or a popular volume for re-educating the home Church in the basics of Christian mission for the new day, or a representative volume presenting an expansion of as many of your insights as possible in all their variety and potential? This required a specific decision before the contributors could be approached. We had the people and the skills to produce any of the three and each is needed.

Ultimately I came to the conclusion, in consultation with a few of my colleagues, that as the volume was a *Festschrift* it should be representative. It ought to reflect the kind of subject that deeply concerns you as the man we desire to honor; it ought to indicate a representative cross-section of the people with whom you have worked (faculty, colleagues, conference and seminar associates, and your graduates— both missionary and national); and it ought to stand on a base of the full range of your own teaching and writing, but point forward to the future, demonstrating where your insights would appear to have us go in Christian mission.

With this in mind, then, and with the blessing of Dr. David Hubbard the Seminary President, I set out to produce something as typical as possible to the regular encounters of your working day at the Seminary. To perpetuate such a memory—it seemed to me—was as sincere and appropriate a birthday gift as we could give you. No-one but yourself can really judge whether or not this *Festschrift* succeeds in being exactly what it is meant to be—not a textbook, not a mission manual, but a memory of a working day, the seminars, the personal contacts, the intellectual encounters and our mutual conviction of the validity of the Christian mission in our day and until He come.

This reminder we give to you, Dr. McGavran, as a keepsake with our congratulations on your 75th birthday. The gift comes not only from the contributors but also from all those scores of others whom they represent and who might well have been asked to contribute. Please receive this gift with our deepest appreciation of your insights and enthusiasm, which have inspired us to go forward with new perspectives in mission.

For and on behalf of all who have worked with you and under you at Eugene and Pasadena, December 1972

A. R. Tippett, Editor

FOREWORD

To commend a book on Church Growth which is being offered by his students and colleagues to Donald McGavran is gilding the lily. The topic is central to the concern of the Church today, and the essays are compelling — none of these authors would dare give less than his best to his friend and mentor.

My reason for adding these few words is selfish. I want to join the editor and authors in tribute to a man who for nearly forty years now has made a singular contribution to the life and growth of Christ's Church world-wide. For most of this time a good share of the debate on mission strategy has dealt with the pros and cons of McGavran's work. He has been lauded, and he has been blasted. But he has not been ignored.

Nor could he have been. His concerns are too pivotal, his arguments too cogent, his foundation is too biblical, his passion is too fervent, his ministry is too fruitful to brook ignoring. His influence, like a stone dropped in a placid pond, has, through these years, moved out in circles that touch the furthest shores.

More than sixty books have been published by his students as witnesses to his zeal and wisdom; his students number in the hundreds and have come from half the countries of the world; the *Church Growth Bulletin,* with its circulation in the thousands, brings his bright and busy pen into the homes and offices of administrators, missionaries, scholars. His counsel is in constant demand in private conversation and public consultation, as church and mission leaders beat a path to his door or welcome him to theirs.

The diversity of topics in the book is itself high tribute to the sweeping range of his interests. Their focus on Church Growth is fitting recognition of the single-mindedness of his mission.

And Dr. McGavran will not be displeased with the exploratory nature of many of the essays. For decades he has set a pace in pioneering; he rejoices when others do the same.

I welcome this book and commend it. Not just because it is an outgrowth of the ministry of Fuller Theological Seminary, and its School of World Mission, where McGavran has served these past eight years, and not just because it salutes the half-century of ministry of an esteemed friend and loyal colleague. I welcome and commend it because it will contribute to the health, growth, and vitality of the Church of Jesus Christ in what must be history's greatest century of mission.

David Allan Hubbard
Fuller Theological Seminary
Pasadena, California

PREFACE

The title, *God, Man and Church Growth,* seems an appropriate one for a *Festschrift* honoring Dr. Donald McGavran. Much of his life, ministry, and literary work has been concerned with bringing alienated man back to God by way of a process of church growth. From the Bible he has come to see this as God's method. The planting of churches—that is, congregations or fellowships in the Lord—and the incorporation of converts from the world for their nurture and then further witness and service. This is how he interprets the Great Commission—discipling and perfecting (teaching all things I have commanded).

After the biographical section, for the benefit of readers who are interested in the man, McGavran, the book falls into five parts. These are intended to bring out the aspects of church growth McGavran recognized and emphasized. Not that he has said church growth comprises five parts, or that he has given equal weightage to them (because at some points he depended on his colleagues) but the program of the institution he founded at the Fuller Theological Seminary in Pasadena, its curriculum and seminars, recognized these specific aspects of missiology—the theology of mission, the theory of mission, the history of the expansion of the Church, case studies in church growth (including obstruction to growth) and research methods.

Many of McGavran's critics have taken one book, which happens to have a single theme, as the basis of their attack on the whole McGavran. Nothing could be more unfair. Therefore it has seemed good to the editor of this *Festschrift* to so structure it that it reflects the regular operational frame of reference of the School of World Mission and Institute of Church Growth (S. W. M.-I. C. G.) which McGavran founded.

Every essay in this volume has been suggested or anticipated in some way in the writings and teachings of Donald McGavran, although sometimes he has only called attention to the matter as an aspect which ought to be developed. In the very considerable editorial correspondence I have insisted that each writer be himself. They have been free to discuss his ideas at length or to use him merely as a starting point, to criticise or develop. In this way one hopes that the total collection of essays will indicate the course that church growth research and theory may be expected to take during the remainder of the seventies. This should disillusion anyone who imagines that church growth is a spent force.

For a decade or so now McGavran's church growth theory has been exposed to friendly and hostile critics. It has passed through a phase of re-formulation and expansion, but the basics have held firm. All the contributors to this volume have been involved somewhere in this process, but there are two or three hundred others who might well have been included, and no doubt there are dimensions which the editor overlooked.

Our thanks are due to other publishers—the Abingdon Press, Fortress Press, Dominion Press, Harper & Row, Collins' Fontana Books, and the International Review of Missions—for the use of material in addition to that in Eerdmans' books. This present book uses the anthropological reference system, and bibliographies are at the end of each article. Donald McGavran's own bibliography is found on pages 43-46. I hope this will be useful to any student who wants to make a deeper study of his missiology.

Pasadena, 1972.

Part I

Donald Anderson McGavran:

Three Portraits

DONALD ANDERSON McGAVRAN

DONALD ANDERSON McGAVRAN

Three items are included in the biographical section of the book because three things seemed essential. McGavran's roots are so embedded in India that someone who had worked with him in that country had to be invited to contribute. Who knows the story of how Donald McGavran became a church growth man better than Bishop J. Waskom Pickett? He tells how he discovered McGavran in the Mid-India Provincial Christian Council investigations on 'mass movements,' of how McGavran's review of his own Christian Mass Movements in India brought them together as researchers in a common theme. He tells of John R. Mott's help in their program. When McGavran put together the report of their joint activities Mott supplied the foreword, pointing out that the book spoke to mission fields much wider than India. Bishop Pickett's article also describes some of the precise problems of India, where McGavran's church growth ideas first developed.

McGavran's studies have reached out from India throughout Asia—the Philippines, Japan, Taiwan. It seemed right therefore to include some comment on McGavran's approaches from the national from South or East Asia. David Liao has chosen to call his contribution "The Orient Awaits an Optimistic Missiology." This is a brief account of what McGavran has meant to him and what he thinks McGavran's message means to the Orient. With so much pessimistic theology coming from certain missionaries who have served in Asia, it is good to have a national saying the opposite.

The third study demands a survey of McGavran's thought as it has developed in the research period since he left India; the organization of his Institute of Church Growth at Eugene, Oregon and how it served as a model for the graduate school of mission now at Pasadena; and the gathering of the present faculty. The School of World Mission and Institute of Church Growth has a concrete entity. If McGavran is still, in a sense, the prophet, he does not stand alone. To dispose of the church growth viewpoint the critic has to dispose of a fairly well-integrated team of men. At many points McGavran depends on them. In anthropology, primitive religion, research techniques, extension training and other dimensions they reinforce his basic ideas. So many of the attacks on church growth have been petty and personal; but McGavran 'short-circuited' this by creating an institution, with a faculty at hand, and hundreds of alumni all over the world. The third essay, "Portrait of a Missiologist by a Colleague" attempts to depict McGavran as a thinker and activist in this process.

As regards his missionary role McGavran says, "Being a missionary is a continuous process. God has had a series of projects for me. As one chapter closes another opens." Clear goals have always characterized his life. . .

Donald H. Gill "Apostle of Church Growth: Disciples of Donald McGavran Roam the World in Search of Facts" WORLD VISION MAGAZINE, September, 1968

1

DONALD A. McGAVRAN:
MISSIONARY, SCHOLAR,
ECUMENIST, EVANGELIST

J. Waskom Pickett

My admiration for Donald McGavran began during my earliest contacts with him. The occasions that brought us together were Missionary Conferences, school functions and community gatherings in that Mecca of Missionaries, Landour, Mussoorie, a delightful, easily accessible summer resort in North India. The time was the middle 1920s. Many needs combined then to draw missionaries from different Churches, Societies and lands of origin to summer resorts in the Himalayas. Among these were vacations, respite from the extreme heat of their stations on the Plains of India during May, June and July, visits with their children who were there in boarding schools for nine months of each year, and need to exchange understandings, concerns, hopes and fears with people of like motivation and purpose who were then, or at some time had been, dealing with more or less comparable undertakings and problems.

Few missionaries spent more than a month there in any year but a succession of Conferences, and school and community gatherings insured valuable opportunities for all visitors throughout those three months.

The Pickett and McGavran periods in Landour often coincided, and I heard Donald make valuable contributions to many discussions. He always seemed to be extraordinarily well-informed and wholly committed to his calling and to his Lord. Like many others I made note of his exceptional interest in the social organization, beliefs and customs of people whom he was trying to serve. Also I realized that he knew, as few did, the facts about every phase of the work of his Church and Mission for the people in the area in which he lived and worked. While appreciating what his seniors, including his parents and an uncle, had attempted, and to some extent had accomplished, he warmed my heart by his eagerness to study afresh all parts of their program, including the principles and assumptions on which each part was based.

Acting on advice given to me by the great missionary statesman, John R. Mott, I had determined to challenge every assumption that I could recognize as underlying the work of my Church in India, not to prove any of them wrong, but to find out, if I could, whether they seemed to be right or wrong as indicated by their results. Dr. McGavran seemed to be doing the same thing in his Mission. In that process I had already reached conclusions that made me reject a number of my initial opinions and accept a number of procedures that I had, at first, regarded with disfavor.

In 1928 I was asked by the National Christian Council of India, Burma and Ceylon to make an extensive, penetrating and objective study of Christian mass movements in India. Under the guidance of Dr. Mott I conferred in New York City with the Institute of Social and Religious Research that was being financed as a subsidiary of the Rockefeller Foundation. The Institute, under the prestigious Dr. Galen Fisher, decided that the study was practical, and if wisely conducted, might prove to be of value to the Church, and through it to large populations, not only in India, but also in other countries. Thus encouraged, I applied to the Institute for a grant that I and my advisors, accustomed to the constant poverty of Missions in India, thought would be adequate.

The Institute thought differently and made further consideration of the application contingent upon the preparation of a revised plan calling for at least twice as much money, and for successful defense of the plan. At length the Institute approved the plan and promised the entire amount for which we asked subject to two conditions—(1) that $10,000 from some other source be obtained, and (2) that in addition to the staff to be recruited in India from Churches, Missions and Universities, a counselor be nominated by the Institute and accepted by the director of the study and by officers of the National Christian Council. An anonymous donor, on Dr. Mott's solicitation, immediately provided the additional money, and agreement on the Institute's nominee as counselor was quickly reached.

Ten representative areas of mass movement activity were chosen for intensive study. They represented eight missions and nine Churches. Instruments of research had to be invented. This required many discussions and much testing. Three and a half years after the study got under way, my book *Christian Mass Movements in India* was completed and published simultaneously in India and the U.S.A.

One of the early reviews brought to my attention was written by Dr. McGavran. He wrote with an enthusiasm traditionally associated with new converts. He certainly had not previously been known as a participant or even as a believer in religious movements then called by such diverse names as mass movements, community movements and group conversions. Other prominent churchmen, ministerial and lay, in India, the U.S.A., Great Britain, Continental Europe and elsewhere were generous in their appreciation of the book. Mission Board executives, university and seminary professors, including sociologists, economists and church historians welcomed the book, commended it heartily and urged supplementary studies. An early feature was an order from one of the Roman Catholic leaders in India for two hundred copies, for study by members of the hierarchy. Strong endorsements from other Roman Catholic leaders soon followed. At a meeting for which tickets were sold in advance, the then Archbishop of Canterbury, Dr. Lang, presided over an audience of seven thousand in the Methodist City Chapel in London. The Archbishop and two eminent Free Church ministers spoke eloquently about the book and advised that it be studied thoroughly. Big interdenominational meetings were held in the Episcopal Cathedral in Boston and in the Marble Collegiate Church in New York City to receive reports on the study. The British Broadcasting Corporation and American Radio Stations gave generously to publicizing the reports.

The National Christian Council and a number of Regional Christian Councils in India offered specific advice on issues, problems and situations that they wanted to have studied. Six supplemental studies were made and two other books were produced. Reports on four areas studied were submitted to the Churches, Missions and Mission Boards most directly concerned, but were not published. Dr. McGavran participated helpfully in the supplementary study of the Sudra Movement into Christian Churches of Andhra Pradesh with public confession of Christian faith and baptism. All of us sharing in that study became excited over the evidence that grew day by day that these new converts from among the Sudras were not being brought to Christ by missionaries from abroad, or by Indian Christians of the Upper Classes, or chiefly by pastors, but by lay converts from the formerly despised Harijans, or Untouchables.

Dr. McGavran then became the chief architect of the plan for a study of Christian Missions in Madhya Pradesh. Dr. John R. Mott, in a foreword for a book that grew out of that study, wrote as follows, "The distinctive and important contribution of this most instructive, stimulating and reassuring book has been that of setting forth with clarity and frankness why the work of so many churches and mission stations has been so comparatively sterile, and why in other cases their labors have been attended with wonderful fruitfulness." Dr. McGarvran wrote the following words that appear in that book before Dr. Mott's foreword—"Dedicated to those men and women who labor for the growth of the Churches, discarding theories of church growth which do not work, and learning and practicing productive patterns which actually disciple the peoples and increase the Household of God." Three editions of that book have been published. In the third edition some revisions and an additional chapter were incorporated. The first and second editions were entitled, Christian Missions in Mid-India. The third edition, broadened and enriched by a chapter by Dr. A. L. Warnshuis, Secretary of the International Missionary Council, is called *Church Growth and Group Conversion.* The additional chapter forcefully and convincingly presents the fact that group conversions have been frequent, normal and solid throughout church history.

Dr. McGavran's participation in the studies of Sudra Conversions in Andhra Desh and of Christian Missions in Madhya Pradesh produced values that are reflected in the ever lengthening series of scholarly, perceptive and productive studies conducted by him, or with his guidance, under the auspices of The Institute of Church Growth. He would object to what I nevertheless think it right for me to say, that so far as I can see, the Institute could not have been established without the scholarship, persistence, executive ability and devotion that are among the rich personality characteristics of this great man. A puzzling feature of church history every generation is that so little attention has been given to the emphasis that Jesus placed upon loving God with the mind. The command "Thou shalt love the Lord thy God with all thy mind" is in sharp contrast to the position against study that many have taken. The mere suggestion that God wants His people to study church growth is sometimes resented. When the study of Christian mass movements in India was first proposed, one of the most respected and successful missionaries then at work in India protested vigorously. In the course of a letter to me he wrote, "I and my colleagues are tired of being told what to do and how to do it. If you have money to spend on such a study I suggest that you pass it on to people who already know how to bring others to Christ but do not have sufficient money to finance their work." However, when the first stage of that study had been completed and he had read the findings and recommendations, this beloved brother expressed his delight and asked that a supplemental study be conducted in his Mission. When that study was undertaken he cooperated most helpfully with results of large value in the area of his work, and in other parts of India and other countries.

Again it is disturbing to read book after book about modern missions without finding so much as a hint about either what helped or what hindered church growth. In many

books the author seems eager to prove that the missionaries
have done everything according to God's leading and that if
no church has come into being it means only that God's time
for saving souls has not come: "The disciples' duty is to
sow the seed and leave it to God to produce." How different
this is from the command of Jesus, "Make disciples of the
nations!"

The first major discovery in the supplementary study
in the above mentioned field was conclusive evidence that
group conversions in that area, followed by faithful pastoral
care had produced radical behavior and character change,
as in many other areas. Groups of Hindus whose ancestors
had accepted and passed on to them the belief that their
Outcaste or Untouchable neighbors should be denied access
to schools and temples now accepted these converts to
Christ as friends and colleagues. Indeed many former
Hindus and a few Moslems had accepted men from these
groups as ministers of the Gospel and their spiritual advisors. Hundreds of Sudras, who as landowners, were men
and women of influence, had been converted and were
zealously urging their relatives and neighbors to accept
Jesus Christ as Lord and Savior. Other hundreds who had
not declared their faith nor sought admission to the Church
were regularly attending church services, and many others
sought opportunity to tell us that these Christians had been
changed in a year or two, and a few even within months
from being "very bad" into being "wonderfully good." A
common remark was "We keep thinking that if Christ can
do such wonders for those people He can do as much and
more for us." And more remarkable yet, perhaps, was the
finding that Moslems too were being influenced to join with
Hindu neighbors in accepting Christ and the ministry of
Christians who came from these Outcaste groups.

But the study revealed weaknesses and failures as
clearly as strength and success. And possibly the finding
of one grave failure may have accomplished more good
than did the discovery of a dozen successes. The failure came from losing hope of success in an early attempt
to persuade Christian converts to abandon ancient marriage
customs and substitute customs that Christians in other
parts of India had adopted. The old marriage custom
was for parents and their caste associates to select

husbands for their daughters, and wives for their sons. Like all other groups in their villages, the sooner a binding marriage arrangement was made and formally ratified in a religious ceremony the better it was thought to be, not only for the young people but for the parents and the two participating families. For in Caste-ruled India a marriage unites the families of the bride and groom far more than in Western countries. The result is that when groups turn from polytheistic Hinduism, with its recurring use of idols, to Christ, they do not easily substitute Christian marriage customs for those that prevailed in the groups to which they were accustomed. When people act singly in giving up Hinduism for Christianity they much more easily substitute the mores of their new fellow Christians than they do when they come in a group. But they lose much of their potential Christian influence.

In this Mission early attempts to introduce Church-approved rules and ceremonies failed, especially because of church opposition to child marriage. The new converts believed that in conditions prevailing in their villages the unmarried girl could not be protected from lustful men, so they persisted in refusing to postpone the marriage of their daughters beyond their tenth, or at most, their twelfth year. The able and most beloved mission super-intendent concluded that he and the Church had to choose between allowing the old idolatrous Hindu custom of child-marriage, conducted and blessed by Hindu priests, and introducing a non-idolatrous ceremony solemnized by or-dained or licensed Christian pastors. He and his as-sociates, for understandable reasons made the latter choice. Their mistake lay in their too quick surrender to despair. Two other major Churches dealing with the same problem on a wider scale, persisted in opposing child-marriage and demanding a minimum age of sixteen for both bride and groom, and were so successful that our studies in their areas showed that members of their Churches had almost completely abandoned the age-old custom of child-marriage and that there were in many of their village congregations unmarried girls of seventeen, eighteen and older. The Superintendent and other minis-ters and leading laymen could not believe us when we told them what we had learned. They had to visit the other areas before they had the courage to change their rules and to insist on a minimum age for marriageable girls.

A veteran missionary, asked what he would do differently if he could start all over on his job as a missionary, reflected the wisdom born of experience and studious observation when he replied, "I would give much more time to studying the people with whom I was to work, and the records, wherever they were available, of those who had preceded me in service, both missionaries from abroad and local people, confident that God tried to lead them each to an understanding of His purposes. And I would seek, day by day, for further guidance from the Heavenly Father."

It seems clear to this writer that the Church through most of its history has been strangely unresponsive to many of the teachings of Jesus, but that now in this twentieth century despite the massive pessimism in which many church members are entangled, the life and activities of the Church are rapidly improving. Today, the Church as a whole is much more Christian than it has been at any time since the first century.

The Church of tomorrow is being, in part, shaped now and I firmly believe that one of the most successful agencies in helping brighten the prospects for more Christian tomorrows is The Institute of Church Growth.

The urgency of church growth is heightened by the fact that the Church now faces a most responsive world. . . . The responsiveness of peoples to the Gospel is sometimes obscured by adjustment to the postcolonial era. . . . Entry has been denied. Missionaries have been sent home. Yet . . . the incontrovertible fact that the number of missionaries working abroad was never larger than it is today is a tremendous testimonial to open doors.

Probably a greater cause for pessimism concerning church growth . . . lies in domestic conditions in Europe and, to a lesser extent, in America. European powers have seen their empires fade away. Public and private worship has declined. The disaster and disruption of two world wars have torn the Church . . . . All these factors have contributed to a feeling that the advance of the Church is no longer a tenable hope for intelligent men . . .

Nevertheless, many lands are responsive, many populations are receptive . . . . More winnable people live in the world today than ever before.

UNDERSTANDING CHURCH GROWTH
pp. 56, 57, 58

2

THE ORIENT AWAITS
AN OPTIMISTIC MISSIOLOGY

David C. E. Liao

No one can work with Dr. McGavran very long without being influenced by his passion and optimism for church growth and learning to suspect non-growth and talk of resistant situations. At least he teaches one to apply critical testing to such claims.

The first change in my church growth thinking came when after studying under him for a while, I began to doubt the "spirituality" of a non-growing church in Taiwan whose members are proud of their spiritual attainment and their principle of stressing "quality and not quantity," an unfair cliche often used by church growth critics who are self-defensive and not prepared to face up to the facts of statistical non-growth. Before long I concluded that my Taiwanese 'perfectionists' are not as spiritual as they think they are, because in spite of their appearance of religion, they have not obeyed the Great Commision of Christ, and have not followed the heart of the loving God "who will have all men to be saved" (I Tim.2:4). God desired quantity as well as quality.

Other churches, desiring growth but failing to attain it, have withdrawn and have become pessimistic. Often, I

14

hear them say, "Hasn't Satan hardened the sinner's heart? "
Hasn't the Lord said that 'straight is the gate, and narrow
is the way, which leadeth unto life, and few there be that
find it'?" Yet this is a dangerous defeatism. Once again
McGavran has caused me to see the fallacy of this kind of
reasoning. Time after time he pointed to this group or that
group which did grow under the same circumstances as the
non-growing community. I came to see that non-growth is
largely due to inadequate approach and strategy rather
than to hardness of heart.

McGavran was also the first one to arouse my interest
in the Hakka people as an ethnic entity, when he expressed
to me his doubt about the alleged resistance to the Gospel
of this peculiar branch of Chinese. This led me into a
special research study, under his mentorship, of the Hakka
people and Hakka Church in Taiwan. That study has fully
convinced me that the Hakka people, as well as many other
so-called resistant groups, are readily winnable, if only
the correct approach be used.

McGavran's approach to the analysis of such cohesive
ethnic units has led to his systemization of church growth
principles, both the positive (growth) and negative (obstruction to growth) principles. They have helped me very much
to understand why there is such a wide diversity of
growth and non-growth among the indigenous churches of
the Orient.

One of these principles is the necessity of developing
church leaders on all levels, especially the local lay
leaders. The fastest growing groups in Taiwan provide a
perfect illustration of this point. Two quite indigenous
Churches have a strong lay leadership upon which to build
the life of the local churches. Their thriving congregations present a vivid contrast to the many tiny struggling
groups of believers pastored by inadequately salaried young
ministers in some of the more widely known denominational,
overseas-supported missions. These static churches, I
believe have a tremendous potential to grow in these days
of spiritual emptiness, if they would only launch out in bold
plans to train qualified lay leaders at the grass-roots level,
and accept them as the mainstay of their church life.

McGavran's thesis that the Gospel is transmitted most
naturally within a homogenous ethnic unit is abundantly

illustrated in the Orient. His people-movement point of
view aptly summarizes how God has used sociocultural
structures and ties to achieve His purpose. One day as I
pondered the fact that the multi-individual way of decision-
making has always been the traditional way of the Oriental
people, it suddenly dawned on me that McGavran is not
trying to promote anything new, but simply seeking to
prevent the individualistic approach (developed to the extreme in the modern western Christian nations) from inter-
fering with God's own great way of bringing millions to
Himself out of non-Christian societies in Asia and elsewhere in the world.

In the light of this, the common people in the Orient
today present a great challenge to those who are "church-
growth conscious." By far the majority of the present-day
static churches in the Orient exist in the middle class or
have become middle-class orientated. This is the more
acculturated or foreignized segment. These western-styled
churches have not grown well among the common people
who constitute the majority of the population. Many large
homogenous units are sociological "new tribes" in which
no church has been planted, or planting even attempted.
What a tremendous growth we could expect, if we should
follow McGavran's principle to develop a gospel approach
and an indigenous mode of church planting appropriate to
each homogenous unit among the millions of the common
people, both urban and rural, in the Oriental countries.

This is McGavran's optimistic missionary philosophy.
It is set over against the 'perfectionist,' pessimistic, self-
defensive, resignation to non-growth. It dares to believe
that large homogenous units of people are currently winnable,
that the Great Commission still speaks to our day, and will
do so until the end of the age (Matt. 28 : 18-20).

This, I believe to be the most important restatement of
missionary purpose in the Orient today. Certainly God has
used McGavran to impart the vision; it now remains for us
who are in the fields to work out the details with untiring
effort, and expect great things from God!

I speak as a son of the Orient, from a part of the world
which has not been slow to criticize the foreign character
of Christianity as given to us by the missionary organization of the west. But McGavran's missiology is biblical

rather than western and the Bible came out of Asia. This I know, because McGavran's church growth principles have been a tremendous help in my own ministry in Taiwan today.

We stand at the beginning of church growth thinking. The biblical case will not change much; but we are only beginning to see the many ways in which the discipling and perfecting are carried on.

"What is the Church Growth School of Thought?"

3

PORTRAIT OF A MISSIOLOGIST
BY HIS COLLEAGUE

Editor

This article is not intended to be a life story. I never met McGavran face to face until I went to work with him in Oregon. Sometime before I had procured a copy of his Ph. D. dissertation to help understanding the Fiji Indians. I had read and used *Bridges of God,* and was reading *How Churches Grow* on my way to Oregon. In 1961 we had an exchange of correspondence, which sprang from an article I had written. I knew him only by his ideas and reputation and I am certainly not the person to write his biography. For the last decade I have worked with him as a teaching colleague, but in our researches we have gone our own ways. I have learned very little of his private life. When his biography is written the person responsible should be one who knows India well because India still conditions his thinking and behavior, in spite of his world vision.

Yet for this volume someone had to write from close association with him in teaching, research, administration and other experiences, especially those concerning the Institute of Church Growth, and the wide coverage of church growth seminars that have been features of his last ten years. Someone had to be able to relate the Oregon and Fuller periods, and trace the development of church growth approaches. This kind of requirement eliminated most of those we might have considered for this article. I hope that Dr. McGavran will forgive my temerity in attempting to interpret his ideas. I know how I hate people trying to interpret me.

After a very brief, formal and not very informative, precis of his life and achievements before going to Eugene, I propose to discuss what I consider to be the three major conceptual contributions of McGavran to missiology. Of course, one cannot pin him down to three things; but it seems to me that these three things tie together the whole complex of his thought. After that I hope to show what happened at Eugene and what is happening at Fuller. Perhaps between them I shall wedge a unit on McGavran and his Critics.

McGavran is essentially a biblical missiologist. The basic pre-supposition of all his writing and debate is the authority of Scripture and his view of authority is evangelical. This is why a liberal missiologist has difficulty in dealing with McGavran, because they have no common basis for discussion. McGavran's use of Scripture is strongly New Testament. He uses the Old Testament very little, a point in which he differs from several of his colleagues. Most of his arguments begin either with the Great Commission or from Antioch. The precedents of the early Church are his guidelines and he is well-versed in the writings of Paul. A person who does not line up with McGavran on these points will have difficulty debating with him.

The three great conceptual contributions of McGavran to missiology in our day are (1) the notion of the people movement, (2) the notion of evangelistic opportunity, and (3) the differentiation of discipling and perfecting. I shall devote a unit of this essay to each of these but they will be recurring themes in the whole paper. I shall try to deal with them in an historical manner, because McGavran was both giver and receiver. Church growth theory has emerged from missionary symbiosis.

*   *   *

Brief Historical Record to 1960

Donald Anderson McGavran was born of missionary parents in India on December 15, 1897. His grandparents also were missionaries. Educated in America he took his B. A. at Butler University, Indianapolis in 1920, his B.D. at Yale Divinity School, New Haven in 1922, and his M.A. at the College of Missions, Indianapolis in 1923. Ordained as a minister of the Christian Church (Disciples of Christ) he returned to India in 1923 by appointment under the United Christian Missionary Society. His first assignment was as superintendent of the mission school system at Harda. Subsequently he served as Director of Religious Education for the India Mission and as its Secretary-Treasurer. From 1928 he served on the Executive Committee of the India Mission. His missionary experience covered a wide range in hospital administration, education and rural evangelism.

In 1936 he took out his Ph. D. at Columbia University, New York, but continued his missionary service until 1955. He speaks Hindi and Chattisgarhee, and translated the Gospels into the latter. He also produced a sound-and-color motion picture, "Constrained by Love" portraying the missionary life. From about 1954 his society began to use him for intensive surveys of church growth in Asia, Africa and the Islands. In 1957 he became Professor at the College of Missions, on loan to visit various institutions to teach missions. He visited Phillips University, Butler University, Christian Theological Seminary, the Drake University Divinity School, Bethany College, Northwest Christian College and The Pacific School of Religion. He also held seminars in Costa Rica, Mexico and in many parts of the United States mainland.

In 1960 he was called by the Northwest Christian College to found the Institute of Church Growth, which commenced operations in 1961.

The Notion of the People Movement

The Mass Movement Study under the Indian N. C. C. sprang from a realization that between 1929 and 1931 from a sample of 145 mission complexes, 134 had a percentage church growth of less than the population. In the other nine a growth of 200% had been achieved, and this growth was by adult conversions. This had been a continuous subject of McGavran's interest and investigation for forty years. It runs like a red thread through the strands of his writing and research. How do you account for growth and non-growth in identical situations where presumably missionaries have been equally faithful?

Pickett's book *Christian Mass Movements in India* came in 1933. It directed attention to the phenomenon we now call the people movement. John R. Mott said of this book, "It is difficult to overstate the faith-kindling power of this modern apologetic." It was this book which brought McGavran and Pickett together.

Mott, who is best known for his concept of winning the world in this generation, was, with respect to this dream of world evangelization, an antecedent of church growth. He supported the work of both Pickett and McGavran. He made an interesting observation in his "Introduction" to Pickett's book:

> It will be surprising if anthropologists and sociologists do not seize upon the data . . . for light on the modification of ancient folkways under the impact of a powerful new force (1933: 6).

They did not do so because of the stresses on salvage anthropology and cultural relativism and the general mood against missionaries on the part of anthropologists at the time. Yet Mott's insight was right. Such group movements certainly do provide a superb data base for the analysis of culture change as scholars like Emilio Willems have demonstrated.

Pickett did not consider the mass movement as an end in itself but rather as a guide for reshaping policy. He regretted the selection of the term and said so in his first chapter. Years later he told me he felt they made a serious error in using the term at all. He preferred group movements (21).

Subsequently Pickett, McGavran and Singh worked together on further studies and *Christian Missions in Mid-India* appeared in 1936 to be reprinted in 1938. McGavran discussed the term and elected to use people movement. In those days, within the context of Indian movements to

Christ McGavran tied the concept up with ideas of brotherhood and social justice:

> The Christian movement has again entered upon one of
> its great battles with entrenched privilege. One of the
> major campaigns against that subtle and ever-present
> enemy of mankind—race prejudice. . . (1938,1,32).

He was writing of the iniquity of Hindu attitudes to Untouchables. He was looking for an answer to the problem of the
depressed peoples of India. He described 2000 Chamar
village leaders urging their people to change their faith,
and he saw the battle for brotherhood and group movements
to Christ as related issues (1938,2,134-135).

In the following decade McGavran developed his theme.
He studied Mandala and Mehra movements, updated the
little book he had done with Pickett and Singh, adding a
chapter from Warnshuis, and published *Bridges of God,*
in which he moved out beyond India, tracing the idea of
people movements from New Testament times down through
history. In *Bridges of God* McGavran was speaking to world
mission, and the book soon became missionary table talk
in all sorts of places. I read it in the Fiji Islands. Many
missionaries said it was a restatement of Roland Allen, but
McGavran has never admitted this. He had read Allen and
cited him, usually with approval, but he could always point
out differences he had with Allen. Yet we must admit the
idea of the "spontaneous expansion of the Church" was very
similar to that of "Christward people movements," Biblically they both drew from the same wells: both are
thoroughly Pauline. As for myself I drew more from the
Gospels, and certainly more from the Old Testament.

I did not hear the term people movement until about
1956, when I read *Bridges of God.* I had long been looking
for such a term for describing the movements of Tonga
and Fiji. I accepted the term at once but I did not like the
phenomenology of a group mind, a term McGavran used in
his book. Not until early in 1962, when I was studying
"Cultural Dynamics" with Homer Barnett did I have the
opportunity of discussing the ethnopsychology of people
movements. He gave me the term *multi-individual;* which
immediately suited us all, especially those who were 'hung
up' over individual conversion and group movements.
McGavran has made use of the term ever since and has

developed it further in his own way.

Over the years McGavran has gathered all kinds of information about people movements by observation and interview. He sets out his views in *Understanding Church Growth* (1970:296-334). The names of Sunda, Krass, Seamands, Major, Gamaliel and Wold are of men he either interviewed personally or corresponded with. I also believe that the meeting of McGavran, Sunda, and myself and our access to Homer Barnett at Oregon at the precise point of time when we were trying to interpret this phenomena in an evangelical but scientific manner was what Newman called a confluence of history as far as we were concerned. Sunda's fresh and dramatic experience in New Guinea, was something outside of India that deeply impressed McGavran. Both his experiences and his photographs illustrated what I knew of Tonga and Fiji by historical reconstructions. Barnett introduced me to the experiments of Sherif, the social psychologist, and the jig-saw pieces began to fall into place. McGavran now began to see something of the wide range of people movement phenomena, that was not Indian in type. He fell to thinking of the various kinds of people movement and worked out a classification, after his method, on a basis of scriptural types (1970:319ff). He was always more concerned with how the church grew and along what lines it was diffused rather than the precise nature of the phenomena. He left the phenomenology to me—I had a group seminar on it this term at Fuller. It was in Oregon that I gave much thought to this—the conversion process, the significance of the symbolic reference points, the phenomenology of incorporation of converts into the fellowship group and the consummation experience. I wrote this up in 1962 and McGavran had seen it and made his comments. I issued a Research in Progress pamphlet in 1967 to try out some of the ideas with a wider critical audience. *People Movements in Southern Polynesia* (1971) needs to be read beside the chapters of *Understanding Church Growth* (1970) and also Sunda's little book, to see something of the total picture of our interaction in 1962 and 1963.

It is difficult to separate our different contributions—McGavran, Sunda, Barnett and myself—and of course the people movement idea matured by interaction. Over the years, especially at Fuller, many missionaries and nationals had added something. We have now learned so much about them that I firmly believe the history of the expansion of the Church needs to be rewritten in the light of new insights.

The Notion of Lost Opportunities

From as far back as the thirties McGavran was troubled by the tragedy of lost opportunities in evangelism. In those days he was watching the turn of events with respect to Dr. Ambedkar and his followers and pointed out in 1938 to the missionary world that a huge movement out of Hinduism was surely about to occur. Would it be into Sikhism, or Islam or Christianity? Eventually it turned out to be Buddhism. Ambedkar had considered Christianity. He was won to it by the New Testament but lost by Christian failure to demonstrate it. McGavran's insight about an imminent religious movement was quite sound. Pickett later discussed Ambedkar's decision in Christ's Way to India's Heart in terms of factors of church growth and obstruction.

The tragedy of lost opportunities came to me in my historical studies of church planting in the Pacific. For example, among the Fiji Indians in the early period doors had really opened, only to be neglected. The same thing happened in Papua in an area I have documented. In each case the excuse given was the same—"No missionaries available: when one arrives we will send him." In Fiji the door closed never to open again. In Papua the neopagan Taro Cult swept through the area along the route of the very villages which had been asking for instruction. So McGavran was saying what I knew well to be true—that ripe fields must be harvested and not all harvesters are Christian. As time went on we all became convinced that the present period of harvesting had a limited duration. Both McGavran and I have made many statements on this. If the Lord takes our missionary role away from us we will have none but ourselves to blame, for hiding our talent in the earth.

Another point which McGavran and I have in common is the difference between missions a century ago and today: namely, the competitive element. A century ago the choice was between animism and Christianity. Today, to use Barnett's term, there are many advocates. People are changing, whether we like it or not; whether we send missionaries or not. But the Gospel is not the only solution advocated today. The point is repeatedly made by both of us, in different contexts. In an article McGavran wrote for the *Christian Herald* called, "Have we Lost our Way in Missions?" he was discussing how good churchmanship, a fine thing in itself, might nevertheless so occupy our attention that we failed to observe the opportunities for evangelism:

> This might be good missions if we had a thousand years and no competition. But we do not have a thousand years. We possibly have only today—and the tremendous competition. If we do not win responsive people, Communism, Hinduism or Islam will.

Part of McGavran's note of urgency in missions springs from this compex of truth. The world is going through rapid change today. It is alive with opportunities. Theologically expressed—fields are ripe unto harvest, and harvesters should be sent into the harvest. This is God's hour. This urgency underlies much of his writing.

At Oregon I was stimulated in the same direction by studies in social change. There is quite a body of anthropological theory on societies coming ready for change. Yet more than mere social factors might be involved. The church growth of history would demand that God be in the picture. In my writing I have related it to the old Wesleyan doctrine prevenient grace. As Wesley said in his sermon of "The Means of Grace," the Holy Spirit goes before us and opens up the way.

McGavran's stress on opportunities and his distress at the Church's failure to do anything about them recurs in all kinds of settings. He weighs administrations, institutionalism, perfectionism, budgets, personnel distribution and many other things against opportunity for growth. He speaks of winnable people. In the last analysis his case for deployment of funds and personnel to winnable fields has an essentially biblical authority in the words of our Lord himself in Luke 10, a missionary passage.

This is a theology of optimism, of hope, of promise, and a belief in man's stewardship under divine authority. Further back beyond this is a belief in the lostness of man without Christ. What more can be desired for the race of man,

than that he should come to know Christ, and how can this
be achieved, if those who know Him turn from the opportunities to share Him with those who are ready to listen?
Every farmer knows that harvests have to be gathered
in when they are ripe. A crop not harvested at the right
time deteriorates and in time becomes useless. The first
chapter in *How Churches Grow* is called "A Blaze of
Opportunity." It ends:

> Opportunity blazes today, but it may be a brief blaze.
> Certainly conditions which create the opportunity—as
> far as human wisdom can discern—are transient con-
> ditions. We have today. Let us move forward.

Many of the countries that were open for mission when he
wrote that are closed or largely closed today. But scores
of new tribes are open and in 1970 McGavran is still
writing:

> Today's paramount task, opportunity and imperative in
> missions is to multiply churches in the increasing
> numbers of receptive peoples of the earth (63).

qualifying it against the tragedy of lost opportunities: "Millions have set their faces like flint against Christ. . .
Nevertheless many lands are responsive. . ." (57).

The Differentiation of Discipling and Perfecting

McGavran migrated, like all of us, from the life of a
field missionary to missionary research. His own organization (United Christian Missionary Society) had him make
a number of surveys into the state of the mission churches
—Congo, Puerto Rico, the Philippines, Thailand, Formosa,
Gold Coast, Jamaica and among the Yakima Indians. When
I met him first he was preparing material on Mexico.

This period of research surveys helped McGavran to
broaden his Indian perspective and enabled him to relate
his experiences to the wider missionary front. Many of his
ideas were confirmed. Here and there he made adjustments.
At some points he saw more clearly the need for classifying
types of missionary strategy. This is manifest in his important book *How Churches Grow,* which is not a book about
people movements, but, as the sub-title suggests, about
new frontiers in mission. The impact of his experiences in
Puerto Rico and the Philippines in particular are evident

here; but he draws his data from all over the world. In
this book we see McGavran emerging as an apologist,
structuring his material so as to be able to point out the
errors of his critics. Hendrik Kraemer called it "an
excellent and much-needed book" that would "evoke many
new problems."

McGavran did create problems, as Kraemer suggested.
He did so because until his time missionary policy was
extremely confused. His own word was fog. But missiology
owes much to him for sorting out the issues, classifying
the various approaches, and forcing the missionary policy-
makers to confront the precise choices before them. Many
of them did not like it. Missionary vested interests were
threatened. But despite all the hard words, policy-makers
have learned much because of McGavran.

In *Bridges of God* McGavran had made the distinction
between the two forces pressing themselves on the Church
—discipling the nations and perfecting the inner life. In
Church Growth and Group Conversion a book about people
movements, he nevertheless devoted the last chapter to
deepening the life of the young church. McGavran told me
that he was astonished at the opposition he had to the basic
idea of *Bridges of God,* and he wrote *How Churches Grow*
to deal with the opposition without mentioning people movements. Here he sees the Church in a state of imbalance.
Discipling and perfecting must be kept in equilibrium. Both
are essential. But—

> There is a constitutional bias toward perfecting. The
> Churches gravitate toward caring for what they have.
> Their inbuilt nature prefers perfecting (1959: 93).

He discusses how excessive attention to perfecting can lead
to legalism and other things. Perhaps we have here a conviction, born of his observations of an ingrown or enclosed
Church, shutting itself off from the world. Many of our
churches were (or still are) just this. It is the Church's
imbalance that forces him into apparent polarity.

Yet never has he neglected the perfecting of the flock.
In *How Churches Grow* he discusses systems for training
leaders and the organization of an indigenous ministry
(132-143). Leadership training has become an essential
aspect of church planting. Since that book he has developed
this subject further (Cassette Tape: "Five Kinds of
Leaders"). His colleague, Ralph Winter, has specialized

in this area and argues strongly that this qualitative dimension is essentially part of the quantitative growth. McGavran has encouraged Winter to develop this aspect of church growth. He also includes the training of lay leaders in his ideas on post-discipling care (1970 : 286-7, 327).

The distinction between the discipling and perfecting is based on the structure of the Great Commission (1955 14-15) and ramifies through all McGavran's writing. For example, when he distinguishes between what he calls biological growth and conversion from the world, perfecting and discipling are implied. To grow properly a church needs both biological and conversion growth. I remember an American minister telling me that this was the great discovery McGavran had led him to. By this differentiation he saw what was (and what was not) happening in his congregation.

McGavran has also frequently pointed out that for a pagan convert the process of being discipled has to come before the perfecting, although of course in a congregational situation both processes are going on at the same time.

Many of my ideas ran beside those of McGavran, but my terms were different, as was my ecclesiology and missionary life story. McGavran would lecture on Gradualism, say. That is the notion that missionary work has to be such as gradually prepares people for readiness for decision for Christ some day (1959 : 102ff). I used to talk about "civilizing to evangelize." He studied it strategically. I studied it historically (Tippett 1971 : 171-196). This is still another aspect of the idea of the futility of trying to perfect before discipling. We found a great deal of this kind of parallelism and we certainly stimulated each other frequently. I am sure that Sunda, Shearer and Read shared in this.

As far back as 1955, when *Bridges of God* had just come off the press and McGavran was readjusting himself to America, impressed by the revolutionary character of the period of history we were entering at the time, he was optimistic and not unaware of its possibilities. He noted with approval a "social spread of Christian responsibility."

> We are taking a new interest in the social, economic,
> and political problems which stand in the way of the
> full development of human personality . . .

He spoke of learning "to live as neighbors" in a world
"permeated with the Spirit of Christ." He recognized the
"problems of international good-will and justice" and
"world peace" and saw these attitudes as speaking to the
Christian world mission. He even admitted that "the
growth of churches is not the whole story," for Christians
had to explore the problems of human life (1955b : 28-29).
Nevertheless he presented two possible approaches to this
developing situation in the revolutionary world. One he
called the philanthropic view of missions, and against this
he set a biblical or dynamic view (33ff). From his Indian
experience he argued the futility of the former and the
relevance of the latter.

McGavran was not in any way intimidated by the dramatic changes he saw taking place and accelerating. Revolutions, he insisted, demand recognition. They demand
evaluation. They open doors for entry (though these doors
are not always recognized). They call for substantial
reinforcement, maybe short-term missionaries, so that
self-supporting churches could emerge (37-39). Thus,
as early as 1955, he was trying to lead his own denomination away from any possible return to the social gospel.
He sought an active possession of any revolutionary mood
of the post-war period for spiritual ends—namely, a new
humanity in Christ. This was thirteen years before
Uppsala 1968, the intellectual battle of which he foresaw
its dangers and potential. McGavran was facing the age
of revolution, fully aware that great changes were coming,
but confident of the abiding strength of Christ and the continuity of his mission in the world:

> There would be no missions, no Church, no Christian
> World Mission, and no revolutionary age if it were
> not for Christ. He is the Rock on which the waves
> break. He changes them. They do not change him.

This he was saying to the people of his own denomination.
To the larger Christian world also he was calling for new
methods for the new age, for departure from static concepts of mission. He was talking of "a change in climate
like the end of the ice age" (1955c:397).

At the same time we were writing on people movements.
Bridges of God appeared then, and also the third edition
of the little symposium, with an article by Warnshuis on

"Group Conversion" added. The title was changed to *Church Growth and Group Conversion.* McGavran saw both the human and the divine side of "open doors," "Bridges of God" or "fields ripe unto harvest" whichever figure was being used. His methodology, however statistical, was never humanistic. The harvest field always reflected the will of God—ripeness meant God's time for harvesting. Harvesting represented man's responsibility. In the response to opportunity man had to know his resources and know how to use them. "The new methodology" he said "simply attempts to cooperate with God."

> If there are more effective ways in which the Church may be planted, or more efficient methods for inducting those now ready to accept their Saviour into the Church, they should be set forth and adopted. One touchstone, in this growing era now upon us, for every methodology proposed is: does it disciple those whom God has called? The second is: does it promise to lead the churches to a greater century than they have ever known? (1955c: 403).

The new methodology depends on differentiating between discipling and perfecting, and seeing that God is leading us into a period of evangelistic opportunity.

The Institute of Church Growth

The Institute of Church Growth (I. C. G.) was commenced under the sponsorship of the Northwest Christian College, at Eugene, Oregon. We owe a great debt of gratitude to Dr. Ross Griffeth for his cooperation. He believed in McGavran's philosophy of mission and started us off as a research body. The I. C. G. was an essential phase in the emergence of our graduate school of missions at Pasadena. We had the advantage of the courses and facilities at the University of Oregon, its truly wonderful library and most helpful professors. Many of us did courses at the university.

The Northwest Christian College provided a number of church growth fellowships and made possible the publication of some of our research—most notably that of Shearer, Read, Grimley and Robinson. The I. C. G. phase of our history provided us with an experimental workshop,

which enabled us to clarify some of our basic terminology
and to fix the direction and methodology. It lasted until
June 1965. Here we had a pre-view of the kind of interdenominational and inter-racial life we were about to be
involved in. We had many adjustments to make—I do
not mean compromises: we had to learn to accept each
other. Much that we learned there has stood by us well
in seminars and orientation courses.

At the I.C.G. we made our first ventures into church
growth publishing. McGavran worked for a while through
a Christian publisher in India, which was all our economic
position permitted. Indeed I believe McGavran was himself out of pocket on this program. However Sunda's
work on West Irian and Hamilton's on the High Andes as
well as McGavran's own work on Jamaica became available in printed form. Later on, as our methods improved
Shearer's *Wildfire: The Growth of the Church in Korea.*
and Read's *New Patterns of Church Growth in Brazil.*
started off what was to become the Church Growth Series
with Eerdmans.

Shearer's and Read's were important works in our history. Shearer's Presbyterian material demonstrated the
importance of documentation and the potential of micro-
filming records and building some kind of data bank. He
also provided superb evidence for McGavran's contention
that over-all statistics of church growth did not adequately indicate what was really going on in the component parts,
or homogeneous units as he (McGavran) called them.
In *Understanding Church Growth* (1970:116-119) he leans on
Shearer's data for this, though scores of subsequent
studies have shown the same thing. Read opened up the
whole area of the study of Pentecostal growth. This raised
a great many questions, which in turn led to the exploration of new dimensions in church growth field research.
Sunda was not a research man, but he came out of the fire
of people movements, was excited about them, and a good
informant. I myself drew much from Sunda, who read my
descriptions of Tongan and Fijian movements, based on
historical sources, and said I was "talking his language."
While McGavran provided us with a systematic approach
to the strategy of mission, and a certain prophetic drive,
I am sure that he was himself deeply influenced by their

discoveries, experiences and data.

As for myself, I think that McGavran's influence showed up most in a series of articles I wrote in 1962 on "Australia's Missionary Outreach in Our Time." The material was accepted for publication in Australia but was not printed— I never discovered why. McGavran (who was so concerned with the urgency of the need, and liked to get things into print quickly) never resigned himself to my historical method, which keeps an almost-completed manuscript on the shelf for years until I am entirely satisfied with the documentation. During 1962 and 1963 I assembled so much church growth writing that it now occupies five bound but unpublished volumes. *People Movements of Southern Polynesia,* published in 1971, was merely an excerpt of this work. McGavran had read this in 1962 and was using a few of the concepts in it. I think we all had a very great influence on each other. Although McGavran was certainly the prophet, church growth was already becoming a corporate thing—even at Eugene.

Another feature of the Institute at Eugene was the facility offered visitors to contribute some input. When the Institute had first opened Bishop Pickett had given the opening address. Subsequently he gave the first series of Church Growth Lectures, later published as *Dynamics of Church Growth.* The following year McGavran decided on a panel rather than a single lecturer. Eugene Nida, Calvin Guy, Melvin Hodges and himself provided a variety of approaches to the subject. This exchange resulted in the publication of *Church Growth and Christian Mission,* which has been widely read. To my deepest regret I had to miss this presentation, as I substituted for McGavran at a Presbyterian Consultation. I always felt that I had been denied a vital experience but I was encouraged that he would accept me as his substitute at an important conference.

Probably the most important event of those years at Eugene was the Iberville Consultation, sponsored by the World Council of Churches in Canada in 1963. They had invited Pickett, McGavran and myself to represent the church growth viewpoint. It was a Consultation on church growth, and we three each had assignments. We met in New York on our way and discussed our position. Several members turned out to be strongly sympathetic to church growth theory, and others went some distance along the road with us. The Consultation issued a formal statement which pinpointed twelve items and approved our pioneering work. We were greatly encouraged. Although the W. C. C. never gave the statement the coverage it deserved, it was nevertheless an important step for us.

In June 1964 I left Eugene to undertake a survey of the churches in the Solomon Islands. While I was in the Solomons the future of the Institute came up for discussion. I had been a Teaching Fellow and McGavran wanted to maintain our connection. He depended on me for anthropological studies and tribal religion. The Fuller Theological Seminary wanted to reorganize its Missions Department, but McGavran was not interested in being a Professor of Missions in a Seminary. The Institute at Eugene had shown him the potential of what he felt the world needed—a research center for experienced missionaries, men who had already grappled with the dynamic of cross-cultural conversion before they came to us. Eventually an agreement was reached: McGavran and myself would go to Pasadena to commence the School of World Mission and Institute of Church Growth (S. W. M.-I. C. G.) as a graduate body. We began to operate in September 1965.

Chapter xix in *How Churches Grow* had been reprinted as a booklet, "Checking Methods Against Actual Growth." It met with a good reception. In this, as earlier in *Bridges of God*, McGavran called for further research in church growth. His position has always been that the more the growth of the church is studied, and likewise the obstructions to growth, the more we will learn about the process, and that good strategy cannot be planned except on a basis of known facts, which show why churches grow or do not grow. McGavran's emphasis on statistics is misunderstood if it be not understood first that he wants them, not for self-aggrandizement but for research, and he wants research that more men may be saved. That understanding was written into the Iberville Statement, which we accepted. Furthermore, the twelfth point of that Statement concerned the need for church growth research. McGavran believed that such research had to be done by men with field experience from various regions sharing things together. The

Institute began in January 1961. I joined 12 months later, attended classes and taught some. The Institute terminated in June 1965. We had learned a great deal. We went to Pasadena with a good experimental model, for which we owe much to the Northwest Christian College.

McGavran's ideas on research are not confined to the activities of his institution. He believes that a percentage of all missionary support should be expended on research as to how the remainder should be spent to produce the maximum of result.

> The time has come for all Churches and their missionary societies to invest at least five percent of their income in planned, continous, purposeful research dedicated to finding out how the Gospel may more effectively be communicated (1966:c).

Realization that better missionary strategy could never be developed for the new age without solid research which exposed why our predecessors succeeded and failed drew me to McGavran. His Institute provided the facilities for this kind of work, and the body of experienced missionaries with whom to interact, compare and test one's ideas. This is what has produced the extensive church growth literature that has come from McGavran's men: not all of equal value by any means but all striving for relevance in the new age of missions.

McGavran and His Critics

For most of the last thirty years McGavran has been in the thick of the battle—the battle being the determination of missionary policy. He has been a prolific writer, but the concentration of his writing has been determined by the nature of the battle rather than his personal bias. Almost without exception his major critics have put it the other way around. They have accused him of stressing quantity at the expense of quality; of being so concerned with the saving of souls that he neglects the serving of human needs; of pushing for church extention and being blind to the needs for social justice; and of relying on human effort instead of the Holy Spirit.

For the last ten years I have worked with McGavran read his writing, witnessed the episodes which have led to his literary outbursts, and have some knowledge of his personal life and faith.   While I do not always say things in the way he does, yet I will defend him stoutly on most of the points at which his literary critics attack him. I had considered listing some here by name and "paying them in their own coin" but of course that would be as uncharitable as they themselves have been. Really they are not worthy of recognition because, by their own writing, they have not listened to McGavran before attacking him—either this, or they are convicted and self-defensive.

On the difference between quality and quantity McGavran has made many statements. From an early stage in his writing, as I have shown, he has distinguished between discipling and perfecting, as two pressures of the Holy Spirit on the Church and two aspects of church growth. Furthermore this has been a biblical rather than a philosophical distinction:

> The discipling of tribes, castes, clans and kindreds is precisely what the Great Commision calls for. The Greek says specifically "disciple the tribes (peoples)." It inevitably adds "teaching them all things." The discipling must be done when God moves on a people's heart to espouse the Christian faith. The teaching is then the continuing task of the Church (1958: 334).

Yet though his critics will cite biblical passages out of context to answer him, none, to my knowledge have ever done so on a basis of his exposition of the Great Commission; which after all, is his mandate for both quantity and quality. Normally one would expect that a rebuttal would deal with the data on which the original argument was reasoned.

Many of the same critics have also raised the point about the planning of man and the work of the Spirit. It is said that numbers mean nothing, our job is to be obedient (proclaim, witness, etc) regardless of results, which are in God's hands. The argument goes on against people movements and against McGavran's attitudes to deployment of funds and personnel. This argument has four or five aspects. First McGavran has a strong doctrine of the Holy Spirit. In *How Churches Grow* he has a chapter on it called "Authentic Spiritual Fire." In most of his writings there is some reference to the Spirit or something which implies it. Second, the argument overlooks the basic fact that McGavran's imagery for a people movement situation calling for deployment of funds and personnel is the biblical theology of the harvest, which God Himself has ripened. This is not man's doing: man's business is the harvesting. I have never seen a critique of peoples movement conversions deal with that biblical argument.

With respect to service and social justice, I must say the critics have been entirely unfair to McGavran because they have repeatedly tried to make him say what he does not say at all, and the issue about which McGavran makes strong demands on every converted Christian is to demonstrate his Christianity in service and social action. I could tell of incidents in his private life that show his own concern. If his critics will read his article "A Plan of Action for Churches," they will discover him making proposals for dealing with the racial problem in America a decade ago when very few programs had been articulated at all. So McGavran is not short on service or social action. He never has been. Away back before the war he was writing a series of articles for *World Dominion* on "The Battle for Brotherhood," speaking on behalf of the Untouchables in India. McGavran has been very vocal in recent years against the confusion of service projects and programs for social justice with evangelism, and against those supposedly missionary agencies which substitute service, or social justice, or mere dialogue, or anything else (good as they may be) for bringing men to decision for Christ. He objects to these good things masquerading as mission, and doing this by the redefinition of the terms mission and evangelism. McGavran believes that men have to be made new in Christ as a first step and that having accepted Christ they must serve and fight for social justice. Both are ongoing ministries of the Church: one discipling, the other perfecting. The distinction is in the Great Commission, and McGavran bases his priority on the words of Jesus to seek first the Kingdom. The critic may argue with his exegesis, but he should not distort what he says.

Criticism, in a way is not a bad thing (except that it does misguide people who like to have thinking done for them). Usually a critic does not notice a writer unless he is getting too near home, making people self-defensive, or threatening programs and vested interests, or hurting in some other way. At the SWM-ICG we do not mind a bit of criticism. Indeed we meet together once a week as a faculty and one of us presents a study to be shot at by others. Two of the studies in this Festschrift received that treatment. And of course, we do not agree on all points. Sometimes we have a lively debate, which leads to drastic revision of the presentation.

However, the thing which has brought us together as a team as far as our respective philosophies of mission are concerned is the major thing that McGavran has been saying —and no critic has ever had the courage to pull it apart. Throughout all his writing and public speaking one hears a recurring clause, borrowed I think from the Presbyterians —"to proclaim Christ and to persuade men to become his disciples and responsible members of His Church." This is the purpose of church growth, and wherever it came from it has become part of McGavran himself. It preserves proclamation (by Divine authority) in an age when the general mood is anti-monological. It insists in persuasion (witness) in dialogue. It seeks a verdict for Christ (personal decision). It demands incorporation into a Fellowship of Believers. It demands responsible "fruit worthy of repentance" as He sends us into the world, as He was sent into the world. No critic can tear apart that kernel of truth without sacrificing the authority of Scripture, and that is our basic presupposition.

Some of his critics have accused him of perpetuating an obsolete doctrine of church extension, yet in their very writing they have never understood his ideas on the nature of the Church. He has been criticized for his concepts of worship on the basis of a one-sentence analogy extracted from its context. Now, one may or may not agree with his views of worship, but any responsible critic will be obliged to ascertain what he believes about the subject first. And his views of the Church also are far from "church extension" in the sense of denominationalism. He argued as far back as 1960 with his own denomination for the validity of other communions, calling them gathered churches; and defining as a gathered church—

> . . . one which Christ gathers. It consists of those who know themselves to be Christian, who intend to follow Christ, and who have placed their faith on him. "Whenever two or three are gathered together in my name, I am in the midst of them" said our Lord. Whatever Christ is in the midst of is a church . . .

Then he subdivided gathered churches into inclusive (who accepted others as valid) or exclusive (who regarded themselves only as the true Church), and finally, he accepted Newbigin's idea that belief in Jesus as Lord and Savior, acceptance of the Bible as Scripture, and manifesting the fruit of the Spirit are valid marks of the Household of God (1960 : 8-9, 25). Some of these dimensions have been developed by Ralph Winter, in his analysis of vertical and horizontal structures of the Church (1969: 74-89), and more recently as modalities and sodalities. McGavran has also compared Gathered Church and People Church (1958: 323-324). Any critic who thinks that the church growth writers have not struggled with ecclesiology and found it far bigger than denominationalism, just has not done his homework. Mostly such critics have set up their own straw men to shoot down.

The School of World Mission and Institute of Church Growth

Dr. McGavran served as Dean of the S. W. M. - I. C. G. from September 1965 to June 1971. Since then he has continued to teach as an emeritus professor. The five years of his administration were formative in many ways, building up an institution, improving the old I. C. G. model, working out degree programs, enlarging faculty and curriculum to recognize all the related aspects and implications of the church growth emphasis in the new age of missions, and welding the whole structure into a fraternal company. We had many problems fitting into the straight-jacket of American educational formalities. We owe much to our new sponsors who have made possible many outreaches we never had at Oregon, but they have not yet grasped our world vision and its implications.

McGavran has made a worthy attempt to define missiology

in terms of a science of mission. A series of church growth seminars across America involves the faculty in regular annual commitments. Visiting lecturers have been drawn into our operations either for one-term courses or for brief lecture series, to expose us all to the wider spectrum of missionary thinking; Stephen Neill, Calvin Guy, Jack Shepherd, John V. Taylor, J. T. Seamands, John Sinclair, David Stowe, Harold Cook, Harold Lindsell and others.

Life at the S.W.M. - I.C.G. is continually on the move. Hundreds of missionaries, administrators, and professors of mission call. Never a week goes by without some influential person dropping in. Maybe we set up a special convocation or have him lunch with the faculty. This all suggests that our present location is more central or strategic, and also that even those who do not agree with the church growth viewpoint feel that they cannot pass it by.

During these five years McGavran began to lean more and more on his colleagues. He had built up a group of specialists at points where he felt church growth had to develop: anthropology, extension training, research methods, theology, the phenomenology of tribal religion, culture and personality, ethnolinguistics and other aspects. To outline all the new lines being currently explored by these men would take a book in itself. It must suffice here to say that no one can dismiss church growth without dealing with a team of men—men as different as they could possibly be, yet bound together with some strong missiological convictions. Furthermore they are all men who have come out of the field situation and have operated in the vernacular languages.

Although McGavran's current writing is still dominated by the same three basic concepts, nevertheless it comes to us in two quite different forms. In *Understanding Church Growth* (1970) he has set out for the first time the panorama he sees. This is a pragmatic study. It shows McGavran as a synthesist. The data base he has received mostly from his men. He himself has tested Shearer, Read, Kwast, Wold and many others and the critic to answer a single paragraph has to read two or three books or theses. On the other hand we have his shorter writing, his many journal articles. These are polemic. Here he is concerned with the philosophy of mission and its perverted forms which threaten the world mission in this day of opportunity. Here he is the same old crusader, seemingly whipping up more and more energy as he gets older.

The *Church Growth Bulletin,* which McGavran still continues to edit, has performed a major service in both directions. Of course it is a house organ in that it presents the church growth viewpoint. Nevertheless it has challenged some important missionary conferences at the point of their policy towards the evangelistic opportunity confronting them, and also in the redefinition of terms like "mission" and "evangelism" so as to rationalize substitutions for the gospel appeal. Occasionally some article from *Church Growth Bulletin* is republished by some major journal of another field. The publication certainly exerts a wide influence across the world. It also permits our trying out new ideas on which we want feedback.

At the time I write these words over eighty missionaries and nationals are doing research here. To have a missionary and national researching the same subject leads to all kinds of discoveries. These researchers come from over forty different boards, missions or churches and have had over five hundred man-years of service (which does not include the seventeen nationals) in over forty different countries, and they speak nearly that number of languages. No professor can interact with that kind of company without it being a learning experience for him and without having his ideas soundly tested.

This is just what McGavran wanted, and the missionary world will have to listen to what this company says to the new era of mission. Several of these men have completed their overseas service and are now professors of mission. They have enrolled here in the Doctor of Missiology program. We retain as much flexibility in elective courses and have experimented in common-interest seminars.

The SWM-ICG complex is probably McGavran's greatest achievement. During his administration a faculty has been gathered. These appointments have considered the shortcomings of the early years. Most of the gaps have been covered. With faculty and men, there probably is not a similar institution anywhere in the world. Its network reaches outwards from the Fuller Theological Seminary to other nearby facilities like the computers of M.A.R.C.

and the publishing program of the William Carey Library. There is no question about the valuable missiological input into this institution. The danger lies in whether or not the missionary administrations of the world will listen to its output.

This article on McGavran as a Missiologist had to be a personal statement. I beg the reader's pardon for so imposing myself on it. That is inevitable in a portrait. This is not a biography. It is what I have seen as I have looked at McGavran at work. I think the other articles in this Festschrift will indicate that church growth has much more to say yet, and that it can speak to the new era of mission.

4

BIBLIOGRAPHY OF

DONALD ANDERSON McGAVRAN

1925 " Sown Field " WORLD CALL 55

1933 "Missionaries and Indigenous Standards of Living" I.R.M. xxii 33-49

1936 "Christ, Christian America and the World" I.R.M. xxv. 116-129
"The Mandala Mission Field." "The Mehra People Movement" and "When the Church Grows" first appeared in CHRISTIAN MISSIONS IN MID-INDIA, edited by J. F. Edwards, later reproduced in CHURCH GROWTH AND GROUP CONVERSION 1955

1938 "The Battle for Brotherhood in India Today" WORLD DOMINION xvi, 1,2,3. 32-36, 132-135, 255-261

1943 "Using the Present Adversity for Advance" I. R. M. xxxii 187-195

1952 "Comity—A Tool" WORLD DOMINION xxx, 37-44

c1954 "Missions in the Coming Era: A Strategy for the Church in Tomorrow's World" (Reprinted, n/d, before BRIDGES OF GOD appeared)

1955a BRIDGES OF GOD, London, World Dominion Press
b "The Church in a Revolutionary Age," St. Louis, Christian Board of Publication. Mimeographed.
c "New Methods for a New Age in Missions" I.R.M. xliv Reprinted.
d "Satan and Missions" WORLD DOMINION xxxiii Reprinted.
e "Discipling Africa in this Generation" D.F.M. Africa Committee, New York. Duplicated paper A744

f CHURCH GROWTH AND GROUP CONVERSION, Edited by McGavran, with contributions by Pickett and Warnshuis, Lucknow, Lucknow Publishing House. (Chapters III to IX are a revision of CHRISTIAN MISSIONS IN MID-INDIA, 1936. Preface, Chapters I and II are new) Reprinted 1962.

1956a "Church Growth in West Utkal, Orissa, India" Indianapolis, United Christian Missionary Society. Mimeographed.

b "A Study of the Life and Growth of the Disciples of Christ in Puerto Rico" Indianapolis, United Christian Missionary Society. Mimeographed.

1958a MULTIPLYING CHURCHES IN THE PHILIPPINES, Manila, United Church of Christ in the Philippines.

b "Have We Lost Our Way in Mission?" CHRISTIAN HERALD Reprinted.

c "What is the Nature of the Church?" RELIGION IN LIFE xxvii, 3, 323-334

1959a "After the First Flush of Success" I.R.M. xlvii, 265-275

b HOW CHURCHES GROW: THE NEW FRONTIERS OF MISSION, London, World Dominion Press

c "Church Growth and Mission Among the Yakima Indians" Ditto copy manuscript

1960 "Of Churches, Sects and Denominations" THE CHRISTIAN, Feb. 21. 8-9, 25

1961a "A Plan of Action for Churches" CHRISTIAN HERALD, Oct.

b "Institute of Church Growth" I.R.M. 1. 430-434

c "Theological Bed Rock in Mission" RELIGION IN LIFE xxx, 4, 603-9

1962a "A Disastrous Almost True Assumption" FAR EAST MIS-SIONARY Reprinted n/d. (Contents must fall between 1960-1965)

b "God who finds His Mission" I.R.M. li 303-316

c CHURCH GROWTH IN JAMAICA, Lucknow, Lucknow Publishing House.

1963a CHURCH GROWTH IN MEXICO, Grand Rapids, Eerdmans Publishing Co.

b "How To Do a Survey in Church Growth," Eugene, Institute of Church Growth. Pamphlet.

1964 "Essential Evangelism: An Open Letter to Dr.J.C. Hoekendijk" W.C.C. OCCASIONAL PAPERS Series iii, no. 2

1964-19-- CHURCH GROWTH BULLETIN, D. A. McGavran, ed.

1965a "Wrong Strategy: A Real Crisis in Missions" I.R.M. liv, 451-461

b "Social Justice and Evangelism" WORLD VISION MAGAZINE, June, Reprinted.

c "What Meaning Does Revolution Have for Christian Mission?" C.G.B. i. 47-51

d "Today's Basic Policy in Evangelism" C.G.B. i. 1-3, 17-18, 29-30, 45-46, 59-60 e CHURCH GROWTH AND CHRISTIAN MISSION D. A. McGavran, Editor Contributors E. Nida, M. Hodges, C. Guy and D. McGavran, New York, Harper & Row

1966a "One Goal or Many?" WORLD VISION MAGAZINE Oct. 9,28

b "Receptivity: Missions' Great Challenge" CHRISTIANITY TODAY, also THE CHRISTIAN. Reprinted.

c "The Church Growth Point of View and Christian Mission" THE JOURNAL OF THE CHRISTIAN BRETHREN RESEARCH FELLOWSHIP Oct. (Bristol) Reprinted.

d "Discipling Precedes Perfecting" C. G. B. ii. 167-168

e "Wheaton's Significance for World Mission" C. G. B. ii, 147-149

f "Why Neglect the Gospel-Ready Masses?" CHRISTIANITY TODAY Ap. 29, 769-771

1967a "Kann Man Das Wachstum Der Kirche Planen?" DAS WORT IN DER WELT No. 1. Hamburg

b "Contemporary Arguments against the Missionary Society" I. F. M. A. STUDY PAPERS, Ridgefield Park, N.J.

c "What About Non-Muslim Resistant Peoples" I.F.M.A. PAPERS

d "The National Church and Resistant Peoples" I.F.M.A. PAPERS

e "Quantifying World Evangelism" C. G. B. iii, 199-200

f "Imperialism and Church Multiplication" C.G.B. iii, 224-225

g "The Passive and Active Role in Mission" C.G.B. iii, 227-8

h "Missions: Passive and Active" THE PRESBYTERIAN JOURNAL, Aug. 2, 9-10

i "Church Growth Eyes on La Marginal" C.G.B., iv, 264-265

j "A Bigger Bang for Your Buck: or How to Get More for Your Missionary Dollar" WORLD VISION MAGAZINE, Dec., pp. 16-17

1968a "Church Growth in Japan" JAPAN HARVEST 18,1, 15-22

b "Church Growth Strategy Continued" I.R.M. lvii, 335-343

c "Will Uppsala Betray the Two Billion?" C.G.B. iv, 5, 1-6

d "Uppsala 'Program for Mission' and Church Growth" C.G.B. v, 333-337

e "Presence and Proclamation in Christian Mission" European Consultation on Mission Studies, Paper No. 8.

f "Prasenz und Verkundigung in der christlichen Mission" Evangelische Missions-Zeitschrift, Aug. 134-146 (Translation of 'e')

1969a "Advanced Education for Missionaries" CHRISTIANITY TODAY xii, 25, 1115-1117

b "Why Consider Polygamy?" and "What Says the Word of God?" in Symposium on Polygamy, C.G.B. v, 350-351, 357-359

c "Evangelism and Church Growth" C.G.B. v, 378-379

    d "Radio and Church Growth" C.G.B. vi, 2, 17-18
    e "Self-Centeredness and the Choke Law: Donald McGavran on
        Hillman & Sapsezian" C.G.B. vi, 6, 25-28
    f Editorial Correspondence and Comments on "Unbaptizable
        Believers in Latin America" C.G.B. vi, 2, 31-34
    g "Church Planting in Europe" C.G.B. vi, 2, 34-35
1970a "For Such a Time as This" unpublished address SWM-ICG
        banquet, Pasadena, Feb.
    b "Crisis of Identity for some Missionary Societies" CHRIS-
        TIANITY TODAY, 722-726, also ADVENT CHRISTIAN
        MISSIONS, July 3-5
    c "The Right and Wrong of the Presence Idea of Mission"
        E. M. Q. 6, 2, 98-109
    d "Church Growth in Europe and America" C.G.B. vi, 6, 73-74
    e UNDERSTANDING CHURCH GROWTH, Grand Rapids,
        Eerdmans Publishing Co.
1971a "The Discipling of Africa in this Generation" Item listed
        above 1955e reprinted in C.G. B. vii, 5, 126-129
    b "Without Crossing Barriers" Symposium with editorial
        comments by McGavran C.G.B. vii, 5, Editorial 135-138,
        "Bring in the Vacuum Cleaner" 147-148
    c "Will Green Lake Betray the Two Billion?" C.G.B. vii, 6,
        149-153
    d "Urban Church Planting" C.G.B. vii, 110
    e "Take Heart Brother Koerner : The Lord Reigns" C.G.B.
        viii, i, 170-172
1972 EYE OF THE STORM: THE GREAT DEBATE IN MIS-
      SION (McGavran, Editor) Waco, Word Books

Unpublished Typescript:

n/d   "The Methodist Church of the Gold Coast"

Cassettes of Public Addresses

1971   "Church Growth Eyes I"
        "Church Growth Eyes II"
        "People Movements"
        "Five Kinds of Leaders"
        "The Crucial Problem in Missions"
        "Without Crossing Barriers: The Mosaic"
        South Pasadena, Wm. Carey Library.

Part II

God's Purpose
and
Man's Responsibility

GOD'S PURPOSE AND MAN'S RESPONSIBILITY

McGavran has always insisted that church growth—namely the conversion of persons to God and the planting of churches or fellowships—is the will of God. To indiscrete critics who ask how he knows what is the will of God, he merely cites Scripture. For example, in Paul's first letter to Timothy, he inserted in parenthesis to amplify the idea of "God our Saviour" the words "who will have all men to be saved, and to come unto the knowledge of the truth." This certainly lines up with the twofold aspect of the Great Commission and McGavran's differentiation of discipling and perfecting.

The idea of our Christian responsibility under God is also a biblical idea. The biblical concept of stewardship is that of a person responsible for his leadership under a higher authority. The elders, or lesser shepherds are to feed the flock of God responsibly ("oversight" is the word used) until the Chief Shepherd comes. The will of God and the responsibility of his stewards are two notions which meet in church growth theology. There are other doctrines which are also implied by this confluence of ideas.

Arthur Glasser, whose responsibility in the church growth team is the theological aspect, presents us with a study of the theological issues raised by church growth. He deals with the doctrines of the authority of Scripture, the sovereignty of God, the doctrine of the Church and the responsibility of man. It is good to have this statement because often these doctrines are taken for granted in church growth writing, and the fact that they are not elaborated does not mean that they are not regarded as fundamental.

Basic theology is involved in the definition of terms—mission, for example, or evangelism. Jack Shepherd, who has been a visiting lecturer at the S.W.M.-I.C.G. discusses the continuities and changes in Christian mission, defining many of the key terms of current missiological controversy, pin-pointing theological issues in which McGavran has been articulate, and he concludes with a focus on the idea of church growth indeed being theology.

Also basic to church growth is the fact of the active role of the Holy Spirit. J.T. Seamands— J.T. as we called him— deals with this divine element in missions, starting from the experiences of the early Church. He discusses the methods by which the Holy Spirit has made the Church grow from within, and to do so in spite of the human situation. He distinguishes between conversion and revival, witnessing and the ripening of harvests—all as operations of the Spirit in the growth of the Church.

Church growth theology is not an arm-chair theology. It relates to humanity, not by speculation or philosophy, but in the dynamics of the existential situation. A methodology for action which calls man to responsible behavior patterns in terms of social and applied anthropology, needs a contact theology, not an arm-chair one. If Christianity is to transform a people's way of life, so that the divine shows through the human in everyday affairs, and Christian mission is to be planned in this direction as well as that of eternal life, then social anthropology and theology have to come to terms. Charles Kraft, who is qualified as an anthropologist, and a colleague of McGavran, has concerned himself with this problem. His article, "Toward a Christian Ethnotheology," wrestles with the basic definitions and distinctions. He distinguishes between the cultural and the supracultural among other things. This is an important article, whether the reader agrees with it or not. It attempts to translate anthropology to the theologian and theology to the anthropologist: something which simply must be done if missiology is to be relevant in what McGavran calls "the new era."

To complete the theological unit of this Festschrift Alan Gates was asked to discuss McGavran's concept of perfection growth. He has chosen to assemble here some of the things McGavran has said about it, together with some of the extensions of the idea from his colleagues, and then, finally to attempt a biblical evaluation. Although McGavran has emphasized discipling more than perfecting in his writing; nevertheless he did make the distinction and has always said that discipling without perfecting, or quantity without quality, was worthless. Many of his critics have failed to recognize this fact, and Alan Gates' reminder of the totality of McGavran's thought at this point is timely.

These features by no means exhaust the theological dimensions of church growth. These, however, have been grouped together under the head "God's Purpose and Man's Responsibility." The doctrine of the sovereign authority of God needs to be balanced with that of the responsibility of Christian man as God's steward in the world. This equilibrium is vital to Christian mission. To consider the former to the exclusion of the latter is to fall into the fallacy of obedience; which leaves one going blindly ahead believing that God will bring the harvest in His time in spite of the bad stewardship of his servants. To consider the latter at the expense of the former leads one into the fallacy of self-sufficiency, namely, that man can save himself and the world by his own wisdom, initiative and technology. The former is not a Christian anthropology. The latter is not a Christian theology. The only way to avoid these fallacies is to remember always that God is Sovereign Lord and man is responsible for his stewardsip under God. Church growth theology stands on the equilibrium of these two doctrines.

World mission today seethes with major theological debate. What, after all, is its theological basis?. . . What is there in God Himself which impels to mission—and would continue to impel, were Christians the poorest and most backward of all peoples? Should any propose to give up missions entirely and leave further Christianization to the younger Churches, we must ask him whether his solution is theologically right. Is it pleasing to God? We seek today for theological foundations.

HOW CHURCHES GROW,
p. 183

5

CHURCH GROWTH
AND THEOLOGY

Arthur F. Glasser

God wills the growth of His Church. A chief and ir-
replaceable element in her ministry is the proclamation
of the Gospel to all mankind and incorporation of those
who believe into her communal life. Only through the
deliberate multiplications of vast numbers of new congregations all over the world will the Church be able to evangelize this generation. When she ceases to perform this
mission, something fundamental is lost in her very essence
as the people of God in the midst of the nations. The church
that does not grow is out of the will of God.

Sweeping affirmations such as these reflect the over-
riding concern of Dr. McGavran and the Church Growth
Movement. Our task is to define the theological issues
that are foundational to this concern. We commence with
the issue of Authority.

✕ The Authority that Defines our Mission

In the Gospels, Jesus Christ says a great deal about
authority and very little about the Church. For a *Festschrift* like this, dedicated to Dr. McGavran—a man who

has vigorously and effectively called the people of God in our generation to mission—it is singularly fitting that we begin with this affirmation. Indeed, we who have had the privilege of intimate and prolonged association with him cannot but bear witness that in his life and work the same proportionate emphasis can be discerned. More central than a concern for the Church and her mission is his solemn awareness of himself as under the authority of Jesus Christ. And this specifically means that he and we are under the obligation to "live according to Scripture" (I Cor. 4:6 RSV).

Indeed, everything stems from the issue of authority. By what right dare Dr. McGavran or any man speak decisively and with finality on one task above all others that should possess the heart, conscience, will and resources of the people of God? Obviously, he must have clear perception of an Authority that transcends the human mind and which impels him to call Christians to the evangelization of the world in this generation. He must have unshaken confidence in the fact that God Himself is the ultimate Authority that embraces all authority, whether in heaven or earth. And he must believe that God has spoken clearly and repeatedly on this matter.

Dr. McGavran postulates the reality of a God who has disclosed Himself to mankind not only through his works of creation and providence but also savingly spoken in the words and events of redemptive history, a history that came to a climax and fulfillment in Jesus Christ. Scripture constitutes the essentials of this divine self-disclosure and is utterly trustworthy, the only infallible rule of faith and practice.

We do not desire to labor this point. And yet, we have no alternative. Many of the most severe critics of the Church Growth Movement affirm that they too are appealing to biblical authority in their condemnation of it. Hans Reudi Weber uses Bible texts to caution against what he terms "nervous fanatical activity," an awareness that "true evangelism may be the cutting down of the numbers of church-members," and an unwillingness to "leave the matter of statistics to God." He is impatient with what he regards as the movement's theological immaturity. Its rejection of universalism is countered with: "The mature

are those who keep firmly to the promise that, in the end
ta panta will be God's." Why take so seriously the concept of the wrath of God? "Is the church the community
of the saved outside of which there is no salvation?"
(1963: 298-301).

In this day of theological double-talk the issue of Authority is not settled merely by stating that one accepts
the Bible as God's Word, and claiming that it is his only
infallible rule of faith and practice. In a sense, this
should be sufficient. But Calvin has warned us in this
connection of a strange propensity in man, tempting him
to "derogate from the credit due to the speaker" (Institutes 1. vii:1). In application, Dr. McGavran would ask,
"What is it but derogation from God's authority, if we refuse to take plain biblical statements at their face value?
The Bible is no purely human book, a miscellaneous collection of the best insights of man. Its several parts
must be interpreted according to their context and coherent purpose, in reverent obedience to the Lord who speaks
through them. Inasmuch as we trust Christ for our salvation, let us also trust Him for the information we need
touching our performance of His mission. In Scripture,
God repeatedly and explicitly defines the mission of His
Church in the simplest of terms."

Without this high view of Scripture and its straightforward mandate for mission, there would never have been
a Church Growth Movement. In essence, mission is "nothing else than the activity of Christ, exercised through the
Church, through which He calls the peoples of the earth
to repentance and to faith, so they may be made His disciples and through baptism be incorporated into the fellowship of those who await the coming of His Kingdom"
(Bavinck, 1960: 62).

We would underscore this fact: the missionary task is
abundantly clear if one humbly accepts the authority of
the Scriptures. Postulate one God, and the implicit corollary follows that His authority must be absolute and final.
Confront Jesus Christ as He is revealed in the Gospels
and you hear Him unequivocally and repeatedly claim this
absolute and comprehensive authority. He never draws
back from its staggering implications. The One who repeatedly claimed that He alone possessed the right of deci-

sion over the eternal destinies of men commanded His Church to declare a message to all mankind by which they may be saved (Acts 11:14). And we should not forget that His deeds of grace and mercy confirmed this authority to such a degree that His enemies, both human and demonic, confessed its reality. "No man ever spoke as this man speaks" (John 7:46).

Throughout the early decades of the Church this dual authority of Christ and Scripture was perceived and acknowledged by His people. Moreover, they uniformly agreed that He so regulated the Church in its beginnings that every precaution was taked to insure that His authority was embodied in a "geniune all-sufficient and authoritative New Testament canon" (Geldenhuys).

What is of tremendous significance to us today is that the New Testament apostles—the authoritative representatives of Jesus Christ—never wavered in their confidence in Jesus Christ and His Gospel as being relevant for the needs of all men. They never deviated a hair's breadth from acknowledging the authority of the Old Testament and the emerging New Testament. So far as they were concerned, the whole Bible was the Word of God.

Down through the history of the Church, whenever men have resisted this authority they have eventually floundered in uncertainty, doubt, confusion and chaos. In every age those who have accepted this Word of God, living and written, have been the vanguard of all efforts to evangelize mankind in Jesus' Name.

In our day when there appears to be such conspiracy to reduce the total mission of the Church to inter-church aid, political action, economic betterment or the quest for social justice, one fact stands out clearly. Those who advocate this reductionism uniformly betray a low view of Scripture. They are highly arbitrary and subjective in their approach to Christ's authority, and water down the apostolic teaching that apart from Christ and the Gospel all men are "without hope and without God."

In contrast, the Christian whose rule of life is Christ and the Scripture manifests the following concerns:

1. He bears witness to Jesus Christ with the deliberate purpose of persuading men to believe on Him as Lord and Saviour.

2. He persuades Christians to receive baptism and enter into the life and witness of the local church.
3. He recognizes that the Church's mission is to multiply thousands of strong, self-propagating congregations throughout the world.

But who is sufficient for such a high order of service? Is not this task far beyond the resources of man, even redeemed men? Even the apostle Paul confessed that he was not qualified to serve as minister of the new covenant (II Cor. 3: 5,6). This brings us to the second theological issue foundational to Church Growth theory.

The Sovereignty that Demands Priority in Mission

When one accepts the authority of Scripture he is solemnized at the picture it portrays of fallen man. Although man retains some of the elements of the divine nature imparted at Creation, he represents terrible loss, moral defilement, ethical distortion, futility and the complete inability to make himself fit for God's Presence, much less His friendship. And always the dark reality that man is under divine judgment. "The wrath of God is revealed from heaven against all ungodliness and wickedness of men who by their wickedness suppress the truth" (Romans 1: 18 RSV). Again and again, in one form or another, this stark fact is plainly affirmed.

Indeed, how can man be saved? It is at this point that another stream of data coursing throughout Scripture takes on significance. It focuses on a God of holiness and grace, working according to a plan whereby the impossible will become possible. God will not be thwarted. He has decreed that in the last day His Son will be supreme in the universe and will be surrounded by a segment of fallen humanity He has redeemed through His Cross and conformed to Himself. This is what Calvin called "the high mystery" of God's sovereignty.

Apparently, without the least element of "rigid arbitrariness" on His part, God feels impelled by his love to gather from mankind—who had forfeited all claims to His mercy— a people for His pleasure. This selectivity of love, this election of a people "before they were created," is a postulate of church growth theology.

At this point one should not come to the hasty conclusion that this inevitably means a "theology of the elect for the elect." Hardly! The Church Growth Movement has drawn missionaries and national church leaders whose commitment to historical biblical Christianity has delivered them from the rationalistic Calvinism which is rigidly double predestinarian. Theirs is a positive theology of redemption for the whole world. They are determined to proclaim the Gospel to all men. Although man is fallen and "dead in trespasses and sins" his rational and volitional faculties have not been destroyed. He is addressable. He can be informed of God's truth, and can perceive its implications. Not that our preaching can change men's hearts. Only by the direct working of God's Spirit can they be brought to repentance and faith.

Sinners can perceive the destructive effects of sin. More, they can avoid the brothel, the saloon, the arrogance of pride. Indifferent people can go to church and hear the gospel. But again, and we must underscore this, only the Holy Spirit can bring God's Presence into their hearts, break their wills and persuade them to seek Jesus Christ.

So then, we do not seek to evade the reality of Election. Indeed, we cannot, although we may not agree as to the precise form it takes. As William Temple pointedly said, "Election is not so much an inference as the only possible reading of the facts when theism is accepted" (1953 : 403).

Why, however, should the reality of God's sovereignty in election be regarded as a distinctive of the Church Growth Movement? Why is it not sufficient to underscore what all evangelicals affirm, namely that man is utterly lost apart from God and cannot be saved apart from His grace? Why not merely embrace the activist's resolution of this mystery by involvement in mission: "Love the sinner, be concerned for his spiritual welfare and secure his conversion by whatever means works!" Why not conclude with the plea that all Christians everywhere open their hearts anew to the constraining love of Christ and devote all their energies to showing Him and sharing Him with their neighbors?

Actually, the Church Growth Movement has taken this profound truth of God's sovereignty and translated it into a dynamic missionary axiom: "Concentrate on the responsive elements of society." It thereby exposes the inadequacy of the pietism that seems to say, "Go where you are sent, even if you cannot expect a harvest." If God is selective in His grace, if Jesus Christ in the days of His flesh deliberately bypassed some to reach others, should not His missionary servants expect His Spirit to lead them to concentrate on winning the winnable? Indeed, one cannot read carefully the Gospels without being impressed with the very deliberate way in which He ministered to the responsive (Matt. 9: 13).

Did the apostle Paul uniformly go to the cities? Hardly! Actually, he concentrated on the Gentile "godfearers" who ringed the Jewish synagogues of the Mediterranean world. As someone has facetiously said, "Paul was not so much a church-planter as a synagogue-splitter." Paul's God was not uniformitarian but selective (Romans 9: 14-18). He chose Jacob in preference to Esau. He constrained some to believe but Pharoah's heart He hardened. And when Paul faced an unresponsive Jewish community he had but one final, terrible word for them: "It was necessary that the Word of God should be spoken first to you. Since you thrust it from you, and judge yourselves unworthy of eternal life, behold we turn to the Gentiles" (Acts 13: 46).

We conclude this section by underscoring this great issue. To speak of the selectivity of God is to speak of election. Little is to be gained from seeking to probe the mystery of God's unscrutable will. One is deliberately disobedient to God when he rationalizes his passivity in Christian witness by appealing to the doctrine of predestination. The aged Dr. Ryland was in error when his hyper-Calvinism made him resist William Carey's simple thesis: "If it be the duty of all men to believe the Gospel . . . then it is the duty of those who are entrusted with the Gospel to endeavor to make it known among all nations." It was not theologically correct for him to say, "Young man, sit down: when God pleases to convert the heathen, He will do it without your aid or mine!" (Walker, 1925: 53, 54).

So then, we are deeply persuaded that God is sovereign in His dealings with men. He makes them winnable. There is a time when His Spirit is peculiarly active in the hearts of men. They become "ripe unto harvest." It is the task of His reapers to translate this reality into a strategy for mission.

We have sought to do this. We believe the deployment

of field missionaries, the allocation of mission and church
funds and the focussing on prayer constituencies should be
a reflection of one's reasonable awareness of where God is
at work. And we are now persuaded that all over the world
where this factor has been deliberately made determinative
of strategy, God has abundantly confirmed with good harvests. Indeed, we feel we have leaped over the inscrutable
mystery that down through the years has provoked endless
theological debate and ecclesiastical division, and have put
our strength where it furthers, not hinders the ongoing of
the Christian mission. In seeking to win those whom God
has made winnable we have not unnaturally gained new
insight into what it means to be co-laborers with God in
the building of His Church.

And yet, we are still left uncertain as to the overall
objective of missionary service. This brings us to the
third theological issue foundational to the Church Growth
Movement.

✗ The Church that Extends the Mission

What is the nature and function of the Christian Church?
There are those that feel that we have yet to define the
Church, despite our constant emphasis on its growth. They
have not fully appreciated Dr. McGavran's concern that the
Movement serve all who confess Jesus Christ irrespective
of their particular polity and churchmanship. In pressing
us to declare ourselves more precisely on this subject,
they have made a caricature of our position by reducing
it to a simplistic absurdity.

On the one hand, we are accused of being so excessively
church-centric in our concept of the missionary task that
we are allegedly unwilling to regard the Church in any terms
other than those which speak of its function. The Church
is merely a witnessing instrument that furthers the Kingdom
of God. It is His instrument for evangelism, nothing more.
Its task is to persuade people to become Christians in order
that they might make other people Christians and so on to
the end of the age. The Church is only a means to an end,
and not an end in itself.[1]

On the other hand, there are those who accuse us of
being preoccupied with church extension in a crass, trium-

phalist sense. No cultural sensitivity, no awareness that the
Church is capable of variation in its local expression and
no concern for the world in its need. In a recent symposium
on world missions embracing both Protestant and Catholics, the Church Growth Movement was charged with being
a "disturbing influence on the image of mission" and then
dismissed with the following, single sentence—

> The strongly western orientation of the Church Growth
> Movement at this time of decolonization and the em-
> phatic dependence upon external missionary personnel,
> when missionary activity is under critical scrutiny,
> raises serious questions about the Church's ability to
> relate to the world   (Scott, 1972:155).[2]

It is difficult to conceive of a statement more filled with
ignorance of the Movement it denounces. One is silenced
by the tragedy of misunderstanding it represents and
offended by its assumptions that the Church Growth Movement is stolidly unaware of the mood of the times and
defective regarding the nature and function of the Church
in the world.

But let us speak positively. If the Church is neither to be
defined simply in terms of its mission and certainly not
in terms of western forms, what is its *esse?* New Testament
writers never speak of the Church without relating it to
God. As G. Johnston says, "As Jesus is the Christ of God
and the Holy Spirit the Spirit of God, so believers belong
to a community that is the Ecclesia of God." In every age,
and up to the present, those who commit themselves to
Christ are being builded together in Him to be a new, universal temple that replaces the particular temple of the
Old Covenant. In their midst God dwells by His Spirit
(Ephesians 2:20-22). It is certainly not a sort of religious association that has been founded by men at some
point in time and has been equipped, governed and maintained
by them ever since. The New Testament Church is an
organism created and kept by Jesus Christ Himself. He is
its Head. He rules in its midst and guards and sustains its
life. As Ignatius said, "Where Jesus Christ is, there is the
Church." It is the divine-human society by which He does
His work in the world.

So then, when we speak of the Church we cannot but
affirm that its fellowship and worship, its adoration of God

and intercessory prayer, its receiving His grace and rejoicing in His gifts, its ministry of sharing with one another and building one another up in the faith—all these are of its *esse.*

The Church glories in one Lord, one Faith, one Baptism. It possesses one common hope. We have no liberty to change it. Because it embraces the people that God redeems, we must contend for a universality that includes the total stratification of mankind. Because God constituted it a unity, we cannot but labor that it be united. Because its calling is essentially missionary, we must plead for the evangelistic priority. "Salvation is inside the Church," said Küng. Indeed, nothing is more important but that the Church grow. This means expansion growth within individual congregations, extension growth and bridging growth to new cultures, near and far. Obviously, we also are concerned with qualities other than membership growth, such as the spiritual growth of Christians, and the qualitative changes of structure with congregations, sometimes referred to as organic growth. Our concerns range widely over all these types of growth. A cursory reading of the titles of church growth publications will confirm this.

The Church Growth Movement represents an understanding of the Church that is biblical, but not innovative in the secular sense. We endorse the hiddenness of the Body of Christ. Only the Lord knows who are truly His (II Timothy 2:19). Those who profess His Name must presume on His grace for their final inclusion among the redeemed. More, we would not identify any one specific denomination with "the Church which is His Body," as some might charge. We stand with the Reformers, however, in affirming that where this hidden Body exists, its presence will be disclosed by certain visible "marks". We do not disagree with the Lutherans who define the marks as "the Gospel purely taught and the sacraments rightly administered." Nor would we fault the Calvinists for adding the mark of order and discipline. Members of the true Body are eager to bind themselves together to maintain the apostolic faith.

Well and good. But these three marks hardly express in their totality the New Testament ideal for the Church. Down through the history of Protestantism they have been debated and trumpeted in defense of ecclesiastical orthodoxy. More often than not, however, Reformation Churches have remained largely indifferent to the mission to which God has called His people. Most Protestant missionary work undertaken during the last century was motivated by the Evangelical Revivals rather than the Reformation. In reaction against this doctrinal imbalance and spiritual failure, the Church Growth Movement has felt it necessary to call attention to this flaw by pouring biblical content into one of the pre-Reformation marks of the Church—its apostolicity.

The New Testament uniformly reveals that the Church is established on the foundation of Jesus Christ and the Apostles (I Cor. 3:11; Ephesians 2:19-22). The Twelve were His authorized representatives. The Christian era was inaugurated by the Holy Spirit when they preached the Gospel, aroused the faith of those who listened and gathered the Church. They established its corporate life and became its most diligent participants. Although we admire their devotion and seek to follow their teachings, we do not believe God intended any succession of their office. The Twelve are dead; they established no succession. And yet, the function of apostolicity remains.

In one sense, the whole Church is called to the same mission that Christ entrusted to His apostles. All who follow Him can be expected to be transformed into fishers of men (Matthew 4:15). We follow Küng (1967:35) in affirming that—

> The Church is apostolic, a true follower of the apostles, when it preserves in all its members continuing agreement with the witness of the apostles, and also preserves a vital continuity with the ministry of the apostles.

In another sense, however, only a segment of a Church may be called to apostolic outreach. In the Acts we find the mark of apostolicity reflected in the development of a sodality within and between congregations (Acts 13:1-3; 15:36-41). Paul and his band were a disciplined, mobile group that performed an evangelistic, church-planting function similar to today's missionary society. When he wrote his great epistle to the four congregations comprising "the Church at Rome," one of his purposes was to stimulate its apostolicity, by drawing it into his forthcoming mission to Spain (Romans 1:5; 15:24).

Dare one say that a Church can reach maturity when its ministry is confined to the neighborhood in which it is located? Apparently Paul didn't think so. Should a 3,000 member Lutheran Church in Japan or a similar sized Mennonite Church in Columbia be encouraged to order the departure of all missionaries from their countries when they have yet to exhibit even the least evidence of apostolicity? And yet, this has been the absurd counsel they have received from missiologists within the conservative evangelical camp! We do well to ask these theorists: "How then shall the millions of Japanese and Columbians hear the message of salvation if you encourage the dismantling and withdrawal of the missionary structure?"

The goal of missions should not be confined to the mere planting of self-contained churches. What good are churches if they are not apostolic? The Church Growth Movement is seeking to hold high the goal of planting churches that manifest the apostolic mark. This means national churches that have developed their own sodalities for both reaching people within their own culture and those in other cultures. The business of missions is the stimulation of every conceivable type of apostolic outreach on the part of churches they plant. Until this is accomplished, they have no right to terminate their service. Only the emergence of a fully apostolic Church marks the completion of the missionary task in a country. And this brings us to the final theological issue foundational to the Church Growth Movement.

The Responsibility Demanded by Mission

Mission is of God. He defines its essence, provides its dynamic, reveals principles for its methodology and sets its goals. But it is not solely of God. It is also of men. Men are His co-laborers. They do the preaching, apply His principles to the cultural context, plant the Church and work out the tactics of its strategy. What does this mean in terms of the attitude they should take toward the human resources that God would harness to achieve this complex task?

We have stated without equivocation that the Church must grow if it is to accomplish the mission of God. One biblical image of growth is peaceful and pastoral; it is borrowed from botany. Another involves struggle and warfare. Much of the New Testament data on the Church in mission may be summarized under the rubric of an army, intimately involved with Jesus Christ in a cosmic struggle to liberate men from the devil's kingdom of darkness. Indeed, the Church has been called into being to fight, using weapons God has provided: truth, righteousness, the Gospel, faith, salvation, the Word of God, and prayer (Ephesians 6:10-20). Their use will demand all the Church's resources of heart, conscience, will, strength and time. It will also involve suffering.

No new languages will be learned, no new "culture formulations" of the Gospel will be defined, no new patterns of congregational life and worship will be created and no new sodalities of apostolicity will be launched and sustained without much effort and considerable cost. It was this realization that pressed the Apostle to say:

> I rejoice in my sufferings for your sake, and in my flesh I complete what is lacking in Christ's afflictions for the sake of His body, that is, the Church. . . We proclaim Jesus Christ, warning every man and teaching every man in all wisdom, that we may present every man mature in Christ. For this I toil, striving with all the energy which He almighty inspires within me (Colossians 1:24, 28, 29).

Dr. McGavran launched the Church Growth Movement by calling for men who would act as "explorers" out to "discover a new world" (1955:154). He recognized that a price would have to be paid if Christians were to rise to their responsibilities in the mission of the Church. He called for indifference to public opinion—total resistance to all pessimistic chatter about the end of the missionary era—and for a variety of forward surges in church growth research, controlled field experiments, missionary seminars, publication ministry and top-level graduate training to produce hundreds of specialists in Church Growth. He specified that this would entail the deliberate harnessing of such secular and relativistic disciplines as sociology, anthropology and history to a creative biblical theology that was capable of challenging this dogmatism of the 16th century Reformers. He called for the forging of a new discipline-missiology. He believed that with this new weapon the "good fight of the faith" would be more effectively fought on all six continents and on behalf of all the peoples of mankind.

Naturally, this call—"the Church must possess for Christ and Mission the best insights of our day, particularly in the behavioral sciences"—was received with mixed emotions. On the one hand, many missionaries responded. Several hundred have received formal training. More than a hundred research studies have been produced. The Movement is beginning to gain momentum. Regional church growth institutes are being established. It is exciting to measure the dimensions of dynamism being released within the Church for the accomplishment of mission in our time.

Of course there are those who do not share our evangelical views and have gone to considerable effort to caricature us as religious imperialists, zealously seeking proselytes and nervously preoccupied with but one scale of measurement, "the bodycount."

On the other hand, there are those within conservative evangelical ranks who challenge the validity of the Church Growth Movement. It seems unspiritual, carnal, worldly. They question the validity of bringing the social sciences to bear on a mission that uniquely belongs to God. Hasn't He "made foolish the wisdom of the world?" (I Cor. 1:20). They cry out: "Pray and preach, love and serve, and the Church will grow under the blessing and activity of the Spirit of God. Do not usurp the place that is rightfully and solely His. Be done with your American, success-oriented gimmicry!"

One recalls the wilderness wanderings of the Israelites. Moses was their able leader. God assisted him by providing a pillar of cloud by day and a pillar of fire by night (Numbers 9:15-25). In that treeless waste all could easily follow this visible sign of Yahweh's continuous Presence in their midst. And yet, the text records that a certain Midianite named Hobab overtook them, and was quickly recruited by Moses to be their guide (Numbers 10: 29-32). This is incredible. What need was there for such a desert expert? They already had the pillar. Does this not underscore the responsibility of God's servants to seek the best human help available for the performance of their mission? Hobabs are welcome in the camp of the Church Growth Movement! Hobabs who have mastered the insights of the behavioral sciences have much to contribute to those who are seeking to disciple the nations. They "serve as eyes for us" (vs. 31).

Conclusion

This is the day of unprecedented spiritual hunger. After extensive correspondence with all classes of society Malcolm Muggeridge bore witness to this fact in the following fashion:

> These (letters) reveal, I think more fully than any public opinion poll or other so-called scientific investigation, the extraordinary spiritual hunger which prevails today among all classes and conditions of people, from the most illiterate to the most educated, from the most lowly to the most eminent. The various moral and theological and sociological disputes of the day, however progressively resolved with ecclesiastical connivance, have nothing to say to this spiritual hunger, which is not assuaged by legalized abortion and homosexuality, solaced by contraception, or relieved by majority rule. Nor will it take comfort in the thought that God is dead, or that mankind has come of age, or even ecumenical negotiations for writing off Papal Infallibility against the validity of Anglican Orders. The only means of satisfying it remains that bread of life which Jesus offered, with the promise that those who ask of it should never hunger again. The promise stands (1969:10-11).

This poses an ancient theological issue we've struggled with again and again. It is the tension between the sovereignty of God and the responsibility of man. When pushed to an extreme and wrongly understood, one can lead to fatalism and the other to naturalism.

And yet, we must be able to respond positively to the criticism of our brethren. It is hardly right to derogate it as introverted pietism or simplistic generalization. More often than not our critics possess a devotion to Christ, His person and His cause, that rebukes us. They work as diligently as the most dedicated member of the

Church Growth Movement. We can only absorb their
criticism, reflect on their alternate suggestions and pursue
the line God has indicated to us. From time to time, however, a church growth researcher turns up evidence that
points to the tragic mistakes made by godly missionaries
in the past.

This brings one a deep sense of pause. On one occasion
while probing the experience of the Church in one section
of Korea, a researcher uncovered a fifteen year period
during which it hardly grew at all. And this despite the
fact that in the same period the growth of the Korean Church
could only be described by the word "wildfire." In this
case, the data base was very detailed and included a microfilm record of the correspondence of the missionaries with
their superiors. Reading this was a solemnizing and illuminating experience. Although no judgments were passed,
one can easily sense the implications of the concluding
summarization:

> It was as if some mysterious force had been holding
> the Church back during those fifteen years, and then,
> when the Church was able to grow, it burst out with
> the force of an unleashed giant, too long held in bondage.
> (Shearer, 1966: 108, 109).

The Church Growth Movement is dedicated to the task
of giving this Bread of Life to all mankind. This task is
biblically defined, divinely sustained, historically vindi-
cated and humanly possible. It is the mission of the Church.

Notes

[1]For a pointed critique of this sub-biblical viewpoint, and with
which Dr. McGavran and his associates would heartily agree,
see Lesslie Newbigin's challenge of Dr. Hoekendijk, THE
HOUSEHOLD OF GOD;   New York, Friendship Press, 1953,
pp. 168, 169.

[2]It is not without significance that the volume containing this
article was the March 1972 selection of the Church Growth Book
Club, despite its criticism of the Church Growth Movement.

Bibliography

Bavinck, J. H.
    1960   AN INTRODUCTION TO THE SCIENCE OF MIS-
              SIONS, Grand Rapids, Presbyterian and Reformed.
Calvin, John
              INSTITUTES, Book 1.
Küng, Hans
    1967   THE CHURCH, New York: Sheed & Ward.
McGavran, Donald A.
    1955   THE BRIDGES OF GOD, New York, Friendship
              Press.
Muggeridge, Malcolm
    1969   JESUS REDISCOVERED London, Collins, Fontana
              Books.
Scott, Roland
    1972   "Motivating the American Church to Greater Support
              for World Mission" in MISSION IN THE 70s.
              Edited by J. T. Boberg and J. A. Scherer: Chicago
              Cluster of Theological Schools.
Shearer, Roy E.
    1966   WILDFIRE: CHURCH GROWTH IN KOREA, Grand
              Rapids, Eerdmans.
Temple, William
    1953   NATURE, MAN AND GOD, London, MacMillan
Walker, F. Dearville,
    1925   WILLIAM CAREY, Chicago, Moody Press.
Weber, Hans Reudi
    1963   "God's Arithmetic," FRONTIER, pp. 298-301.

Christian missions in the lands of Asia and Africa are coming to the end of an era. The entire conduct of missions must be thoroughly re-examined.

The Great Century of Christian Missions may well be followed by a Greater Century of the Christian Churches. As the churches of Christ all around the globe, the older churches and the younger churches banded together, recognize the primacy of discipling those peoples who have been called of God, and as these churches resolutely refuse to be turned aside from this harvesting of ripened grain, there may well result a century of expansion such as has not yet been seen.

BRIDGES OF GOD,
pp. 3, and 158.

6

CONTINUITY AND CHANGE
IN CHRISTIAN MISSION

Jack F. Shepherd

The primary purpose of this essay is to discuss the definition of mission. Consideration of strategy, methodology and structures requires a balanced perspective between continuity and change; but this is not so in a definition of mission, where a vital continuity of meaning is essential. Change or deviation in this respect will lead to compromise and confusion.

It seems appropriate that a volume dedicated to Donald McGavran, who certainly has won distinction as an advocate of creative and radical change in missionary methodology, should include an article that pays tribute to him for his discerning and steadfast faithfulness to the "Unchanging Mission," as Douglas Webster has called it (1965:ix).

Some of us have been uncomfortable with the expression "Church Growth theology." Nonetheless, we would honor McGavran as one who certainly is contributing to that which another great missionary scholar is calling for the need of the hour. In the notable and well deserved Festschrift to R. Pierce Beaver there are two references to a challenging assertion he made to an important missionary conference in 1968. Gerald Anderson quotes Beaver's words: "The

great task and major role of missiology today is to clarify
and define for a confused and lukewarm church the meaning
of mission in an age both ecumenical and secular." (Danker
& Kang, eds., 1971:137). In my judgment McGavran is
doing this. What he means when he speaks of mission is
simple and clear. He has been criticized as being "simplistic," though that seems gratuitous. Perhaps his eagerness to dispel "the semantic fog" arising in current
pronouncements on mission may have resulted in his appearing to oversimplify. Some contemporary advocates
of change in the meaning of mission have produced such
vague and complex redefinitions that McGavran's call to
mission may sound just too simple by comparison. However, this simplicity has about it the ring of Biblical authenticity.

It might be enough in this essay to criticize the changes
introduced in ecumenical vocabulary that seems to be in
dangerous discontinuity from the New Testament "idea of
mission," as Warneck called it. (1901:9). This would not
please or satisfy McGavran. He is the modern missions'
gadfly "on the right hand and on the left." He has been
quick to say, beginning with the first issue of *Church
Growth Bulletin,* "Conservative missions are as foggy as
liberals" (Sept. 1964). Who else would turn from the searching accusation against the World Council of Churches that
Uppsala might "betray the two billion" to raise the same
question for IFMA and EFMA as they would convene G.L.
'71?

McGavran is a man who represents a continuity in the
meaning of mission that should not only command our
respect and commendation, but call us to identify with him
in his commitment to the one Biblical mission. I am seeking to do that in what I say here.

This is not offered as an exposition of McGavran's
definition of mission. It is rather a modest attempt to
reemphasize the elements that are essential to the New
Testament idea of mission. These, I am wanting to affirm,
cannot be omitted or modified if our mission is really in
continuity with God's mission. Having reviewed these as
the New Testament norm, I want to pursue a point on which
McGavran has repeatedly and industriously commented.
Unfortunately, he does not seem to have been heard or

understood. He has tried to rescue the word and concept
of mission from those who want to apply it to everything
the church does and even employ it as a synonym for the
word "church" itself. *(Understanding Church Growth,*
1970: 49, 72, 356). That kind of protest is particularly
critical of some ecumenical notions of mission, but there
is a corollary to it which is a special concern of mine.
We need to work toward greater precision in the definition of mission so that we limit and sharpen the claim we
make for consistency and continuity with the New Testament. We must acknowledge that there is some of that
"rosy fog" floating around when we say "Our mission is
here and everywhere and everyone is a missionary any-
way," just as there is when the claim is made, "The church
is mission and so is all it does."

What We Mean by the Biblical Idea of Mission

1. The Biblical "Idea"

The useful phrase "idea of mission" was called to my
attention by the editor of this volume. Whether Warneck
had it in mind or not, and he probably did, it serves to
do several things. It affirms the presence of the mission's
theme in Scripture even though the word is not explicitly
utilized. That the word itself did not come into ecclesiastical vocabulary until the 13th century *(Planning for Mission,* 1966: 39; cf. Hahn, 1963: 10) does not invalidate the
claim to Biblical authority and definition. The idea is
there.
    To speak of mission in these terms also allows for that
continuity of a single missionary purpose in the whole of
Scripture, Old and New Testament, of which a host of Biblical scholars has written (Blauw, Bavink, Rowley, etc.).
    The identification of the source of the pervasive mission
idea as being in God Himself, His love, will, purpose,
power and acts is delineated in the "missio Dei" theme
(cf. Vicedom, et al). McGavran identifies with that concept, but having recognized the divine initiative he is quick
to emphasize that God has purposed to accomplish His
mission through human instrumentality (1970: 31).
    McGavran, like many others (Zwemer, Kraemer, Stott,
etc.), accepts the missionary commandment of our Lord

as the final comprehensive explication of the Biblical idea of mission. The expression "Great Commission Missions" must be a special McGavranism. He broadens this idea by speaking of the "Great Commision as given by Paul," especially in Romans 1:5 and 16:25, 26 (1970: 62). To accept Biblical authority in a literal and serious way is to recognize that the profound, dynamic idea of mission which permeates the Bible comes to have specific and explicit form as it progressively unfolds in Scripture and climaxes as the New Testament mandate for the church's mission.

2. The Singularity of New Testament Mission

In the context of a discussion of four views of mission, which are certainly to a significant extent mutually exclusive, Hans Margull concludes that today we must "accept a plurality of views of mission" (IRM, Jan. '71: 57). He goes on to speak of a plurality of forms of missionary activity which is not at all problematic. However, if the Biblical idea of mission is in clear view in its basic essential elements, it is one mission. Ronan Hoffman, a Roman Catholic missiologist, seems to understand Hahn's statement that "the earliest Christian view of mission is by no means homogeneous" as suggesting a kind of plurality or ambiguity in the New Testament idea of mission. (Cotter; 1968: 23). This hardly seems consistent with the solid, comprehensive definition of mission with which Hahn concludes his study (1963: 155).

Though McGavran (and his associates at Fuller School of World Mission) find it logical and proper to retain the 's' for certain important usages, he agrees with the trend toward "Dropping the S." The editorial announcing the disappearance of that sacred sibilant from IRM makes a point essential to the right definition of mission. "The mission of the church is singular in that it issues from the One Triune God and His intention for the salvation of all men. His commission to the church for this mission, and the given responses of particular churches in particular situations to the commission manifold" (IRM, April '69: 142).

Having said that McGavran stands for "unchanging

mission," it is appropriate to leave this point with Webster's
fine declaration of it (1965: ix).

> I do not believe that the Church's mission, its essential
> mission, changes with the date. Its mission is the same
> in the 1960s as in the 1860s or the '60s of the first
> Christian century. What changes is the context of the
> mission, the shape and mood of the world in which it
> has been discharged. There is only one mission. It is
> God's mission to the whole world through his Son, his
> Spirit, and his Church. Neither its meaning or its goal
> can ever change. It springs from eternal love; it con-
> cludes in eternal salvation. But the ways of carrying
> out this mission are determined very often by a variety
> of historical situations, by the questions men ask, the
> needs they feel, the forces that condition them. These
> are the variables. The Christian mission and the
> Christian Gospels are constants. Both are given. For
> this reason nothing particularly new can ever be said
> about the Gospel of the mission in everchanging frame-
> works, because presuppositions and assumptions are
> always fluid, not merely from one time to another but
> but from one society to another. It is this kind of cir-
> cumstantial mobility which makes necessary restate-
> ments of the meaning of the Gospel and the meaning
> of mission.

3. Contradictory Pluralism in Mission's Definitions

If it is correct that there is a Biblical idea of mission
and if as many besides these alluded to here are insisting
it is one mission, how is the diversity of multiplying definitions to be accounted for? McGavran has been called
censorious when he has protested the framing of novel
definitions of mission that introduce compromising change
from, rather than loyal continuity to, the classic meaning
of mission. Many of us were in his corner, sharing dis-
may and alarm, in reading the Uppsala statements *(C.G.
Bulletin,* May '68: 3):

> From beginning to end the document is studded with
> the word mission. It is titled Renewal in Mission. Its
> first sentence reads, 'God has set out on His mission
> to men in Jesus, the man from Nazareth.' Its second

main sub-section is entitled Freedom for Mission,
and affirms that 'Renewal for mission is the work of
the Spirit.' But, while the word mission is repeatedly
used, its meaning is nowhere that of communicating
the Good News of Jesus Christ to unbelieving men in
order that they might believe and live.

The post-Uppsala ambiguity over the meaning of mission is exemplified in the Margull article mentioned
above. This noted scholar presided at a Seminar at the
University of Hamburg entitled "Introduction to the Understanding of Mission." The project was to examine four
views of mission which are described as "representative
and theologically constructive." (1971: 50-57)

With the stated Biblical idea of mission as a criterion,
the four views may be seen as moving out in deviation
from the central norm. I would rate them with Freytag's
evangelical view at the center. His emphasis is in clear
continuity with the Biblical idea (cf. Beyerhaus, 1971:18).

The view of Vatican II is next. Like McGavran I have a
sincere measure of agreement with the Decree on Mission.
(1970: 356). Nonetheless if Fr. Jean Danielou is a reliable
interpreter of its meaning, this view, as might be expected,
would be off center, particularly in its ecclesiological
basis (Cotter, 1968: 11-22).

Even further out is Hoekendijk's view which is so
avowedly anti-"church-centric" as to have engaged him in
running debate with McGavran *(C. G. Bulletin.* v. 1, 1964:
25-26). In this Margull seminar, Hoekendijk's "signs of
shalom," which are pointed out as concretizing mission,
are interpreted so as to practically identify mission with
social and political revolution. I want to believe that this
is stretching Hoekendijk's view beyond that to which he
himself would consent. Without appearing to disregard or
oppose any of these "signs of shalom," it must be insisted
that these are not in themselves mission by any New Testament standard of measurement.

The fourth view is Tillich's. It is suggested in the
article that his approach to mission is similar to that of
Rahner with his concept of "anonymous Christians." This
became a philosophical speculation that looses from any
sound theological mooring. It may be mentioned in passing
that the Roman Catholic scholar Fr. Prudencio Damboriena

offers a sharp rebuttal to Rahner's view in the Beaver Festschrift. He also warns against some of the views of Hans Küng whose writings have such strong appeal for some of us (1971: 85).

The offering of such a wide variety of views of mission is part of our contemporary confusion over mission. This modification and shift has been developing since Edinburgh 1910 (Scherer, Anderson), but it is only in the last two decades that official changes in the definition have manifested such distinct discontinuity from the New Testament commission. For example, Pierce Beaver, in the introduction to the volume of the writings of Rufus Anderson, says, "Until at least the 1950s no American mission agencies or missionaries ever openly questioned Dr. Anderson's aim for the mission: namely, the fostering of self-propagating, self-governing, self-supporting churches." (Beaver, 1967: 38). McGavran's view of mission is directly in the tradition of Anderson and of his great contemporary Henry Venn (1970: 336). The continuity of this view of mission must be maintained and promoted over against the kinds of substitutes that are being circulated.

4. The Elements of New Testament Mission

It is strikingly evident that appeal can be made to Biblical authority for mission by people who end up with vastly different ideas as to the work they should be doing. It should be possible to describe mission in terms of elements essential to it. Then it would be logical to say that the objective of mission is to do these things. Until they are done, mission is not completed.

The Frankfurt Declaration has a convincing statement on seven "basic indispensable elements of mission." This affirmation which is in the Freytag tradition is complete and fully acceptable as a definition of mission. Some of its presuppositions have been stated here in different ways. Though the seven Frankfurt points are all indispensable, the test of the integrity of mission can be given without using all of them (Beyerhaus, 1971: 107).

What McGavran has offered as an attempt to "define mission narrowly" really includes basically three elements. Mission is "an enterprise devoted to proclaiming the good news of Jesus Christ and to persuading men to become His disciples and dependable members of His church" (1970: 34). The three elements of mission are a) proclamation of the gospel; b) with the objective of persuading men to accept Christ and become His disciples; and c) to teach them to participate responsibly in the life of a church. This is certainly a church-centric view of missions. Scherer may speak more truth than he intends when he says, "It is currently the most eloquent statement on behalf of church-centrism and, with its vision of fantastically multiplying churches in what Dr. McGavran calls 'Africasia,' a kind of 'last hurrah' for the spirit of Edinburgh 1910" (IRM, 1971: 125).

For McGavran, the primary form of the church is the local congregation. This means that the objective of mission really does not come out as multiplying churches or congregations. If these are churches in which the Word is truly heard and the Spirit is at work, they will be self-propagating, to use that historic word. McGavran is surely on the side of the Spirit according to that account of the "three-self formula" which says the mission society is interested in self-support, the young church is interested in self-government, but the Holy Spirit is interested in self-propagation!

If there is to be continuity of meaning when Christian mission is spoken of, the elements of proclamation, persuasion to discipleship, and development of growing churches must all be present. These are minimal requirements for mission. Those who neglect them or denigrate them should be honest enough not to try to describe their enterprise as mission.

Distinguishing Mission from Other Aspects of the Church's Total Ministry

Stephen Neill's discerning complaint has been frequently repeated, but constantly disregarded. The sort of things noted above are distressing reminders that, "if everything is mission, nothing is mission" (1959: 81). It is difficult to determine which tendency in defining mission is most problematic. Mission can be made so inclusive that engaging in some action broadly classified

as mission may seem to justify leaving other aspects un-
done. On the other hand it can be defined very narrowly,
as I am attempting to do. Then there is the danger of being
misunderstood. To restrict certain activities and services
of the church from the category of mission may be con-
strued as saying that they are insignificant or improper.
It is perilous after having sought to define mission to go
on to distinguish it from other aspects of the church's
ministry. To do so is not to make judgmentally discriminating comparisons but to attempt to keep things in perspective.

How did mission get broadened out so that for some it
has come to include everything the church does; at least
"everything she does outside her four walls" (1970: 49).
There are two evident reasons for this.

1. Confusing Our Mission With "Missio Dei"

There is great meaning in the fact that as we participate in Christ, we participate in His mission; or that the
mission is really God's though we have a share in it. This
is sound and serious theology and provides the only proper
foundation for mission. However, this cannot be taken to
mean that the Christian mission is to be equated with all
that God purposes to do in history.

There might be a sense in which we can say all of God's
acts are part of His total mission, but that is the sort of
usage that is too general. Is there not a kind of distinc-
tiveness in the word "mission" that would suggest redemptive activity rather than the divine work in creation, providence or even revelation? My point is not to minimize
God's acts in creation and history. I want rather to say
that these are not best described as mission, in spite of
the moving expressions about creation and the New Creation which seems to sparkle in the Uppsala documents.

If we begin describing all that God does as His mission
and then see all that we do that relates to righteousness
and good as being mission, we will soon lose sight of something essential in our concern with things that are good. We
may have come to the time when there is a reversal of what
Max Warren warned against in speaking of "the historic
tension" we face in following *The Calling of God*. He says:

"God is primarily creator and only in the second place redeemer. It is part of our human self-centeredness which insists on seeing God almost exclusively in terms of redemption. It is salutary for us to remind ourselves that redemption is concerned only with an episode in God's creative activity, an immensely important episode, costly to God, vital to men, but still only an episode" (1944:15). That is a truth that we conservative evangelicals need to listen to with special care. However, for the present day activist generalizers of ecumenical mission, redemption is hardly considered as a saving work of God distinct from his creative activity in nature and history. Salvation becomes humanization, and mission is then social action to improve man's present life situation. There is the danger of being misunderstood and misrepresented, as McGavran frequently is when he speaks critically of those who promote mission as "Christian presence," "working for secularization," "witnessing to Christ by kindly deeds," "industrial evangelism which seeks fo improve laboring conditions," and "discerning God in the revolution and lining up with Him" (1970: 358). We must insist that no one concerned with mission can avoid or ignore their Christian moral obligations in relation to such issues, but it neither fulfils the demands nor defines the responsibility to call everything of this sort "mission."

I believe we best conceive of "missio Dei" as God's *redemptive* activity. What we are to do to share in it is clearly specified in the New Testament. We can communicate more clearly, in my judgment, by making further distinctions within the total of the redemptive ministry of the church. Mission is a crucial and even the "first" part of that total ministry, but it is only a part. We need to work toward greater specificity and less generality in defining our missionary obligation.

2. "Letting the World Write the Agenda"

It must be admitted that in the area of mission the most stimulating and exciting things being written are by people who are in some sense related to the ecumenical movement. Many concepts borrowed from Hoekendijk, Niles, Blauw, Beaver and many others have been provocative and enriching. The emphasis on "The Church Inside Out" has caused us to look at the world more seriously and sensitively. It is the object of God's love. It is the oikoumene toward which the apostolate is directed (Hoekendijk: 1964).

However there is a very real danger in letting our mission take its shape around the felt needs of the world. We can go astray from God's real purpose in seeking "to define mission in terms of the Christian challenge and response to the longings of the three billion inhabitants of our globe" (Potter, 1968: 36). Our mission is not just concerned with the needs the world feels or can express. The Gospel defines man's need and offers a solution whether or not man senses or acknowledges the need. His problem is sin. His need is salvation. Neither of these things is adequately and finally provided for at the level of humanization.

When the mandate for mission is derived from and guided by the revolutionary styles and goals of present-day movements, whatever good and value they may have, it will not stand under judgment of the New Testament.

Tippett is right in his criticism of Scherer's tendency to consent to an authority in mission that is "churchly" rather than Biblical (1969: iv). The contemporary threat is that the church will borrow its sense of mission from listening to the world so as to "scratch it where it itches" rather than hearing the Word of God in its commission to mission.

3. Priority Requires Particularization

The failure to be particular enough in definition has limited effective communication of truth and assignment of responsibility in relation to the things of God. For example, "Christian" and "church" are both words that have come to have such general meaning as to make them difficult to use. Now "mission" faces a similar threat and "missionary" is also beclouded with ambiguity and equivocation. Can we not limit the idea of mission to stated specified things so that it has clear and particular meaning? If mission is to have a place of priority in the life of a believer or a church, it cannot simply be everything that is done. It must be an activity defined in a particular way if it is to have a real place of priority.

The word that best sums up the comprehensive activity of the church is its "service" or "ministry" as we have it in Ephesians 4:11, 12. If our present-day mission is in continuity with the apostolic aspect of that total ministry, then it should continue to have a *first* place. We must know what it is we are talking about if we are to give it a real place of priority. This is the reason Beaver is calling for someone to make clear the meaning of mission for today's confused and lukewarm church.

A rather striking example of setting mission in the context of the church's whole ministry is reflected in a moving quotation from Karl Barth. It is striking to think that this is a kind of "last word" from Barth. We may quarrel with other things he had to say, but in this case we can give him the last word. This is out of a note by Jacques Rossel in IRM at the time of Barth's death (1969: 227):

> The next to last paragraph of Barth's Dogmatics is devoted to the Holy Spirit and the Sending of the Christian Congregation ('Der Heilige Geist und die Sendung der Christlichen Gemeinde'). It contains Barth's Theology of Mission. Barth distinguishes five types of services the congregation is sent to perform: It is sent to praise God, to preach His word, to teach it, to evangelize and to engage in mission. Barth takes here the word 'mission' in the traditional sense of the church being sent into the nations to witness the Gospel. This sending being according to Barth 'the very root of the existence and therefore of the whole ministry of the community,' and Barth goes on: 'In mission the Church sets off and goes (porenthetes, Matt. 28:19) taking the essentially and most profoundly necessary step beyond itself, and beyond the dubiously Christian world in which it is more immediately set, to the world of men . . . the Word which God has pronounced in Jesus Christ concerning the covenant of grace which he has concluded with it is still alien and must therefore be taken as a new message. (Church Dogmatics IV, 3, p. 874). We leave it to the reader to reflect upon this deep definition of the Church's mission.

Distinguishing Mission from Evangelism

Most of my criticism so far has been directed against the kind of change of the concept of mission that is most frequently heard on the ecumenical side of the mission's community. In the McGavran manner I must balance out with some conservative evangelical self-criticism. Are we keeping a strong vital strain of continuity with historic and New Testament mission? or are we tolerating compromising and eroding changes not just in vocabulary but in our basic outlook?

We certainly are not offering very strong rebuttal to proposals that sound like abandonment of overseas mission in favor of long needed involvement in social action in the nearby ghetto. What I am pleading for is a both/and response rather than an unfaithful either/or. We will never correct or compensate for our missionary disobedience by any amount of social action. Saying it is all the same mission only compounds the problem.

Admittedly we must do more about this than discuss the meaning of words and the relation of particular items in Biblical interpretation. It is true that many a great cause has been compromised by equivocation over words. Nothing is as practical as a good idea clearly expressed. What can we do in this matter of working for a clarification of words like "mission" and "missionary"?

1. We must be alert to the problem

For good and proper reasons we have made shifts in our mission vocabulary. For one, we also have dropped that "s." Incidentally, it may be that the conservative Interdenominational Foreign Mission Association was way ahead of its time in 1917 when it used the singular in naming the organization. That was a good number of decades before anyone else made the move "from missions to mission." A proper coordination of the two terms, as in "The mission of missions," makes real sense. There is, however, a kind of stigma of illegitimacy, or at least anachronism, that can come to be attached to the word "missions" so that the wealth of meaning and challenge it used to convey is lost.

Then there is the taboo word "foreign." It would be well

for all of us to wise up and drop it from our departments, societies, and associations. It undoubtedly has the threat of a pejorative quality. But in the combination of "foreign missions" it may have made some things clear in a forceful and demanding way. All this is now repudiated along with colonialism and imperialism.

Then there is the word "missionary." For a time that was treated with disdain or rephrased in odd disguises. However, the most effective means of completely obscuring its claim and meaning is the sentimentalism that heroically asserted that "everyone is a missionary." Perhaps, as Neill laments about the overgeneralized use of mission, pretty soon nobody is a missionary.

2. Keeping Mission in Its Place

The place to begin, it seems to me, is in delineating the particular function of mission as an aspect of the total ministry of the church. This can only be suggested here in a general way, but it deserves the attention and labor of scholarship in exegesis and hermeneutics, as well as theological and historical studies. Some have attempted to put diakonia, kerygma, koinonia altogether in the "shalom" of mission which, instead of becoming concrete, almost evaporates in near mythical and poetic themes.

We must try carefully to distinguish all of these. We dare not lose any aspect of the life style and standard of the mature responsible believer. We can best define standards of behaviour and responsibility by conscientiously setting out all of the varied areas and aspects of the life of discipleship and the ministry of the church. Then we can point toward the need for involvement in all of the things we are to be and do as Christians. The big issue in contemporary discussion of these matters is the relation of service to mission. Some make them synonymous.

In order to avoid a tense polarization, we often insist that mission inevitably includes service. For example, John Stott worked out the helpful equation: Mission equals Witness plus Service (C.G.B., Nov. 1968: 39). That is not the kind of formula with which once can argue and yet does it not allow for the possibility of saying you cannot fulfil your witness in mission without some supplementary service? In a sense of course that is true, but would it not make for greater clarity to say there are two or, in the case of the Stott equation, three different things for which Christians and the church have responsibility? However, each one can be defined and distinguished the one from the other, even though they have a kind of inseparability, in a proper Christian sense.

3. Distinguishing Mission from Evangelism

The whole issue of "service" in Christ's name is an especially sensitive one today. Debate about it almost always seems to become tendentious. A better example of the way in which definitions become clearer when they are reinforced by precise distinctions is in the attempt to distinguish mission from evangelism.

a. The multiple faceted ministry or service of Eph. 4:11.

The key passage on the ministry of the whole church is certainly suggestive of the varying functions within the total ministry of the church. These can be defined as: apostolic, prophetic, evangelistic, pastoral and didactic. There is much support now for the claim that "apostle" could very well read "missionary." This properly puts the emphasis on apostolate rather than apostolicity. In any case this passage, along with I Corinthians 12-14, points to a distinct division of functions within the one ministry.

b. The contemporary call for clarification of the relation between evangelism and mission

I have been encouraged to pursue the study of this matter in spite of impatient rejoinders about arguing over words and semantic niceties. Three notable comments from respected authorities relate to this issue:

Paul Rees utilized a fascinating title for a lecture series he gave at North Park Seminary in 1966. He called it "Evangelism and Mission: The Elements of an Equation." He began with the comment, "If I have refrained from an outright equating of the two words, it is partly because of the still fuzzy boundaries of definition that surround them."

He goes on to make a point which I am trying here to raise questions about. "In the light of the New Testament, evangelism and mission are, if not indistinguishable, at least inseparable" (1966: 8).

In 1968 John Stott raises the same question in his probing the Uppsala position. He comments on some of the "uncomfortable questions" he has to ask (1968: 38):

> These inner contradictions are all, in their different ways, expressions of a more fundamental cleavage which Uppsala left unhealed. Precisely what is 'mission'? The word occurs in many places in Section Two but it nowhere is clearly defined. Evangelicals have something to learn here. We have too easily assumed that 'mission' and 'evangelism' (like the cognate adjectives 'missionary' and 'evangelistic') are interchangeable synonyms. But is this so?

In Stott's exposition he suggests that mission may be "wider than evangelism." It is in this connection that he proposes his equation: "Mission plus Witness equals Service." This is an interesting proposition and would be fruitful for study. However, in spite of my profound respect for John Stott, I am inclined to think we can achieve greater clarity by distinguishing mission from both evangelism and service.

The call to define the relationship of mission to evangelism is sounded in the Beaver Festschrift in connection with the passage to which an allusion has already been made. Beaver outlines the problems that confront those who undertake what he calls the "major role of missiology today . . . to clarify and define . . . the meaning of mission" (1971: 137, 138).

> The major problems with which it must wrestle are these: the relationship between Christian faith and other religions, the relationship between faith and culture and the relationship . . . between the worldwide sending mission and local evangelism.

Beaver has discussed in a helpful way this relationship between mission and evangelism in a chapter of *The Missionary Between the Times* in which he urges that mission today should be a vital succession to and continuity with the New Testament mission (1968: 1–43).

Gerald Anderson, who includes this important statement in the Beaver Festschrift, adds some items for the task of missiological definition (1971: 138):

For instance there is the dilemma created by the opposition of 'Christian presence' to 'Christian proclamation.' There is the polarity between evangelism and social justice, between mission and service, and between conversion and dialogue. And there is the need to define and describe more adequately the distinctions between mission, witness, and evangelism.

c. Toward the definition of mission in distinction from evangelism

It would be pretentious even to appear to offer the closing observations of this essay as an answer to the question raised about the relationship between witness, evangelism and mission. Perhaps I can, with a kind of modest dogmatism, borrow the title of the Margull seminar and conclude now with a suggestion for a new approach toward an "Introduction to the Understanding of Mission." My timidity is not produced by equivocation about the claim I am making. It comes out of the realization of how presumptuous it is to propose such a sweeping revision of the vocabulary of mission at this late date.

In spite of these considerations I offer this exercise in definition. Let us get mission in focus by narrowing it down instead of broadening it out. Let witness, evangelism and mission be seen as three concentric circles with mission in the middle. Though you cannot have mission without evangelism and witness, not all evangelism and witness properly fits the category of mission. I know what I am saying is in contrast to Stott's suggestion that mission is "wider than evangelism." In my view it is narrower and more specialized.

Let me try to set the three things out in a comparative statement:

Witness can be regarded as the most general in the sense of its inclusiveness. Will anyone deny that witness is both verbal and non-verbal? Scripture certainly bears that out. The works of the Lord and His followers bear witness as "signs and tokens of the Kingdom." The power of the Holy Spirit which makes us His witnesses surely does not have to do only with what we say or talk about. A convincing case can be made for the fact that witness has to do with truth and fact that have been apprehended in experience. But even Christian witness is not limited to reporting in message form that which has been seen and heard. Our witness is every manifest expression of what we are and do and know. Now Christian witness can be narrowed down to personal verbal confession or testimony, but the word itself is best understood, especially in this comparison, as inclusively general.

Witness is also general in terms of those who are to engage in it. Every believer is to be a witness. There is a kind of frustratingly fuzzy ambiguity in saying, "Every Christian is a witness." As a matter of fact this is true in the sense that, if he identifies as a Christian at all, in every situation he is a witness in either a positive or negative sense. That witness includes what he says, what he does, and what he is.

The third aspect of witness that relates to its being general or comprehensive in terms of this discussion is that it is individual. It is perilous to begin distinguishing things that are individually Christian rather than corporately Christian, but I think this can be done in speaking about witness. In my judgment this is not so in the case of either evangelism or mission. They are aspects of the total ministry of the church. They have an ecclesiastical emphasis and relationship that witness need not have, simply because it is so general and inclusive. It seems to me it could be correct to speak of Christian witness that had no particular reference to "church."

However, any "witness" that can properly be described as "evangelistic" or "missionary" has to be saying, or at least implying, something about the church. In trying to make this what may appear to be an artifically exacting point, I am disagreeing with what Beaver points out was a "fundamental principle" of Rufus Anderson's view of mission. Anderson insisted that mission is a responsibility of the individual believer, not of the church. I want to make that claim for witness, but not for mission.

Evangelism gets defined and redefined with warmth and eloquence at one or another of the ever increasing number of conferences and Congresses. Even as I engage in this little exercise, I am convicted by the thought that if we spent the time on evangelistic witness that we do in defining and conferring about evangelism, the task of world evangelization would be nearer completion.

I will not therefore add or quote any of the multiplicity of great definitions. Any that I would accept or agree to would need to include emphasis on an explanation of the Gospel, with the intention of persuading a person to accept Christ and follow Him in the obedience of discipleship, a part of which is responsible participation in the congregational life and witness of the church. In this I am agreeing with the concerned Indian Christian who says, "The church is part of the Gospel." I understand that to mean the local assembly of believers.

Evangelism is partial, incomplete and truncated, if it is seen as calling men to Christ in terms of an individual, metaphysical, vertical participation in "the invisible Church" without any reference to the local visible company of believers. If there is that not inconceivable situation in which "the church" in a place consists of that one believer who seeks to share Christ in evangelistic witness, then in my model you will have not just evangelism taking place but mission also. Before spelling that out, I want to repeat this point. You cannot call men to Christ in evangelism without calling them into the fellowship of the church with you. That last prepositional phrase may have an element of idealism, but I think it is Biblical.

We may think it is more fitting to "win souls" with the Four Laws or some other proven technique and then say it will be good to go to the church of your choice. Or we may refer "our converts" to the kind of congregation or "mission" (sic) in which they would fit socially, economically or racially. If I am hinting at reality here, then I am pointing to a kind of evangelism that is compromising and superficial. Evangelism "in depth" should have a witness that says, "Come and confess Christ as your Saviour and Lord and serve Him along with me in this church. Join the family, be a part of this 'household of God.'"

My point may be exemplified by suggesting that we need this emphasis in relating to "the Jesus people." We must say to them, "You can only properly follow Christ in the

ordered fellowship of a congregation of believers where
baptism is administrered and the Lord's Supper is served."
This also means that as churches we must be open to any
whom we acknowledge to be in Christ with us. To call what
we do evangelism, if it just gets people "saved" but stops
there, so as not to get involved in controversial things like
the sacraments and church "membership," is to operate
below the standard of the New Testament. Evangelism is a
call for action in response to the Good News of the Gospel.
This is primarily a vertical response toward God. It
should also involve on the horizontal level a voluntary
integration into the community of believers.

Now let me attempt to say finally that I think that mission
may be defined even more narrowly than evangelism, although all of the elements of evangelism are necessarily
present in mission.

Mission, as I have already said, is defined with sufficient
clarity by McGavran. It has been implied that the elements
of McGavran's "narrow" definition have been emphasized as
essential elements of evangelism. Does it make sense at
all, then, to try to further distinguish the two? I think it
does.

My affirmations of finality are not unlike Paul's, but I
will end the attempt to make this point by suggesting three
particulars in which I think we can usefully distinguish
mission from evangelism and be in loyal continuity with
the New Testament.

First, there is the constantly emphasized element of "the
sending." Evangelism is done directly by the believer in
his relationship to his own church and its outreach as well
as in its own cooperative efforts with other congregations
and evangelistic enterprises. A Christian can be directly
involved in evangelism at the various levels of individual
witness, group activities, church meetings, regional cooperative efforts, or Graham-type crusades. In all of this
multiplicity of levels of evangelsim, he may be directly
involved in one way or another.

A characteristic and distinctive element of mission is
that it is essentially "a sending." It is carried out for the
individual believer and the local congregation indirectly by
those whom it delegates and sends " to the regions beyond."
Obviously, the frontiers and boundaries of the "regions

beyond" are relative and variable. The home base is everywhere. But mission means that for every believer and every
church there is "a foreign field" to which he reaches out
not in direct evangelism but through the acknowledged and
approved agents of mission who are sent out. This sending
is not that broad sense of being sent by God into the world
as the Son of God was, and as all who are sons of God
through Him are. The "sending of mission" is a particular
part of that general "sentness." In mission God sends His
servants through and by means of His church into the world.
Here my support of the God-Church-World model is
evident.

Now a word about the "world" toward which churches
reach out in the sending mission. It is not that immediate
and adjacent world which is the context in which the congregation carries on its life of worship, fellowship, teaching,
service, and witness. That world, the shape and size of it
being determined by the location and composition of the
congregation, can be reached in direct evangelism of one
sort or another.

Mission has as its objective the reaching out to the world
beyond that immediate and accessible one. Obviously there
are many points at which these worlds intersect and overlap, but every church everywhere is failing in fulfillment of
the sending part of its total ministry unless it is providing
for ways in which individual believers can be involved together in participation in "sending mission" to the "regions
beyond" their own world.

There is a characteristic and need that identifies those
areas or "worlds" which we are required to discover and
reach out to in the sending mission. They can be defined
in Biblical terms: "where Christ has not been named"
areas of which we must say, "How shall they believe in Him
of whom they have not heard," places where men "know
not God and do not obey the Gospel." This is the world,
the *oikoumene*, that McGavran yearns over with such pas-
sionate concern. This is the world of the two billion that
Uppsala does appear to have betrayed and GL '71 may
neglect in their preoccupation with the techniques of mission
rather than the objects of it.

Some may need to be reminded that McGavran did not
dream up the term, the "two billion," as he has some of

his other quaint neologisms. It was the sober scholar and churchman, Stephen Neill, who concluded his great little Penguin, *History of Christian Missions,* by saying (1964: 575):

> It is still the case in 1963 that one-third of the people in the world have not so much as heard the name of Jesus Christ, and that another third have never heard the Gospel presented in such a way as both to be intelligible and to make on them a demand for personal and existential decision. There is still plenty to be done.

That world of the lost two billion is accessible in part to the direct outreach in evangelism of existing churches. Most of it will only be evangelized if churches are faithful in massive, agressive and imaginative sending mission, as Beaver has said.

In addition to the sending mission and the receiving situation (and what makes a person a missionary is not the place to which he goes but the fact that he is "sent" in mission), a word needs to be said about the other distinctive of mission, its strategic objective. That is, and has forever been, at least since the launching of "great commission missions," the planting and multiplying of churches.

Evangelism is the direct attempt and plan to call people to serve Christ within the structure of existing congregations. Mission sets out to see the church brought into being where it does not yet exist in visible congregational form.

Another distinction would need to be made in comparing mission with conventional denominational expansion into worlds already occupied by other churches of believers who are in the Body. But that is another big issue in itself. It is sufficient to say that mission, even though the word is strangely missing from the five commissions, has as its aim the establishment of churches. These churches, which are the products of mission, will then become centers for direct evangelism and also that representative sending in which they reach on out in mission to the regions beyond them.

When you get to the very center of the core of mission, as it is distinguished from the larger circle of evangelism and the even more comprehensive one of witness, the key issue is multiplication of churches. That suggests that Donald Anderson McGavran is in the apostolic succession

of vital continuity with the New Testament idea of mission.
It may yet be proved that "Church Growth" is theology.
I hope this essay has at least pointed out the good sense
and consistency of saying   "Multiplication of Churches is
mission!"

Bibliography:

Beaver, R. Pierce
    1969   THE MISSIONARY BETWEEN THE TIMES, New
            York, Doubleday
Beaver, R. Pierce (ed.)
    1970   TO ADVANCE THE GOSPEL, Grand Rapids, Eerd-
            mans
Beyerhaus, Peter
    1971   MISSIONS, WHICH WAY?, Grand Rapids, Zondervan
Cotter, J. P.
    1968   THE WORD IN THE THIRD WORLD,   Washington,
            Corpus
Danker, W. and W. J. Kang (eds.)
    1971   THE   FUTURE   OF   THE   CHRISTIAN WORLD
            MISSION,   Grand Rapids, Eerdmans
Hahn, Ferdinand
    1965   MISSION IN THE NEW TESTAMENT, Naperville,
            Ill., A. R. Allenson
Hoekendijk, J. C.
    1966   THE CHURCH INSIDE OUT, Philadelphia, West-
            minster
McGavran, D. A.
    1970   UNDERSTANDING   CHURCH   GROWTH,   Grand
            Rapids, Eerdmans
Margull, Hans J.
    1971   "Mission '70—More a Venture than Ever" IRM.,
            LX, 50-57.
Neill, Stephen
    1954   CREATIVE TENSIONS, London, Edinburgh House
    1964   HISTORY OF CHRISTIAN MISSION, London, Penguin
Rees, Paul S.
    1966   "Evangelism and Mission: The Elements of an
            Equation," Lecture, North Park Seminary.
Rossel, Jacques
    1969   "Karl Barth is No More," I. R. M.. LVIII, 227-228.
Tippett, A. R.,
    1969   VERDICT THEOLOGY IN MISSIONARY THEORY,
            Lincoln, Lincoln Christian College Press.

Potter, Philip
1968   "Renewal in Mission," CHURCH GROWTH BULLETIN, V, 2, 36.
Warneck, Gustav
1892   MISSIONS TO THE HEATHEN, Copenhagen.
1901   OUTLINE OF A HISTORY OF PROTESTANT MISSIONS FROM THE REFORMATION TO THE PRESENT TIME, Edinburgh.
Warren, Max
1944   THE CALLING OF GOD, London, Lutterworth Press.
Webster, Douglas
1965   UNCHANGING MISSION, Philadelphia, Fortress

Periodicals:

CHURCH GROWTH BULLETIN, School of World Mission, Fuller Theological Seminary, Pasadena
INTERNATIONAL REVIEW OF MISSION, Commission on World Mission and Evangelism of WCC, Geneva

The growth of the Church is always brought about by the action of the Holy Spirit. As in the New Testament Church, so today, the Holy Spirit leads, convicts of sin, converts, builds up, selects missionaries and thrusts them out to ripened fields. The concern of Christians today must be to understand the workings of the Holy Spirit and to be open to His leading. We talk of factors producing readiness to accept the Savior—but who produces the factors? It is largely the Holy Spirit of God. We but describe the way in which He acts. He upbuilds the Church, extends and nurtures it. Men are the channel through which He works.

HOW CHURCHES GROW,
p. 55.

7

THE ROLE OF THE HOLY SPIRIT IN CHURCH GROWTH

John T. Seamands

Although Dr. McGavran emphasizes the significance of the cultural factors which either stimulate or obstruct church growth, he is quick to recognize that the primary cause of church extension is the divine factor, namely, the operation of the Holy Spirit in the lives and affairs of men, recognizing the Church as a divine institution, not so much an organization as an organism. It is a living fellowship where the Spirit of God is present and working, not just a club where members pay dues and attend meetings.

Several years ago an interesting program on the radio amplified a variety of sounds several times beyond the normal volume. One of the sounds was that of a precision watch, claimed by the announcer to be "the world's most perfect time-piece." The watch ticked away: "click-clack, click-clack, click-clack." Later in the program, the announcer said: "Now we want you to listen to the heart-beat of the world's champion mile-runner, Bob Mathias." There followed the steady throb: "lub-dub, lub-dub, lub-dub." The sound of the "click-clack" and "lub-dub" reminded one of the difference between an organization and an organism.

The watch is a mechanism consisting of several parts put together by man, to tell the time of day. The heart is an organism, created by God to sustain life in the human body. The Church of Jesus Christ is not a "click-clack," a man-made organization, but a "lub-dub," a Spirit-created organism which throbs with life and imparts life. The organization in the Church will only be a means to an end, and not an end in itself or a substitute for life and mission.

The Holy Spirit and the Early Church

The Holy Spirit brings the Church into being, sustains its inner life, renews it from time to time, empowers it for mission, and causes it to grow. This is readily seen from a careful study of The Acts of the Apostles, which is a manual on both the Holy Spirit and the Church, and indicates the role of the Holy Spirit in the Church.

On the Day of Pentecost, when the Holy Spirit was poured out in His fulness upon the early disciples, Peter, now empowered by the Holy Spirit, testified to, and exhorted the crowd that gathered together, his hearers "were cut to the heart," and said to him and the rest of the apostles, "Brethren, what shall we do?" Then as Peter called them to repentance and faith in Jesus Christ, three thousand of the crowd "gladly received his word and were baptized" (Acts 2:37-41). Thus the Church came into being. From that point we observe a close relationship between the Holy Spirit and the Church.

The Holy Spirit endued the disciples with power for witnessing and preaching. "And they began to speak as the Spirit gave them utterance . . . Then Peter, filled with the Holy Spirit, said unto them . . . and they were all filled with the Holy Spirit and spoke the word of God with boldness . . . and with great power the apostles gave their testimony to the resurrection of the Lord Jesus" (Acts 2:4; 4:8, 31, 33).

The Holy Spirit also guarded the purity of the Church. When Ananias and Sapphira sold their property but turned over only a part of the proceeds to the Church, Peter rebuked them and said, "Why has Satan filled your heart to lie to the Holy Spirit? How is it that you have agreed together to tempt the Spirit of the Lord?" There was such a profound and overwhelming sense of the presence of the Holy Spirit in the congregation at Jerusalem that evil could not be tolerated (5:1-11).

The Holy Spirit called and commissioned the first missionaries in the Church at Antioch. "While they were worshipping the Lord and fasting, the Holy Spirit said: 'Set apart me Barnabas and Saul for the work to which I have called them.' Then after fasting and praying they laid hands on them and sent them off. So, being sent out by the Holy Spirit, they went down to Seleucia. . . "(13:1-4).

The Holy Spirit also guided the missionaries indicating both where to go and where not to go. The Spirit commanded Peter to go to the house of Cornelius at Caesarea (ch. 10). The Spirit ordered Phillip, the evangelist, to go down to Gaza (8:26-40). The Holy Spirit forbade Paul and Silas to go into Asia and Bithynia, but instead led them to Macedonia (16:6, 7, 9, 10). The Spirit led Paul to return to Jerusalem in spite of impending danger (20:22, 23).

In times of persecution the Holy Spirit comforted the Church. "Walking in the fear of the Lord and in the comfort of the Holy Spirit (the Church) was multiplied" (9:31).

The Holy Spirit guided the early Church in matters of administration. Commenting on the momentous decision made at the first council in Jerusalem, Peter declared: "It has seemed good to the Holy Spirit and to us . . ." (15:28). When Paul was admonishing the elders of the Ephesian Church, he solemnly reminded them that the Holy Spirit Himself had made them guardians of the flock (20:28).

Finally, the Holy Spirit played a significant role in the outreach and growth of the early Church. In addressing the enquirers in Jerusalem who gathered on the Day of Pentecost, Peter told them very clearly that they also could receive the gift of the Holy Spirit (2:38). Then when they believed and were baptized and continued daily in the apostles' doctrine, in prayer, and worship, "the Lord added to their number day by day those who were being saved" (2:47). In a short while the original three thousand converts had increased to five thousand (4:4). When the time came to elect the first deacons of the Church at Jerusalem, the apostles insisted that, among other qualifications, they should be men "full of the Holy Spirit." The very next sentence tells us that "the word of God increased; and the number of disciples multiplied greatly in Jerusalem, and a great many of the priests were obedient to the faith" (6:1-7). When Saul was converted on the road to Damascus and there followed a period of freedom from persecution, Luke the historian, tells us that "the church throughout all Judea and Galilee and Samaria had peace and was built up; and walking in the fear of the Lord and in the comfort of the Holy Spirit it was multiplied" (9:31).

The history of the Church down through the centuries only serves to underline and illustrate the facts that are recorded in the Acts of the Apostles. Over and over again we observe the significant role of the Holy Spirit in the life and outreach of the Church of Jesus Christ. This is especially true in the historic "mission fields" of the world.

The Holy Spirit and Conversion

Only as the Holy Spirit has convicted men of their sin and made them new creatures in Christ Jesus has the Church come into being in these lands. Well do I remember being invited by a group of outcaste Hindus in the village of Tegur in Belgaum District in India, to share with them the Good News of Jesus Christ. After several visits and sessions with them, they began to see their sin and their Savior, and eventually declared their faith in Christ by public baptism. The transformation in their lives was real. Their old habits and behavior were gone. They had a new purpose and dynamic in life. The inner change was followed by outer change. They cleaned up their personal appearance, tore down their old mud huts and built new homes. They gave of their time and resources to help build a chapel for worship. They started a school and began to educate their children. They borrowed money to buy lands, and soon became economically independent. Today there is a small but thriving congregation in that village. This was the work of the Holy Spirit.

Dr. McGavran has repeatedly pointed out that a "people (or group) movement" often starts with a key-man who gets soundly converted, stays in the area, weathers the persecution, and then begins to win his relatives and friends.

The conversion of Ko Tha Byu, a criminal, under the ministry of Adoniram Judson, started a group movement among the Karen tribes in Burma that today constitute one of the great indigenous churches in Southeast Asia. The conversion of a dark, lame Chuhra named Ditt, led to the ingathering of almost the entire community of Chuhras in the Sialkot District of the Punjab (now in Pakistan). Similarly, when a Madiga (outcaste) named Yerrguntla Periah was converted and baptized in the village of Talla Kondapad, a movement began which in the course of three or four decades led to the transformation of hundreds of thousands in the Telugu-speaking area of India.

Commenting on these Christward movements, Dr. McGavran writes:

> We not only affirm it, but go further and claim that the vast stirrings of the Spirit which occur in People Movements are God-given. We dare not think of People Movements to Christ as merely social phenomena. True, we can account for some of the contributing factors which have brought them about; but there is so much that is mysterious and beyond anything we can ask or think so much that is a product of religious faith, and so much evident working of divine Power, that we must confess that People Movements are gifts of God (McGavran, 1955: 81).

The Holy Spirit and Revival

The working of the Holy Spirit has not only been a decisive factor in the birth of the Church, but also in its growth.

Sometimes spectacular church growth has followed in the wake of revival, as the Holy Spirit has awakened a sleeping Church or revitalized a dead Church. There is the ever-present danger of second and third generation Christians drifting into nominal Christianity, of losing their sense of mission and becoming a self-satisfied and ingrown church, of losing the message and power. Periodically the Holy Spirit has to call the people of God back to repentance and faith and a personal experience with Christ. He has to purify and empower believers. He has to call the whole Church again to be obedient to the Great Commission. Without such refreshing periods the Church would certainly die.

Revival and church growth are not always linked together. At times, church growth has taken place apart from revival, sometimes revival has not resulted in church growth, and sometimes church growth has led to revival. But often the two have been inseparable. As the people of God have been quickened with new life by the Holy Spirit and have regained their sense of mission to a lost world, they have gone out to share the Good News of Christ with those outside their fellowship, and naturally, this has led to church growth.

One of the best illustrations of this fact was the famous revival in Korea at the opening of this century. In his book, *The Christians of Korea,* Samuel Hugh Moffett writes:

> It was a spiritual revival, explosive and spectacular, sweeping through the peninsula from 1903 to 1907, that touched off the massive ingathering of the church and permanently stamped its character with revivalistic fervor (Moffett, 1962:52).

The revival began rather quietly in a week of prayer and Bible study for missionaries in Wonsan, led by a Canadian Methodist doctor, R. A. Hardie. In the course of his Bible studies, Dr. Hardie felt compelled by the Spirit to go before his fellow missionaries and later before a Korean congregation to confess "with shame and confusion" his own "pride, hardness of heart and lack of faith." From Wonsan revivalism spread and reached its climax at a great evening meeting in Pyongyang, in 1907, when scores of Christians publicly confessed their sins and received a fresh touch from the Holy Spirit. In five short years the membership of the Korean churches increased fourfold, from approximately 50,000 to 200,000. In the words of Samuel Moffett, "the revival was the spiritual seal on the founding charter of the Korean church."

The most recent and spectacular illustration of revival-and-church-growth has come out of the Evangelical Christian Church on the island of Timor in Indonesia. In the 1930s large numbers of people began to come into the church from the interior regions of the island. The Christianization occurred so rapidly, however, that the church did not have sufficient personnel to instruct all the new members. In 1964, out of a population of a little more than one million, some 450,000 of the inhabitants belonged

4·7·4·17

to the church. The number of pastors at that time was only 103, far too few for the task. The spiritual state of the churches, therefore, was almost catastrophic. The former pagan beliefs, the magic and sorcery, the promiscuity and alcoholism, all continued to prosper together. One might say that Timor had never been evangelized, only Christianized.

In July 1965, David Simeon, teacher in a Bible school in East Java, arrived on Timor with a team of students. He started to hold evangelistic campaigns in two strategic cities. The team's message was one of repentance, rebirth, and sanctification through the Holy Spirit. The campaigns were immediately followed by a huge outpouring of God's Spirit. The people brought their fetishes out of their houses, piling them up in heaps and burning them. A wave of cleansing swept through the ranks of the Christians. But more important still, the Lord called many of the islanders and used them to spread the fire further.

As a result of the purification and renewal of the Timor Church, scores of witness teams and gospel bands were formed, fanning out across the island. Through the power of the Holy Spirit countless miracles of spiritual transformation and physical healing took place. Within three years almost 200,000 people from the pagan community were converted, baptized, and brought into the fellowship of the church. Today the membership of the Timor Evangelical Christian Church stands at 650,000 (Koch, 1970).

As Dr. McGavran so aptly points out, revival that takes place within people movements is far more likely to produce rapid church growth than when it breaks out in gathered-colony congregations at mission stations. I have personally witnessed this fact a number of times on the mission field. In 1947 I witnessed a wonderful revival in the central Methodist Church at Belgaum, India. Many of the members entered into a new experience with Jesus Christ. The whole congregation was lifted to a new level of spiritual life. An increase in stewardship and giving was one of the lasting results that ensued. However, the revival in the city did not result in any noticeable growth in membership, either locally or in the surrounding villages. One of the major reasons for this situation was the fact that almost all the members were second or third generation Christians;

their fathers had come into the church as isolated families;
and the members themselves had no family ties nearby.
In the same year revival broke out in the central Methodist Church at Bidar, about 300 miles to the east. As in
Belgaum, many in the congregation experienced the new
birth. The whole church was renewed and empowered. But
unlike Belgaum, the next two years produced a large
number of new converts in the surrounding area. As a
result of a new lay-witnessing movement, in Bidar District,
6,690 were converted and baptized during 1947-48, while
in the adjoining Chitaguppa District an additional 3,088
added to the Church. The main reason was that the members in the central church at Bidar had strong family ties
with fellow-caste members residing in the surrounding
villages. With a new sense of concern and responsibility
they went out to witness to their new experience and to
win their relatives to Christ. Thus the church grew.

The Holy Spirit and Witnessing

The above illustration helps to point out another area
in which the Holy Spirit plays a significant role in church
growth, namely, that of lay witnessing. Jesus promised
his disciples: "You shall receive power when the Holy
Spirit has come upon you; and you shall be my witnesses
in Jerusalem and in all Judea and Samaria and to the end
of the earth" (Acts 1:8).
From the very beginning, the Church has always grown
primarily through the witness of the people of God. Church
history proves this over and over again. And this is as it
should be. The New Testament shows that the work of
evangelizing the world was intended to be done, not simply
by the clergy, but by the whole membership. Take the
Book of Acts and search it for evidence of the place and
power of believers acting together for the spreading of the
Good News. You will be surprised at what you find. Too
long we have fixed our attention on the individual evangelists
Peter, Paul, Barnabas, Silas. We have overlooked the
collective strength of those Spirit-filled men and women
who felt that each one of them separately and all of them
jointly had a share in this common witness to the Savior-
hood and Lordship of Jesus Christ.

Look at some of the lay witnesses in the Book of Acts: Stephen, a waiter on tables, who disputed with the Jews in the synagogue and became the first martyr of the Christian Church; Phillip, another waiter, who became a leading lay-evangelist in the early Church; Lydia, a seller of cloth, who was a leading member of the church at Philippi; Aquila and Priscilla, tent makers, who expounded the way of Christ more fully to an eloquent preacher of the Word; and Luke, missionary doctor, who gave us his biography of Christ and the history of the early Church. But we must add to this list a multitude of un-named followers of Christ, who, when they were scattered abroad through persecution, went everywhere preaching the Word (Acts 8:1-4). Some of these disciples went to Antioch and established a great church that eventually became the center of a significant early missionary movement (11:19-26).

The secret of this dynamic lay movement which led to spectacular church growth was that Christ, through the Holy Spirit, had transformed their lives and endued them with courage and power to witness effectively for their Lord. Without this enduement they would have failed. With it, nothing could stop them.

Two things stand out with clarity in the Book of Acts: the irresistible missionary expansion of the early Church, and the power of the Spirit in that expansion. The missionary witness and movement begins at the precise moment of the descent of the Holy Spirit, and the place and power of the Spirit to that witness are repeatedly attested throughout the book. No wonder Wilkenhauser formulates the theme of Acts as "The universal expansion of Christianity begun in the power of, and effected by, the Holy Spirit" (Wilkenhauser, 1921:15).

In his book, *Pentecost and Missions,* Harry Boer argues the interesting thesis that the phenomenal expansion of the early Church is not to be found in her conscious obedience to the command of Christ, but in her spontaneous response to Pentecost and the decent of the Holy Spirit. The Great Commission was not a fully meaningful ingredient in the missionary thinking of the early disciples, and they made no strong appeal to this command, and held no rallies or gave any "pep talks." Witnessing and mission were the free, natural outflow of the indwelling presence of the Holy

Spirit in the lives of the Christians. Only then did they
begin to act on the instructions of the Lord. Pentecost
made the Church a witnessing Church, and this witness
was spontaneous, immediate (Boer, 1961).

If we were to put this truth into a simple formula, we
might express it thus: Church growth may result from a
lay witnessing movement; lay witnessing is the result of
the inner working of the Holy Spirit; therefore, the Holy
Spirit and church growth are inseparably linked together.

There is perhaps no finer demonstration of this truth to
be found in present-day missions than that of the growth
of the Church in Latin America through the Pentecostal
movement. With their strong emphasis upon the ministry
of the Holy Spirit in conversion and sanctification, together
with their emphasis on the baptism of the Holy Spirit and
on spiritual gifts, the Pentecostals have witnessed a remarkable lay witnessing movement that is sweeping thousands of converts into the fellowship of the Church. Every
church member is expected to be a witness for Christ;
every congregation is expected to be a center of evangelism.
Pentecostal Christians are witnessing on the streets,
conducting Bible study classes in the homes, confronting
people in the jails, hospitals and factories. As a result,
laymen are not only winning individuals to Christ, but
also establishing new congregations. Everywhere the Church
is growing.

The Pentecostal example in Latin America was largely
responsible for the development of the Strachan theorem
which led to the inauguration of the Evangelism-in-Depth
program on the continent. The theorem states: "The
expansion of any movement is in direct proportion to its
success in mobilizing its total membership in continuous
propagation of its beliefs." With its slogan of "total mobili-
zation for total evangelization" the program is now producing spectacular results in many of the South American
republics.

The Holy Spirit and Ripened Fields

The Holy Spirit plays an important role in another
aspect of church growth. McGavran has repeatedly emphasized the fact that in any given land, society is not single

but multiple. It is made up of a vast number of sub-societies, each having its own structure, culture, and status. In other words, society is usually not like a uniform wall with one color of paint. It is more like a mosaic with a variety of colors and shapes. The missionary often finds himself working in one particular piece of the mosaic.

The significance of all this is that just as crops grow differently and ripen at different times in different soils, so each piece of the mosaic, or each sub-society, ripens and becomes responsive to the Gospel at a different time. Peoples and societies vary in receptivity. Whole segments of mankind resist the Gospel for periods—often very long periods—and then ripen to the Good News.

Factors which affect the responsiveness of a people are innumerable. They may be political, religious, cultural, sociological, or economic. Such items as migration, conquest, nationalism, natural disasters, depression, spiritual vacuums, and social disintegration are some of the myriad forces that affect the degree of responsiveness. Wise missionary strategy suggests that, while we do not abandon resistant peoples, at the same time we should concentrate our resources in personnel and finances upon those peoples who are receptive to the Gospel. That is, we must harvest ripened fields.

Now whereas McGavran emphasizes the various human and cultural factors that affect the receptivity of men and societies, he is quick to recognize that the chief of them all is the divine factor, namely, the operation of the Holy Spirit in the lives and affairs of men. In the paragraph quoted at the beginning of this chapter he writes: "We talk of factors producing readiness to accept the Savior—but who produces the factors? It is largely the Holy Spirit of God. We but describe the way in which He acts." McGavran is right. It is the Spirit who opens the hearts of men, illumines their minds, convicts them of sin, and draws them to the Savior. Without the imparting of this "prevenient grace" all our human efforts would be in vain.

The Holy Spirit, of course, does work through the human factors. He never works in a vacuum, but through the structures and laws of society. Sometimes he even takes the wrath of men to build up His Church.

The most recent and powerful demonstration of this

fact is probably found in the exceptional growth in Java, Indonesia, during the last five years. In the pre-dawn hours of October 1, 1965, the Communist Party of Indonesia made a sudden and determined effort to take over the government. They ringed the President's palace, captured the Djarkata radio station, and brutally murdered six army generals. General Suharto, however, providentially escaped, rallied the army at the last hour, and quickly crushed the Communist coup. Then the populace, enraged at this attempt to betray the nation, turned upon the Communists in savage revenge. In the mass slaughter that followed during the next three months, at least 400,000 Communist party members and sympathizers were unmercifully killed. As a result the Communists suddenly found themselves as a people without a country, without a cause, and without a "god." Thousands of disenchanted Communists lost what they believed to be the spiritual foundation for their lives. They were thrown into a spiritual vacuum. Disappointed and confused, they now began to seek some new basis for their lives.

It was right at this point of human despair that the Holy Spirit stepped into the picture, brought His influence to bear upon the political and spiritual confusion, and prepared the hearts of hundreds of thousands of Communists for the acceptance of the Good News in Jesus Christ. As a result, thousands of these ex-Communists have come to faith in Christ during the past five years and have entered the fellowship of the Church. Furthermore, thousands of Muslims have also turned to Christ in Indonesia during this period, for as the murderers of their Communist enemies, they were seized with an overpowering sense of guilt from which they desperately sought relief. Many of them discovered that forgiveness is only possible through Jesus Christ.

The importance of this for Christian Missions is that Christians must be concerned to understand the workings of the Holy Spirit within, and in spite of the human situation, and to be open to His leading. We must work where the Holy Spirit is working. We must go to peoples whose hearts have been prepared by the Spirit for the preaching of the Word. We must harvest fields that have been ripened by Him.

We are indeed grateful to McGavran for calling us to renewed faith in the Holy Spirit and to a new understanding of His significant role in the life and growth of the Church. Christian Mission is not a human enterprise, but a divine movement led by the Holy Spirit. He is the Originator, the Promoter, and Sustainer of Christian Mission. Through Him the Church takes birth, maintains its inner life and strength, and reaches out to people of all lands. We must be "filled with the Spirit," cooperate with His workings, and depend upon His power. We are shut up to the alternative—Pentecost or failure. For the human spirit fails unless the Holy Spirit fills.

BIBLIOGRAPHY:

Boer, Harry R.
 1961   PENTECOST AND MISSIONS, Grand Rapids, Eerdmans
Koch, Kurt
 1970   THE REVIVAL IN INDONESIA, Baden, West Germany, Evangelization Publishers
McGavran, Donald
 1955   THE BRIDGES OF GOD, London, World Dominion Press
Moffett, Samuel Hugh
 1962   THE CHRISTIANS OF KOREA, New York, Friendship Press
Wilkenhauser, A.
 1921   DIE APOSTELGESCHICHTE UND IHR GESCHICTWERT, Munster, Germany

Church growth must be founded on sound theology. . . It must also take sociology into account. . . God desires church growth; it takes place among men.

The Church will grow differently, not only in each different culture, but in each of the many homogeneous units. . .

The functioning organism—the "one Church"—is in fact a fellowship of Churches each growing in its own homogeneous unit.

By ignoring social stratification and disregarding homogeneous units and webs of relationship, they (Western Churches and missions which ignore sociology) constantly diminish the effectiveness of their presentation of Christ.

The linguistic and ethnic differences can be recognized and used as highways of the Spirit. . .

CHURCH GROWTH AND CHRISTIAN MISSION,
pp. 69, 71, 76, 78, 80.

8

TOWARD A CHRISTIAN ETHNOTHEOLOGY

Charles H. Kraft

Among the significant accomplishments of Donald Mc Gavran is the establishment of the missionary research and teaching institution at the Fuller Theological Seminary.

Dr. McGavran early saw that what has come to be called "church growth theory" would lean heavily upon the disciplines of theology and anthropology. Thus competence in both disciplines came to be a prerequisite for faculty members at SWM-ICG and a major goal for those being trained. However, it is neither advisable nor possible for us to keep the disciplines separated or even to label our course offerings one or the other. In training for mission, when we deal with man in culture—ordinarily an anthropological topic—we cannot do so without reference to insights derived from theology. Nor can we usefully treat the relationship between God and man—a theological topic— without reference to an anthropological understanding of the place of culture in human experience. We have just not been able to keep the disciplines distinct. Nor has it been possible for us to make use of the totality of either discipline.

At certain points we have found it necessary to recognize a fundamental incompatability between certain of the tenets of the two disciplines as well as a certain lack of relevance to our concerns with respect to some of the goals and subject matter of each discipline.

The original intention to "harness" anthropology and theology to the missionary task, as McGavran is fond of phrasing it, foundered to some extent on the twin rocks of general incompatability and lack of total relevance. It has thus become a necessary part of the thinking of the SWM-ICG faculty to develop a theoretical perspective that is at once properly integrative and properly discriminating with respect to the disciplines of theology and anthropology. The purpose of this paper is to outline the dimensions of the undertaking.

The Name of the Proposed Discipline

Ours is a day when reaction to the increasing specialization of certain major disciplines and their consequent isolation from each other has led to the initiation of a number of inter-disciplinary approaches to areas of study which, due to the fact that they lie at the periphery of more than one of the established disciplines, have often been neglected. Thus, with the developing of the widespread interest in the non-Western world (and wealth and leisure to pursue it) a number of "cross-disciplines" have sprung up between areas of study heretofore specializing on a single aspect of Western culture and the relevant part of cultural anthropology. There are now, for example, areas of study known as ethnohistory, ethnomusicology, ethnolinguistics, ethnopsychology, ethnobotany and the like which attempt to study their subject matter from either a cross-cultural or a non-Western perspective.

Thus we may conceive of a cross-discipline, labelled *Christian ethnotheology,,* that takes both Christian theology and anthropology seriously while devoting itself to an interpretive approach to the study of God, man and divine-human interaction. From theology such a discipline would draw understandings of eternal (absolute) truths relating to each of the areas it treats. From anthropology it would draw cultural (relative) truths and perceptions concerning

these areas. Such a discipline would have both a theoretical and a practical component, the latter of which might
consist largely of the "harnessing" both of anthropology and
of theology for the purpose of bringing about more effective
cross-cultural communication of the Gospel of Jesus Christ.
Note that this proposal is for a specifically *Christian
ethnotheology*, based pointedly on a wedding of *Christian*
theology with anthropology. There are other theologies
which might form the theological component of a more
broadly conceived discipline. And it might be that at some
point the proponents of these theologies would want to
develop such a study. The aim here, however, is not that
more broadly conceived discipline but one that is of specific
relevance to those who take Christianity seriously.

However, Christian ethnotheology would not simply
serve as a handmaiden of missions. It would as well serve
the needs of any person or group who sought to retain belief
in an absolute God (as anthropology does not) and a responsible yet culture-bound man (concepts on which theology is
generally weak). Within Christian ethnotheology, for example, the pressing problem of what is absolute and what
is relative in human experience can be worked out. And any
insights into this problem would be of much wider relevance
than simply to missionary work. One (perhaps the) major
application of Christian ethnotheology, however, would be to
Christian missions.

The study of Christian ethnotheology is not new, however.
The proposed label is the main innovation. The informal
development of such a discipline has been underway at least
since the early fifties, notably through the efforts of
E.A. Nida, W.A. Smalley, W.D. Reyburn, J.A. Loewen and
others associated with The American Bible Society (Trans-
lation Department). The journal *Practical Anthropology* has
been perhaps the major participant. Books such as Nida's
Customs and Cultures (1954) and especially *Message and
Mission* (1960), Luzbetak's *The Church and Cultures* (1963),
McGavran's *Bridges of God* (1955), and *Understanding
Church Growth* (1970) have played an important part as well.
Furthermore, the studies going on in such institutions as
The Kennedy School of Missions (now unfortunately defunct),
the Anthropology Department of Wheaton College, Jaffray
School of Missions, SWM-ICG and elsewhere has to a great

extent fallen into this category.

Not all students are able to achieve integration of the various elements or the necessary balance between the relativism of anthroplogy and the absolutism of theology. Many, going to the theological extreme, have absolutized some western cultural approach to Christianity and sought to convert people to that particular expression of Christianity. Others, however, led to the opposite extreme by an unguarded exposure to anthropology, have virtually relativized the essentials of Christianity, as if Christianity were but one of the myriad of cultural expressions of religion. Certainly the need for a balanced, integrating approach to the subject matter of theology and anthropology is urgent.

Why Can This Not be Done as a Part of the Study of Theology?

Ideally it should be possible to treat Christian ethnotheology as a subdiscipline of theology. Indeed, it is hoped that in the not too distant future the administrators of theological institutions will see the great urgency for the kind of serious approach to such problems as that of absolutivity versus relativity that is to be a major focus of Christian ethnotheology. But at present, it appears, Evangelical Theology at least is more concerned with defending its basic tenets than with developing them.

Christian ethnotheology would, for example, examine all of the basic formulations of Christian theology to determine just which of these formulations represent eternal Truth and may, therefore, be presented to the Christians of another culture (or subculture) as essential parts of Christianity, and which represent discussable theories or interpretations of such Truth, and therefore should be regarded in a cross-cultural situation as the attempts of the Christians of a given culture to come to an understanding of eternal Truth. A disturbingly high percentage of the formulations of western theology seems to fit into the latter category. As the theologian F.R. Tennant admits—

> . . . the doctrine of Original Sin is not contained in the Old Testament and the only unmistakable presentation of it that can be found in the New does not appear to have been the starting-point for the first framers of

the ecclesiastical doctrine. Tertullian set out from stoic psychology, Origen from the institution of infant-baptism and also from the myth of Plato concerning the fall of the soul from the celestial sphere into earthly life (1962: 22,63).

Thus Christian ethnotheology would attempt to distinguish carefully what in Christian doctrine is supracultural revelation from God, (defined below) and what is the cultural "enclothing" of this revelation in terms meaningful either to those who originally received the revelation or to those in another culture (e.g. ours) to whom it has been transmitted in the Bible and interpreted by theologians. In so seeking to understand the message it would be necessary to divest the theological interpretation of such modifications as the pervasive influence of Greek philosophy on western theology and the tendency to adsolutize certain elements of western culture by attributing them (often wrongly) to Christian influence on our culture.

The study of Christian theology has a long and venerable history within western culture. Western theology however, has become so specialized in approaching reality from a single valuable and necessary (philosophical) perspective that it seems unable at present to adequately tackle certain problems which have only recently begun to attract our attention. Typically, for example, western theology is apt at describing eternal verities, such as the attributes of God, the sinfulness of man and the faith-remedy for man's plight. However, it is not nearly so able to deal with questions such as: What is the permissible range of valid human perception of God? Or, what is the permissible range of valid human response to God? Or even, what changes in behavior are preconditional to a relationship with God? Nor is western Theology very helpful in providing Christians with a principled approach as to which of the commands of Scripture speak most significantly to a twentieth century American. What, for example, is the principle by means of which one decides that the Old Testament injunction against stealing is to be strictly obeyed but the New Testament command that women cover their heads when praying (I Cor. 11:5, 10, 12) may be ignored?

When both the students of Theology and those to whom they seek to communicate Christian truth share a degree of cultural homogeneity and experience many such questions do not seem pressing. When one attempts to proclaim the Gospel message relevantly to those of another culture, however, one is faced with these and myriads of unexpected questions that our theology has not taught us to deal with. How, for example, does one explain the difference between the stealing and head covering commands to an African who has come to understand that since the Bible is God's Word its commands are to be obeyed, yet observes that not a single missionary woman covers her head when praying? One such African once said to me, "You missionaries live by a different Bible than the one you give us!" Likewise, is the permissible range of valid human perception of and response to God wide enough to allow those of mission lands to identify with the Christian God and to respond to him in their own way. Or must Christianity set up a competing system, which presents God in terms only of our Christian perception of Him, advocates response to Him after our patterns, and recommends or requires behavioral changes in them that make them behave more like us?

The strengths of our theology lie in the fact that it has been developed especially to deal with the problems in western culture, and to do so in a way that we regard as appropriate. Thus since our culture demands it, western theology is absolutistic—we demand that there be only one right way to do or think about a thing. There can be no such thing as differing, but equally valid theologies, systems of church organization, patterns of witness and preaching, understandings of moral behavior, etc. Our culture tells us that there is only one right way—the rest are heretical. And this absolutism is applied not only to doctrines which are clearly expressions of asbsolute Truth (such as the fact that God created the universe) but, frequently, also to the much more discussable matter as to exactly how God did what he did. We often reason, for example, that since God could have created the universe in seven literal days, therefore, he must have done it that way.

Furthermore, western theology tends to be monocultural in its perspective—often looking at the biblical cultures (especially Greek culture) as direct antecedents of our own and interpreting biblical events as if they form a part of a historical and cultural continuum which has over thousands of years at last progressed to the pinnacle on which our "Christian (or nearly Christian) culture" stands. In keeping with our western philosophy of history, many westerners see our culture as the product of such cultural development, denying our real cultural roots among the illiterate pagan tribes of western Europe in favor of a much more flattering (and recorded) Greek (and sometimes even Hebrew) ancestry. Western theology, furthermore, springing as it has from Greek philosophy, has adopted almost entirely philosophical models of thought. As F. R. Tennant has said, "the very terms and conceptions ... into which the relatively undefined traditional beliefs of the early Church . . . (were cast) were supplied by Greek philosophy" (1962 : 22, 63). Theology has therefore focused mainly upon thought, reason and the propositionalization of Christian truth and experience. And this is all well and good as long as one is living within the culture which feels that philosophical abstraction is the appropriate mode to apply to theologizing. But there are other methods of abstracting from experience (ritualizing, for example, is a very common method in many cultures as it was among the Hebrews) and there are many other forms of philosophy than the one(s) we know.

Under the influence of philosophy, theology has often taken a negative attitude toward what it has understood to be culture—usually on the basis of an incorrect identification of culture with "the world" which, according to certain Scriptures, is a source of stumbling to the Christian. Nor does it take a positive attitude toward more informed (often anthropological) treatments of culture since they tend to start from a relativistic position unacceptable to theology. Thus, unless western theology shows a greater flexibility, it would seem that the creation of a new discipline integrating theology and anthropology is called for.

Why Not Simply Look to Anthropology
for Ethnotheological Insight?

If it is true that western theology would be unreceptive to the spawning of Christian ethnotheology it is perhaps doubly true that anthropology as we know it does not provide a friendly atmosphere for its development, for much anthro-

pology completely relativizes God and theology. In spite
of indications of a certain wistfulness on the part of some
anthropologists for some sort of standard of measurement
as between cultures, anthropology has by and large turned
from any possibility of dealing with absolutes.

Christian ethnotheology in the hands of anthropology,
therefore, would be reduced to a mere study of competing
but equally valid approaches to the understanding of the
Supernatural. It would thus be undistinguishable from
studies such as comparative mythology or "primitive"
religion. This is not what is intended here. Christian ethnotheology would seek to avoid relativizing God every bit as
much as to avoid absolutizing culture.

Furthermore, anthropology as it has developed within
its own form of increasingly naturalistic western culture
itself betrays its own form of culture-boundness in that it
refuses even to consider the possible existence of absolutes
(other than "universals") either within or outside of culture.
Christian ethnotheology believes in absolutes—not as
western theology proposes perhaps, but far more than
anthropology admits.

Contributions of Theology and Anthropology to Christian Ethnotheology

Christian ethnotheology needs both disciplines—the one
to inform it concerning absolutes, the other to deal with
culture, man and even God at the level of human perception.
The statements of each discipline, however, will have to be
evaluated in the light of the other. The ethnotheological
conclusion then, may side with either, both, or neither of
the source disciplines. For example:

Theological Understanding	Anthropological Understanding	Ethnotheological Understanding
1. God created man.	People of each culture create their own god(s) as an ideali- zation of themselves.	God created man. Man perceives God in terms meaningful in his culture. This human perception will always be in- fluenced by culture and sin.

2. God reveals himself to man.	Man thinks he receives communication from a supernatural source.	God reveals himself to man in terms appropriate to man's cultural perception.
3. Christianity absolutely valid (tends to define Christianity in western philosophic terms)	Christianity but one of many valid cultural expressions of religion (sees no absolute model, only cultural expressions of Christianity)	Supracultural Christianity absolutely valid. Must be distinguished from its cultural expressions and transmitted apart from them.
4. Western culture more Christian than other cultures.	All cultures valid and relatively comparable to each other in terms of their ability to cope with reality.	All cultures usable by God as vehicles for his inter-action with man.
5. Man pervasively sinful and needing redemption.	Man the product of his culture.	Culture the vehicle of Satan as well as of God. Man and culture pervasively sinful and needing redemption.

It may appear from the above chart that Christian ethnotheology leans more heavily on theology than upon anthropology. This is to some extent true, especially with regard to basic theological tenets such as 1, 2, 3, and 5 above. However, it should be noted that in every case above the statement of ethnotheological understanding involves a mention of the place of culture in the understanding. And, since theology virtually ignores culture; this is a contribution from anthropology. The areas of concern of the two disciplines may be diagrammed as follows:

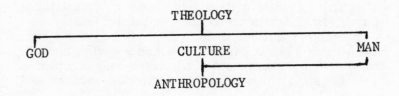

Or alternatively, we may see theology dealing with man encircled by God, anthropology with man encircled by culture, but Christian ethnotheology as treating all three thus:

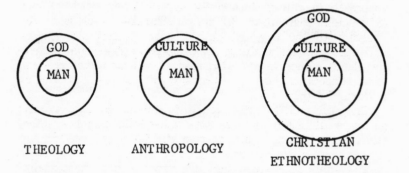

THEOLOGY   ANTHROPOLOGY   CHRISTIAN
                                        ETHNOTHEOLOGY

Theology, as it were, reduces the place of culture to insignificance (mainly, of course, due to historical reasons). Anthropology, on the other hand, refuses to consider an absolute God. Hence the need for a more balanced approach.

The Cultural and the Supracultural

One of the major quests of Christian ethnotheology will be the understanding of what in Christianity is absolute, supracultural and valid for any church at any time, and that which is cultural, relative, and valid for a single culture only. God of course, is supracultural. He stands outside of culture and is not bound by culture unless he chooses to be bound by it. Man however, is immersed in culture and unable to escape his culture-boundness.

God however, from outside of culture reveals himself to man in terms meaningful to culture-bound humanity and elicits from at least certain men responses acceptable to Himself. He indwells certain human beings, leading them to act within the cultural context on his behalf and even once became a human participant within a culture himself. And some of his interactions with men have been recorded— interactions which happened in particular cultures and were recorded in particular languages and collected in case-book fashion in a Book which in translated form has come down to us.

And it is this document preeminently that provides for us both the demonstration that God chooses to meet man where he is culturally and the source from which we seek to discern that which is supracultural—which was only relevant to the original participants in the interaction. Likewise we learn from an ethnotheological approach to the Bible something of what God is willing to start with, with respect to human perception of Himself and supracultural Truth.

One approach to this aspect of ethnotheological investigation would be to seek to fill out the following incomplete illustrative chart. Note that in the left hand column are listed certain supracultural truths, while the larger right hand column is divided into two parts labeled "less ideal" (at the far right) and "more ideal." This is to show the

SUPRACULTURAL TRUTH (The Mind of God) Absolute Truth	CULTURAL PERCEPTION OF SUPRACULTURAL TRUTH Growth in Relative Understanding		
	More Ideal Understanding		Less Ideal Understanding
The Great Cardinal Doctrines of Scripture God exists	Close, Personal		Distant, Impersonal
God interacts with man	Direct and warm	Direct but cool	Indirect Judgmental
Man created in God's image	Understanding implications		
God accepts man on a basis of faith	Well-nigh total commitment		Small, kernel faith
Don't steal	Coveting equals stealing	From anyone	From ingroup
Don't commit adultery	Lust equals adultery	With anyone	With married person

possibility of differential perception of supracultural truth from within the cultural context and of the possibility of movement from a less ideal to a more ideal (i.e. more close approximation to the supracultural model) understanding of the mind of God in each matter. Note however, that the line between cultural perception and supracultural truth is uncrossable (at least this side of heaven).

Cultural Relativism in Ethnotheological Perspective

One of the most important tasks of Christian ethnotheology (and a primary reason why this discipline is of wider relevance than simply to Christian missions) is to deal with the matter of the doctrine of cultural relativity from an informed Christian point of view. I would like by way of illustration to outline the method in which the suggested discipline would deal with this issue.

Cultural relativism is a doctrine developed by anthropology which maintains that "each culture may be evaluated only in its own terms" and therefore, "it is objectively impossible to distinguish worldwide levels of cultural progress" (Beals and Hoijer, 720). That is, cultures are to be regarded not as assignable to some level of overall superiority or inferiority to other cultures, but rather as more or less equal to each other overall and of equal validity to their own members. Each culture therefore, is valid for those immersed in it but not for those of another culture.

"Cultural relativism," said Melville Herskovits, one of its most active advocates,

> is a philosophy which, in recognizing the values set up by every society to guide its own life, lays stress on the dignity inherent in every body of custom, and on the need for tolerance of conventions though they may differ from one's own. Instead of underscoring differences from absolute norms . . . the relativistic point of view brings into relief the validity of every set of norms for the people whose lives are guided by them, and the values these represent.

"The very core of cultural relativism," he continues, "is the discipline that comes of respect for differences—of mutual respect" (Herskovits, 1951:77).

"CULTURAL RELATIVISM"

This doctrine is therefore, on the cultural level, what personal acceptance is on the individual level. It recommends that, rather than moralizing about the good or bad in the given culture (or in the given individual), the proper attitude to take has nothing to do with whether or not one approves of the behavior of that culture (or individual). Nor does it imply any change or desire for change of the evaluator's behavior in the direction of the cultural (or individual) behavior being considered. It simply means that one should take seriously, respect and accept the culture (or the individual's behavior) as in some overall sense valid for those immersed in it.

The previously prevalent attitude (against which this doctrine developed) was that of the cultural evolutionists who, strongly influenced by the traditional ethnocentricism of western culture, and the attempts of scholars to apply Darwinism to social theory, "saw individual cultures mainly as illustrative of particular stages in a world-wide evolutionary sequence" (Beals & Hoijer, 1965:720) with our so-called 'civilized' (European) cultures at the top and the technically less developed cultures arranged in descending order down to the most 'primitive.' This ethnocentricism was developed in the crucible of a society which tends "to arrange objects on a single scale of value from best to worst, biggest to smallest, cheapest to most expensive, etc." (Mead, 1947:113)—a society which insists on evaluating all other perspectives toward life either as black or white, good or bad, superior or inferior. Since "judgments are based on experience, and experience is interpreted by each individual in terms of his enculturation" (Herskovits, 1948: 78), cultural difference is interpreted by Euro-Americans as cultural inferiority.

> In a culture where absolute values are stressed, the relativism of a world that encompasses many ways of living will be difficult to comprehend. Rather, it will offer a field-day for value-judgments based on the degree to which a given body of customs resembles or differs from those of Euro-American culture (Herskovits, 1948: 78).

However, while much of the western world holds (at least nominally) the relativistic viewpoint, the western Church (reinforced by monocultural theology) and the rest of the population retain the evolutionary position. Often the western Church has falsely equated cultural and moral relativism, rejecting the former on the presupposition that any relativism is a threat to Christianity and/or the Euro-American way of life. Furthermore, much of western Christianity associates a supposed superiority of western culture to western Christianity, and this has led to the diffusion of the evolutionary, ethnocentric view of the cultures of mankind.

Yet Christian applied anthropoligists, studying the cross-cultural operations of the Church, have considered what Nida calls a position of "relative cultural relativism." This position does not deny the presence of absolutes but relates all absolutes to God, who stands outside of culture, rather than to any cultural expression, description or exemplification of a God-man relationship (be it American, Greek or Hebrew). "The only absolute in Christianity," says Nida in what may be an overstatement, "is the triune God. Anything which involves man, who is finite and limited, must of necessity be limited, and hence relative" (Nida, 1954: 282).

Nida and other Christian ethnotheologians see a "Biblical cultural relativism" as "an obligatory feature of our incarnational religion," asserting that "without it we would either absolutize human institutions" (as theologians often do) or, going to the other extreme (as anthropologists often do), we would "relativize God" (282). This biblical relativism maintains that the absolute God in his interaction with man takes into account the relativity of the human situation in at least three respects. His expectation with regard to human beings is conditioned and therefore relative with respect to: 1) The endowment and opportunities of people (Mt. 25: 14-30; Lk. 12: 48). 2) The extent of revelation (Rom. 2: 14; cf. Lev. 24: 20; Deut. 23: 6 and Mt. 5: 38, 39,44). 3) The cultural patterns of society (e.g. the Old Testament sanctions slavery (Lev. 25: 39-46), trial by ordeal (Num.5), polygamy (2 Sam. 12: 7,8) and divorce (Deut. 24: 1-4). None of these were sanctioned in the New Testament, while divorce was challenged (Mt. 5: 31-32, Mk. 10: 2-12). Paul sought to be "all things to all men" culturally (I Cor. 9: 20-21). (Also contrast Gal. 2: 11-16 with Acts 21: 24, and Acts 16: 3 with Gal. 2: 3).

"Biblical relativism" Nida continues—

> is not a matter of inconsistency, but a recognition of
> the different cultural factors which influence standards
> and actions. While the Koran attempts to fix for all
> time the behavior of Muslims, the Bible clearly
> establishes the principle of relative relativism, which
> permits growth, adaptation and freedom, under the
> Lordship of Jesus Christ. . . The Christian position
> is not one of static conformance to dead rules, but of
> dynamic obedience to a living God (1954: 52).

However, many persons (Christians and non-Christians)
assume that if cultures are relative, the proclamation of
Christianity across cultural boundaries is invalid. "What
right have we to change their culture?" they ask, "They
are happy as they are." These questions imply two false
assumptions, 1) that the primary aim of cross-cultural
proclamation is to destroy culture patterns, and 2) that
Rousseau's "happy savage" exists.

While one could not contend that everything done cross-
culturally in the name of Christianity had avoided culture
change in some way or other, or that it had not often led
to physical hardship; nevertheless ethnotheologians would
challenge both the above assumptions. Beyond the fact of
the wide diversity in cultures, there are other facts of
commonality that need to be focused on. Some of these,
though long implicit in theology of the human condition,
are now receiving attention from certain anthropoligists.
These commonalities provide Christian ethnotheology with
an anthropological as well as a theological base for cross-
cultural communication of the supra-cultural Gospel, without the necessity of culture change as a presupposition.

The respected anthropologist, Walter Goldschmidt of
UCLA, for example, states that "people are more alike than
cultures . . . There is" he continues, "a good deal of evidence that, for instance, the average Zuni and the average
Kwakiutl man behave a good deal more like each other than
the normative patterns of the two cultures are alike." He
suggests that this recognition be interpreted not merely as
"an expression of the limitations of culture," but as an insight into "the nature of man *to which culture must adapt*"
(Goldschmidt 1966: 134-5. Italics mine). Relativity, therefore, though applying to cultures does not apply to basic man.

Goldschmidt then goes on to specify a series of general-
izations concerning cross-cultural human similarity which
suggest (among other things) that they may be universals:
1) the presence of deep dissatisfaction, selfishness, exploi-
tiveness and conflict in every culture and 2) a longing for
escape from all of this into "some kind of symbolic eternity."
Furthermore, he asserts, the presence of communal groupings which involve individuals in patterns of activity in
which they share with other persons is not (as Montague and
others have suggested) to be interpreted as indicating "that
man is. . . fundamentally a loving creature," but rather, as
indicating that humanity needs institutional devices "to
preserve society against the essential self-interest of the
human individual" (136).

An Integrated View of God, Culture and Man

By drawing insights from both theology and anthropology
Christian ethnotheology may arrive at conclusions concerning both the relativity of culture and the essential oneness
of mankind, including his lostness in sin—in spite of the
cultural differences in perceptions and expressions of this
sinfulness. Drawing from theology alone our discipline may
arrive at conclusions regarding God's provision for man's
need and the supracultural condition (i.e. faith) for meeting
that need. We then turn to anthropology for the techniques
of cross-cultural communication of this supracultural
message in terms meaningful within the hearer's culture.
Basic to the employment of these techniques is the understanding derived from anthropology that the hearer's culture
is valid and logical and must be taken seriously by the
communicator. Furthermore understanding derived from a
culture-conscious interpretation of the Bible, that a supracultural God is willing and anxious to accept any culture
(without pre-condition) as a vehicle of His interaction with
culture-bound man is an axiom of ethnotheology.

On a basis of these and other insights arrived at through
the study of Christian ethnotheology the matrix can be
developed that will issue in the kind of integrated approach
to God, culture and man that has been tabulated on the next
page.

CHRISTIAN ETHNOTHEOLOGY

	GOD	CULTURE	MAN
A	God Exists Outside of Culture Supracultural-Transcendent	Cultural Diversity a Fact	Basic Human Similarity a Fact
B	God Ordains Culture To restrain human self-interest To channel human potential as areas for His inter-action with man	Functional Relative Validity of Culture Each Culture More or Less Adequate Reflects Man's Organizational Ability	Human Total Involvement In Culture
C	God Provides Ultimate Meaning for Man	Culture Always Lopsided Reflects Man's Sinfulness	An Individual's Culture Can Never Provide Complete Satisfaction
D	God Desires to Answer Man's Problem, No Matter How He Perceives It	Each Society Defines Its Own 'Hangups'	An Individual's Perception of the Problems and Their Answers Are Culturally Determined
E	God Seeks Man	The Ultimate Answer to Cultural Lopsidedness Comes from Outside Culture	An Individual's Perception of the Supracultural Is in Terms of His Own Culture
F	God Will Be Found by Those Who Diligently Seek Him (Hebrews 11: 6)	Cultural Lopsidedness Challenges People to Seek God	An Individual's Search Is Culturally Channeled
G	Missionaries Are to Serve Both as Discoverers of the Culturally-Expressed Need for God and as Proclaimers of the Answer	Culture Contact Is Often an Instrument for Stimulating this Search	The Individual's Perspective May Be Broadened, His Discomfort Increased and/or His Search Ended

BIBLIOGRAPHY:

Beals, R. L. and H. Hoijer,
    1965   AN INTRODUCTION TO ANTHROPOLOGY, New
            York, Macmillan
Goldschmidt, Walter
    1966   COMPARATIVE FUNCTIONALISM: AN ESSAY IN
            ANTHROPOLOGICAL THEORY, Berkeley, Univer-
            sity of California Press
Herskovits, Melville J.
    1948   MAN AND HIS WORKS, New York, Alfred Knopf
Mead, Margaret
    1964   ANTHROPOLOGY: A HUMAN SCIENCE, New York,
            Van Nostrand Ch. 9, originally an article in 1947
Nida, Eugene A.
    1954   CUSTOMS AND CULTURES, New York, Harper &
            Row
Tennant, F. R.
    1962   "Theology" in ENCYCLOPEDIA BRITTANICA, v. 22

The second stage in the establishment of a Christian civilization is "teaching them all things." For the sake of convenience we shall condense these words into another term, and say the second stage is that of Perfecting the People. This is the bringing about of an ethical change in the discipled group, an achievement of a thoroughly Christian way of life. . . All that great effort of the churches . . . with holy living and with social, racial and political justice is part of the process of perfecting.

BRIDGES OF GOD,
p. 15.

9

PERFECTION GROWTH

Alan Gates

Donald McGavran began using the term *perfection growth* shortly before writing *Bridges of God* (1955). He referred to the process of leading multiplying churches into Christian maturity and spontaneous outreach. The idea, if not the term, was much older than that. He was facing the pheno-menon of large groups of tribal and outcaste Indians turning to Christ and was concerned that they should become con-gregations and receive Christian nurture, which he used to speak of under the general term of Christianization. More and more since then he has been concerned with great numbers of people turning to Christ in group move-ments: making-disciples of the tribes. And always behind this was the presupposition that they would be formed into churches. Planting churches implied perfecting or maturing (as the scriptural word is sometimes translated). Those who have criticised McGavran's emphasis on quantity have quite wrongly ignored the qualitative base on which his quantitative studies stand. Perfection growth is essential to the total experience.

The following is a brief review of the ideas of Donald McGavran and his co-workers on the subject. Both the numerical and maturing aspects of church growth theory spring from biblical roots—Matt. 28: 18-20—and the confrontation of "people movement churches" rather than the slow-growing churches within resistant societies.

McGavran and Perfection Growth

From the thirties, working with Pickett and Singh, McGavran formulated his ideas on Christianization. Their original work was reprinted later with a chapter on "Group Conversion" by Warnshuis under the title *Church Growth and Group Conversion.* In the final chapter of that book McGavran discussed the nature of Christian nurture in the rapidly multiplying churches. It should be profitable in an article on perfection growth to sum up the component parts as McGavran (1936: 111-115) saw them at the time. These were:

(1) Training in worship:
The rich meaningful worship of the Christian Church is the birthright of every Christian group. Daily worship of God is invaluable in the achievement of Christian consciousness (111) . . .They should be trained till their worship is regular, inspiring, well attended and participated in by all (112).

(2) Training of honorary national leaders:
Amongst the first duties of those to whom God has committed the spiritual care of a beginning people movement is that of discovering, training, and keeping at work its honorary leaders (112).

(3) An organized pastorate:
The best of the people being saved should be trained both as catechists and as ministers (112). He went on to warn against the dangers of training centers, which make a graduate unwilling to return to his rural setting. He also accented the necessity of training leaders from among the people being discipled.

(4) The teaching of stewardship:
The habit of . . . giving will not establish itself. It must be taught as God's provision for His Church (113)

(5) The teaching of Christian truth:
     Christian truth should be taught to both adults and
     children in worship, special instruction, institutes
     and by other means (114).

(6) The establishment of Christian customs:
     Christian burial, marriage, festivals, symbols,
     pictures, greetings, postures in worship, attitudes
     toward the castes, treatment of women and children
     . . . all these Christian customs need to be estab-
     lished (114).

(7) The practice of Christian witness:
     The group of converts is constantly faced with
     caste fellows who are intensely interested in the
     fact that 'our folk have become Christian.' They
     may hate it. They may like it. But they will not
     be indifferent to it. The new convert should be
     taught to bear his witness clear and unwavering
     in the midst of the kind of comment his own vil-
     lagers are likely to make (115).

Within the same context of nurture for new people movement churches, McGavran also stressed the need for a
church building in which to worship. Normally "group
movements may be expected to multiply churches." Here
we glimpse an idea which was to become increasingly
prominent in McGavran's thought, namely that all forms of
Christian nurture should eventually lead to further discipling.
In other words, those received into the fellowship today
must be discipling tomorrow. Christian mission is an
ongoing business.

From the beginning of his church growth writing McGavran's thoughts turned to sociological and anthropological
dimensions and related to the various local ways of life.
Converts had to live and mature in their own social worlds.

In *Bridges of God* (1955:15) McGavran made the distinction between discipling and perfecting. He defined
perfecting as:

> . . . a bringing about of an ethical change in the dis-
> cipled group, an increasing achievement of a thoroughly
> Christian way of life for the community as a whole,
> and the conversion of the individuals making up each
> generation as they come to the age of decision.

Perfection growth is thus the second stage in the establishment of a Christian society, the natural sequel to discipling
a people from pagan society, and it implies (in this context)
a large enough group of converts to function as a congregation. In the great commission (Matt. 28:19-20) the apostles
were commanded to make-disciples (one word and a verb)
"teaching them all things." It is from this second injunction
that McGavran has drawn his concept of perfection growth.

Although he distinguished discipling and perfecting as
two separate stages he recognized that "the second stage
overlaps the first, but it cannot precede it without destroying it" (1955:16). A people in the early stages of turning
from idols cannot be expected to demonstrate "evidence of
an ethical change or dedication of Jesus Christ, which some
Christians in the older churches have not yet achieved"
(15).

If requirements for baptism and church membership
other than faith and repentance be forced upon individuals
within a people movement, then the danger of halting or
disrupting such a movement can be great. Growth in Christian maturity must come in the second stage as proper and
adequate shepherding is provided. McGavran takes great
pains to demonstrate the importance of perfection growth
for the ongoing of people movement churches. To the early
critic who questioned the motivation which turns large
numbers to Christ, McGavran would cite the well-docu-
mented findings of Pickett, that—

> . . . the motives which lead people to Christ in people
> movements are those that lead individuals anywhere
> to Him (1936: 16).

McGavran saw the real problem as not, "how people movements begin" but "what to do with them when they come."
And this is precisely where perfection growth becomes
the name of the game.

In 1959 McGavran touched on perfection growth in *How
Churches Grow* in a discussion on "the pressure to perfect"
(93-101). However this was a negative passage, the focus
being on the danger of perfecting at the expense of discipling,
his point being that the two had to proceed together.

While the term is little used in other parts of *How
Churches Grow*, nevertheless, he was dealing with ideas
germane to perfection growth in parts Four and Five in

which he discussed leadership and organization (122-125). There was, however, little extension of the basic ideas already found in his earlier writings. The importance of his writings in 1955 was that he defined more precisely the meaning of perfection growth, and by basing it on the second part of the great commission, he theoretically distinguished it from discipling (making-disciples).

By 1959 McGavran was developing his ideas on leadership in perfection growth, that the church might be not merely nourished but also trained in outreach. At this time he was advocating a program with three levels of leadership: two ordained and one lay. The ordained leaders divided between churches of the classes where the average income would be "2,000 pesos" and churches among the masses of "400" average income (1959:139). The third class was unpaid lay leadership and was made up of "deacons . . . elders, teachers and youth workers, secretaries and treasurers, board members and choir singers" (1955:139). Such lay leaders would serve both in the inner life of the Church and its outward aspects of expansion.

By 1965, he had expanded his number of levels of leadership to five. Distinction was made between lay workers who operated in the inner life of the church and those who helped in outreach activities outside. A fifth level of leader was the well-trained multi-lingual person operating at national and international levels of church life. This shows how McGavran's ideas of leadership were growing step by step with the programs of indigenization and nationalization of the churches over this period, and also under the influence of his post-Indian research.

In *Understanding Church Growth* (1970), perfection growth is touched briefly under the title "post-baptismal care" (325-329), and post-baptismal shepherding is stressed. One new line of thought not fully developed in his earlier works is the relationship of perfection growth in young people movement churches to subsequent times of revival:

> Adequate post-baptismal care. . . regular worship, instruction by sermon, crises met under guidance of older Christians, living in the presence of the righteous God, and feeding systematically on His Word, all lift the community to a place where revival. . . becomes possible for large numbers (1970: 328).

The above resume of McGavran's writing on perfection growth should be sufficient to demonstrate his great concern for the spiritual quality of church growth in reply to his uninformed critics who talk of "quality being more important than quantity." McGavran has always insisted that the two must go together, and the Church must be concerned about each. Let his own words sum it up:

> To be sure, some fast-growing Churches have been scandalously neglected. The practical problem of how to assure adequate Christian nurture for inflooding multitudes is always keen. Nurture must be provided. Genuine Christianity is essential to church growth (1965: 235).

McGavran's Colleagues and Perfection Growth

McGavran has not stood alone in this battle. Some of his colleagues have also defended his position. For example, Tippett, a social anthropologist has related theological and anthropological dimensions to church growth theory. Indeed he made use of the precise words of the critics— "quantity and quality." In an article "Church Growth or Else!" (1966) he applied the expression *quantitative, qualitative* and *organic* as descriptors of church growth, designating "evangelical expansion," "internal growth in grace within the fellowship" and "the emergence of an organized indigenous church (1966; 12). These he insisted had to be kept in *equilibrium* and in *continuity* (1968: 12). This sociological model is in harmony with McGavran and indeed was intended to reinforce the idea of perfection growth (Tippett, 1969: 127). In his book, *Church Growth and the Word of God* (1970: 26-27) the same writer finds his base for qualitative growth or perfecting in the New Testament. Here we are shown that Jesus directed his followers to the importance of maturity (Matt. 5: 48); Paul stressed perfection as the mark of the man of God (III Tim. 3: 17); the local group of worshipping believers must also grow in maturity in Christ (Eph. 4: 11-12) and so on. He is careful to note that perfection growth is a concern of both the individual and the group.

Another term used by Tippett is *incorporation* (1969: 106 ff). Incorporation "concerns belonging." This concept bears upon perfection growth at the point of how and when one brings converts of a people movement into a new group with which they may identify. Group movements to Christ in many lands give evidence of the danger of leaving converts for long periods of time without providing a new communal society within the church. People must know where they belong. Whether they be baptized upon the basis of burning fetishes and renouncing old religions, or whether they be required to give evidence of understanding a certain number of doctrinal truths, it is imperative that the Christian advocate involved assume full responsibility for providing some sense of belonging to new converts. Of the person in a communal society Tippett says—

> He knows who he is and where he belongs. He has his personal rights and knows what they are. He has his responsibilities and knows what they are. He knows his relationship with people in other statuses. Because he knows these things he can go about with confidence (107).

When such a person is converted, Tippett insists, he must be incorporated into a group where he feels he belongs. Only thus can he grow in grace. This is an anthropological way of dealing with perfection growth. In the same passage Tippett speaks of the need for a *consummation* of a people movement. This is another term which calls for further work of grace in the convert from paganism. He has used this term since 1962, but its best treatment is in his most recent book on people movements (1971) in which it is a major entry in the index. This is a phenomenological approach to perfection growth.

While Tippett refers to organic growth as distinct from qualitative, it nevertheless includes areas such as organization, training of leadership, creation of new roles and functions to match the changing needs of an ongoing Church, all of which I believe McGavran would include within perfection growth. We may, therefore, consider the idea of organic growth as an extension of the basic perfection growth idea.

Finally, we do well to heed Tippett's warning against "perfectionism;" that attitude of self satisfaction and perfectionism which "shuts off a congregation from the world, encloses it (and) robs it of outreach" (1970:64).

This is not perfection growth: rather it is the mark of a dying congregation.

Leadership training has always been considered a crucial part of perfection growth in people movement Churches. Probably no single man has contributed more to this one dimension of church growth in recent years than Ralph Winter. Before joining the faculty at the Institute of Church Growth, Winter was largely responsible for the pioneering of "theological education by extension" in Guatemala.

The relationship between extension and perfection growth may not be immediately apparent. Essentially, extension education is a means of providing theological education for laymen without dislocating them culturally or geographically. Obviously there is nothing magic about extension as a method. Neither will large attendances at such a program necessarily result in perfection growth. However, if the laymen trained are concerned to propagate the Gospel, then their further training and ordination should exert a salutary influence over the Church. With better trained men in the churches, men raised and proven within homogeneous units, there is good reason to expect a quickening of the life of the Church, improvement of patterns of worship, increased outreach to surrounding peoples, the sum of which is bound to result in a maturing influence upon the church as a whole.

The impact of extension education in the United Presbyterian field in Guatamala can be appreciated from the following: Three years after extension began, one hundred students were in training as against ten to fifteen a few years earlier. The range of students in training had broadened out to include the whole social spectrum from rural Indians to professional men in the cities. Eleven regional centers were serving two Indian sub-cultures, rural Spanish communities, three urban centers and one group of professional men (1969: 74). Today, the Guatamala program, at the graduate level alone, is training more students than all the rest of the seminaries in Latin America put together. The impact of this increased coverage of theological education upon the quality of church growth is considerable.

Winter has chosen to define church growth not so much in terms of "qualitative versus quantitative" but rather in

terms of "how growth itself takes place." While his definitions are not primarily related to what we have called
perfection growth, nevertheless they suggest another perspective from which perfection growth may be regarded.
He sees church growth as being either "expansion" "multiplication" or "bridging." The first term designates the
growth of a single congregation into a larger membership.
The second term refers to the establishment of new congregations within a homogeneous unit. The third points to the
starting of new congregations in homogeneous units foreign
to the home base. This could include anything from crossing
of tribal barriers to crossing the ocean.

Biblical Implications

McGavran and his colleagues have all operated from a
biblical base and Christian convictions. From different
approaches they have insisted that the idea of perfection
growth (by this or any other name) is an ongoing element
from the great commission. From the anthroplogical,
phenomenological and educational we now turn to a deeper
analysis of the biblical base.

We now return to the words of Jesus "teaching them to
observe all things whatsoever I have commanded you" and
ask just what did our Lord include in the "all things?" This
was McGavran's *locus   classicus* for defining perfection
growth. How then should we understand the implication of the
terms "teaching" and to "observe" for together these words
make up the Church's mandate for maturity.

Of all 95 occurrences of the verb didasko in the New
Testament about two thirds are to be found in the Gospels
and Acts. The Gospels indicate that teaching was one of
the prominent features of Jesus' public ministry. The
form of Jesus' teaching was according to the tradition of
Judaism, with expositions from the Torah (Matt. 5: 21 ff)
or at least starting from some Old Testament passage
(Luke 4: 16 ff). However His teaching was never restricted
to the Law alone. Nor was Jesus patient with the lifeless
casuistry of current religious teachers, which failed to
consider the life situation and needs of the one being
taught, teaching the Law for its own sake, and elevating
knowing above doing.

The whole of Jesus' teaching was ordered with a view to
bringing man into harmony with God and neighbor (Matt.
22:31ff). His teaching was always directed to the will of man
and called for a personal verdict for or against the will of
His Father. As early as Mark 6:30, Jesus was instructing
His disciples to teach. Finally, Jesus made the continu-
ation of this teaching to be the life task of the disciples
(Matt. 28:20). A. B. Bruce reminds us that the form of the
verb (present participle)

> . . . implies instruction is to be a continuous process,
> not subordinate to and preparing for baptism but con-
> tinuing after baptism with a view to enabling disciples
> to walk worthily of their vocation (1951: 340).

Turning now to the "all things," we are faced with the
problem of deciding the scope and content of what Jesus
intended to be taught. Perhaps one may assume that
(following the authors of *The New Testament Speaks*) the
all things "are precisely the things recorded in Matthew's
own Gospel" (Barker et al, 1969: 263). If one agrees with
them that "Matthew may be regarded not only as a Gospel
. . . but also as a book of the teachings of Jesus intended
primarily for use in the Church's task of instructing
Gentile converts"—for which a good case is made—then,
we may proceed with some confidence to determine the
"all things," assured that these represent the areas in
which perfection growth must take place.

The Gospel of Matthew falls into five clear divisions,
each including a separate block of didactic material.
Each of these five sections ends with a formula: "And it
came to pass when Jesus had finished all these sayings"
(7:28; 11:1, 13:53; 19:1; 26:1). We may now distinguish
five broad categories of teaching which make up the "all
things." The first section (Matt. 5:1-7:27) includes Jesus'
Sermon on the Mount or His teachings on the ethics of the
Kingdom. New believers accordingly are to be taught the
higher ethic of the law of Christ and His kingdom. Here
God's new children must learn those general principles
governing human and Christian relationships, together with
the safeguards against the violation of God's law in the
name of free grace.

The second passage of "all things" is found in Matthew
10:1-42 and deals with Jesus' charge to the Twelve as they

go out to preach in the cities of Israel. This is His teaching on mission and builds on what has been said about ethics. Those who would be true disciples of Christ must learn of the cost of persecution and the need for radical commitment from this missionary discourse.

The third unit (13:1-52) takes up the parables of the Kingdom, its nature, and destiny. These parables show how the kingdom has come in the Christ event. Despite small and hidden beginnings it will yet come in fulness.

The fourth passage (18:1-35) covers matters of discipline within the Church. God's people are to live together under His authority, bound together in the ties of mutual love and forgiveness.

Finally, in the Olivet Discourse, Jesus speaks about eschatology (23:1-25:46). The Christian community must learn that it lives in the shadow of His coming. Jesus will return as Son of Man depicted in various metaphors like a bridegroom for a wedding, the returning lord of a manor, a thief in the night. He will reward both the evil and the just, according to their desserts. Meanwhile each Christian must give good account of himself in terms of stewardship over talents given him for use.

Having defined the general scope and content of the "all things," we come finally to the admonitions of the Master that what we teach must then be observed. This is "to keep" or "to preserve" that which is committed to one's trust by appropriate use. The meaning here includes both the idea of obedience and practice. The teaching, says A.B. Bruce (1951: 340) is not something one has to know but something to be practiced, "the aim is not orthodox opinion, but right living."

The "all things" cover all aspects of Christian faith and life. Centered in the teachings of Jesus they yet root back into the Old Testament tradition. They are to be taught as Jesus taught, aimed at the will, and calling always for a personal verdict. In this way, there will be an ever increasing conformity of the whole man to the will of God and the image of Jesus Christ. The promised result is nothing less than His continued presence "Lo I am with you always."

We see then that perfection growth in the light of Matthew 28:20 is primarily a problem of teaching right belief and right living; covering the five areas of ethics, mission, kingdom truth, church discipline and eschatology.

Finally, the definition of what represents true Christian maturity in each different culture pattern is difficult for a cross-cultural worker to determine. Furthermore, we may well ask if there ever can be a mature congregation unless members are continually being won and brought into the fellowship. As Shenk points out, "every church is a mixture of both mature and immature members"(1971: 9). And this is as it should be. Discipling and perfecting go on together. As the newly-discipled are helped to grow in grace, they are sent forth themselves to make-disciples. There is no other way to carry out the requirements of the great commission. This is what McGavran and his colleagues have been saying all the time.

Let me gather together a few points which I consider worthy of summation. Perfection growth is a useful term, a biblical one, standing on the commission of our Lord. Perfection growth pertains to both teaching and observing, learning, sharing and doing. Physical facilities and methods are secondary, and should be directed to the commissioned goals, not become ends in themselves. The scope of things taught embraces both the cultural and evangelistic mandates, and brings the whole man to God. Perfection growth is a corporate thing: someone should always be being incorporated for fellowship and learning, and someone should always be reaching outwards in service and mission. From the signs of the times (especially the wide-spread people movements of our day) we anticipate the need for more and more perfecting programs in the years that lie ahead. You cannot have people movement intake without being responsible also for perfection growth.

BIBLIOGRAPHY:

Barker, G. W., W. L. Lane, J. R. Michaels,
    1969   THE NEW TESTAMENT SPEAKS, New York,
            Harper & Row
Bruce, A. B.
    1951   THE EXPOSITOR'S GREEK TESTAMENT, Michigan
            Eerdmans. Vol. I
McGavran, Donald A.
    1955   THE BRIDGES OF GOD, New York, Friendship
            Press
    1959   HOW CHURCHES GROW, London, World Dominion
            Press
McGavran, Donald A. (editor)
    1964-9 CHURCH GROWTH BULLETIN, Vol. I-V, South
            Pasadena, William Carey Library
Pickett, J. W., A. L. Warnshuis, C. H. Singh, D. A. McGavran
    1962   CHURCH GROWTH AND GROUP CONVERSION,
            Lucknow, India, Lucknow Publishing House
Shenk, W. R.
    1971   "A Church is Mature When ... ? INSIDE LINE, John
            Bender (Ed.). Elkhart, Indiana, Mennonite Board of
            Missions Bos. 370, August
Tippett, Alan R.
    1966   "Church Growth or Else!" WORLD VISION MAGA-
            ZINE, February.
    1969   VERDICT THEOLOGY IN MISSIONARY THEORY,
            Lincoln, Illinois, Lincoln Christian College Press.
    1970   CHURCH GROWTH AND THE WORD OF GOD,
            Grand Rapids, Michigan, Wm. B. Eerdmans Pub. Co.
    1971   PEOPLE MOVEMENTS IN SOUTHERN POLYNESIA,
            Chicago, Moody Press
Winter, Ralph D. (editor)
    1969   THEOLOGICAL EDUCATION BY EXTENSION, South
            Pasadena, William Carey Library

Part III

God's Work
in
Human Structures

GOD'S WORK IN HUMAN STRUCTURES

The theology which calls for Christian man's mission and ministry in the world (for as the Father sent him into the world so he sends us into the world) commits him to action within the structures and institutions of human life. The Incarnation itself demonstrates this. Even as God made it, the earth was structured —day and night, the four seasons, seed time and harvest; but when He gave it over to mankind other structures emerged— families, tribes, occupational patterns, inter-communication networks, markets, governments, hamlets, cities—evidence of man inter-relating with man in his conquest of the earth.

If theology discloses the purposes of God for mankind in this human situation, the theory of mission may be regarded as the method whereby Christian man transmits that word from God to secular and pagan man. In this part of the Festschrift we have, as it were, the pert plan of how this theology may be applied in the human situation. The theory of mission must stand firmly on the theology of the Word, but it must show how application can be made in the structures and institutions of human society. It must come to grips with anthropology, sociology and psychology, and it must recognize that the human situation is always changing. It must consider the social mechanisms of decision-making and culture change, of acceptance and rejection, so that Christian man may be both enlightened and warned about his presentation of the Gospel.

This section of the book commences with an aggressive survey of McGavran's pragmatic missionary strategy from C. Peter Wagner. He looks at objectives, progress evaluation, mobility opportunities, functional methodology, all of which he pulls together in the notion of church-centeredness. This is a forward-looking statement reflecting McGavran's view that we are in the "sunrise, not the sunset of mission."

Roy Shearer, the psychologist of the church growth team, gets more 'meat' in a few short pages than many writers do in a whole book. He discussed the notion of receptivity, and the diversity of motivations that bring people to the acceptance of Christianity. The Christian is the advocate—following Barnett's terminology (1953). He advocates a method of testing situations for recognizing potential responsiveness. This is a good example of relating church growth theory and data to the methodology of another discipline, and as such, it suggests the ever-widening range of missiological theory in the seventies.

The editor's essay takes Calverton's anthropological theory of cultural compulsives as applied to social thought, updates it for today (when applied anthropology has a firmer status), and discusses, among other things, "cultural relativism" as a compulsive in anthropology, and what this means for missiology.

Bill Read wrestles with a concept he has from sociology. He wants to describe church growth in terms of modernization. He reminds us that church growth does not take place in a vacuum; that social change is inevitable; that human societies are passing into a new age; but that the Church is, or should be involved in the process. Our mission is in the world and to the world, and there has to be a new day in Christian mission, with an organization and a methodology adequate for that modern world. For this reason he wants to state the principles and procedures of church planting and growth in sociological terms of modernization. If this can be done a whole new area of research procedure and techniques would be open to us.

Cal Guy was assigned the difficult task of relating missionary administration to field situations. This is an objective look at things by a professor, who has travelled widely round the missionary world. By way of contrast, Stan Shewmaker's study is subjective. This man came from a static field situation, studied church growth methods, rethought his own position, modified his techniques; and the Holy Spirit truly blessed the faith which was ready to take up the task again with new methods. We could have included this in the Case Studies section, but he is included here to press the point as part of church growth theory, that taking time off to do an honest, critical survey, based on sound research method, is the best way of acquainting oneself with the real situation. McGavran has always said that theory has to be measured against concrete facts. Shewmaker is typical of many men who took off time to study church growth, and returned to situations that had been static, to modify methods and to start planting churches.

The essay on ethnolinguistics is by McGavran's colleague, Charles Kraft. He opens up a huge area for study, which most of us had probed a little during our missionary service. But this is the first time, I think, it has been set forward as a field of study in the discipline of missiology. Directly it represents a research area crying out for attention. Indirectly it has major consequences both for the training of missionaries and for the forms and structures of the indigenous Church. As a cultural anthroplogist and a linguist, Kraft can handle this well. Missionaries who master this article will be well on their way to mastering their ethnocentricity, and will be ready to serve with nationals in partnership, or as servants of the national churches.

Theory is often pushed aside as dull and uninteresting, but we can never do without it. Something has to come between the theological base we have from Scripture and the human situation in which we proclaim the Word. The Word is true. But the true Word can be so badly presented and so ethnocentrically injected into cross-cultural situations, that it receives rejection instead of acceptance, and doors may be closed for generations. A wrong theory of mission can have devastating results. We must never forget that Christian man is called to proclaim God's Word and to do God's work in human structures.

Individuals, congregations, Churches and Missions, boards and older Churches, all in their own spheres need to cultivate the habit of measuring "church-growth achieved" and regarding it as one of the most significant factors in the world mission. Only then can they rightly estimate the value of theories of mission, forms of organization, and methods of operation. Measurement is not easy. It cannot occur automatically. Yet it must be done if the younger Churches are to enter into their heritage and the world mission is to fulfil its high calling. The effort required will be abundantly rewarded.

HOW CHURCHES GROW,
p. 154.

10

PRAGMATIC STRATEGY
FOR TOMORROW'S MISSION

C. Peter Wagner

> Christian mission wanders in a rosy fog of vague
> objectives and promotional hopes. Its objectives are
> frequently phrased in words— utreach, extension of
> the Gospel, witness, opening a province, beginning a
> work, carring on mission work—as vague as they are
> wide. 'Outreach'—to what end? Beginning what kind
> of 'work'?
> Instead of ambiguous and slippery terms, Christian
> mission needs to speak positively and exactly about the
> growth of the Church. Not what missionaries did, but
> how churches grew. Not national trends, but how
> congregations arose. Not nationalization, urbanization,
> devolution and mechanization, but how well are we
> getting on with discipling a particular part of a parti-
> cular nation. Not 'what do they eat,' but 'have they
> confessed Christ' ? (1964: 10-11).

In the very first issue of *Church Growth Bulletin,* , Donald
McGavran set the tone for a new pragmatism in missionary
thinking with the pithy words quoted above. Regardless of
the form which a particular mission strategy might assume,
McGavran would ruthlessly haul it before the bar of

missiological judgment, asking the stinging question: has it produced?

Produced what? For McGavran the question of priorities in missionary objectives has never been negotiable: faithful obedience to Jesus Christ as Lord implies bending all efforts, energies, and resources above all in bringing men and women to follow Christ in true discipleship, and to join themselves together in the fellowship of local churches. This is not some vague and misty goal which easily evades measurement and evaluation. People and churches can be counted. If tens are being won where thousands could and should be won, the particular strategy fails the test of pragmatism.

At a gathering of friends of the School of World Mission, McGavran also said:

> We devise mission methods and policies in the light of what God has blessed—and what He has obviously not blessed. Industry calls this 'modifying operation in light of feedback.' Nothing hurts missions overseas so much as continuing methods, institutions, and policies which ought to bring men to Christ—but don't; which ought to multiply churches—but don't; which ought to improve society—but don't. We teach men to be ruthless in regard to method. If it does not work to the glory of God and the extension of Christ's church, throw it away and get something which does. As to methods, we are fiercely pragmatic—doctrine is something entirely different (1970: 3)

Statements like this make many who are currently engaged in one form or another of Christian work highly uncomfortable. A pragmatic approach is risky because for some it is threatening. If carried through it can burst pride, expose weaknesses, uncover slothful stewardship, and hopefully stir up enough concern to initiate in-depth reevaluation of certain hallowed programs. As the so-called "church growth debate," which has now spread to many parts of the world, eloquently accentuates, pragmatism in missions can easily produce strong reaction and harsh criticism.

Some of the criticism against McGavran's "fierce pragmatism" has taken the form of spiritual judgments. It is thought by some that true Christian work depends so entirely on the intangible ministry of the Holy Spirit that it cannot be geared to pragmatic considerations. Pragmatism seems to these critics to be a very earthy way of doing God's business.

This is why we need to stress that pragmatism can, in fact, be consecrated. While human methods undoubtedly may all too easily intrude and become obstacles to the free working of the Spirit of God, at the same time a practical approach can profitably be mixed with spirituality in proportions that please God and that better accomplish His purposes. Spiritually speaking, only a pragmatism which is Spirit-directed and Spirit-filled can be considered as a characteristic of Christian work. The Holy Spirit cannot be left to one side, superceded by human means.

The glory for any results which come from the Lord's work goes to the head of the body, Jesus Christ. What the members of the body do, they do only in obedience to Him, and they acknowledge full dependence upon Him. Once God's will is known, however, it should be implemented by His people in the most efficient and effective way possible. Why else would Christ have taken so many pains to draw the distinction between "wicked and slothful servants" and "good and profitable servants" as He did in the parable of Matthew 25? When the judgment came there, it was based on some pretty hard-headed pragmatism. There is no reason to suspect that Jesus demands any less of us when it comes to missionary strategy today.

Pragmatic missionary strategy, properly related to the Triune God, is characterized by five major components;

1. A Well-Honed Set of Objectives

On the preliminary and theoretical level, a lack of proper goal-setting has been perhaps the major retarding factor in modern missions. Typically, missionary objectives have been vague and imprecise. Few other contemporary professions would allow such shoddy planning on such a wide scale. How laymen who demand that explicit objectives be set in their own businesses or professions continue to invest the money earned there in a missionary enterprise which has largely been careless about objectives is one of the more curious phenomena of contemporary Christianity. Somehow they have been conditioned to believe that God does not want Christian workers to define objectives and subsequently measure success or failure according to whether they have accomplished them or not.

Naturally, the danger that wrong objectives be set cannot be denied. But infinitely greater is the danger that no objectives at all be set. Hesitancy to set precise objectives in missionary work may often be traced to a lack of faith in God's dealings with His people. Overstressing the transcendence of God, the mysterious working of His providence, and the sovereignty of the ministry of the Holy Spirit, all of which are true and good Christian principles, can too easily squeeze out other equally valid elements of God's way of relating to His servants. God has not set His church adrift without some pretty definite navigational principles. The Bible, the Word of God, gives Christian workers clear indications of what God's will for them is, and what God's own objectives in Christian work are. God has given us enough information in the Bible to allow missionary strategists not only to articulate objectives, but to enjoy a good degree of assurance that they are the right objectives because they reflect God's revealed will.

Not enough attention has been paid to basic definitions in missionary circles today. Very few missionary leaders, to say nothing of grass-roots missionaries, are able to give precise definitions of such seemingly elementary terms as "mission" or "evangelism" or "disciples." Enticing as it might be, the purpose of this essay is not to develop these terms in detail—they are given only as illustrations of an unfortunate state of mind in modern missions. Some question the value of struggling with definitions at all, assuming that such terms mean the same thing to all people and are clearly understood. Not so.

To some, "mission" simply means anything good the church does. Digging canals, teaching literacy, distributing powdered milk, immunizing against polio, scattering tracts from airplanes—all these activities and countless others have at one time or another been called "mission." The ambiguous, but widely-promoted slogan that "the church is mission" has added to the confusion in many circles. It is quite different from the more dynamic and more biblically-oriented definition that insists that missions properly constituted will invite all men everywhere to become

disciples of Christ, form themselves into Christian churches,
and in turn proclaim Christ and plan still other churches.

"Evangelism" can be defined in one of three general
ways, and even missionaries who accept the biblical definition of mission may be working toward quite different
evangelistic goals, according to their understanding of the
term. Those who define evangelism simply as "Christian
presence" may live among a people for years, may establish rapport with them by good works of one kind or another,
but may never get around to telling them that God loves
them, that sin has blocked this love and made them enemies
of God, and that God demands that all men everywhere repent of their sins and trust Christ for forgiveness. Nevertheless they call their silent witness "evangelism." others
may communicate the message to others, but with communication itself as their objective. They feel that all those who
hear the message of the Gospel have been "evangelized,"
whether they respond or not. Not so, claims a third group,
not satisfied with stopping at proclamation only. Evangelism to them means actually bringing a man or woman to
new birth in Christ. Anything short of this may have been
a good evangelistic attempt, but not a successful evangelism in terms of the proper objective.

When a person is brought to Christ and becomes a new
creature, he is then a "disciple," according to one understanding of the New Testament concept. Some, however,
have narrowed this term down to the place where it signi-
fies not simply a Christian, but a Christian who has gone
on and reached a certain level of maturity or sanctification.
This definition is important for missionary strategy, since
the very bedrock of God's revealed will for missionary
goals is to "make disciples" according to the Great Commission (Matthew 28:19-20). Until you have clearly defined
"disciples" you will have difficulty knowing whether you
are "making" them or not.

The list of key terms which need sharp and accurate definitions prior to setting goals for any missionary work
could be expanded. But the point has been made that without definitions a missionary will have difficulty in knowing
just where he is headed, and he who aims at nothing usually
hits it.

Those who support, administer, or perform missionary

work should insist on seeing objectives in writing. Vague
and meaningless terms such as "a work," "witness,"
"reaching people," or "outreach" should either be carefully
explained or eliminated from missionary vocabulary. Separate sets of long-range and short-range objectives need to
be drawn up for every missionary ministry, either by a
multi-field mission board or by an independent couple living
back in the hills.

Meaningful objectives cannot be written, however, without
certain essential input. No one can tell where he should be
going until he is sure of where he is and where he has been.
Amazingly enough, most missionaries cannot tell you this
with any degree of accuracy. "Oh, our mission has not
stressed statistics," they will say. While this statement
may seem innocuous, think it through. It is about as
serious as having the altimeter in an aircraft fail while
flying through a peasoup fog. Much of the resistance to
goal-setting comes about as a result of this very thing.
Missionaries are either ill-prepared or unwilling to do the
nitting-gritty research which is essential before they can
begin to write objectives.

On all levels, the church must condition itself to make
the sacrifices necessary to produce what solid research is
needed as the basis for properly honing future objectives.
Churches, denominational agencies, interdenominational
mission boards, and associations of missions should ear-
mark a minimum of five percent of their annual budgets for
research. Missionaries should discipline themselves to do
whatever is necessary to draw an accurate statistical picture
of what is happening on their particular field, and such
analyses and reports should be required by superiors.
Without the realism, vision, courage, and hard work needed
to produce missionary objectives, tomorrow's mission will
flounder in sinking sand.

2. Ruthless Progress Evaluation

Once proper objectives are set the major hurdle toward
a pragmatic missionary strategy is passed. But even the
most carefully-formulated objectives cannot be taken for
granted.

Although it has not been the custom to do so, the words

"success" and "failure" could be effectively applied to missionary work. If the objectives are being accomplished the missionary work is a success, otherwise, why not be realistic and call it a failure.

No one can make such a judgment without a careful system of evaluation. Missionary work, like business, can be deceptive on the surface. Businessmen who think all is going well because of much activity, effusive praise, slaps on the back, and superficial optimism, then who suddenly discover that expenses have been exceeding income are jolted by the prospects of bankruptcy. More missionary work may be close to bankruptcy than any of us care to believe.

Some evangelical missions suffered this kind of a jolt when the results of the most extensive study of the Protestant Church in Latin America was published in 1969 under the title *Latin American Church Growth* (Read, Monterroso, and Johnson 1969). For years they had considered themselves among the most evangelistic of the missions working there, the ones really producing church growth. Then the published research exposed the fact that the churches associated with them in most cases were growing more slowly than the Pentecostals on one hand and the historic denominations (including Seventh–Day Adventist) on the other. Happily the IFMA and EFMA missions working in Latin America reacted positively to this unsolicited progress evaluation and called an emergency consultation of leaders in Elburn, Illinois, in 1970. The resulting "Elburn Recommendations" eloquently illustrate the good effects that such a level-headed evaluation can produce.

One of the admissions made by most of the Elburn delegates was that such an evaluation was too long overdue. It should not have taken them by surprise. They realized, as all involved in missionary work should, that they could have been doing this right along. Effective progress evaluation must be properly planned and scheduled. While perhaps not as frequent, it should be considered as much an obligation to a Christian worker as Sunday church attendance. Too often even those who have good intentions put research off for "someday soon." Other good activites crowd the schedule, and even when the time for the annual report to the mission board or the field conference comes up, only a few hastily-compiled statistics are thrown together to meet the deadline.

In a day when world events seem to be pointing to the soon return of our Lord, when the population explosion has aleady given us two billion human beings yet to become Christians and with more to come, it is time that a new note of responsibility be introduced into the missionary enterprise. How can this be done? Experience has shown that it will probably not be initiated by grass-roots missionaries. There are three reasons for this: (1) they are not convinced that progress evaluation is a high priority activity, (2) progress evaluation requires more hard work in the area of statistics and analysis than they are willing to invest, and (3) they intuitively feel threatened by an intrusion which may end up in casting a shadow over the effectiveness of their own ministry through the years. Therefore, any new movement significant enough to bring missions in general to a higher level of effectiveness in carrying out God's purpose in the days to come must come from the top, either from mission executives who have the courage and stamina to bring this about among those who are following their leadership, from pastors who can see missions from a broader perspective without emotional involvement, or if need be from the army of Christian laymen who support missions financially either directly or through their churches and who understand the value of objectives and progress evaluation from experience in their own secular involvement.

3. Mobility in Changing Circumstances

One of the obvious results of a progress evaluation may be to inform a missionary or even a whole mission that it is on the wrong track. When this happens, the most effective missions will already have a built-in flexibility so that they will rise to a challenge rather than cringe from a menace.

In very few cases will progress evaluation reveal that a mission has always been ineffective. Most often it will simply show that the mission has not kept up with changing circumstances. The world has moved ahead, but the mission has stood still. Certain missionary methods effective in the fifties are found to be inadequate in the seventies. Mobility has been lacking.

In order fully to understand the theological perspective of changing circumstances in missionary endeavor, the concept of God as the "Lord of the harvest" must be strongly emphasized. While the doctrine of the sovereignty of God can conceivably be twisted to stultify missionary motivation, when seen in the proper missiological light divine sovereignty it is at once a comfort and a challenge. The sovereign God prepares the soil for the seed to be sown. As the Parable of the Sower illustrates, not all fields are equally fertile. The history of missions shows that down through the ages God prepared one people here, and another people there for the fruitful reception of the Gospel message, and when the Go pel has been faithfully preached there, fruit has come forth thirty, sixty, and one hundred fold. Conversely, when the Gospel seed has been sown on soil which has not been made ready by the sovereign God, little or no fruit has resulted.

Not even the most erudite theologian can explain why God does this, why He seems to prepare one soil and not another. The Spirit moves like the wind, which cannot be brought under human control. But missionary strategists who have had experience in working with the Lord of the harvest have developed a sensitivity through which they can discern the signs of the times, and detect where God has prepared soil for fruitful evangelism. Their efforts, energies, and resources are then directed there, the seed of the Word is planted, and God gives the increase. They are pragmatic enough to take a long, second look at supposedly fertile fields, when a progress evaluation is made, show that the harvest has been scant.

At this point mobility is necessary. As farm laborers in the United States know, the wheat harvest begins in May in the South and continues through August in the North, but if they want employment they have to be in the right field at the right time. There is no work for them in North Dakota in May; they can spend a whole month there and not harvest a bushel.

It is not an easy task to convince missionaries that mobility will greatly increase their productivity. But if missionaries could be as mobile as the wheat harvesters, a much more significant portion of the two billion could be won for Christ in our decade.

God often uses secular instruments to accomplish His purposes. He used Cyrus and Pharaoh in dealing with His people in the Old Testament days. He may also use rulers today, or revolutions, or natural disasters, or migrations, or urbanization to prepare masses of people for the message of Christ. Wise missionary strategy will be conditioned to recognize the hand of God when it moves, and to move with it into the productive fields where people will become disciples of Christ and churches will be multiplied.

4. A Functional Methodology

Locating the fertile soil will not alone guarantee a pragmatic missionary strategy. Diagnosticians of church health often discover that the reason disciples are not being made in a particular field lies in the methods used. The fact that other churches are growing vigorously on the same soil would indicate that the methodology of a static church needs some fresh examination.

Fertile soil, therefore, can be misused and become unfruitful. Any farmer knows that he can go wrong by sowing too much seed, not properly spacing the rows, cultivating too early or too late, applying wrong proportions of fertilizer, allowing pests to multiply, or moving in to harvest wheat with a cornpicker. If he makes any of these mistakes in methodology, he does not wonder why he gets little or no fruit. By the same token, missionaries can blunder in their methodology in numerous ways. Without attempting to be exhaustive, by way of illustration, we will mention four of the more common pitfalls in missionary methodology.

Choosing the wrong soil in an otherwise fertile field. Statistics on the growth of the church in a certain geographical region may show that the soil of a country or a state or a province is generally fertile, and that the sowing of the Gospel seed can be expected to bring forth a harvest. But unless the people in the region are completely homogenous, more refined soil testing needs to be done. Probably the church will be growing among certain kinds of people, but not among others. In some cities the working

class and residents of the newer districts are responsive
while the university students and upper class couldn't
care less about committing their lives to Christ. If making
disciples is the mission's goal, good methodology will
gravitate toward the more fertile patches of soil within a
given field, and see a proportionate share of God's blessing.
    Using an individual approach in a group-oriented culture.
Many Western missionaries have a difficult time understanding that other peoples may be less individualistic than
they. Individual action on important matters is repugnant
to many cultures of the world. Family and clan unity seems
every bit as important to them as eternal life. When a
missionary violates this principle and takes the one-by-
one approach, he should not be surprised that his ministry
is unfruitful. Because it seems like an easy road, and
because it may work in the homelands, some missionaries
begin evangelistic work with women and children, supposing
that the fathers will come later. In one case, leading
children to Christ without proper consultation with the
parents brought the wrath of a tribe down so fiercely upon
the missionaries that they lost their home, their airplane,
their belongings, and their opportunity to win an entire
people to the Lord.
    Employing institutions as pre-evangelism. It is diffi-
cult to generalize on the matter of the effectiveness of
institutional work in missionary strategy because such
projects as schools and hospitals have borne fruit for the
Kingdom in some places. Where they do, they represent
good methodology. In many other cases, however, they
have produced very little fruit through the years, and as
evangelistic methods have failed the test of pragmatism.
At times they have been justified as instruments of so-
called pre-evangelism, based on the hope that they would
generate such Christian good will among otherwise resistant
peoples that the Gospel would eventually spread. In many
cases this has not happened in an entire generation or
more, but the institution in the meantime has become so
embedded in the missionary operation as a whole that it is
practically impossible to abandon. The objective you have
set for your mission is social service, but if making
disciples is your objective you should look for a better
method.

Failure to communicate the Gospel message. Many missionaries who do not take the pains to master the language and culture of the people whom they intend to evangelize, preach and preach and write home about what a difficult field they are working in. In one case missionaries preached the Gospel in the official language in a town for twenty years with seven conversions. When they left a local evangelist moved in, preached in the dialect, and within months had a growing church of one hundred. The soil was fertile all the time, but a poor methodology blocked healthy church growth.

One of the most valuable exercises for a missionary is to make a careful study of evangelistic methods currently being used in his area, determining which methods God has obviously blessed, and which methods He has not. If he acts on what he discovers, he may find that he has developed a strategy which will bear abundant fruit.

5. A Church-Centered Mission

It was no coincidence that the particular emphasis in missiology which Donald McGavran brought about was labeled church growth. Churches are the most tangible products of missionary work, more so even than individuals. The normal outcome of evangelistic work is the salvation of people who gather together in churches. Planting churches which vigorously reproduce themselves is the goal of pragmatic strategy.

Interdenominational missions have brought immeasurable blessing to people in all parts of the world. Their horizontal structures have been used by God in magnificent ways. But they have certain built-in weaknesses, one being that by nature they tend to be weak on ecclesiology. Some have overcome this tendency and have planted large and healthy churches in the Third World. Others have shied away from the church and assumed the role of "service" missions. A revealing study recently made by a prominent member of an evangelistic basketball team which had toured the Orient for many years showed that 86% of the ministry of that group had been unrelated to the church. This is not untypical of service missions.

If evangelism (as contrasted, for example to theological

education or social service or a missionary children's school) is the stated objective of a mission, the church must not be bypassed. Churches should be planted, nurtured, and brought to maturity, maturity being understood in part as the church itself becoming involved in its own responsibility in winning the two billion to Christ. The strategy needed for tomorrow's mission will not only use the growth and multiplication of churches as a primary criterion for its own effectiveness, but will impart a hunger for an equally pragmatic strategy in the churches it plants.

Is there room for pragmatism in missions? Yes. We need more, not less, of it if we hope to meet the challenge of tomorrow. As McGavran has said, we are not in the "sunrise of missions." A glorious daytime of abundant harvest lies right ahead. Many are predicting the greatest ingathering of reborn Christians into the church that history has ever known during the decade to come. God has many requirements for those who would share in the fullest blessings of the harvest. One of them is that His servants courageously approach the opportunities ahead armed with a Spirit-directed, pragmatic missionary strategy.

BIBLIOGRAPHY:

McGavran, Donald A.
    1964   "Nothing but the Truth," CHURCH GROWTH BULLE-
            TIN, Vol. 1, No. 1, September 1964, Eugene, Institute
            of Church Growth, pp. 10-11
    1970   "For Such a Time as This," Unpublished address
            given at Fuller Theological Seminary buffet dinner,
            Pasadena.
Read, William R., Victor M. Monterroso and Harmon A. Johnson
            LATIN AMERICAN CHURCH GROWTH,   Grand
            Rapids, Eerdmans

There are many other situations where techniques. . . . . could be tested while being used. This could be done with little further cost once the concept of research in growth seized the minds of the leaders of missions. It would give us enormously valuable information.

BRIDGES OF GOD
p. 153

11

THE

PSYCHOLOGY OF RECEPTIVITY

AND CHURCH GROWTH

Roy E. Shearer

The opportunity is not "to carry on church and mission work," says Donald McGavran in *How Churches Grow* (1966:5) but to church the responsive unchurched in as great numbers and as rapidly as possible. Whenever church growth occurs, everybody tries to find reasons for the growth. Among the more common reasons offered are: "the Church grew because there was good preaching," "the Church grew because of a revival," and "growth happened because the right missionary methods were used." These reasons are often given with some justification, but all too frequently the real key to growth is mentioned only in passing, or maybe not at all. The key to growth is the preparation of the people to be receptive to the Good News.

Research in church growth has shown that when people are ready to receive the Gospel, they will respond to the most stumbling of presentations. However, people who are not ready to receive the Gospel will reject it even though it is presented with the most brilliant argument and the most sophisticated means available. An extreme example is the high resistance of Moslems in the Middle East to evangelism connected with education, hospitals, or the Gospel presented through literature, radio or any other means. On the other hand, when the inhabitants of certain parts of Indonesia turned receptive, the Gospel ran faster than the professional advocates, because the people passed the Good News on ahead of both the national and foreign missionaries.

McGavran has pointed out in his writing that people are never equally receptive throughout the world nor are they equally receptive across time. People become receptive or resistant to the Gospel in different eras. Furthermore, since God is working in history and in the hearts of men, He is continually turning peoples receptive to Himself somewhere in the world. We know that God chooses to reveal Himself or to remain hidden:

> No one knows the Son except the Father, and no one knows the Father except the Son, and those to whom the Son wants to reveal him (Matthew 11: 27). (Good News for Modern Man)

In addition, history confirms that God has prepared people to receive His Gospel with great response in many different places. C. G. Jung has said—

> Christianity itself would never have spread through the pagan world with such astonishing rapidity had its ideas not found an analogous psychic readiness to receive them (1960: 152).

No attempt will be made to unravel the mystery of why only certain people at certain times become receptive, unless perhaps to suggest that in the divine economy of the harvest and in His wisdom, God has not expected His harvesters to have all the fields ripe at one time.

Receptivity to new ideas has been studied by the anthropologist Homer G. Barnett (1953: 378ff.). Included in his research on all aspects of innovation is his study of the process and causes for acceptance and rejection of new ideas or of innovation. His general description of acceptance is a good account of the process of acceptance of the Gospel. Barnett shows that acceptors to a new idea are basically unsatisfied with their lives as they are; acceptors desire something new. So it is with acceptance of the Gospel. A gospel acceptor has to be unsatisfied with his current life-style before he will change his religious orientation.

Barnett (1953:378-380) finds that there are three characteristics of people ready to receive a new idea: (1) they will receive the new idea only if it satisfies a want better than some existing means; (2) the reception of this idea depends in part on the previous life experience of the person; and (3) dissatisfaction may be a pervasive attitude in some individuals.

Evidence that this theory holds true for the Christian Church is seen in the fact that most of the converts to Christianity in the last century (who were not raised in Christian homes) have not come out of one of the great religions where there was a strong satisfying set of beliefs. Rather, most of the Christians of the new world have been won out of animism, which is not satisfying to the people. Often modern science (including education and medicine) has helped animists to become dissatisfied with their belief in spirits and makes them ready to turn to another religion.

The gospel advocate can promote this dissatisfaction among a population where he wants to effect a religious change. If he can convince his hearers that he has something desirable, then he has produced the want that will lead to receptivity and change.

Often, however, what the advocate says has little bearing on the reason of receptivity. Many people in India became Christians for social reasons; they wanted to better themselves. Pickett (1933:155-197) shows that they became sound Christians after enumerating a great many different motives for their initial interest in Christianity. Many Koreans turned to Christ because the Church represented a political force to combat the Japanese colonialists. Many people have turned to Christ because of a need for physical healing. The list of reasons is endless. Thus, while the gospel advocate any influence the hearer's dissatisfaction with his own lot, there is overwhelming evidence that men and women have turned to Christ in responding to the preaching about salvation. Those who came were in no way rejected. The important thing is they came and God has used this kind of receptivity to build some strong churches.

If receptivity truly is an important factor in the spread of Christianity, then adequate tests of this receptivity must be produced. Up to the present time the only such adequate test is a growing religious body. Wherever we see a growing church, we can be sure that the people in that area are receptive to religious ideas.

Wherever we see a growing non-Christian religion, we can be sure the people in that place are potential receptors of the Gospel. This test of religious receptivity is useful, but limited because it is a measure after the fact. Many years go by before we can determine if a people are receptive by watching the Church grow.

Is there no better way to test receptivity? Yes, I believe there is a better way but it will take much dedicated, skillful research and much money. Psychologists have long been assessing the attitudes of people. This skill in assessing attitudes should be harnessed for the mission of the Church. A conversion-readiness questionnaire could be carefully constructed with standardization and validation procedures currently used for the best of the nearly two thousand psychological tests available.

To be useful, the questionnaire should be scored to read out and estimate (a) the amount of dissatisfaction a person has with his culture, (b) the amount of dissatisfaction he has with his present religion, (c) the strength of bond with his family and clan, (d) the amount of freedom the respondent has to change, and (e) the part his family or clan group plays in a decision to change. Other scales could be discovered during the process of validation which would indicate aspects of receptivity.

If this test were translated into many languages and properly administered with sampling procedures, valuable data for pinpointing the segments of a population that are receptive to change would emerge. The test would also indicate the better approaches for eliciting greatest response. Within segments of a population this test could show which cross-section by age, occupation, or other group is most receptive; church planting could then be aimed at that specific group.

The effort put into the construction of such conversion-readiness scale presupposes a shift in evangelistic policy from what McGavran calls "the effort to do good work for all people," to the concentration of one's limited resources on what he calls "winning receptive people." History is full of examples of evangelistic effort blind to the implications of great receptivity. In Korea, around 1900, the people of the northern section were especially ready to turn toward Christianity, yet the resources and Christian workers were spread out evenly over all Korea as if the evangelistic policy were aimed at geography rather than people. Extra personnel and extra funds were requested to help with the great harvest in the north. The denial of this request may have kept some who were ready from having a chance to hear the Gospel. This is a tragic—even a sinful error. Sometimes we call it equalitarianism.

Down to our own times there is evidence that, following the Second World War, the people of Japan were receptive to the Gospel but the opportunity was lost. The Church there is still trying to become more than a small minority. Yet Soka Gokkai growth indicates a readiness to respond to religious persuasion.

The use of a better test of receptivity assumes a change in attitude of evangelism strategists so that they recognize that a growing church among receptive people is a good sound church. Generally churches which have grown rapidly have maintained good quality. God has changed Christians with initial inadequate motivation into spiritual men. There is probably no rapid statistical church growth where the church is not also growing in quality.

Those concerned with winning men and women to Christ must reorder their priorities. Instead of endeavoring to create new techniques, gimmicks or catchy ways of presenting the Gospel, let us concentrate on scientifically finding which groups of people are receptive. When these people are found, a growing church planted in their midst will be the proper Christian response to the Great Commission of our Lord:

> Jesus drew near and said to them: I have been given all authority in heaven and on earth. Go, then, to all peoples everywhere and make them my disciples: baptize them in the name of the Father and of the Son and of the Holy Spirit, and teach them to obey everything I have commanded you. And remember! I will be with you always, to the end of the age (Matthew 28: 18-20).

BIBLIOGRAPHY:

Barnett, H. G.
    1953   INNOVATION: BASIS OF CULTURAL CHANGE, New York, McGraw-Hill Book Co.
Jung, C. G.
    1960   ANSWER TO JOB, (Trans RFC Hull) Cleveland, World Publishing Co.
Pickett, J. Waskom
    1933   CHRISTIAN MASS MOVEMENTS IN INDIA, Lucknow, Lucknow Pub. House

Each theory (of mission), arising from biblical and theoretical grounds, is formed in the light of what seems necessary and possible at that particular period. The warp of theory is biblical; the woof is contemporary conditions...
Thus theories of mission are formulated, modified, and discarded as theologians wax and wane, and history flows through new country.

"Theory of Mission" in CONCISE DICTIONARY
OF CHRISTIAN WORLD MISSION, p. 595.

12

CULTURAL COMPULSIVES

Alan R. Tippett

In this paper I purpose taking the anthropological theory of *cultural compulsives,* as developed by V. F. Calverton in 1930, restating as much of it as is required for the paper, interweaving a few elements of religion and Christian mission in terms of his thesis and picking up the theme where he left off in 1930.

The Manifestation of Cultural Compulsives

The writings of Charles Darwin and E.B. Tylor met some of the intellectual and emotional needs which were felt by many people in England and other places in the sixties and seventies of the last century. Their writing in biology and anthropology articulated something that was already there — a demand for an explanation of human progress and civilization. As we look back on the historical situation it is easy to understand how, in spite of the resistance of some theologians and conservative scientists, western man began to restructure his interpretation of his world and himself in terms of evolutionary theory. The history of English literature shows that this had been coming slowly for almost a

century, and now the time was ripe. The preceding century
had seen the worlds of Africa and Oceania exposed, revealing new races, with strange customs and unknown languages.
Explorers and navigators published accounts of their journeys and voyages. The age of modern missions had commenced. The battle against slavery had been settled in
Britain. Civilized man was faced with the phenomenon of
savage man—not in ancient history, but in the same contemporary world as that in which he himself lived.

British shipping had suffered so much at the hands of
savages in the Pacific that English commerce gave support
to Christian mission to speed up the civilizing of the offen-
ders. Travellers and missionaries (especially the latter)
wrote thousands of reports about the people they met and
their social institutions. The romantic ideas of the arm-
chair philosophers about "the noble savage" were stimulated by the same historical factors, but did not in any way
disillusion the English commercial and missionary constituencies.

This confrontation of savage and civilized man raised
the significant quesion of their precise relationship. It
became a matter of popular and academic concern. In this
intellectual climate the biological idea of the survival of the
fittest seemed to speak to the problem of the emergence of
human society. A social theory based on a biological analogy was natural. If man could be conceptualized as the climax of a biological evolution, it had to be modern western
man of the 1870s. Similarly western civilization had to be
the climax of cultural evolution, for in the struggle for survival the fittest came out on top. The savages discovered
by explorers and navigators, and described by the missionaries, were surely a "lesser breed," who had survived only
in the marginal regions of the world—its remote islands
and dense forests. Thus is the puzzle of human origins,
both biological and social, the savages became 'guinea-
pigs' for anthropological research, and the early anthropologists worked over their themes of marriage patterns,
law, religion, kinship and lineage, in terms of evolutionary
sequences. Which came first: matrilineal or patrilineal
descent? Did religion begin with a belief in souls, with ancestor worship, or totemism or a high God? Everywhere
men sought the sequence of human progress from savagery

to civilization. We speak of this now exploded theory as unilinear evolution. Even the early variants of evolutionary theory, like the parallelists who based their theory on the idea of the psychic unity of man, still fell for this basic fallacy that civilized man is the supreme climax of the evolutionary process.

This had all sorts of consequences. For example, if western civilized cultural constructs were the climax of the process then the idea of private ownership, of individualism and monogamous marraige were validated as the most developed cultural forms. The argument, of course had a serious fallacy, yet in its day it enjoyed great popularity. And, if I may add a point from my own personal experience, I would use the example of the Comparative Study of Religion, in which the idea emerged of religious evolution from the lowest animist forms, upward through the great religions to their crown and completion, which was Christianity. Of course the world's religions cannot be placed in an evolutionary sequence, either as a reality or an abstraction. Each has its own independent development, its own 'revelation' and its own unique history. My own training for the mission field forty years ago was based on this very fallacy. It was the basic frame of reference of most of our textbooks, and even in the years I have been here at Fuller I have read articles in current critical journals written under the same delusion, so that I am amazed at its tenacity.

Calverton takes some of these civilized notions—the idea of private property as fundamental to social life, and the monogamous family as the corner-stone of society and social existence and so on—and asks what made them so acceptable when they are fallacies or at best only half-truths.

From unilinear evolution he turned to another approach to monogamous marraige, namely that of Westermarck, who in 1891 argued that it was right because it was natural. He devoted twenty pages of his article to the "rationalization of monogamy as the natural form of human marriage which was foisted upon the nineteenth century world by anthropological dialectic." Westermarck claimed that monogamous marriage was "rooted in man's primeval past" and he spoke of a monogamous instinct "from some ape-like progenitor." Calverton raises the question with respect to Westermarck's thesis: "Why should a man's doctrine become so widely accepted when his evidences were so flimsy and fallacious?" Then he discusses the research and evidence that existed at the time which showed that the gorillas were not monogamous, but polygamous or at least promiscuous. This is not aimed at Westermarck, but at the audience of critical scientists who accepted the thesis against the evidence.

The idea of monogamous marriage as natural, like the notion of unilinear evolution was long accepted in spite of the evidence against them. He asks what were the cultural compulsives responsible for this.

The evolutionary doctrine of Lewis Henry Morgan in particular which left monogamy as the ethical ultimate was taken for their own purposes by radical critics, like Engels, Kautsky and Plechanov, who fitted it into their own doctrine of social evolution and used it to attack the western institutions of the day. Thus there arose a new socio-intellectual need for the defence of existing institutions. Thus Westermarck's thesis provided a rebuttal to the critics:

> Influenced by the middle-class culture of his day, and the necessity of defending its institutions by every device of logic, his (Westermarck's) mind reverted to that evidence which tended to justify those institutions, and endow them with a natural origin and continuity (Calverton, 1931:13).

To this end, Calverton claims, he distorted his evidence to prove his case, and after discussing further its biology he concludes:

> Westermarck's statement about these animals was uncritically accepted by most of his contemporaries during the generation that followed . . . because his doctrine supplied the need of the time, a protection against those doctrines that threatened middle-class supremacy in the field of ethics and economics . . . they became at once part of the cultural defence of the era (1931:14).

This was a cultural compulsive for the establishment, just as Morgan's theory found its cultural compulsive among radicals because it "supplied the dynamite for the fortification of the proletarian position" (p. 25).

Cultural compulsives are the "vested interest in a cultural complex" (p. 24). They indicate not the validity or

falseness of a theory, but the importance of its social meaning. History is full of them. In my own recent research,
for example, I have asked myself why the gross manipulation of Hawaiian history in James Michener's supposedly
historical novel received such wide-spread acceptance in
this country. A little research in the press of the time
reveals two factors which together created the cultural
compulsive. First, it supplied information about the newly-
constituted State of Hawaii for people who were somewhat
ignorant in this area and therefor met a felt need: and
second, it provided fuel for the contemporary fire of anti-
puritanism and appeared to validate the current mood
against missionary ethnocentricism, it fitted the popular
philosophy of "Missionary, Go Home," so that the public
was ready to believe the A.B.C.F.M. missionaries were
just exactly the monsters Michener depicted. The gulli-
bility of the public was not confined to those who wanted
to believe ill of the missionaries. About once a year some
missionary writer reveals how he has taken Michener "hook,
line and sinker" and builds a paragraph in an article on
some error or misunderstanding he assumes to have been
established by Michener. The emotional reactions of the
audience to certain episodes in the film version of *Hawaii,*
again reveal the cultural compulsives. *People wanted to
believe ill* of the unpopular missionary.

Cultural Compulsives and Social Thought

Now let me return to Calverton. He pointed out that
the source of power of the cultural compulsive is not the
truth or falsehood of the doctrine, but its "adaptability to
other interests." Human nature being what it is, our battle
with cultural compulsives is inevitable. Social history
provides us with thousands of examples. We cannot deny
their existence, but we need to identify them for what they
are. This applies in all aspects of social thought, including
anthropology and missiology. Books like *Honest to God*
and *The Secular City,* both of which operate on the basis
of serious fallacies, are not nearly as important as the
cultural compulsives which made them best sellers. The
value of such books to us is that they bring out latent feelings we may not otherwise be able to identify and we be-

come aware of the climate in which we ourselves have to
operate. The battle grounds of missionary theory—Christian Presence, Development, Humanization—are good
examples in our own discipline, not because of the conference declaration or some published symposium but
because of the general temper in the churches at large
which make such presentations credible—that is, the latent
cultural compulsives.

Calverton pointed out that the existence of cultural compulsives made objectivity in the social sciences impossible;
that one could only be objective in his collection of facts,
not in their interpretation:

> Interpretation necessitates a mind set, a purpose and
> an end. Such mind-sets, such purposes, such ends,
> are controlled by cultural compulsives (1931: 29).

Thus the circle where the mind-set is controlled by the
current mood against monologue and proclamation Christian
presence writing is inevitable. On the other hand if the mind-
set is the Great Commision then the Christian public, which
appeals to Scripture instead of the individual, will be disposed to listen. All we write here is accepted or rejected
to a large extent by the existing cultural compulsives. I
said "to a large extent" because I am speaking here of
anthropological (that is, human) factors. The matter of
divine compulsives is another subject, even though the
psychological outworkings have many similarities.

Cultural compulsives are essential to social thought.
They give it cohesion, meaning and direction. "Anthropology" says Calverton again, "becomes of value, not because it collects facts about primitive peoples, but because
those facts have meaning for our civilization" (1931: 29).
Therefore it becomes important that we shoud recognize
the cultural compulsives in all social science. Experiments and invention are open for acceptance more when
they meet a desperate need. Awareness of the compulsive
keeps us discerning, critical and flexible.

Cultural Compulsives and Applied Anthropology

The idea of anthropology having "meaning for civilization"
implies that anthropology should be applied. Although
Applied Anthropology as a discipline is comparatively

recent, the concept has been in anthropological writing from the beginning. As far back as E. B. Tylor we meet statements like this:

> The study of man and civilization is not only a matter of scientific interest, but at once passes into the practical business of life. . . . it may guide us in our duty of leaving the world better than we found it (Barnett, 1956:1).

Nowadays we have a large bibliography of books and articles and several technical journals to indicate the establishment of Applied Anthropology as a discipline in itself, with sub-sections like Directed or Planned Change, Educational Anthropology, Medical Anthropology and Missionary Anthropology. Yet despite the obvious validity of the idea of applying anthropology, the discipline has had to fight for its existence. I should like to develop this, taking Calverton's model a step further. He argued that Morgan's evolutionism received acceptance by the social radicals because it fitted into their social theory and permitted carrying the evolutionary process a step further. Then to counter this, Westermarck rationalized his theory of a monogamous instinct from primeval man. This too was acceptable because it reinforced middle-class institutions. So we have here an encounter of compulsives.

Even as Calverton's book was coming off the press there was emerging a new surge of interest in cultural relativism. The best example of relativist writing in the early thirties was Benedict's Patterns of Culture, although the precise doctrine of cultural relativism in anthropology was not really formulated until Herskovits gave a whole chapter to it in Man and His Works in 1951. Both these works were significant in their day but the cultural compulsives were different. According to Redfield the idea of cultural relativism can be pushed back as far as Westermarck (Redfield, 1953:144). This is a good example of how long an idea can exist in a more or less dormant manner, and how it takes a compulsive situation to make it dynamic. Benedict's relativism declared that all cultures were equally valid. We are to value "all of them" not "none of them" (1934a:256-257). She demonstrated how normal behavior in one society was abnormal in another (1934b). She did not hesitate to criticize western culture contact

for destroying culture, as her famous Digger Indian passage indicates (1934a: 19-20).

Herskovits (1951: 63) defined cultural relativism as a
principle in these terms (Italics his):

> Judgments are based on experience, and experience
> is interpreted in terms of his own enculturation.

The study raised many related issues and set the stage for
much to come. He asked if any absolute moral standards
existed at all, or are all morals culturally conditioned, and
as at a given point of time. In the same essay he popu-
larized the term ethnocentricism, as the primary mechanism for all value judgments. He defined this as "the
point of view that one's own way of life is to be preferred
to all others (1951: 68). He challenged the assumption
that the cultures of non-literate peoples are inferior and
questioned some aspects of the concept of progress. He
argued against the "deceptive simplicity" of the terms
primitive and civilized. None of these ideas are basic in
Applied Anthropology, yet it was the cultural relativists
who challenged the rightness of applying anthropology in
cross-cultural programs of human betterment.

Contemporary with the American configurationists like
Benedict, British anthropology was developing the culture
contact approach.   Mair, Hunter, Schapera, Richards,
Fortes and Malinowski met in the late thirties for the
methodological study of culture contact. Most of this theoretical development implied methods based on applied anthropology. Schapera (1938:27) pointed out that the missionary had to be regarded as a factor in tribal life in
the same way as the chief and magician. Richards (1938:
59) spoke of the "sphere of co-operation between the anthropologist and the 'practical man'." Malinowski (1938:
xix-xxiv) saw the new situation in terms of a new autono-
mous entity, which recognized the inter-relating of administrator, missionary and trader with the traditional roles
of tribal life. All these have to be interpreted in the light
of the fact that solutions were still being sought within the
structures of colonialism. Some of the best known early
British applied anthropologists were administrators or
missionaries. They had the compulsive that within the
structures of Government and Missions some solutions
had to be found. Their work moved in the direction of

independence, but once independence of a nation or a Church was achieved the question of applied cross-cultural anthropology changed. The cultural compulsive was moved from the colonial government and mission to the national government and the Church.

Cross-cultural applied anthropology was most used in American anthropology in connection with technical aid and the Point Four Program in particular, and a most useful body of literature has come out of this. Books like Arensberg and Niehoff's *Introducing Social Change, The First Look at Strangers* by Bunker and Adair, Erasmus's *Man Takes Control,* Niehoff's *Casebook of Social Change,* Spicer's *Human Problems in Technological Change,* to mention only a few of them, all seem to me to be discussions of problems of innovation, but based on the implication of the rightness of applying anthropology for human betterment. In the first book on the list, the title implies this: *Introducing Social Change,* as also the dust jacket claims, the basic term "change agent" and such comments as:

> The change agent wishing to transfer a new idea to the
> people of another country must . . . deal with the world
> of values (Arensberg & Niehoff, 1964: 48-49).

Probably the most important statement on the application of anthropology to missionary goals (more particularly in medicine and education) was F. E. Williams' *The Blending of Cultures.* This came from the Government anthropologist in Papua in the Australian Mandate—a contemporary of Benedict's *Patterns of Culture,* but he had been employed by the Government since 1922 and was a fine anthropologist. A pact, known as "The Canberra Agreement" between Australia and New Zealand concerned the cultural problems of Oceania and incorporated the phrase "anthropological investigation." As Felix Keesing (1963: 373-398) pointed out this is applied anthropology being used for solving administrative, missionary and commercial problems.

As long as cultural relativism remained a recognition of the uniqueness of different cultures and the reference points for change were found within those cultures, so that planning was intelligent, it was in harmony with the goals of applied anthropology. However, by the fifties when Herkovits made his statement the compulsives of colonial situations were weaker. Some independence movements were generating heat. A new set of compulsives had arisen in many situations which were still colonial. Cultural relativism assumed a new mood. Both administrators and missionaries were being told to go home.

Contemporary with this rising mood for independence came an emphasis for objectivity in anthropology. Ethnocentricity became a loaded term. Missionaries became the scape-goats for lectures in the universities. Cultural relativity became the popular theme. Any idea of absolute values was rejected. The idea of using anthropology for guiding administrations and missions in their ethnocentric purposes was hotly debated. The anthropologist was to make his objective study and not to get involved. This challenged the very foundation of applied anthropology. It was a popular cultural compulsive and it still exerts a strong influence over anthropologists trained in the fifties. Fortunately anthropology had many penetrating thinkers to examine the issue.

> It was easy to look with equal benevolence upon all sorts of value systems so long as the values were those of unimportant little people remote from our concerns. But the equal benevolence is harder to maintain when one is asked to anthropologize the Nazis or to help a Point Four administrator decide what to do for those people he is committed to help. The Point Four man is committed to do something to change that people, for he cannot help them without changing them (Redfield 1953: 145-146).

He goes on to call cultural relativism the "doctrine of ethical neutralism" and to argue that this does not mean "ethical indifference." Commenting on Kroeber's statement that "there is no room in anthropology for a shred of ethnocentricity, of homini-centricity" (1948: 841), he frankly admits that his preference for the humane values of Euro-American civilization and his desires for the well-being of the human race would bring him under those designations.

When Herskovits denied the existence of absolutes he did not close the door to universals. Two anthropologists, Murdock (1945) and Linton (1945) have done research seeking common denominators in cultures. Linton spoke of an "emergent science of man" to identify and use such universals for the good of mankind. But the rank and file of cultural relativists have indeed made it ethical neutralism and non-commitment. This would never have been possible had it not been for the cultural compulsives of the present mood against the establishment and against authority.

In 'my book' the fallacies of cultural relativism lie in the following:

1. It makes no allowances for the fact and the nature of continual culture change. It is a survival of static structuralism. It does not recognize that mechanisms for the control of change are built into social structure, and that people who undergo change borrow, accept and modify ideas from outside.

2. It does not allow for the time element in change, that the patterns and processes acceptable in a given culture today differ from those of a century ago, and that societies resistant to change yesterday may be responsive today.

3. It does not allow for the fact that in any culture change, directed or spontaneous, the people themselves are the innovators. The so-called agent of change can never be anything more than an advocate.

4. It does not allow for the fact that just as an individual has his being within a social context, so each society also exists in a context. The group has to survive in the world context and cannot live in isolation.

5. It does not allow for such processes as urbanization, or nationalization, where social and linguistic groups are being welded together in a total complex with some new values.

What I am saying is that the whole concept of cultural relativism as it is often presented in anthropology is unrealistic in the dimension of cultural dynamics. Applied anthropology—could not proceed without recognizing the relativity of cultures, but part of that relativity is the diverse mechanism they have for changing their own structures and values. We have to follow the road of the relativist but may God help us not to bog down there. It was Felix Keesing, one of the greater applied anthropologists of two decades ago, who pointed out that effective change had to be planned with reference points within the culture being changed, nevertheless he approved the place of persuasion in directed change, even to the extent of indicating "where a given culture should be most malleable" (1963: 393).

Keesing's son, Rodger, likewise has no illusion about non-committed relativism. The recognition of cultural diversity is a way to understanding needs and operations. It is a means, not an end. This is what he says:

> Many anthropologists would urge that cultural relativism is not a position one can ultimately live with—but that it is a position we need to pass through in search of a clearer vision. By wandering in the desert of relativism, one can sort the profound from the trivial, examine one's motives and conscience, customs and beliefs. Like all vision quests, it can be lonely and dangerous; but it can lead to heightened perceptions of ourselves, of what it is to be human, and what man could be if he would (Keesing, R. and F., 1971: 127).

Walter Goldschmidt in his book *Comparative Functionalism* (p. 138) in a different context, has said the same thing: we have to go by the way of cultural relativism but that is by no means the end of the road.

This somewhat long discussion on cultural relativism and applied anthropology was stimulated by the idea of an encounter of cultural compulsives. This is an encounter within anthropology, but it is one of considerable consequence to a missionary anthropologist, for the validity of his discipline stands on the validity of applied anthropology, and the validity of applied anthropology stands on the validity of the diversity and uniqueness of cultures. Of course the Christian mission has another validity, but missionary anthropology is an orientation and a methodology, requiring anthropology validation. The popularity of cultural relativism, as an end in itself in the fifties and sixties, has run out its welcome in the developing nations, although still popular in this country. Indigenous communities are no longer willing to be treated as guinea-pigs for experiment. They are saying, if you are ready to help us in the way we ask of you, you may stay, but otherwise, "Anthropologist, Go Home!" A new cultural compulsive is emerging. I wonder if this is what lies behind Roger Keesing's prediction that we may have to turn to the library and not to the

jungle for advanced anthropological research, and that a
professional degree, higher than the M. A. but less-demand-
ing than the Ph. D. may be required to train teachers of
anthropology (1971: 406).

Cultural Compulsives and Christian Mission

When an anthropologist says—

> It would be unwise, for instance, to advise missionaries
> to use their influence to discourage the replacement of
> cattle by money, etc., etc (Wagner, 1938).

I think it implies two things—(1) that missionaries need
anthropological advice, and (2) that anthropologists have a
legitimate role in giving wise advice to missionaries. It
would be better however for such advisers to be proficient
both as missionaries and anthropologists, and this seems
to call for a field of missionary anthropology. In that
applied anthropology has withstood the pressure of non-
committed cultural relativism, and started on the course
of developing educational and medical anthropology, I think
we may also assume the relevance of missionary anthropology. This calls for an awareness of possible cultural
or missiological compulsives.

Let me give an example. A few years ago I was engaged
in researching New Britain church growth. I was studying
the records of my own church in the years of rehabilitation
after the war. Our plant and work had been badly hit by
enemy action. Every male missionary on the field at the
time of the invasion had died, and the buildings were completely destroyed. The indigenous Christians 'went bush'
and many survived and continued to worship but all vestige
of the mission was obliterated. I was working through the
records of the home board of the time, and I came across
a presentation to the Church at home on the rehabilitation
program. The writer had manipulated the Great Commission. He was a fine fellow—I knew him well—and an honest
man. His message proclaimed that our Lord commissioned
us to go, to preach, to teach, to heal, and now (in the face
of the ravages of war) to build. His main motive had nothing
whatever to do with the Great Commission; he 'piggy-backed'
a huge rebuilding program on the words of our Lord. What
is more, the board re-established the paternalistic institu-

tionalism which the war had really given them a chance to
be freed of: so that I am not at all sure the Lord was saying
"Build!" Not only did a good missionary write this in
sincerity, but the board secretary and editor of the missionary journal accepted it (and wrote a supporting paragraph), as did the ministry and the congregations all over
the country. Not one single person appears to have objected
to this appalling exegesis. The point is, of course, that I
cannot imagine this getting by in my Church at any other
time. It was accepted because of the cultural and missionary
compulsive—a situation of physical devastation and a
desire to restore missionary operations.

I can give many reasons why that rebuilding program
was a great mistake. It is just here that a little missionary
anthropology and a church growth investigation, dovetailed
together, could have redeemed the situation. This is what
Calverton (1931: 30) meant by urging the social scientist
(and the missionary) to—

> be on his guard against accepting Westermarck, or any
> future Westermarck, because he (the missionary) has
> become part of his cultural compulsive.

and again—

> . . . awareness of the compulsive nature of social
> thought should make it possible for the development of
> a little more flexibility and a little more criticism with-
> in the radius of the cultural compulsive itself.

That is one example of a bad decision having been made
on the basis of a cultural compulsive, when good researching
might well have revealed the fallacies. This is what church
growth is about and many other examples could be cited.

Applied anthropology has now been recognized for
thirty years in this country with an official society and
journal "devoted to the solution of practical problems of
human relations in fields of business and political administration, psychiatry, social work and wherever else human
relations play a part" (Smith et al, 1970: 81). Its goals
assume that people with social advantages have a responsibility to the less fortunate, but aid should be given within
the frame of reference of the recipients. The best way to
give aid is discovered through research, and for this a
methodology has been developed. If people are to have a

new educational pattern with new subject matter, and a new health orientation or a new and more relevant religious belief, in any given culture, the innovation should be related to the culture pattern itself, and so presented by the agent of change or advocate that it will receive positive acceptance without serious cultural dislocation. The underlying assumption is that the group must be understood and any change must still meet its felt needs. The ethics of guided innovation imply responsibility to both canons of the discipline and the welfare of the target group. If there is to be a missionary anthropology, it has to locate itself within such a frame of reference. There is still some pressure from cultural compulsives against such a thing as missionary anthropology, from the cultural relativists of the non-committal variety, and from materialists who are just as ethnocentric as the most puritan, their religious indicator merely being at the negative pole. You cannot be negative or nebulous with respect to religion when dealing with people for whom religion has always been a basic configuration. For this reason some anthropologists take the attitude that, until a people becomes scientific materialist, they must have a religion (e.g. Hogbin, 1935: 31-32).

Applied anthropology, and therefore missionary anthropology, has an ethical dimension, what Nadel called a "worthwhileness" (1958:264). The sociologist, Horowitz, says that when a social science (and he is dealing with anthropology as much as sociology) suppresses a commitment to ethical perspectives for the sake of, say, objectivity, it leads to a series of disastrous consequences—an indifference to problem solving, unconscious ideological distortions, a neglect of scientific evaluation in value theory, and an identification of objectivity with indifference to ethical judgments. (1959:30-45)

One would be hard pushed to find a better example of a cultural compulsive being brought to bear on Christian mission than the recent *Barbados Declaration* (W.C.C. 1971). This statement is a vicious attack on the missionary work among the American Indians. While I would not defend these missions for all their mistakes of the past, many missionary bodies are certainly now aware of them and are actively correcting them. The anthropologists who made the declaration have taken their stand on a particular conceptual cultural relativism, based on a salvage anthropology, which is out of step with current reality. The declaration posed an application of the theory of cultural relativism, which (if it could be applied at all) could bring nothing but fragmentation to the American nations, including the United States, would perpetuate tribal isolationism and eventual extinction, and set a course of discord for many years to come.

This is out of step with current anthropology, which is moving towards such concepts as the unity of humanity, the interaction rather than the isolation of societies, and concepts of progress which demand anthropologically oriented assistance in technical aid, welfare, medicine and education. Medical aid, education and poverty correctives undermine magico-religion. Anthropology has come to see this has to be, but even agnostic anthropologists cannot visualize religionless society and react against cultural voids. Culture change, a major area of research, is geared to planning within the idea of the progress of ethnic groups, discrete but relating. The Barbados Declaration ignores this. Its political, anti-colonial, anti-western bias blasts Christian missions under the presumption that they can be nothing but western and colonialist. The confusion of Christianity with western colonialism, either imperialist or economic, can be a powerful cultural compulsive against us.

Finally I should like to point out that I have kept this discussion within the regular orbit of anthropology, its values and its criteria. In anything missionary there is, of course, another dimension, namely the nature of the Christian mission itself which stems from an authority outside of anthropology. Each sub-type of applied anthropology has such a body of directives unique to itself. But in as much as we speak of missionary anthropology, we are asking how that body of spiritual and scriptural directives may be advocated for acceptance without cultural dislocation. The cultural compulsives set against us presuppose this cannot be done. Missionary anthropology demonstrates how it can be done with a minimum of disequilibrium.

The point was made by the Wilsons in *The Analysis of Social Change,* a book which assumes the inevitability of social change and the expectation of ultimate benefit by it, that—

> Disequilibrium is not inevitable in the change from
> primitive to civilized—a moving equilibrium is pos-
> sible—but a degree of disequilibrium is unavoidable
> if the change. . . be very rapid (Wilson, G. & M. 1945:
> 167).

Frequently, especially in people movements, religious change is rapid. This is why church growth places so much stress on the consummation of such spontaneous expansion, on the preservation of indigenous forms in indigenous churches. the planting of groups with the same structural and leadership patterns as the culture pattern, and the use of the vernacular. To maintain this moving equilibrium missionary anthropology advocates such procedures as the use of functional substitutes. This has been more developed in church growth writing than in any secular anthropology. We hope that sound research along these lines, bringing theory and case studies together in mutual validation, will help to recapture the status of Christian mission in aca-demic circles and dispose of some of the pressures of the cultural compulsives which stimulate the will to believe ill of the missionary cause. I may point out again that mis-siology is in step with applied anthropology, for has not Gutorm Gjessing (1968:397-402) pressed the relevance of this discipline by arguing that (1) Anthropology, as a social activity, has a responsibility to society, (2) it cannot live in isolation from reality, and (3) ethically it is to serve humanity. In making available its skills and knowledge to mankind anthropology validates its entity as a discipline. In the religious sphere Christianity can be rated by the same criteria, and this is quite in line with the terms of the Great Commission. Of course, if Christianity does not show a responsibility to society, if she lives in isolation from real-ity, and if she has no world vision, she may be declared to to be irrelevant. That she has often fallen under this con-demnation cannot be denied; and to this extent we may have ourselves contributed to the build-up of cultural compul-sives against us.

Therefore I take some encouragement from the point Calverton made that cultural compulsives are essential for the progress of social thought. If I did not feel the oppres-sion of a half-truth and also the current will to believe ill of Christian mission I should never have written this paper.

NOTES:

1 "Modern Anthrop. & the Theory of Cultural Compulsives"
   appeared in PSYCHE, was reprinted in Amer. Journ. of Soc,
   and eventually became the leading article in THE MAKING
   OF MAN.
2 From Coke's mission in 1786 to 1813 five missionary societies
   were founded in Britain and also the R.T.S. and B.F.B.S.
3 For more detail see Tippett: PEOPLE MOVEMENTS IN
   SOUTHERN POLYNESIA, pp. 76-77, 176ff and also end-notes
   referring to those pages.
4 If all the descriptive material in the extant missionary accounts
   sent to Britain and Australia from Asia, Africa and Oceania
   were brought together the world would be astonished at this
   great reservoir of essential anthropological data. These reports, correspondence and missionary journals were published
   under the head of "Missionary Notices" or "Missionary Intelligence" in the denominational and ecumenical journals through
   the last century, quite apart from manuscript material.
5 The noble savage theory of Jean Jacques Rousseau claimed
   that the ills of civilization could be cured by man's return to
   his primaeval state, where clothes, houses, work and government were not needed and man enjoyed perfect freedom as an
   undomesticated brute. More space might have permitted my
   discussing this 'myth' in terms of cultural compulsives.
6 R. Keesing's revision of CULT. ANTH. NEW PERSPECTIVES
   IN CULT. ANTH. goes on to show the need for such wisdom
   in a world where political and religious dogmas are advocated
   (p. 127).

BIBLIOGRAPHY:

Arensberg, Conrad M. and Arthur H. Niehoff
   1964   INTRODUCING SOCIAL CHANGE: A MANUAL FOR
          AMERICANS OVERSEAS. Chicago, Aldine Publishing
          Company.
Barnett, H. G.
   1956   ANTHROPOLOGY IN ADMINISTRATION, Evanston,
          Row, Peterson & Co.
Benedict, Ruth F.
   1934a PATTERNS OF CULTURE, New York, Houghton
          Mifflin Co. (Mentor edition used.)
   1934b "Anthropology and the Abnormal" in Haring, PER-
          SONAL CHARACTER AND CULTURAL MILIEU,
          pp. 182-201
Calverton, V. F. (ed.)
   1931   THE MAKING OF MAN, New York, The Modern
          Library
Gjessing, Gutorm
   1968   "The Responsibility of the Social Scientist" CURRENT
          ANTHROPOLOGY, 9, 397-402

BIBLIOGRAPHY (cont.)

Goldschmidt, Walter
    1966   COMPARATIVE FUNCTIONALISM, Berkeley, University of California Press
Herskovits, Melville J.
    1951   MAN AND HIS WORKS: THE SCIENCE OF CULTURAL ANTHROPOLOGY, New York, Alfred A. Knopf
Hogbin, H. Ian
    1935   "Sorcery & Administration" OCEANIA, 6,1 pp. 1-32
Horowitz, Irving Louis
    1959   "Social Science Objectivity & Value Neutrality" in PROFESSING SOCIOLOGY, pp. 30-45
Keesing, F. M.
    1963   "Applied Anthropology in Colonial Administration" in Linton, THE SCIENCE OF MAN IN THE WORLD CRISIS, pp. 373-398
Keesing, Roger M. and Felix M.
    1971   NEW PERSPECTIVES IN CULTURAL ANTHROPOLOGY, New York, Holt, Rinehard and Winston, Inc.
Kroeber, A. L.
    1945   ANTHROPOLOGY, New York, Harcourt, Brace & Co.
Linton, Ralph
    1945   "The Scope and Aims of Anthropology" in THE SCIENCE OF MAN IN THE WORLD CRISIS, pp. 3-18
Malinowski, Bronislaw
    1938   "The Anthropology of Changing African Cultures" in METHODS OF STUDY OF CULTURE CONTACT IN AFRICA, pp. 92-105
Murdock, G. P.
    1945   "The Common Denominator of Cultures" in Linton, THE SCIENCE OF MAN IN THE WORLD CRISIS, pp. 123-142.
Nadel, S. F.
    1958   THE FOUNDATION OF SOCIAL ANTHROPOLOGY London, Cohen & West
Redfield, Robert
    1953   THE PRIMITIVE WORLD AND ITS TRANSFORMATIONS, New York, Cornell University Press
Richards, A. I.
    1938   "Village Census in Culture Contact" in METHODS OF STUDY OF CULTURE CONTACT IN AFRICA, pp. 46-59
Schapera, I.
    1938   "Contact Between European and Native in South Africa: Bechuanaland" in METHODS OF STUDY OF CULTURE CONTACT IN AFRICA, pp. 25-37
Smith, Allan H. and John L. Fischer (editors)
    1970   ANTHROPOLOGY, Englewood Cliffs, Prentice-Hall.

BIBLIOGRAPHY (cont.)

Tippett, Alan R.
    1971   PEOPLE   MOVEMENTS   IN   SOUTHERN   POLYNE-
            SIA: A STUDY IN CHURCH GROWTH, Chicago,
            Moody Press
Wagner, Gunter
    1938   "Culture Contact and its Practical Applications" in
            METHODS OF STUDY OF CULTURE CONTACT
            IN AFRICA, pp. 92-105
Westermarck, Edward Alexander
    1891   HISTORY   OF   HUMAN   MARRIAGE,   London, Mac-
            millan Co.
Wilson, Godfrey and Monica
    1945   THE ANALYSIS OF SOCIAL CHANGE, Cambridge,
            University Press
World Council of Churches
    1971   "The Declaration of Barbados"

The missionary enterprise has not yet experienced the degree of growth which is possible. The magnitude of opportunities for church growth would be considered by most Christian leaders as beyond the bounds of possibilty. Yet the world teems with unsuspected opportunity.

As concentration of resources on growing points comes to be the strategy of missions, we shall find ourselves in a new era of advance.

BRIDGES OF GOD,
p. 112

13

CHURCH GROWTH
AS MODERNIZATION

William R. Read

Studying church growth under McGavran in Eugene in
1962 after ten years evangelism in North Minas, Brazil,
I realized the importance of receptive pockets. I came to
call them "high potential areas." I also became aware of
the different processes of change as church growth case
studies from other parts of the world were presented for
our consideration. I realized that the Christian Church over
the world had mostly grown by the spontaneous expansion
of homogeneous groups, and that anthropological tools
existed with which to analyse the processes of such social
change.

When I came to bring these insights to bear on my own
field of Brazil, I had to gather statistical data. From 1955
the Brazil Census Bureau had reported religious figures
annually. Here I found data to examine by church, state,
and region, which permitted me to extract a record of the
growth of each Protestant Church for a decade. In time
patterns and links emerged in the statistics, which demanded specific reading and investigation. I discovered
that in this church growth, which I certainly believed to be
of God, there were, nevertheless, structured patterns, processes of change and openings for innovation.

I now began to direct my efforts to specifics, data checking and interviewing, assisted by a fellowship grant. This resulted in the book, *New Patterns of Church Growth in Brazil*, after another term on the field. This work revealed a wide range of growth differential among the Churches of Brazil, and seemed to indicate a relationship between growth potential and rapid social change. This has led me to think more about the mobility of people in Brazil and the diffusion of innovations, and the conditions propitious for those innovations. This anthropological term "innovation," in church growth parlance, is frequently "religious conversion," and thus my theme had come to be the relationship of high potentiality for acceptance of biblical (that is, non-Christopagan) Christianity and rapid social change.

With the aid of another grant I now worked in a team project over a wider area of the Latin American world. The results of our combined efforts have appeared as *Latin American Church Growth* (Read, Monterroso & Johnson, 1969). About a third of this report dealt with the relationships of church growth and the dramatic processes of acculturation. This analysis revealed that Brazil was certainly the focus for such a study. The book is merely a summary of the total data collected, but Part IV describes some of the cycles of transition and development which reflect how dynamic the situation really is. Opportunities and potential for growth begin to stand out. Part VI, "Evangelical Prospects" speaks to the missions and national church leaders about the opportunities waiting to be discovered if one has the eyes to see them.

When I returned from my research experiences to field evangelism it was this time to an urban area—Porto Alegre. Fourteen counties had eight fast-growing cities with a ten-mile radius of this urban complex. The demographers have projected that its million or more people (1968) will have increased to ten million by the year 2000. This kind of megalopolis growth calls for a new type of planning. It is alive with possibilities. Its organization and physical structures will be quite modern, and the people who migrate into the complex will find themselves in a strange new world, where even survival itself will depend on adaptability and innovation. The churches planted in this modern world will need to be modern at least in form and structure. The methods of planned evangelism will need to be relevant to the modernized world. Only the Gospel itself is sure of remaining the same as it has been. The leaders of the churches I found in Porto Alegre were already articulating a new set of church growth in their world of steadily accelerating change. I had the feeling that the opportunities could be lost. I had this feeling all over Latin America. If the high potential opportunities are of God—and I believe they are—we might well ask what is our responsibility as His stewards.

In 1970 I became involved in the MARC/MIB Brazil Project,* the twofold goal of which is (1) to provide the churches and missions of Brazil with basic information essential for planning strategy for the evangelization of Brazil, and (2) to demonstrate that evangelization is more effective when those engaged in it have "fellowship around the facts." The project gathers and classifies the facts so that churches and missions can examine their progress, understand the trends and patterns, perceive the mistakes and recognize the new opportunities. The project recognizes the current investigation within the frame of reference of modernization. Although we have a focus on Brazil, much of what we discover applies to Latin America at large.

The purpose of this paper is to discuss church growth within the conceptual framework of what the sociologists call modernization. Our research shows patterns of church growth synchronizing with, and reflecting the process of modernization in the different regions of Brazil. I am postulating that the notion of church growth as modernization should be a useful conceptual tool for planning missionary strategy.

The Changing Fabric of Society

The concept of modernization is used by some scholars to describe the many faces of dynamic social and economic change, including the complicated processes of interaction

----

*MARC, Missions Advanced Research & Communication Center.
MIB, Missionary Information Bureau.

within and upon the fabric of society. Sociologists use this conceptual framework to analyse societies and groups moving from rural to urban situations. Demographers, economists, political scientists, geographers, anthropologists and historians have used it to describe the basic elements of society in transition—social, cultural and economic. In each discipline of the social scientists some writer has used this frame of reference for a major analysis. Myron Weiner (1966) brought together the statements of twenty-five scholars with different points of view on the subject. They agreed that modernization was "the most challenging problem of the twentieth century.

The essential core of modernization is the assumption that societies, like people, can outlive old forms, that metamorphosis is a natural process, and that survival depends on adaptation to the changing environment. Modernization is thus a process into the modern world, whereby human societies change so they can interact with the life forces about them. This leads us on into the study of how those changes take place, what happens in society as a result of those changes and, once it is established that the change is good, how it can be accelerated.

The question now arises as to whether or not this concept offers us anything in missiological theory. We must not look at church growth merely as an effort of the church to survive in the face of forces which would annihilate it, but rather how the potential of a new situation may be captured. The church is not struggling for life. It is a struggle in life. It has to achieve new and relevant forms to perform its Christ-given ministry to mankind. In this sense I think we can use the concept of modernization for church growth investigation.

Implications of Modernization
in Church Growth Theory

Modernization conceptualization relates to the study of church growth in the writings of Donald McGavran at a number of points, although he has not employed the term. In *Bridges of God*, his first definitive statement of the church growth viewpoint, the idea at least is stated (e.g. pp. 65,105,142,155). In his enthusiasm to present an account

of the people movement approach to missions as a method
that God has singularly blessed in the evangelization of
tribes and nations since Pentecost, in contrasting this
approach with the mission station approach, he reveals his
awareness of our problem:

> . . . . The tens of thousands of students who journey to
> the West for education, the flood of publications in all
> the major languages of the land, the advent of the movie,
> the loud-speaker and programmes of social education,
> the sensitiveness to foreign criticism, the intensive
> desire to prove their own nation the equal of any on
> earth, and the resentment felt at foreign leadership—
> all these presage the end of an era. . . . (1955: 65)

Although I have taken this out of its context for a purpose
other than that for which McGavran was using it, I do so
because it shows his awareness of both the complex of
world forces responsible for current rapid social change
and also that the old day of missionary techniques was far
spent.

A very few years later he was speaking of "a change of
climate like the end of an ice age." He said:

> The world today is a new and strange place. Men and
> women long attached to old faiths and loyalties are
> now confronted with new scientific truth, world civili-
> zation, new visions of abundant life, principles of
> democracy, and the revolutionary revelation of God in
> Christ. Jolted out of old adjustments and set social,
> political, economic and religious patterns, they are
> searching for better, truer, or more satisfying ways
> (1959: 1).

The grinding glacial processes of traditional societies on
the move into the modern world and into Christian potential,
present us with a new age. McGavran was now writing of
great opportunities for growth around the world. Since
then he has been lecturing on strategy and "hard, bold
plans" for the new era of Christian mission. The burden
of his prophetic message sounded out through the sixties
against the pessimistic chatter of his opponents. Although
he has not forsaken his people-movement hopes for the
tribes nevertheless, he has become more and more aware
that:

> The rush to the cities is on, and within the next few
> decades perhaps three-fourths of the human race will
> be born, live and die in urban rather than rural areas
> (1970: 278).

Understanding Church Growth sums up his teaching of the
sixties, and has a forward look into the seventies with a
whole chapter on the problems of winning the urban situations—"growing still enormous." He finds models in
Brazil and Chile and calls for research by "social scientists
in the service of the great commision."

I believe that such social scientists might well work within the frame of reference of modernization. An impressive
bibliography is now being assembled, with theoretical concepts, with many identified processes, patterns of measurement and a varied and flexible methodology. It should be
possible to adapt these theoretical sociological insights to
specific practical missiological situations.

Closely related to the notion of modernization is the
study of the diffusion of innovations, either on the personal
level as in conversion (as developed by the church growth
writer, Tippett) or as a historical process as Everett
Rogers has shown. The latter has identified seven major
research traditions (1970:23). Yet despite their close
relationship there has been little interaction between them.
The diffusion of innovation is thus seen to be an interdisciplinary field. Church Growth has been described in
terms of both diffusion and innovation. It seems to me that
these could be utilized within the field of modernization.
All fields, instead of being merely prospected, could be
properly and jointly mined. Why should it be left for purely
secular sociologists to discover and interpret the religious
dimensions of the changing world?

Church Growth and Modernization

- McGavran has always insisted that church growth can be
best understood when case studies are compared with the
graph of growth. Thus the record of time factors, historical events, policy changes and such matters are checked
against the rise and fall or plateauing of the graph. This
raises such questions as why the phenomenal growth of the
churches in Gold Coast between 1907 and 1912 synchronized

with the cocoa boom. This, of course, is not to say that other factors were not also involved. The cocoa boom itself would be a complex set of factors. However, my point is that a cocoa boom is a modernization factor, and it seems to have had a bearing on church growth. A study of the cocoa boom might break down into component parts, which could then be investigated one by one with respect to church growth.

A large number of published and unpublished church growth studies now available indicate that, under God, some remarkable growth has been achieved by policies which we might well call "planned modernization." Students of church growth frequently unearth convincing data of the significance of environmental, social and anthropological factors, as for example, with respect to the accelerated growth of Pentecostal Churches in Latin America (Kessler, 1968:302). Thus it becomes essential for missionary researchers to acquire more and more anthropological and sociological knowledge and to examine their church-planting programs in terms of these values. McGavran has long been aware of this and set out from the beginning to add anthropologists to his team of colleagues. Yet these men approach the subject from different angles. When I think of modernization I think of an embracing concept that could draw them all in, and wider still geographers, demographers and scientists with other techniques for measurement. Church growth is a wide subject—as wide as the great commission. The resources of the social sciences for this kind of research have scarcely been tapped.

Neither do I exclude the theological dimension. The process of modernization must be understood as God's activity in the world today. Once we accept that, we have to interpret it in terms of church planting, God being what He is, and the Scriptures saying what they do about His purposes for man. The church planter operates as God's agent of change in the processes of modernization, in biblical terms, His steward.

I now propose to draw together a few ideas that have been expressed by church growth writers and show how they seem to have potential within the frame of reference of church growth as modernization.

Tippett (1967:330-331), in discussing the growth of churches in a South Pacific town shows that the direction of the diffusion of ideas is not necessarily from the urban administration center towards the rural areas. There is an important flow of conceptual constructs from the country to the town or city when people migrate that way. The key to understanding the character of newly-planted rural churches in the city may be found in this important process which conditions the modernization. However the church in the city has to find its own identity in the changing scene: it is no longer rural and not typically urban, and of these migrants we are told:

> They receive many shocks. Their lives are suddenly open for re-evaluation. Thousands of innovations are thrust before them for acceptance or rejection. . . yet a real indigenous church can emerge in this very type of situation. . . (333)

The same writer has also analysed certain rural communities in Ethiopia where the process of modernization is taking place at a rapid rate. Flying low in an M.A.F. plane he recorded

> an intensification of agriculture, an improvement of methods of cultivation, an increased distribution of iron-roofed houses and a growing opulence (1970: 226).

Taylor (1962:16-17) and McGavran (1963:41) have attempted to classify the types of community in Mexico, pointing out how the opportunities for growth differ in each. McGavran says:

> Effective discipling of the ten Mexicos requires keeping abreast of changes in each section. . . Christian mission is being carried out in a rapidly changing social order. What is not often recognized is that this rapid change influences receptivity and hence is important to church growth (41).

Scores of similiar cases could be cited from church growth case studies, from modernization in the nomadic way of life in Africa (Kjaerland 1971) to urbanization studies in New Guinea (Fugmann 1969). It must suffice to say that this kind of church growth writing is within the context of modernization, though they seldom use the term.

Ralph Winter, the historian of the church growth team, has pulled back the curtain on the last twenty-five years, the historic retreat of the West when almost seventy-five nations received their independence (1970). The degree of nationalization, modernization and church growth in these emerging countries of the Third World is waiting to be charted. Winter describes the prelude for a surge of modernization. Never has there been such a period in history so open for new ideas—never such an opportunity and never such a responsibility. In his theological writing Tippett speaks of prevenient grace, of God working in societies preparing them for reception of the Gospel. He also discusses how societies change, and the missionary role, in the process of modernization (1969:98, 109).

Thus it seems to me that a great deal of church growth writing could be quite simply gathered together within the concept of modernization. I have some attachment to the term because it so well expresses the conviction that the day of old missionary methodology has gone by and if the churches are to grow in the modern world they need new forms and have to meet new problems. We are "tied up in the bundle of life." We have to modernize.

Modernization has to be clearly distinguished from modernism. Modernization is a methodology. Modernism is a theology. Church growth theology is biblical and conservative. The problem of modernization is how to communicate the old Gospel to a modern world in modern forms. Latourette saw these changes coming in the thirties and called for the latest techniques and a scientific approach (1932:532). After the war, Myklebust (1951:8) spoke of "the revolutionary present" and the need for "re-thinking missions" in terms of principles and structures.

Church growth writers have said all this and more. A study of their writing reveals a steady development of ideas over a decade and a half. Each new work shows an improvement in their methods. Their awareness of the passage from one era to another lines up with the notion of church growth as modernization, or church growth in modernization. This sociological frame of reference permits planning for a new age. The world that lies before us needs the Church, and in particular the kind of Church which can fit the biblical analogies of salt and light in a modern world.

BIBLIOGRAPHY:

Fugmann, Gernot
1969   "Church Growth and Urbanization in New Guinea,"
        Pasadena, Fuller Theological Seminary, School of
        World Mission, M. A. Thesis
Kessler, J. A. A. Jr.
1968   "Hindrances to Church Growth" INTERNATIONAL
        REVIEW OF MISSSIONS, 57: 298-303
Kjaerland, Gunnar
1971   "Planting the Church among the Nomadic Borana,"
        Pasadena, Fuller Theological Seminary, School of
        World Missions, M. A. Thesis
Latourette, K. S.
1932   "Research and Christian Missions," INTERNA-
        TIONAL REVIEW OF MISSIONS, 21: 532
McGavran, Donald A.
1955   THE BRIDGES OF GOD, New York, Friendship
        Press
1959   HOW CHURCHES GROW, London, World Dominion
        Press
1963   CHURCH GROWTH IN MEXICO, Grand Rapids,
        Eerdmans Publishing Co.
1970   UNDERSTANDING CHURCH GROWTH, Grand
        Rapids, Eerdmans Publishing Co.
Myklebust, Olav G.
1951   AN INTERNATIONAL INSTITUTE OF SCIENTIFIC
        MISSIONARY RESEARCH, Oslo, C., Tybring-Gjedde
Read, Wm. R.
1965   NEW PATTERNS OF CHURCH GROWTH IN
        BRAZIL, Grand Rapids, Eerdmans Publishing Co.
Read, Wm. R., V. M. Monterroso & H. A. Johnson
1969   LATIN AMERICAN CHURCH GROWTH, Grand
        Rapids, Eerdmans Publidhing Co.
Rogers, Everett M.
1969   MODERNIZATION AMONG PEASANTS: IMPACT
        OF COMMUNICATIONS, New York, Holt, Rinehart
        & Winston
1970   DIFFUSION OF INNOVATIONS, New York, The
        Free Press
Rogers, E. M., J. R. Ascroft and N. G. Roling
1970   DIFFUSION OF INNOVATIONS IN BRAZIL,
        NIGERIA AND INDIA, East Lansing, Michigan State
        University Press
Taylor, Jack E.
1962   GOD'S MESSENGERS TO MEXICO'S MASSES,
        Eugene, Institute of Church Growth
Tippett, A. R.
1967   SOLOMON ISLANDS CHRISTIANITY, London, Lut-
        terworth Press
1969   VERDICT THEOLOGY IN MISSIONARY THEORY,
        Lincoln, Lincoln Christian College Press

BIBLIOGRAPHY, (cont.)

Weiner, Myron
    1966   MODERNIZATION: THE DYNAMICS OF GROWTH,
              New York, Basic Books, Inc.
Winter, Ralph D.
    1970   THE   TWENTY-FIVE   UNBELIEVABLE   YEARS,
              South Pasadena, William Carey Library

They (executive secretaries) usually administer several fields and do not become intimately acquainted with the people in any one of them. They converse with missionaries and church leaders in English, and since they are responsible for many kinds of work, automatically guard against undue interest in particular ones. Their chief duty is the recruitment of missionaries and the raising of the budget in the sending land, and for this they need and specialize in not diagnostic but promotional materials.

Nevertheless, some executives are becoming students of church growth, and more of them will. Accurate and extensive knowledge of how churches grow is essential for any administration which intends to carry out the Great Commission. The day is coming when knowledge of the natural laws—one might say the science—of church growth will be part of the qualifications for office of any church or mission administrator.

UNDERSTANDING CHURCH GROWTH,
p. 126.

14

HOME ATTITUDES, ADMINISTRATORS AND FIELD REFLECTIONS

Cal Guy

Pity the poor administrator. Any discussion about the role of the missionary leader, particularly those men in the very top levels of decision making, should begin by looking at the dimensions of his difficulties. They are truly beyond the knowledge of any person who has not occupied the chair. One aspect of his responsibility, his ability or inability may be apparent to the person on the outside who deals from his own limited area of interest. But the total package can be known only by the person in the middle who catches the pressure from all sides and often can do little more than absorb it.

If politics is correctly described as "the art of the possible," perhaps missionary administration. ought to be described as the art of the impossible. The various skills required for the job range from superior saint to kind counselor, from perfect projection planner to master-maker of definite decisions. One ability or skill is quite likely to work against the other. The kind counselor, so essential to the survival of part of his staff and field corps, may enter into internal warfare with the decision maker. Indeed each of these roles ought to be held in proper dynamic tension by the others, but realization of the conflict will be helpful to the administrator and anyone who might be so bold as to evaluate and advise him.

This description of capacities and conflicts will be enlarged and defined later in the chapter. Everything said is intended to be a kind but careful examination of the administrative role which must be examined in the light of the dilemma in which the person with this much responsibility, authority and humanness finds himself.

Perhaps the humanness is the most necessary and at the same time most dangerous part of his equipment. Before and after he is an administrator he is a human being. Created within everyone of us is an innate desire to be acceptable to, liked by other persons. Even the best decisions can be subjected to the worst of interpretations and when this happens the sensitive human being can draw scant comfort from his title. He bleeds, and the probability is that he bleeds more painfully than the man who has just been hired to sweep the floors and mow the lawn. Grown men don't cry, we've all been told. It should be restated that they don't cry in public. The inclination to tears probably never disappears. The deep rooted desire to please and placate all people may work wonderfully in favor of the relationship to his field troops and his home constituency. On the other hand it may exert tragic, destructive pressure on his ability to make difficult decisions and to project long-range plans.

Another aspect of the problem of the missionary administrator is the fact that administration, which covers a large range of responsibilities, has become a field for highly trained specialists. They draw some fabulous salaries after they have completed some highly specialized training and have exhibited the desirable abilities. The top executive is a key figure in the success or failure of any public corporation as the history of the Ford empire will reveal clearly. Decisions made at the top are the most important ingredient in the health of a huge operation. Criteria for selecting these decision makers can be rather clear in the business world. In the world of church and mission they are often blurred beyond recognition.

Nearly everyone has been enlightened by the statement

of the Peter principle: A man is promoted to the point of
his maximum inefficiency. The illustration most easily
understood is about the auto mechanic who can tune an
engine until it purrs beautifully. As a mechanic with such
a skill he is quite likely to be selected as shop foreman
when a vacancy develops. But his skill as a tuner of engines
does not relate at all to the skill of organizing the work of
the shop until ten other men can tune them. And so he becomes a disaster as a shop foreman because he always has
his head under the hood of a car, getting his principal
satisfaction out of making it run to perfection, when he
really needs to be keeping ten men supplied with assignments, directions, parts and leadership. "Maximum inefficiency" he has in the new assignment but who could
have predicted it? And who can change it? With the best
of intentions he assumed a responsibility for which he really
had no aptitude, but who could have known that a man so
highly skilled in one particular operation could be so sadly
without skill in the very next step.

The choice of men to lead the troops in missions is
subject to all of these problems to an accentuated degree.
The committee to select the executive will usually be quite
remotely related to his actual performance at the adminis-
trational level. Trustees of mission boards are usually
located in the U. S. A.; the primary work of missions is
overseas; it is a very rare group of trustees who has in
depth acquaintance with field operation. Something of
statistical performance may drift back home but little
or nothing of interpersonal successes and failures. Successes and failures—successes perhaps; failures not very
likely.

The primary knowledge that the selecting committee is
likely to have is of platform and promotional ability, since
these are the levels at which the constituency is usually
exposed to the overseas missionary and mission board
executive. Sometimes personal piety may be the chief
recommendation for administrative leadership. It is of
immense value in the task at hand unless it provides refuge
from the hard reality of leadership and effective, tough-
minded decision making.

Perhaps an illustration at a point so difficult and yet so
very important will help. "A certain administrator fell

among thieves." No, really not among thieves; he fell among the conflicts in an organization which many people traced to the failure of leadership to chart guidelines of adequate clarity and strength to keep day by day internal functions from great confusion. There was very little restriction on personal freedom. Each employee was able to do that which was right in his own eyes. In the resulting confusion staff members began to accept positions which were subject to fewer conflicts and stresses.

One well meaning trustee gave advice to one obviously discontented staff member: The top man in your organization is a good man. The only thing wrong with your relationship to him is your failure to pray with him. Seek him out personally, spend some time with him in prayer, and all of these conflicts will evaporate.

The unhappy one ignored the advice, accepted employment elsewhere, and submitted his resignation. He was soon accosted by the advice giver who insisted that the action he had taken in resigning was drastic and unnecessary. "You didn't do what I told you to. You didn't go pray with the man in leadership."

The reply was to the point: "Sir, in your business men operate some expensive machines. You can choose a man from the crowd, kneel down beside that machine and pray with him from sunset to sunrise. But, after you've done that, and when you get up off your knees, you still have to ask this fellow one more question—can you run this machine?"

There is little doubt that this particular administrator has a reputation for real piety. He was, in many respects, a good man but selection of a man to fill the role of an administrator because he's a good man without having regard to his planning, executive, decision-making ability can be tragic. The part that genuine piety plays is important but this can be devastating if substituted for adequate leadership.

Why all this talk about the administrator? Primarily because he gathers up in his person the existing situation at home and relates it to the field; because, more than any other person, he creates the field situation and explains it, justifies it, or sells it to the home constituency; because his office and his person create a unique exchange of influences running in both directions. It is important to understand him because he is both maker and victim of his situation, both molder and captive of prevailing opinions. He carries an enormous responsibility. Through him we can read part of the prevailing situation and, by an accurate judgment of his stewardship, can make predictions about the future.

Pressures

After a brief attempt to understand and to sympathize with the administrator we can move on to relate the thrust-counter-thrust from home to field and back again through the way these impinge upon the person who is the titular head of the movement. In his person and his office he cannot, of course, gather up the total stream but enough of it can be seen in its confluence in his office to make it a useful vantage point for viewing the whole.

A primary pressure upon the entire mission scene is the operational theological perspective. This is often far different from the textbook statements of it. Eloquent exposition from the pulpit and thoughtful theological treatises from the school have some effect upon, but do not usually accurately reflect, the operational theology of any home constituency. This is such a broad river that it defies any immediate alteration by the use of words. It probably is an accumulation of centuries, at least of generations. "Operational theology" is often at variance with theoretical or academic theology. It is this operational pressure which usually influences the administrator and the field program.

The cutting edge of the theological presuppositions for mission is found in the concept of salvation or conversion or whatever is defined as the priority need of the receiving community. Controversy and debate about the "lostness of man" have a rising or falling barometer if judgment is based upon the words that are printed about them. The chances are good that one type of emphasis will flow out of the training centers through their contemporary graduates and another will mark the main stream of the constituency. The most vital effect of this broad stream upon mission today is in its creation of an attitude toward conversion. In some quarters it is probably characterized now more by indifference toward conversion than by antagonism, although some of that is present. Its effect is found in increasing emphases by budget and planning upon other priorities.

The real point of this discussion is to suggest that performance and attitude on the field are bred and nurtured at home. They are affected to a fair degree by the later stages of training but probably the basic attitude is imbibed in the process of identification with the home culture. At times there is deliberate rejection and dramatic reversal, but usually performance is based on the actual level of operational theology of the home constituency. If this is composed primarily of the concept of Christian "presence" as over against decision, of cultural values as either superseding or equaling conversion this is likely to mark the field program. In all too much of the life of the home church the honest, driving urge to call men from darkness to light has been lost in busy work which keeps the machinery running. This trend is likely to be accentuated rather than diminished on the field.

Its effect upon mission is easy to read in modern developments. Men who are professors of missions at divinity schools of two large denominations report that their chair may not endure until their retirement. Each of them reports not one single student in preparation for vocational missions. Each of them says his teaching load must be made up by courses offered in peripheral fields. This is a clear barometer of the theological climate and its effect upon the rate of church growth on the mission field can be accurately discerned. Where there is no drive to call men to decision for Christ here at home there is little reason to send men abroad, and certainly there is little likelihood that men sent out of this climate will call men to conversion there.

It is at this point that the rapid shift in appointing and supporting field missionaries is deriving its momentum. Groups with a passion for "finding"—as contrasted with "searching" without any compulsion to find—are still of the opinion that the vocational missionary is needed in today's scene. They are expanding. Those without this verdict theology are withdrawing at a frightening pace.

For this, as well as every other part of the field

program, it can be said that we accurately reflect ourselves overseas. "Like father like son"; "as is the mother so is her daughter"; the travail of Zion at home will predict with a high degree of accuracy the birth pangs overseas.

A particularly persistent pressure upon the administrator is in the realm of promotion. It is a necessary role; it certainly is a fascinating one; and it has the possibility of capturing the major interest of able men. It also has the devastating possibility of creating the field program. Instead of asking what God requires of us in obedience in projecting guidelines for operation the prostituting question about what the home constituency expects may intrude. In this case we switch from asking what is biblically sound to what is promotionally profitable. Only the Father Himself can compute the extent to which basic Christian priorities have been thwarted by this drive for survival and expansion. To whatever extent these criteria define the field program the Christian conscience develops cramp colic and the organization is likely to spend all too much of its time hunting a bottle of paregoric.

Perhaps it should be said clearly, out of deep conviction, that the best promotion grows out of the best field program, honestly conducted and honestly presented. There is something about the informed, devout Christian heart which resists manipulation and cries out for an honest relation to the facts of life. Every person connected with mission would be wise to take into account the potential perversion of programs calculated to reach the pocketbook of the constituency instead of the souls of the lost sheep.

It should be said in honesty that no leader can completely change or defy the preferences and deeply held convictions or prejudices of his constituency. He can surely modify them. This limits the administrator and the field missionary to some realistic degree to fulfilling the basic expectations of the supporting constituency. If there is great conflict here between role and identity somebody suffers a breakdown and the entire program is crippled in the process.

The competitive pressures upon the leader and his entire organization are subtle but real. Sometimes the goal is to produce visible statistics which mark at least a degree of progress over earlier years. It may call for a better record in second priority matters than some rival ecclesiastical organization. It is sadly true that some people do not work by conviction but seem to be strongly motivated by competition. It is a very inadequate, subspiritual motivation, able to warp both program and spirit. In true Christian love no workman is in competition with any other. Obedience to the highest claim of the lordship of Christ is essential to spiritual health.

It would be interesting to know (and only the Judgment can fully reveal this) to what extent the pressure of creating a personal record affects every one of us in the Kingdom. In earlier days there was maintained some discrete distance between the death of a person and his monument in the form of a building with his name on it. That kind of reticence seems to have disappeared with the last buggy horse in the country. But it is not necessary for so obvious a personal goal or personal notoriety to be a part of the drive. The pressure to achieve in order to be known as an achiever can affect everybody at home and abroad. About the only remedy is to read the pressure well, to avoid it like the plague to whatever extent this is possible, and to be careful not to be driven to false goals in order to erect personal monuments.

Another real confluence of home-field influence is at the point of establishing priorities. Again the prevailing home environment is likely to make primary impact. If expansion has turned to contraction and the move to consolidation is dominant at home this will be the major thrust on the field. The discouragement of slow growth or no growth strongly stimulates the drive to pool limited resources in order to look more productive. The call for genuine Christian love, a true ecumenism of Christian fellowship, was never more desperately needed. A summer spent among the Christians of Indonesia in 1971 found these unsophisticated people speaking out again and again for relationships with all of the people who love Christ. They were ill content to be ghettoed off into separate, competing groups. This urge had the ring of a profoundly Christian impulse, one stirred by God himself. But this is different from the effort to reorganize and unite existing weaknesses. The priority of Christian love is undebatable; the priority of trying to merge that which is too small to make an impact even in its total collection can be self-defeating.

Two defeated groups do not merge into one winning team. But the drive to unite can supersede the drive to expand and, to a frightening degree, it has done so in today's world. Another priority which often seizes control is the drive toward devolution. There is not any choice about entering into an honest partnership and a biblical servanthood in connection with work overseas. Devolution in truly spiritual terms is not only long overdue, it ought never to have been necessary. Advice from a man named Roland Allen could have prevented the kind of unseemly dominance which the missionary force has exercised until it has stirred up the demand for radical, immediate and sometimes bitter devolution. The real question as it affects administration is not whether this process will move on or not. It is "a river in spate" and nobody is going to dam it up. The important issue is whether we shall brand as success developments made necessary by failure of the Christian to treat another as his brother to the extent that men who have been dispossessed in their own homeland in every position of meaningful leadership rise up at last in indignation to demand what should have been given them in brotherly consideration. Successful devolution is a matter of spirit and the exercise of true Christian brotherhood would not only meet the demand; it would do much to eliminate the conditions which gave rise to it.

The administrator relates with vast importance to the field in the matter of prerogatives, personal and corporate. Administration in the broadest sense can include the unspoken demands of the home constituency. These can range all the way from the demand that they be allowed the privilege of indiscriminate giving to the privilege that all giving carry with it a degree of automatic control. The people who give and the people who direct the distribution of the gifts have within their hands some enormous powers, enough to frighten any saint.

Personal prerogative can express itself in determination to implement decisions without adequate concern for the welfare of those upon whom the impact will be most profound. It can express itself in leadership by preference instead of leadership by principle. There is the possibility of a prerogative of preferential treatment for my field, my special project, my closest friends—missionary and national.

Biblical objectives and brotherly courtesy surely should outweigh personal preferences in influencing decisions.

Another point of powerful pressure where the home front makes an overwhelming impact on the field program is in the process of trying to make them look and act like us—always, of course, for their own good. Everyone knows that the seat of all wisdom and righteousness is found in the place of his own location. We're much like the elderly lady who was born and reared in Boston. A visitor inquired if she had ever traveled. "Of course not. There was no reason to. I was born here." This completely understandable preference for that which is familiar and its transference into the judgment that all these are right has devastating effect upon the development of a local initiative, local judgment, and local patterns of church life.

One of the major battlegrounds of conflicting opinions of right and wrong, of permissable or beyond the pale of acceptable custom is in the question of polygamy. The home constituency has made its judgment that polygamy was wrong. Once that assumption has been made we seem morally justified in using nearly any expedient necessary to break up this pattern. And break it up we have through the edicts and decrees of boards and field missionaries alike. It has all too seldom occurred to us that we are required by Christian love as well as by simple courtesy to walk very softly into the emotional lives of other people and to be very slow to jerk up large segments of these interpersonal relationships by the roots.

It seems that the African first reacted with some fear to the almost universal demand that he get rid of these extra womenfolk around his house. Those who were inclined to do so really didn't find any "Christian way" to do it, so they were stuck with the problem—and these extra women. The longer the missionaries were around and the more the Bible became available to Africans the less inclined they were to accept the judgment of this Westerner. When they learned that Solomon had seven hundred wives and three hundred "cucumber vines" their confidence in collective missionary judgment was shaken indeed. Home front pressure had imposed demands of Victorian morality on primitive people. God's leadership and patience are working out answers in a more gradual and effective way.

Leadership

Everyone who has any connection with missions is aware
of the complaint of the candidate that mission board qualifications demand a Charles Atlas body, an Albert Einstein
mind, a spiritual vitality like Paul, and a personality like
Dale Carnegie. With that much going for you nearly anybody
can be appointed, so they say.

However much the statement is exaggerated there is a
bedrock reality connected with it: Ideals for leadership at
every level are and ought to be pitched as high as possible.
The profile for the administrator is therefore admitted to
be an ideal one. The reality of the fact is that no one is
available for the role but a human being, and human beings
do not fulfill this completely idealistic representation.
Therefore we'll pitch the ideal and settle for the nearest
approximation to it.

The most important qualification, since this is administration at the highest level, is effective leadership in many
different directions. One of these directions is in a charismatic impact. In the fall of 1971 a newspaper article was
commenting on the lack of this quality on the national scene
in the United States. The tone of the discussion was almost
a wall of despair at the absence of leadership that could
raise the level of the country's life to above normal performance and expectation. The writers were dealing
specifically with the able, mechanical, but non-charismatic
leadership of our president. Nixon was classified as a good,
solid man. He was not viewed as able to stir any pulse to
a beat above normal. Contrast was drawn between him and
John Kennedy. The evaluation of Kennedy's record admitted
a poor performance level, but praised the power he had to
lift the mood of the country. We'll opt for a record which
matches the lifting quality of the person but admit need for
charismatic leadership.

In the missionary administrator this goes beyond the
personality cult into a deep spiritual life, one which has
enough warmth about it to affect the temperature of a total
operation. This also defines one of the most important
roles of the missionary leader: Enspiriting the troops.
The level of spiritual vitality at home is, admittedly, dis-
tressingly low; overseas the general tone is lower and the

missionary is inevitably affected by it. Few people have dealt realistically with the destructive impact on his spiritual vitality of the total situation into which the field missionary is projected. Since we are entering a new day of honest confession, we shall be hearing more about this. (Read *Stop Treating Me Like God* by Levi Keidel) Up to this point, it has been relatively hidden, but it is one of the most devastating factors in missionary performance. To sum it up: The level of spiritual life which projects a missionary into his place of service is often inadequate and the likelihood is that the situation itself will lower it still more; therefore the role of the administrator must take this reality into account and must include adequate measures for dealing with it in its total projection.

Another level in the profile of the leadership is the ability to live in today's world, to benefit by yesterday's experience but to project realistically and hopefully into the future. The world of church-mission has an overwhelming tendency to live on past accomplishments, to enshrine the leaders of the last generation and to copy rather than enlarge and modernize their patterns.

Again reference to the Ford empire can furnish illustration for this creative role on the part of leadership. The person in the Ford organization who dreamed up the concept of the Mustang is worth $100,000 a year to the company without ever tightening a bolt on the assembly line. If the person who needs to create these vast patterns of change and improvement is caught spending his time on the production line instead of at the drawing board he should be accused of waste of valuable resources. It's about as sensible to use a howitzer to shoot a house fly.

A school superintendent in the old South years ago— depression time—was found one day sitting on a wornout stair tread nailing a piece of tin over the hole. He prided himself on saving the school district some money. He could have hired a thousand men at that time for $2.00 a day to do the same thing, and do it better, while he could have been projecting plans for upgrading the entire school system. "Don't send a boy to do a man's work" is a wise injunction, but it is equally unwise to use high powered talent to do day by day mechanics when its most useful function is projecting into a productive future.

It is extremely difficult to combine in one person the far visioned dreamer (the person who can gather together in his own mental processes forces of the past, present, and future in order to project them to meet developing trends) and the person who can expedite and implement these dreams. The functions may be so different as to call for two persons. Part of the problem in the two persons solution arises in the fact that the dreamer, the planner of tomorrow is rarely free to project his plans if the person who must put them into effect has veto authority over them. Every one of us knows the deadening effect of a heavy work load on the more creative aspects of life. Interpersonal relationships suffer when exhaustion is the usual physical symptom of the parties involved; the pulpit ministry of a preacher will become dull, perhaps deadly, if he is so busy discharging necessary pastoral duties that he has no genuine energy for creative thinking for both message and new concepts of ministry for his congregation. Likewise the role of the missionary or missionary executive is often bankrupted by over work (or perhaps the wrong choice of what to do) so that the more vital tasks of leadership suffer at the hands of the more easily performed routines.

Important to the functioning of the troops on the field is a high IQ in the proper places. We usually define that to mean "intelligence quotient" but in this kind of responsibility it is far more important to have a high "idea quotient." This takes some natural ability, some time, some careful reading for intellectual stimulation, some searching of soul before the Lord, and enough physical energy left from other tasks to spend time and effort to develop the ideas which, under encouraging conditions, can be the product of a fertile mind.

A trusting partnership with many people is necessary for the production and implementation of new ideas. The ideas ought to be welcomed as they float in from unexpected sources. Eugene Nida suggested that the idea man is usually closely regulated if not seriously distrusted by the person who is in charge of deciding what changes will be tolerated in a given society. The person who makes this kind of decision may be the chief, the governor, or the administrative officer of an organization. The two roles are indentified as *innovator* and *censor.* If the censor uses the blue pencil too much he can destroy innovation. If the innovator is too wild and has too free an access to the organizational machinery he may cause damage by failure to introduce new processes with due caution. These relationships need to be kept in delicate balance. Fortunate indeed is the missionary organization which combines the innovator and the censor in creative balance in one person.

Once the ideas have come through these processes great faith in the ability of other people in the organization to implement them is important. Perhaps it is not necessary to have too many idea men but it is necessary for those who sanction change to give great freedom of implementation to those who must work it into the current processes. This requires great maturity on the part of the person who might be the object of criticism if these innovations backfire. It requires a great deal of personal security so that consequences can be taken rather calmly in case the necessary process of change runs into temporary setbacks. It requires a person willing to share both credit and authority.

Conclusion

The home constituency is usually thought of as furnishing men and money for the overseas operations. It is inevitable that, in connection with this, will go some of the basic concepts, preferences and prejudices of the home constituency.

Beyond this obvious contribution to mission there is urgent need for the home constituency to create a spiritual climate which sustains the right of advance in mission rather than expecting these currents of spiritual life to flow from the field operation into the sending churches. There is a strong call for enough authentic Christian life here to validate the message which we preach there. The administrator represents a focal point at which most of these forces come into play with help or hurt to the overseas program.

Perhaps at this point in the final lines of the chapter personal reminiscence about D. A. McGavran will be acceptable: *Bridges of God* from his pen had been published before I met him. He was on deputation ministry to Brite

College at Texas Christian University in Fort Worth when
Dr. Bill Hall, professor of missions there introduced him
to me and my classes at Southwestern Baptist Theological
Seminary. Because of my appreciation of *Bridges of God*
I met him eagerly and found the personal contact very
rewarding.

On that trip he had with him the manuscript of *How
Churches Grow.* The ideas in it were so helpful that students
and missionaries deserved a chance to read them. His
judgments on priorities and programs were important and
helpful. But he had discovered that evaluation, even of the
most valid and kindly nature, was not welcome everywhere.
It was proving difficult to get *How Churches Grow* published.
It was not a negative book. He was insisting that everything
being done be examined, some priorities established, and
improvement sought in every way and place.

Sometimes the truest friend is the one who for adequate
reason points out the areas which need attention. Sometimes
he goes beyond pointing and uses the surgeon's knife.
Surgery is never pleasant, is often painful, but necessary
in many circumstances. McGavran has been a judge, a
surgeon, a critic in the highest sense of the term and always
a warm friend of mission. He has done all of us in the field
of missions real service. His insights have particular
value to every administrator.

His ministry to missions can perhaps be summarized
by the passage from the Proverbs 27:6, "Faithful are the
wounds of a friend; but the kisses of an enemy are deceit-
ful."

If a bit of preaching is in order, let this be the sermon:
The trends away from church planting into vague activity
have been carefully described in many ways by this field
missionary-seminary professor. His warnings have been
given in order that the ripe harvest be not lost in the field.
Many of us have cause to be grateful for his lessons. We
shall be profiting by them for a long time.

The tribe . . . must be recognized and welcomed as a significant political and social entity in the new Africa. Even if a hundred years from now tribes should cease to exist, they are a powerful part of the contemporary scene. A mode of mission must be perfected which converts not only individuals but "individuals in society." The adult power structures of most villages and wards must be made up of Christian men. The mature men who control each ward and village should not be complacently left pagan, in the expectation that in time they will die off.

UNDERSTANDING CHURCH GROWTH,
p. 23.

15

NEW APPROACHES TO MISSION
(Tonga, Zambia)

Stan Shewmaker

"A mode of mission must be perfected," said McGavran (1970:23) "which converts not only 'individuals but individuals in society.'" A few missionaries have appreciated the importance of the Tonga culture pattern for the Church of Zambia and have written on the subject, but the majority have either remained unconcerned about, or opposed to it. They have been unaware of the groupness of the people among whom they were working, and oblivious to the idea of discipling "individuals in society."

Hitherto the usual mode of mission has been the school approach. This was individualistic in that young boys and girls were extracted from their society and kept isolated from their "heathen" environment; hopefully long enough for them to become solidly Christian. But becoming a "real" Christian too often meant ceasing to be Tonga. This form of Christianity attracted comparatively few permanent adherents. Today only nine percent of all Tonga are actively Christians.

Once they left the artificial atmosphere of the mission school, multitudes of young Christian graduates, under pressure from pagan power structures and relatives back in the village, reverted. Hundreds of others migrated to the cities looking for white collar jobs. Nearly all laid aside their Christian training and experience as irrelevant and powerless in their new situation, and became secular. Losses in Church membership have been high. The Church of Christ, which is not different from other Churches and missions in this respect, has during the past twenty-five years retained only 16 percent of those baptized. These facts, which were revealed by a 1968 church growth survey (Shewmaker, 1970), demand a fundamental change in mission strategy and emphasis.

In 1969 a group of missionaries of the Church of Christ began to implement a new approach to discipling the Tonga and to perfecting Tonga churches. This new terminology and approach to missions was developed to meet the need for a new strategy and emphasis in mission by Donald McGavran (1955). This paper describes a practical attempt to apply these principles among the Tonga of Zambia.

Discipling

This approach to mission gives top priority to the rapid discipling of people. Thousands of Tonga must be persuaded to give their lives to Jesus Christ now and "to become responsible and committed members of His Church." In order for discipling of any magnitude to occur, the Good News of God in Christ must be taken to the locality, (1) where the people are, and (2) where they are most receptive.

Traditionally missions have required that people (usually school children) come to them. But this traditional method must no longer be regarded as tenable. No longer can unrelated individual school children be extracted from their society, to be superficially doctrinated with foreign values and forms in mission schools. History has repeatedly illustrated the futility of this approach.

Jesus Christ must become the Saviour and Lord of adult men and women in village after village and in kinship group after kinship group. This means that missionaries will have to go where these adults live and must abandon the isolation of mission stations.

The Gospel must be so presented that non-Christians can see clearly that not only is it possible, but it is indeed the best way of life, to be a redeemed Tonga child of God, who is part of a Spirit-filled Tonga church, which sings Tonga hymns and applies Tonga biblical interpretations and Christian experience to felt Tonga needs and problems.

Requirements for effective communication of the Gospel on this deeper level of Tonga experience demands that each missionary speak Tonga fluently. This is a primary objective for wives as well as husbands. Furthermore, valuable anthropological data and insights which may have some bearing upon church growth are gathered daily and shared periodically. Each member respects Tonga cultures and recognizes the importance of understanding, as much as possible, what conversion to Christ actually means to a Tonga person. He knows that only in this way can his witness and teaching strike chords in Tonga hearts.

Discipling among the Tonga during the 1970s requires a determined and concerted effort to plant churches. But church planting had not been stressed before, and this necessitated a radical change of direction from the school approach. Though thousands of school children and other individuals had been baptized in institutions and villages, little thought had been given to the organization of these new-born Christians into specific self-sufficient and ongoing congregations.

The effect of this shift to direct evangelism in the larger context as the main thrust of mission in the Church of Christ can be observed in the statistics. The total number of Tonga congregations has grown from thiry-seven in 1968 to fifty-four in 1971. Church membership (now 2,100) has increased by 60 percent, during the same period. If the current rate of growth under God be continued until 1980, we could have a total membership over 10,000 (Shewmaker, 1971).

With practically no previous church planting experience to draw on, national Christians and missionaries are spending much time in prayer together, in seeking the power and leading of the Holy Spirit as they plan and execute new ways of discipling receptive villages. The discipling of Saibalengu village is typical of the way one of these plans was implemented successfully in the planting of a new Church.

When the headman, the only Christian in the village,

invited a team of missionaries and national evangelists to
preach, the leaders of the churches within a ten mile
radius were notified of the headman's desire and were
requested to pray specifically for the conversion of the
Saibalengu village. Christians who had relatives there
expressed a particular interest. Thus the awareness of the
possibility of a church in Saibalengu was linked with the
ramifications of the extended family.

The team of evangelists which had accepted the challenge
of presenting Jesus and His way to the village prayed until
midnight every night for a week, demonstrating a group's
concern for a group. They not only prayed that the Holy
Spirit would fill them with power and wisdom, but that He
would also prepare the hearts of the people of Saibalengu
village for the message of Jesus, for the "field" could hardly
be harvested until the harvest was ripe.

The team arrived at sunset on Saturday evening. After
the evening meal they explained to the adult men of the village the purpose of their visit. Thus they began operations
within the normal authority structures of the village. Jesus
Christ was presented but there was no call for decision.
The evangelists then requested and were granted permission
to speak to the whole village the next day. The basic essentials of the Christian faith were presented to the assembled
villagers, and the matter was placed in the hands of the household heads. After deliberation, two men stood and expressed
their decision to give their lives to Jesus Christ. Seven
young people followed their lead. All were immediately baptized, and communion was observed that afternoon for the
first time in Saibalengu village.

Before the team left, the man who had been the first to
decide for Christ (a polygamist with a seventh grade education) purchased a Tonga Bible. He wanted to start preaching that same week! Within six weeks he had persuaded
most of his fellow-villagers to become Christians, among
them his two wives. He baptized them all himself. A week
after his conversion he was enrolled in a thirteen-lesson
post-baptismal course designed for new Christians. As he
completed each lesson, he taught it to other members of
his congregation.

This account of the way a village turned to Christ follows
the pattern that McGavran has called a "web movement"

(1970: 174), and reveals several new principles currently operative in the evangelization of Tonga villages:

1. Prayer support is solicited from all concerned Christians in the surrounding area. Prayer has become a fresh and indispensable dimension of evangelism.
2. The power structure of the village is approached first, on the supposition that it will lead the village in its decision for or against Christ. The "words of God" now enter a village the same way as does any important message from the chief; first, the headman hears; then the men, then the remainder of the village.
3. Penitent polygamists are accepted into the full fellowship of the church upon confession of faith in, and baptism into, Jesus Christ, on a basis of repentance rather than knowledge.
4. The emergence of responsible local leaders is encouraged from the start of the new congregation. These ministers are then reinforced by regular preaching and teaching on the part of missionaries and national evangelists.
5. These leaders are enrolled in a thirteen-week new converts course as soon as possible after their conversion. This is an effort to give substance to their decisions and to help them grow rapidly in their new life in Christ—the dimension of perfecting.
6. Non-Christians are urged through personal witness, instead of merely through public proclamation on Sundays, to repent and accept salvation in Jesus Christ. Given this freedom, Christians invariably show more concern and urgency for converting their relatives. They don't wait for "evangelistic experts" to persuade them.

Other factors are accelerating the spread of the Christian faith in some areas of Tongaland. One of these is the process of cultural change within the tribal social order which, to many Tonga Christians, is interpreted as a sign of the imminent end of the age. Basing their convictions on New Testament eschatological passages, they press forward as never before to seek and save the lost before the end. Their efforts are culturally directed towards their

pagan kinsmen. Non-Christian Tonga are becoming increasingly receptive to their message because of this same
social stress. Headmen and adult men, who form the power
structures, are reaching out for this new life of hope and
security by inviting men to their villages to tell them the
"words of God."

A second contributing cause of this church growth is the
rising awareness of the presence of the Holy Spirit in their
midst and in the program of evangelism. The lack of this
awareness in the past was undoubtedly due in large part to
the fact that the Tonga Church of Christ mission has held
to a weak theology of the Person and work of the Holy Spirit.

Another factor (more significant perhaps to an African
than a westerner) is the dream. Two examples will suffice.
A Christian leader in a dream saw an old village headman,
who had once been a Christian, beckoning him to his house.
Unable to sleep for the remainder of the night, and believing
he had been "given the thought" by God, the church leader
rode his bicycle five miles to speak to the old man and
to urge him to return to his first love. After three hours of
prayer, hymns and tears, the headman was led back into
his Father's house and into the full fellowship of the Church
—after 31 years of rebellion against his Lord!

A pagan woman, who had apparently been resisting
Christianity for some months, dreamed that she was being
baptized in a large pool of water. Early the next morning
she inquired if there were someone who could baptize her
and was told that the nearest Christian was nine miles away.
Thereupon she persuaded her husband to transport her by
bicycle, found the Christian who explained the Good News
and upon her profession of faith, baptized her that same day!

A fourth factor which is accelerating the discipling of the
Tonga is the impact of healing as a result of Christian
prayer. At least two villages have become interested and
then receptive to the "words of God" after someone in the
village was healed when Christians prayed for him. By
giving God all of the glory, the witnessing Christians convinced their friends and relations that their God is the one
with all power and that His is the best Way.

In view of the present rate of evangelization, some national Christians and missionaries foresee that the missionary's present role in the *discipling* of the southwestern part

of Tongaland, known as Tokaland, will be nearly complete by the end of 1974. By this is meant that (1) half of the adult population of the area will be actively Christian; and (2) there will be a church meeting within walking distance of every village. Although much discipling will remain to be done, the missionary role will have shifted toward the *perfecting* of the churches and toward the discipling of other areas of Tongaland.

Perfecting

Jesus commissioned His apostles to go into all the world and make the nations and tribes His followers and to baptize them. But this was not all. They were then to teach these new disciples understanding of and obedience in everything He had taught them during his public ministry.

Dr. McGavran makes use of the term *perfecting* to describe the many activities that are involved in this most important process of post-baptismal care and teaching. He lists some of the more prominent of these activities under three categories: (1) the instituting of regular worship; (2) the securing of a place to meet; and (3) the systematic teaching of God's word to both literate and illiterate Christians. He believes that for young congregations to continue for long with no regular meeting-place is to court disaster, because even illiterates and semi-literates can and should be taught liturgically. Memorizing important Bible passages and hymns to be used repeatedly in worship is an effective way to teach illiterate converts. These will provide them with spiritual confidence, a sense of security and hope in hours of stress (McGavran, 1970: 326-327).

What Paul called the "perfecting of the saints . . . for the edification of the body of Christ (Ephesians 4:12) has been assigned a priority second only to that of discipling. The history of missions is replete with examples of how dynamic movements to Christ have been halted because of a disproportionate emphasis upon either discipling or perfecting. Therefore missionaries and African Christians involved in direct evangelism in Tongaland realize how vital it is to maintain a proper equilibrium between these two aspects of church growth. Ways must be found to halt the staggering reversion rate of the years gone by.

While a growing group of Christians, impelled by the Holy Spirit, are going forth to compel men to accept Christ as Savior and Lord, others are planning, writing, and teaching courses designed to strengthen and establish the faith of the new converts.

The first of these thirteen-week courses is a 150-page lesson book entitled *First Steps in Christian Faith* written specifically for the Tonga situation. It has already been taught to the leaders of 25 percent of the Tonga churches who are now being instructed. Each leader was urged to equip others for a life of service to Christ even as God had enabled him to be equipped. As these men develop spiritually, they will become better shepherds than would ever have been possible by depending solely on available missionary personnel.

Work has already begun on the second phase of post-baptismal shepherding. A three-year theological course designed to give emerging church leaders a more advanced and balanced Bible orientation than is provided by the new converts course is being prepared. This extension leadership training program (ELT) is being written on the fourth grade level and will be available to all leaders selected and recommended for training by their own congregations. These unpaid and self-supporting ministers will pay most, if not all, of the production costs of the materials used in their training.

From the very beginning Tonga teachers are being incorporated into the ELT program as instructors. This should enable perfecting to keep pace with church planting. It should also provide these men with the experience and the opportunity for personal development that will enable them to build into the Tonga Church an independence of thought and Biblical interpretation which has not been encouraged before. As Tonga Christians are given the tools for interpreting God's word, they are urged to interpret it in the light of their own experience and not to remain dependent upon a small band of missionaries or a few prominent national ministers. This is a deliberate break away from the somewhat paternal policy of the past.

Although missionaries will continue to work vigorously both in discipling and perfecting they will become an increasingly smaller part of the total evangelistic and perfecting work of the national Church.

In addition to the development of courses for new converts and the ELT program for leaders, groundwork is being prepared for the writing of a range of diverse religious literature. Zealous new Christians soon exhaust the present vernacular religious library of some 15 booklets and long for more. Therefore in an effort to provide something as quickly as possible, Zambians are being encouraged to write tracts and booklets in Tonga on relevant topics like "Witchcraft and Christianity," "Christ and Evil Spirits," "Patterns of Worship in the Tonga Church," and many others. Also desperately needed are such Bible study aids as a simple concordance, a Bible "question and answer" booklet, and a brief theological word book.

Many of these new approaches to winning the Tonga for Christ owe their formation, at least in part, to the writing and teaching of Donald McGavran. Each member of this missionary group responsible for this application of church growth principles in Zambia has studied under him. They have not only been profoundly influenced by his missionary principles and procedures, but by his consistent concern for the salvation of the "two billion" which he somehow manages to transmit to his students and readers.

This is my personal tribute that no single individual has played a more prominent role than McGavran in bringing about a shift from the unproductive school approach of the past to the dynamic church planting approach which is now being applied to discipling the Tonga people of Zambia.

BIBLIOGRAPHY:

McGavran, Donald A.
  1955   BRIDGES OF GOD: A STUDY IN THE STRATEGY
            OF MISSIONS, London, World Dominion Press
  1970   UNDERSTANDING CHURCH GROWTH, Grand Rapids,
            Wm. B. Eerdmans
Shewmaker, Stan
  1970   TONGA CHRISTIANITY, South Pasadena, Wm. Carey
            Library
  1971   "Church Growth in Butonga" Mimeographed.

. . . the language of the heart is difficult to stamp out. It is learned from the mother's lips and spoken in the home. It is an inner sanctuary where the outside world cannot penetrate. It is jealously guarded because it enhances a sense of peoplehood.

As the Church spreads throughout the earth, she is constantly dealing with hundreds of millions who live in two worlds. In some she speaks the heart language and flourishes, in others she presents the Gospel in a standard language and languishes.

UNDERSTANDING CHURCH GROWTH,
p. 193.

16

CHURCH PLANTERS
AND ETHNOLINGUISTICS

Charles H. Kraft

Dr. McGavran is fond of saying that folk like to be with people of their own kind, and that people like to worship in their own language—the language of the heart. He has built into church growth theory the assumptions that rapid, solid church growth is most likely among linguistically and culturally homogeneous groups, and that the most effective form of cross-cultural communication is in terms of the language and cultural concepts of the target people. Furthermore he advocates the translation of Scripture into the "heart language" as a basic for Christian mission.

Ethnolinguistics frequently comes into focus in the study of helps and hindrances to church growth and in the training of missionaries. The linguistic dimensions of culture, or the cultural dimensions of language are relevant both to church planters and to the planted churches. Specific areas of ethnolonguistic study are: a people's linguistic behavior to their overall conception of reality; the range of linguistic and cultural problems involved in cross-cultural preaching, Bible translation, missionary language learning, etc.; the use of specialized language or style (e.g. honorifics) for worship, prayer, singing, teaching, medicine, or for addressing persons of differing social status, sex, age, etc., or on special occasions; cultural attitudes towards one's own language, dialects and world languages; natural and directed change of language, particularly under the impact of religious diffusion, etc.

The effective church planter needs to understand the differences between the system of logic of, say, Euro-American culture and that of non-western culture, lest he simply assume either that he can communicate effectively from the base of his own perception of reality, or that inability of the listeners to understand such communication is an indication of deficiency or inferiority on the part of the listener and/or his culture. The influence of a body of naive writing on the logic of other cultures is still very much with us. Such writing uninfluenced by the insights of ethnolinguistics concerning the differences in cultural perception of reality, and the variety of equally valid logics developed on the basis of these differences, employed such now-discredited terms as "primitive mentality" and "prelogical thinking" (Levy-Bruhl 1910; 1922 and comment by Bidney 1967: 157-8). The church planter first has to accept the validity of such differences, to seek to understand and to work in terms of the system of logic of the receptor culture.

Now let me outline ethnolinguistic methodology before developing a few areas for investigation. These areas are 1) The reality of perceptual differences between members of different language communities, 2) the need to take culturally-defined perceptual differences seriously in cross-cultural communication of the Gospel, 3) the need to take culturally-defined perceptual differences seriously in Scripture translation and interpretation, 4) ethnolinguistics and the development of an indigenous Christian theology, and 5) Christianity and the conceptual transformation of language.

Ethnolinguistic Methodology

Ethnolinguistic method is a combination of approaches developed by such disciplines as linguistics, anthropology, semantics and folk-lore, with a few original techniques of

its own. The greatest originality within the field has, however, related more to the conclusions arrived at than the
methods employed. For example, in attempting to learn
as much as possible concerning the world view and value
system of a given culture one might look first at any ethnographic and/or linguistic descriptions for clues as to which
particular areas of grammar, mythology, vocabulary, folk-
tales, proverbs, epithets, aphorisms, onomatology, slang
and the like would be most likely to be fruitful.

A study of proverbs, for example, will prove fruitful
since in most societies (especially, but not limited to, pre-
literate societies) proverbs play a prominent role in education and social control. Ethnolinguists collect and classify them according to themes. The particular emphases
that culture focuses on its own values in the process of en-
culturating its children may be learned from such classifications. A plethora of proverbs recommending the patient
acceptance of things as they are, in Hausa for example, shows
that this society places a high value on that attitude.

Fables, mythology, epithets and other types of folklore
may also be classified and ordinarily will reinforce the
impressions gathered from the study of proverbs, their
major difference being functional rather than content. Mythology tends to be direct with respect to values. Fables
tend to be less direct in stating both world view and values,
except for the proverb-like moral attached to them. Fables
however illustrate the application or misapplication of the
culture's principles of conduct and drive the point home
in a way that a simple statement cannot do.

Studies of vocabulary likewise point up such things as
the value system of a culture. Cultural foci may be discovered by statistical listing of vocabulary items. For
example, Arabic languages contain approximately 6000 terms
for various kinds of knives, indicating the high value of the
knife in Arabic cultures. Similar conclusions may be drawn
from lists of camels among the Arabs, or some among the
Eskimo, or technological, medical and scientific terms in
Euro-American languages.

Beyond this ethnolinguists classify and analyse (using
semantic techniques) the particulars of such cultural foci
as indicated by vocabulary counting. They study the indigenous valuing of various terms and semantic categories

(e.g. those valued or tabooed), and observe contrasts between semantic organization in different languages. For example, many cultures identify but three primary colors while others may recognize up to eleven without becoming technical (Berlin & Kay 1969; Burling 1970). Specialized groups, especially occupational groups, develop many more precise distinctions (dyeing, weaving, etc.), using terms not known to the majority of people in their own culture.

Through such semantic studies ethnolinguists are able to learn about culture-specific perceptual categories of varying relevance for cross-cultural communication. Perception of color, shape, heat and cold (which may be four rather than two, as in Hausa), for example, though important in cross-cultural communication are ordinarily not so crucial to missionaries and other advocates of culture change as are such things as the indigenous perception of the hierarchy of non-material spirit forces and activities, or the indigenous habit of analogizing from material or concrete concepts to abstractions. Even so, the more the less crucial differences in perception are understood, the more intelligible and effective will be the cross-cultural communication.

An ethnolinguistic approach to grammar may also help to discover a people's world view. For example, a given language specifies in its verbal inflection the kind of action (completed, continuing, potential) rather than the time (past present, future) of the action. We presume that the former culture places a higher value on the nature of that action than on the time of it. Hausa requires the same construction for "I was going," "I am going," and "I will be going." There is greater similarity between these performances of "going" than in our time-conscious culture, and this difference relates also to the perception of reality and the values attached to them. Once a Nigerian who was to meet me at two o'clock did not arrive until five, and when I commented on the time factor he incredulously replied "But I have come." He interpreted our agreement in keeping with his own value system and focused on the "come" part of the action and could not fully understand my pique.

By these and similar techniques ethnolinguists probe the depths of the perceptual differences between peoples of differing cultures.

The Reality of Perceptual Differences Between
Members of Different Language Communities

The American anthropologist and linguist, Edward Sapir,
was among the first to focus attention upon the reality and
depth of the perceptual differences underlying the linguistic
differences between peoples of different linguistic communities. In a now famous quote, he wrote in 1929:

> the "real world" is to a large extent unconsciously
> built up on the language habits of the group. No two
> languages are ever sufficiently similar to be con-
> sidered as representing the same social reality. The
> worlds in which different societies live are distant
> worlds, not merely the same world with different
> labels attached (209).

This challenges the assumption of many monolingual
Americans that languages are simple, different but equivalent codes applied by different peoples to the same reality,
and that the major problem in becoming fluent in another
language is merely learning to substitute the vocabulary of
the new code for the old.

Sapir, Whorf and their followers have established the
fact that each language provides and defines for its users a
particular form of logic, a mold for the thought of its users,
a peculiar frame of reference different from the speakers
of any other language (Henle, 1958: 1, summarizing Whorf).
Even more indicative of the differences between the world
views of the members of different linguistic communities,
however, are the contrasts between their grammatical
categories. In contrasting Hopi with "Standard Average
European," for example, Whorf lists five points of grammatical divergence representing major broad areas of
conceptual non-compatibility between the cultural perspectives of the two linguistic groups—plurality and numera-
tion, physical quality, phases of cycles, temporal forms
of verbs and the expression of duration and intensity.
Speakers of SAE languages—

> tend to see the world in terms of things, the things
> themselves built up of a formless stuff given a deter-
> minate form. Non-spatial entities are conceived by
> spatial metaphor (Henle, 1958: 15).

On the other hand, the Hopi seem—

> to have analyzed reality largely in terms of events
> (or better "eventing"), referred to in two ways, ob-
> jective and subjective. Objectively, and only if per-
> ceptible physical experience, events are expressed
> mainly as outlines, colors, movements, and other
> perspective reports. Subjectively, for both the physical
> and non-physical, events are considered the expression
> of invisible intensity factors, on which depend their
> stability and persistence, or their fugitiveness and
> proclivities (Whorf 1941, Carroll 147).

On the basis of the comparison of world views underlying Hopi and SAE grammatical categories, Whorf concludes that "Concepts of 'time' and 'matter' are not given
in substantially the same form by experience to all men,
but depend on the nature of the language or languages
through the use of which they have been developed" (Whorf
1941, Carroll 158).

The Need to Take Culturally-Defined
Perceptual Differences Seriously
in Comminicating the Gospel Cross-Culturally

If culturally-defined perceptual differences between peoples of different cultures are real and deep, communicators
of the Gospel must take them seriously. E. A. Nida points
out in *Message and Mission* that people tend to assume they
mean what they think they mean, even in their native tongue,
when the "hearing" of the message actually depends on the
experience of the hearer. "The way in which the receptor
'decodes' the message has as much effect upon its meaning
as the way in which the source 'encodes' it" (1960:1,34).
The cross-cultural communicator must be asking continually
"What are the hearers hearing?" This ethnolinguistic problem is of particular concern to missionaries since the
eternal destiny of human beings is at stake.

If the speaker (missionary) and hearer (potential convert)
are of different cultures the potential for miscommunication
is great. The greater the difference of cultures the greater
the probability of misunderstanding. In much of Africa, for
example, the well-meaning missionary who presents Jesus
as the Good Shepherd may discover to his chagrin that

people have understood that Jesus never grew up, since in their society only young boys or the mentally incompetent tend sheep. And such non-identity of the meanings attached to similar forms is a frequent cause of cross-cultural miscommunication.

The book of Acts records several other examples. In the healing of the cripple at Lystra (Acts 14:8-18), the action of Paul and Barnabus was 'saying' "God is concerned with alleviating the suffering of the cripple." The people interpreted the event in terms of their own frame of reference, and assumed that since only gods could heal, these men were "gods in the likeness of men," or "in human form," and proceeded to worship Paul and Barnabus. At Athens (17:18) the response of the philosophers, "He seems to be setting forth new gods" was a judgment based on their own cultural background. Fortunately in each case Paul got the kind of feed-back to see that his message was misunderstood, and he was able to adjust or simplify it so that at least he was better understood.

Contemporary examples can be mutiplied endlessly. A young Liberian, a product of western missionary schooling gave me his understanding of John 3:16 as follows: "God so loves Europeans that He accepts as Christian an African who turns his back on his own customs and becomes converted to western culture." Of course no missionary had ever said such a thing. But the total effect of his understanding of the missionary message and operation was this distorted form. Unfortunately nothing was done to remedy the misperception until it was too late, for concluding that Christianity was a purely western religion the man had rejected it, as he explained to me.

Within their own cultural framework the missionaries had spoken accurately, but this young man was receiving their word in his own conceptual framework. Let me tabulate what was said and heard:

1. Christ is the way to a right relationship with the one True God.	1. They bring a foreign religion competing with our indigenous religion for my allegiance.
2. Accept Jesus Christ and you will have God's power.	2. Convert to western culture and I shall have God's power.

3. God is concerned about your health.	3. God endorses western medicine and condemns African medicine.
4. God wants you to be better educated in order to better know and serve Him.	4. If I go to school, I can become a God-blessed, powerful European.
5. Follow Christ to have real life.	5. Follow Christ to be a European.

These and many other misconceptions came pouring forth from this man. The real tragedy lay, not only in the misconceptions, but the fact that they went uncorrected, because the missionaries neither took his culturally conditioned perception seriously, nor solicited the feedback which could have led to their correction. (Acts 14:14)

The effective cross-cultural communicator must work within the culturally-defined frame of reference that permits proper communication and, if need be, the correction of miscommunication.

The Need to Take Culturally-Defined Perceptual Differences Seriously in Scripture Translation and Interpretation

Another crucial area is the translation and interpretation of the Bible. This involves the missionary, not in two, but three or four cultural frameworks. The Bible records God's revelation as it was perceived in Hebrew, Aramaic, and Greek language and culture. Our own perception of this revelation, however, is pervasively affected by our Euro-American culture. We translate and interpret the revelation into appropriate linguistic and cultural forms of still another culture.

The translator or interpreter must "be constantly aware of the contrast in the entire range of culture represented by" the source and target languages (Nida 1945:194). He must also be on his guard against interference from his own linguistic and cultural background. For example, through English we understand New Testament injunctions to continuing trust (such as John 3:16) as "once-for-all" action which many of us have experienced. Thus we translate faith as an act at a single point of time rather than a continuing commitment.

The Hausa language possesses a "continuative aspect" similar to the Greek "present tense," but the translation does
not employ the continuative. It uses the Hausa equivalent
for the Greek aorist, giving the popular English meaning
rather than the Greek. Again, the translator or interpreter
can go astray if he strives for formal rather than cultural
equivalence. Striving for literalness rather than functional
equivalence has produced many misleading translations,
both in the great historical versions and the missionary
translations.

Ethnolinguistic insight into the nature of language, cultural conditioning and cross-cultural communication has
led to a new understanding of what "correctness" in translation is really about. "Correctness must be determined
by the extent to which the average reader for which a translation is intended will likely be to understand it correctly"
(Nida & Taber, 1969:1), rather than by some literalistic
criteria, perhaps because of respect for the Scriptures,
focus more on the forms of the original text than on the meanings to be conveyed to the hearers. But biblical languages
(and cultures) must be seen to be human (rather than super-
human), though treated reverently. "The writers of the biblical books expected to be understood" and are not well-
translated, however motivated, if the original meaning is
obscured (7-8).

An ethnolinguistic approach to Bible translation and interpretation, therefore, paves the way for greater intelligibility
of the message and consequently for a lower degree of
dependence upon outsiders such as the missionary for its
interpretation. This is good for church growth since it
enables young churches to move rapidly toward indigeneity.

Ethnolinguistics and the Development of Indigenous
Christian Theology: A Case Study from Africa

Among the pressing concerns of indigenous Christianity
is the need to develop Christian theology based upon the
indigenous, rather than the western world view. Given that
there is an absolute theology beyond culture, the dual facts
of 1) the vast perceptual differences between cultures, and
2) that God has chosen to reveal Himself within the cultural
context, have resulted and will result in a variety of cul-

turally-conditioned understandings of theology (such as those of the West, of India, Latin America, Africa, etc.) none of which should be regarded as absolute, but all of which can contribute to a less culture-bound understanding of the supracultural God and His workings. Since God seeks to interact with human beings of each culture in terms maximally comprehensible to them, we may assume He is in favor of the development of theological understandings within each culture that will facilitate this end. Missionaries, therefore, should encourage the indigenization of theology, so that peoples of every culture may have, what Welbourn terms "a place to feel at home" (Welbourn & Ogot, 1966).

In Africa, at least, missionary endeavor has been focused primarily on western theologizing, which disregards the cultural factors underlying this process and tends to equate with supracultural absolute models. Of the Baganda, John V. Taylor wrote that "missionaries preached from within the culture of the nineteenth-century Evangelical Protestantism—or nineteenth-century Roman Catholicism—while the Baganda heard from within the culture of the traditional African world view" (1958:253).

Welbourn says of the founder of an African independent church, that Kivuli wanted a home, with rational structures and thought-forms within which he could conceptualize his Christian theology; yet he and his countrymen had been presented with an often irrelevant "prefabricated" theology, based upon the concerns and "rational structure" of another culture in which the people could not feel at home. For this reason thousands have split off from missions in quest of relevant theology.

Yet the culturally sympathetic missionary can assist in this worthy goal (as indeed an increasing number are) by taking seriously the insights and methodology of ethnolinguistics. The African, John Mbiti, in a recent volume, *New Testament Eschatology in an African Background* demonstrates the value of this approach for coming to grips with both the problem of extricating Africans from the maze of western theology and that of attempting to develop an African theology to feel at home in.

Mbiti focuses primarily on an analysis of the Akamba understanding of time and history, and the implications of this for their perception of the message already delivered,

and for the development of an Akamba African theology
based on ethnolinguistic data from which he examines "the
inner, more profound, question of what Christianity has meant
in this African situation" (23). In doing so he seeks:
   (a) to see the conceptual background of the Akamba;
   (b) to find what has been taught and received as the
       Christian Faith, and the methods employed in its
       propogation;
   (c) to assess the impact of such teaching upon the
       people's total understanding;
   (d) by bringing together both traditional concepts and
       the New Testament, to see what light is thrown by
       each on the other; and
   (e) to draw some theological implications of the whole
       picture (23).

Mbiti's method of presentation involves five steps: 1)
"Analysis of Akamba traditional concepts related to eschatology;" 2) a theological presentation of the New Testament
teaching on the subject under discussion; 3) the teaching of
"the main evangelizing agent among the Akamba"on the subject; 4) a discussion of "how Akamba Christians may have
understood (or misunderstood) the Christian teaching, and
with what results or consequences;" and 5) the drawing of
"conclusions and deductions, some of which are purely
theological while others tend in the direction of practical
issues of evangelization" (3-4). In this way he treats such
topics as "Time, History and Eschatology of the Sacraments,"
"The Nearness of the Spirit World" and "The Resurrection
as Corporate Eschatology." At each point he contrasts New
Testament, Akamba and missionary concepts in an
enlightening way.

Mbiti pleads for the right to develop an indigenous
theology, and demonstrates the need for it, recommending
ethnolinguistic methods in laying the foundations. Whether
or not he has succeeded in this, he has certainly proved
the need for an Akamba Christian theology, and pointed up
areas of investigation within the language and culture,
which will have to be probed in the development of such a
theology. An indigenous Christian theology will be affected
by both language and culture, but on the other hand "to
introduce eternal realities into African thought is to introduce something not only new but revolutionary" (Mbiti

1969: 182). However, it is all important just how this 'revolution' is brought about, for—

> The eschaton must invade the African world, not destroy or colonize, but to fulfil, to inject into its cosmology Christian realities. Africa has an Eschatology, but it has no teleology, and this is an area where Christian Eschatology can make a radical contribution to God's natural revelation in Africa. Eschatology without teleology is as empty as a house without furniture (181).

Mbiti also recommends as another end where change is needed "the sacraments of Baptism and the Eucharist (which) present themselves clearly as areas where temporal and eternal realities meet, and the media through which the temporal may catch glimpses of the eternal" (181). He goes on to suggest that Africa should discover the theology of the Sacraments "and apply it to the work of evangelization, for the ground is already prepared" (182).

Mbiti's own language and culture are beginning a kind of linguistic and cultural transformation, and the Gospel itself brings about. In the following section we shall look back on the process of conceptual transformation that Mbiti seeks, as it has occurred first in Greek, and then in Fijian.

Christianity and the Conceptual Transformation of Language: A Case Study from Greek and Fijian

Another area for ethnolinguistic consideration is that which takes place in the language of a people under culture contact. Such culture contact stimulates expansion, re-definition and replacement of vocabulary and conceptual categories of a language and maybe even modifications in the grammar.

English, for example, has had prolonged contact with French in a context where French has been regarded as the more prestigious. This culture contact with its prestige factor and the English predisposition to borrow has resulted in the large number of French words and even certain grammatical features in English. But borrowing is only one of the methods by means of which a society changes its linguistic habits. The processes of expansion and replacement of vocabulary through borrowing are well understood. What is not so well understood, but of greater importance to church planting is the process of linguistic transformation that occurs when words and concepts already present in the society are redefined, or otherwise expanded in scope, to accommodate the "new wine" of the innovative influences. Typically the forms of the words and concepts remain virtually the same, but the meanings attached to them, and the uses to which they are put, change in accordance with the requirements of the new concepts and situations introduced into the culture.

This process is another normal feature of linguistic change and adaptation. A language, like culture, adapts to changes in the reality with which it deals. Meanings change in denotation and connotation. The English word "manufacture" (meaning "made by hand") was "transformed," via the Industrial Revolution and mass production, into a symbol implying large scale, and semi-automated production of consumer goods. The term "turnpike," originally a turnstile-like device to obstruct the enemy in a narrow passage, came to mean a device at the entrance of a toll road in a non-war situation. When these roads gained more focus on tolls, the term "turnpike" came to signify the road, even when no toll was required. "Education" changed from "child-rearing" to "formal schooling" (Mead: 1943, rep. 1964: 164). Many other examples could be cited of conceptual transformations as a result of changes in culture.

Some of the most striking examples of linguistic transformation, however, have come from the introduction of Christianity into a culture. The Greek word *agapao* (and its derivatives), for example, was transformed from a word the "etymology (of which) is uncertain, and its meaning weak and variable," a word which lacked "the power or magic of *erao*" and "the warmth of *philein*" and often meant "no more than 'to be satisfied with something'" (Kittel, Vol. I, p. 36) into the distinctively Christian word for love which to Paul was "the only vital force which had a future in this aeon of death" (p. 51) and to John "the principle of the world of Christ which is being built up in the cosmic crisis of the present" (p. 52).

Likewise the translators of the Septuagint chose to transform the word *kurios* into the Greek equivalent of the Hebrew

Yahweh rather than to employ *despotes*, "which was also possible and perhaps more natural in terms of current usage" (Kittel, Vol. III, P. 1802). Kurios was not, apparently, at that time widely, if ever, employed with reference to God, or even to the Greek gods, meaning "Lord" merely with reference to one human being who held legal rights over another. Then when presumably under the influence of the Septuagint, the process of transformation had gotten underway, "it was in common use only in certain places where it corresponded to native, non-Greek usage" (p. 1051). In these areas, however (especially in Egypt), the word came to be "particularly used in expression of a personal relationship of a man to a deity, whether in prayer, thanksgiving or vow, and as a correlate of *doulos* (slave) inasmuch as the man concerned describes as *kurios* the god under whose orders he stands" (p. 1052). Thus the way was paved for the use of the term with reference both to God and Father and to Christ with the implication of "the personal, legitimate and all-embracing sovereignity of God" (p. 1088) clearly stamped upon it.

Thus likewise was a word like *ekklesia* transformed from meaning simply "the lawful citizenship rights" (Tippett, p. 12) customarily "summoned and called together by the herald" (Kittel, Vol. III, p. 513), into the distinctive designation for the Church of Christ both in its local sense (I Cor. 1:2) with regard to the Church Universal (I Cor 10:32), and later, with reference to "one of the household Churches (I Cor 16:19) which were springing up throughout the Graeco-Roman world" (Tippett, p.14). And the same type of transformation took place for term after term, concept after concept in Greek as a result of the birth and development of Christianity in a cultural setting where Greek was the language employed.

But Greek was far from the only language within which this kind of semantic and conceptual transformation has been stimulated by Christianity. The introduction of Christianity into culture after culture in our own day (not infrequently combined with massive westernization) has resulted in strikingly similar linguistic adaptation in hundreds of the languages of the world. Wherever, for example, a Christian preacher or Bible translator has chosen to employ an indigenous rather than a borrowed term for God, for forgiveness, for love, for faith or for any of the distinctive concepts of Christianity, the process of Christianity-stimulated linguistic transformation has begun.

Thus, at least for Christians of the Kaka and Bulu tribes of southern Cameroun, the perhaps ill-chosen term Ndjambie which referred to an impersonal, mythical cosmic spider is being invested with meaning-transforming denotations and connotations because of its adoption by the Christian Church as the designation of the Christian God (see Reyburn 1957). This term was chosen, according to Reyburn, because "there is no better native term...and a foreign word would be lacking entirely in the few equivalences which do not exist" (p. 192). Some translators in an attempt to avoid syncretism, according to E. A. Nida (1947), have elected to employ a borrowed term for God on the assumption "that the native people will automatically come to understand by the borrowed word . . . exactly what we understand by the same term." This approach, however, is not usually successful since "in almost every case the native will immediately try to equate this new name of God with one of the gods of his own religious system" and may end up with some sort of understanding like that of the Aztecs, who equate Dios with the sun and the Virgin Mary with the moon, and consider Jesus the offspring of the two. "Before the translator realizes it, instead of being able to fill an empty word with the proper meaning, he has a name which has already been given a content from the pagan religion" (p. 205).

Much better is the approach that recognizes that "in terms of the native culture the Greek word *theos,* the Latin *deus,* and the Gothic *guth* could hardly be termed exact equivalents to the concept of God as taught in the Bible." They were, however, generic terms rather than names of particular specific gods such as Zeus, Jupiter or Woden each of which was associated with "a great deal of legend as to the individual peculiarities, excesses, and immoral actions of the particular gods." The generic terms, however, which "designated any important supernatural entity" were taken by the Christians and "by context and teaching made (to) apply to only one such entity (p. 206). Nida recommends that this "transformational" approach be that employed in similar situations in today's languages, and lists a series of questions that translators should ask concerning the indigenous term(s) they may be considering to represent basic Christian concepts.

Tippett (1958:27-55) details a number of different aspects of what I am calling the process of linguistic transformation as a result of the penetration of Christianity into Fiji culture and language. This penetration, having started in 1835, is of long enough duration for us to safely assume that the observed changes are of permanent significance. Among the large number of words taken over by Fiji Christianity from the pre-Christian religion were words for sacrifice, prayer, worship, atonement and offerings. Though the major transformation seems to be the Christian usage of words, it is clear from the derivations that the elaboration of these concepts within Fijian Christianity has involved considerable transformation. Though, for example, the concept was transformed to apply to the bringing together of men and women alike in common gathering though, true to other patterns in the culture, to this day there is a segregation of the men and women within the gathering to their respective portions of the building.

A second type of transformation prominent in Fiji Christianity was the extension of the meanings of certain common words to expose Christian meanings. Among these are the verb "to pour out," formerly used of liquids only but within Christianity now applied also to the pouring out of the Holy Spirit, "a concept common in Fijian prayer to this day" (p. 35). An apparently greater degree of transformation has taken place in the extension of the word originally denoting the extinguishing of a fire first to "wipe out" then to "erase," (as of a blackboard) and eventually to cover the concept of forgiveness. This latter extension of meaning provided for Fijian Christianity the long-sought solution for an adequate translation of such passages as "forgive us our sins" in the Lord's Prayer which, until about 35 years ago had been rather unsatisfactorily rendered, "Do not be angry with us on account of our sins." Incidental, though important, changes in meaning have taken place in the words for "human flesh," once a highly prized food now reduced to a term of abuse and that which once meant "a desire to eat human flesh" but now means "a desire to eat fish."

In certain cases it was felt important to produce new

constructions to adequately represent the new concepts. These were of two types: word extensions (grammatical rather than semantic) and word combinations. Among the former is the word for missionary or minister which, though a term for priest was available, was wisely constructed from the Fiji verb "to send" resulting in a term parallel to the Greek *apostelo* meaning (literally) "the one sent forth with an important message" (p. 37). A similar type of construction has proven a worthy choice to translate the word "Gospel" since it both incorporates the "good news" concept and avoids the possibility of confusion with indigenous tales and oral traditions.

Among the conceptual transformations brought about through word combinations, the outstanding example, according to Tippett, is the combination of the terms for "bad" and "habits" or "customs" to represent "the idea of sin as active and continuing evil" (p. 38). The transformation of the term meaning "bad" as an adjective but "war" as a noun has proceeded so far that an expression that once meant "the land is at war" has now come to mean "the land is evil," since "Christianity has changed an era of internal wars into an era of peace, and the meanings no longer needed have dropped out of use" (p. 38). The ramifications of the semantic transformation have enabled the construction of combinations such as those meaning "hating one another," "to slander" and "to cause another to sin" (p. 39). Similar transformations are illustrated for word combinations involving the Fijian word meaning "true." And since "basic concepts like evil . . . and true or truth . . .change all aspects of daily life . . . a shift in meaning or depth or tone in one of these key root words will ramify throughout all private and social life. Truly then it may be said that the Church by giving new meaning to words like sin, truth, right, honor and many others, has charged a secular vocabulary with a spiritual quality" (p. 40).

There were, in addition, "words from the old way of life which were taken by the Church and deliberately changed for use in a new way" (p. 41). Among these were the term for God which, in spite of the fact that these people have been monotheistic for many years, must still occur preceded by specifiers such as "the" or "our" as symbols of the fact that the term once applied (without such modifiers) to the deities of Fijian pre-Christian polytheism. The term employed by Christians for "blessed" or "happy," further, is that once applied to the happiness believed to result from a form of snake god worship. Perhaps the most dramatic change of all, however, underlies the word presently employed for Christian singing which once designated the chants and dances performed before and after wars of revenge at the completion of which it was customary to torture, kill and prepare as food any prisoners taken.

As implied above, some of the conceptual transformations stimulated by Christianity required the introduction or production of completely new terminology. Some few of these terms were borrowed. Among such borrowings were names for unfamiliar fauna and flora, e. g., *sipi* (sheep), *ose* (horse), *sita* (cedar), names of foreign places and people and the names for certain of the completely new cultural elements introduced, e.g., *sakaremede* (sacraments), *papitaiso* (baptism), *same* (psalm), *tevoro* (devil) and *lotu* (church, Christianity—from Tonga). More frequently the label for the new concept was constructed from indigenous Fiji vocabulary items. In this way the Christians produced organizational terms such as minister (mentioned above), catechist, village teacher, lay church officer, preacher; terms labeling aspects of their religious experience such as an "inquiry concerning the way of life," "piety" (meaning literally "habitually at prayer") and the term with accompanying proverb labeling the Gospel as something so astonishing and exciting that "it had to be expounded far and wide, to be shared, to be communicated" (p. 46); and "the terminology of a new ethic" including expressions based on the word for spirit such as evil-spirited (i.e., angry), covetous, true-spirited (i.e., generous), cool-spirited (i.e., unenthusiastic), hot-spirited (i.e., enthusiastic), pity-spirited (i.e., merciful), long-spirited (taking a long time to act), little-spirited (discouraged). Another set of constructions can now also be made with the word for behavior (generally signifying the effect in behavior of the bent of the person's spirit) and the word for the mind (signifying basic attitudes).

Certain grammatical constructions have also come to be employed in new contexts because of Christianity. Among these is a "reciprocalizing prefix" the use of which has enabled the construction of terms meaning to be the same good disposition towards one another, "to love one another," "to know one another," "to hate one another," "to help one another," "praying for one another" (i.e., interceding), "being well-disposed toward each other" (i.e., peace) and "mutual help." Similarly a suffix or postposed word meaning "together" or "of the same kind" enabled constructions meaning of the same spirit, of the same mind, or the same behavior, or, when employed with verbs, pray together, weep together or sing together. "By means of such constructions Christianity was able to develop a sense of Christian relationship and also fortify her demands for the corporateness of the Church, and for this reason that number of combinations was greatly increased and the language enriched" (p. 52).

In summary, Tippett lists nine important aspects of the contribution of the coming of Christianity to semantic transformation of the Fiji language. And the fact that this type of thing has happened and should happen again in multitudes of other languages makes this summary and the following conclusions highly relevant to Church planters around the world. These points are:

1. The Church took over the linguistic forms of the native people and found her doctrine and ethic expressible in the constructions and thought-forms of the people, and there followed great semantic development within the indigenous heart of the language.

2. Foreign borrowings were restricted deliberately.

3. Many words from the pre-Christian liturgies and sacrificial ritual were preserved because they contained basic elements of worship, not confined to one religion; but these were charged with new meaning as the indigenous theology was developed in the light of scripture translation and Christian experience. Many new combinations were developed.

4. In some cases these words were re-interpreted in the light of the new religion, but in others they were given completely new meaning.

5. Some significant choices had to be made between old words for use in the new. The choice between the word meaning "priest" and the construction

message "the one sent forth with an important message" as the designation for minister or missionary, for instance, is seen to involve the nature of
the Church ministy—was it to be priestly or apostolic. The semantic study shows the Fijian Church
captured the true apostolic concept, and this had
social implications.

6. The Church widened the Fijian lexicography by means
   of word-combination, and thereby assisted the development of an indigenous ethic and theology. The
   doctrinal potential of the language was discovered
   and exploited.

7. Both morphological devices and endemic thought
   forms were used for the development of this potential, and words were found for concepts like incarnation and transfiguration, but are nevertheless
   conditioned by the scripture narrative. There is
   real semantic development here.

8. The Church is found to have developed her own original and unique terminology in three respects—
   a. arising from her constitution and organiza-
      tional power.
   b. growing from her ever-widening religious
      experiences.
   c. arising from the demand for a terminology
      of Christian ethics.

9. By the reduction of the spoken language to written
   form, the translation of the Scriptures, composition
   of hymns, preparation of a catechism and the writing
   and printing of other books the Church has standar-
   dized the language, and expanded its vocabulary so
   that it is quite adequate for the Christian experience
   of its members. Secular vocabulary has been charged
   with spiritual significance and the moral quality of
   many acts is indicated by the word root and morpho-
   logy much more obviously than in English (pp. 53-55).

In conclusion Tippett points to the similarity between the
processes of ethnolinguistic change and development (what
I have labeled linguistic "transformation") in Fiji and those
we can trace in New Testament Greek. He refers to these
processes as "a continuity of the forces and factors that
operated in the Apostolic Church" (p. 57) and suggests that

we have here a method of God's work with man. So
much there is to glorify Him, which lies dormant in
life, awaiting the right mind to discover it and give it
to mankind. Nothing brings home this truth better than
the study of biblical and ecclesiastical ethnolinguistics. . . (pp. 56-57).

He goes on to suggest that in these modern continuations
of the Book of Acts (i.e., the young Churches) we are able
to observe and participate in something truly exciting and
truly different from the experience of our "home" churches,
for these churches

are still in the testing period, they have not yet fully
developed their theological and ethical potential, there
are spiritual and linguistic resources they have yet
to discover and exploit, there are experiments of faith
going on that have yet to be consolidated and interpreted,
and there are experiences being worked out which will
ultimately be reflected in new terminology. In the Young
Churches (I speak generally, not of Fiji in particular)
we are today able to observe the apostolic mission in
action, and the Faith that is being forged today in one
place in the face of Communism, and in another in the
face of Caesar-worship and Roman persecution, because it is both experiential and apostolic. The home
Church is fortunate in being able to observe these movements in our time, and might well question herself
about the nature of her theology (is it mere accumulated
tradition, or growing from a vital experience?) and
whether or not we have a clear concept of her apostolic
mission, and again whether or not her ministry is a
commission or a career. She may not be able to answer herself satisfactorily, but the questions should be
asked and answered nevertheless. Again, looking forward, we should ask whether the old world of Western-
ism has a sufficiently apostolic religion to face and
explore and control the . . . atomic age?
The persecutions of Rome were overcome only in
an apostolic faith, and likewise the forces of Druidism,
and the same applies to the cannibalism and widow-
strangling and patricide of Fiji. It would seem that only
a church with apostolic faith and commission is likely
to survive Communism, and surely nothing less will
be required for the control of or survival in the atomic
era.
History reveals how churches have developed and
been sorely tested. Some have survived and some have
been exterminated. Their experiences have been reflected in the literary records they have left, not merely

narrative but in the very words they have selected to use. Historic periods of spiritual growth have always been likewise periods of semantic growth. We see this in the words of Jesus, of Paul, of Augustine, of Coverdale, and Tyndale, of Luther and Calvin, of Wesley, and of Hunt and Hazelwood in Fiji. Furthermore, periods of real religious strength growing in experience are reflected in semantic growth in the indigenous vocabulary, by the discovery and development of terminology with strong apostolic affinities (pp. 57-59).

Conclusion

We have surveyed but a very few of the areas in which the perspectives of Ethnolinguistics can make solid contributions to various aspects of the planting and growth of the Christian Church throughout the world. If missionaries and others engaged in the cross-cultural communication of the Gospel approached their tasks naturally on the basis of these understandings, there would be no need for a study such as Ethnolinguistics to be a part of the training of Church planters. The fact is, however, that it is precisely at the points where ethnolinguistic study can be of assistance that much of the insensitivity and misunderstanding that have unfortunately, characterized a number of missionaries have occurred.

If, for example, prospective church planters instructively understood the depths of culturally-defined perceptual differences, there would be no need to labor the point. Or if there were no (or even few) people of mission lands who had misperceived the message of Christianity to be advocating mere cultural substitution, it would not be necessary to point to examples like that of my misled Liberian friend— an example that we all would rather not believe is common— as if his misperception were widespread (which unfortunately it is). Nor is it pleasant to allude to the fact that the lack of ethnolinguistic understanding had often resulted in Scripture translations and approached to theology that compound rather than clarify cross-cultural misperception. It is however pleasant to end this paper with a case study demonstrating the constructiveness of an approach that apparently applied ethnolinguistically informed insight to the solution of the problems raised earlier in this paper.

Both the negative and the positive illustrations, however, speak eloquently to the extremely high importance for missionaries (whose ultimate aim is the planting of rapidly-growing churches which are thoroughly indigenous) to be trained in the insights and methodology of the cross-discipline of Ethnolinguistics. This would permit them to 1) better translate or assist in effective translation of the Scriptures, 2) more intelligently and sympathetically assist and encourage the development of indigenous approaches to theology and 4) through all of this function as catalysts in the process of linguistic and cultural transformation through the "inculturating" of supracultural Christianity deeply into the conceptual heart of culture after culture around the world.

BIBLIOGRAPHY:

Berlin, Brent and Paul Kay
    1969   BASIC COLOR TERMS: THEIR UNIVERSALITY AND
             EVOLUTION, Berkeley, University of California.
Bidney, David
    1967   THEORETICAL ANTHROPOLOGY, 2nd edition, New
             York, Schocken Books.
Burling, Robbins
    1970   MAN'S MANY VOICES, New York, Holt, Rinehart
             and Winston.
Davis, Linnell
    1968   THE USE OF THE BIBLE IN THE KAMBA
             TRIBAL SETTING, Unpublished thesis, Fuller Theo-
             logical Seminary, Pasadena, California
Henle, Paul (editor)
    1958   LANGUAGE, THOUGHT AND CULTURE, Ann Arbor:
             University of Michigan Press, (references to paper-
             back edition, 1965)
Hoijer, Harry (editor)
    1954   LANGUAGE IN CULTURE, Chicago: University of
             Chicago Press
Kittel, G. (editor)
    1964-65 THEOLOGICAL DICTIONARY OF THE NEW
             TESTAMENT, translated by G. W. Bromiley, Vol. I,
             1964, Vol. III, 1965. Grand Rapids, Eerdmans.
Mbiti, John
    1969   "Eschatology" in Dickson, K. A. and P. Ellingworth
             (eds.) BIBLICAL REVELATION AND AFRICAN
             BELIEFS, London, Lutterworth, pp. 159-84
    1971   NEW TESTAMENT ESCHATOLOGY IN AN AFRI-
             CAN BACKGROUND, London, Oxford.

Mead, Margaret
    1943   "Our Educational Emphases in Primitive Perspective"
            AMERICAN JOURNAL OF SOCIOLOGY, 48:633-9,
            reprinted in Margaret Mead 1964, ANTHROPOLOGY
            A HUMAN   SCIENCE, New York, Van Nostrand
Nida, E. A.
    1945   "Linguistics and Ethnology in Translation Problems,"
            WORD, 1:194-208
    1947   BIBLE TRANSLATING, New York, American Bible
            Society
    1960   MESSAGE AND MISSION, New York, Harper.
Nida, E. A. and C. Taber
    1969   THE THEORY AND PRACTICE OF TRANSLATION,
            Leiden, Brill .
Reyburn, W. D.
    1957   "The Transformation of God and the Conversion of
            Man," PRACTICAL ANTHROPOLOGY, 4: 185-94
Sapir, Edward
    1929   "The Status of Linguistics as a Science," LANGUAGE,
            5: 207-14
    1931   "Conceptual Categories of Primitive Languages,"
            SCIENCE,   74: 578
Taylor, J. V.
    1958   THE GROWTH OF THE CHURCH IN BUGANDA,
            London, S C M
Tippett, A. R.
    1958   THE INTEGRATING GOSPEL, Unpublished manu-
            script, Methodist Theological Institution, Davui Levu.
Welbourn, F. B. and B. A. Ogot
    1966   A PLACE TO FEEL AT HOME, London, Oxford
Whorf, B. L.
    1940   "Science and Linguistics," TECHNOLOGICAL RE-
            VIEW, 42: 229-41, 247-8, reprinted in Carroll 1956,
            pp. 207-19
    1941   "The Relation of Habitual Thought and Behavior to
            Language" in L. Spier, A. I. Hallowell and S. S. New-
            man, LANGUAGE, CULTURE AND PERSONALITY,
            pp. 75-93, reprinted in Carroll 1956, pp. 134-59

Part IV

God in Human History

GOD IN HUMAN HISTORY

When Donald McGavran was still little known outside of India and he was about to publish *The Bridges of God,* it was the historian Kenneth Scott Latourette, who saw the potential of the church growth viewpoint, not only as a means of coming to grips with the new age of mission, but of interpreting those periods of history when the Church had bounded ahead in people movements. He described *The Bridges of God* as "a breath of air."

Three principles stand out in McGavran's view of history. First, human history provides the stage on which the divine drama has been and is being enacted. Second, the written records of history, including reports, journals and statistics, contain the source material for the reconstruction of how and why Churches did or did not grow. Third, the church growth case studies being produced by his graduates (and including several essays in other parts of this book) are, to use his own words "a new genre of writing church history."

The Bridges of God starts with the action of God in New Testament history—the group movements of the Early Church (1955: 17-35), which were activated by the Holy Spirit (p. 18). Then he follows through the sweep of the centuries, speaking of the subsequent movements as "God-given" (p. 68).

His historical methodology for church growth case studies is found in *Understanding Church Growth,* pages 131-140 in particular. For this section of this *Festschrift* two men were asked to deal with the writing of history. Dr. Kessler has been a guest lecturer at the School of World Mission and is the author of a carefully documented Mission-Church study on Peru and Chile. He tells of how he goes about writing a history of an emerging Church, of how to fix on major issues in the history, of note-taking, library research, drafting and polishing the final manuscript. He writes within the missiological frame of reference—giving the people the Gospel, helping the development of the national Church, and finally giving them the stimulus "to reflect on their own development."

By way of comparison this should be put beside Dr. Kwast's essay. Their experiences in documentation have been quite different—we might call them the historical and the ethnohistorical. Kwast explores the use of both historical and anthropological methods for the collection and appraisal of historical documents in church growth research. This is a valuable statement, in which he exposes both the satisfactions and the problems of using various kinds of primary sources, both from missionary and vernacular origins. Here and there he lays down important criteria for evaluating material. His locus is West Cameroon in the last century.

Another contributor is Dr. Edwin Orr, well-known writer on the subject of the history of Revivals. He asked to write an historical study bearing on some aspect of missiological theory. We decided on the relationship of evangelism and social action. The essay serves to illustrate how theory cannot stand alone. It is subject to historical validation. This study presents a long stream of cases in which evangelical movements were followed by "fruits worthy of repentance" in the form of reform and social action. Orr preserves the distinction made by McGavran that the Holy Spirit worked through both evangelism and social action, but that the latter should not stand alone as a substitute for the former. McGavran's many statements about this are due not to an imbalance so much as to concern for the manifest facts of Christian practice, that much so-called mission is in reality social action isolation—a masquerade or a substitute.

Dr. Winter, whose provocative approach to history has introduced a new vitality into this discipline at SWM-ICG, grapples with the need for cross-cultural perspective in Christian history. In the process he reminds us of such problems as "cultural pluralism" and "culture change," which are very much with us still, although they have not always been allowed for adequately by church historians. He calls for a re-formulation of our philosophy of history, which is in step with the changes taking place in missiology at large.

So long as mankind is divided by separate languages, "One Church" can be a reality in a special sense only . . . the "One Church"—is in fact a fellowship of Churches each growing in its homogeneous unit . . . Each homogeneous unit flourishes under its own leaders . . . Each piece of the mosaic develops a Church which grows at its own rate, has its own problems, and flourishes best under its own leaders and with its own organization.

CHURCH GROWTH AND CHRISTIAN MISSION,
pp. 76, 77, 78.

17

CHRISTIAN HISTORY IN
CROSS-CULTURAL PERSPECTIVE

Ralph D. Winter

A great deal of Donald A. McGavran's insight can be traced to the unique advantage he had of growing up in India. There before his eyes were not only the expectable ethnic-linguistic divisions of the sub-continent (whereby every given geographical area has its own regional culture) but he early encountered the world's most rigidly stratified system of social classes. The very fact that India's castes long constituted a highly visible quasi-official structure meant that his perspective as he traveled in other parts of the world remained highly sensitized to social barriers (arising from other than racial and linguistic differences) even in places where no overt social categorization existed. This is why on occasions he has been accused of reading into a situation social differences that did not exist. It may be that in some such cases he has merely pointed out differences people wished to hide or ignore. As a matter of fact, many nations too long have looked down on India's overt social prejudice without recognizing their own covert castes.

In any case, one of the durable common denominators among those associated with McGavran in the amorphous church growth school of thought is their own parallel sensitivity to the central importance of the profound cultural diversity within the community of mankind. This sensitivity is the basis of what may be called here cross-cultural perspective, a perspective which undoubtedly informs and pervades all of the chapters in this book. Cross-cultural perspective goes to the very heart of Christian theology and historiography as these disciplines have developed across the centuries, since it sheds new light on the problem of unity versus uniformity as we see it in a historic dimension.

Examples of the Problem

Not so long ago representatives of the Lutheran World Federation went to great lengths to persuade the Batak Christians of Northern Sumatra to subscribe to the Non-Altered Augsburg Confession.

One millenium earlier, on another mission frontier in the middle of another island (not nearly as large as Sumatra) a small group of men earnestly tried to persuade a Celtic Christian leader that he ought to subscribe to the Roman way of acting out the Christian faith.

In these two cases the advocates of uniformity were only partially successful, since the group being persuaded retained a good deal of autonomy and naturally preferred their own way of doing things. In both cases the advocates were not readily able to distinguish between the universal and the particular elements in their own faith. In both cases the Christian faith had grown up and become quite well established without any insistence upon the forms which were later presented so persuasively.

Historically speaking, however, more often as in the Reformation, advocates of a foreign formulation of Christianity are at first successful and do not until much later face the insurgent nationalism of the surviving cultural tradition which eventually demands its own indigenous Christian formulation.

In the Philippines, for example, the Roman tradition swept in along with a colonial power, and while a great amount of painstaking and quite enlightened mission work was conducted throughout the whole of the Philippines, there eventually came a time when an immense sector of the Philippine church under Bishop Aglipay declared its independence from Rome in much the way that Luther had. Ironically, the American seizure of the Philippines almost smashed the movement as the new colonial masters forced all properties to be returned to Rome. Even so, the Philippine Independent Church endures to this day as the largest non-Roman church in the country.

These are only a few of dozens of examples which demonstrate one of the most unique and surprising things about Christianity—that it is by nature a faith that both welcomes and encourages cultural pluralism. In this sense, if it must be called a religion at all, Christianity is the only world religion of this kind. This little understood fact is clearly perceived only by means of what is also rare: cross-cultural perspective. First, let us discuss what cross-cultural perspective is, and then proceed to indicate some of the bright new hues which Christian history takes on when viewed from this angle.

A Biblical-Historical Analysis
of Cross-Cultural Perspective

Cross-cultural perspective is not a new skill required of us by the sudden smallness of the modern world. You might say that God has always had cross-cultural perspective since He was the One who was pleased to create the diverse *ta ethne*—the various tribes and tongues and families of mankind. But fallen man has never clearly seen things from God's point of view. It is almost a truism that the languages of man, apart from those affected by Christian insight, rarely if ever possess words for mankind in the generic sense. Typically, languages divide the world into *us* and *them*. We are the humans and those others are the non-humans. We are the Jews and they are the Gentiles. Even the most primitive tribes employ this semantic distinction.

Yet man has not always been content with this kind of implicit blasphemy. We recall how exercised Alexander the Great was over the diversity of his new far-flung domain. He launched one of history's most novel experiments when he married off 10,000 of his own soldiers with Middle

Eastern maidens. The Romans allowed a great diversity in their empire for practical reasons, but they never solved the problem of diversity on a theoretical level and never surmounted the ethnocentrism of their hierarchical political structure. It is not suprising that the Roman mentality, perhaps bolstered by the earlier Alexandrian idealism, encouraged the development of a culturally monolithic Christianity. There have been great arguments about where the center of Christendom should be located—Rome, Constantinople, Rheims, Canterbury—but the assumption is always that there had to be some one specific place as a center. This in turn implied cultural uniformity.

One of the most striking uniquenesses about the Bible is that it both recognizes the endemic xenophobia of Jew against Greek and nation against nation, but it goes on to propose a breath-taking solution. It says in effect that God can not only speak Hebrew, but Greek; that is, God was not only able to reveal Himself among and to the Hebrews in their language and culture, but the essential revelation was just as capable of being clothed in the words and cultural forms of the pagan Greeks.

Literally hundreds of parallels can be traced between almost everything that is said or done in the early Christian tradition and what is found in the environment of the ancient world. In its theological terminology, for example, Christology became a strong rope of three weak strands. One strand derived from the Hebrew apocalyptic concept of a *Messiah*. Another was the term for *Lord* *(kurios),* which had long been employed by the mystery cults of Eastern origin and also in the Roman emperor worship. The third prominent strand was the Greek philosophical concept of the *Word (logos)*. Each one of these key words in the Bible is thus paralleled by an identically pronounced word in the non-Christian environment. These parallels between the Bible and the ancient world have been disputed by some who feel it desperately important to maintain that early Christianity in all its forms was entirely unique. But those who would attempt to chip away at specific parallels between Christian and pagan forms are not only fighting a losing battle, but—in terms of cross-cultural perspective—are also fighting the wrong battle.

For one thing, we must not suppose that the message of

Christianity, clothed in the new garments of the Greek world,
was damaged by this new clothing. This supposition is the
consistent and understandable but erroneous assumption of
the Jews (even many Christian Jews) in ancient times and
still today. Some Christian scholars have stumbled on the
cultural differences and classified Paul's gospel a new religion rather than the essential Jewish revelation in Greek
clothing.

Cross-cultural perspective does not in itself prove that
there was distortion; it does not insist on the real possibility
of distortionless cross-cultural communication. With this
perspective, then, we are not startled that so many pagan
words or forms were employed, or that it seems really possible for the Christian message in its essential integrity to
be faithfully transmitted. Even those who are most eager to
detect the employment of new forms must admit that the new
forms are generally given a new twist and a modified meaning. Where no modification has taken place, the unmodified
meaning of the adopted forms is not necessarily something
which is in conflict with Christian truth.

Secondly, we are not suggesting that there is something
so magical about the Christian message that post-biblical
attempts to clothe it in new words and forms have always
been successful. This is very important to say. The fact
that "reclothing" can be accomplished, that it has been
done, that it must be done, does in no way imply that the task
is easy, or that it involves no dangers, nor does this mean
that beyond the Bible there have never been any mistakes
in the process. As a matter of fact, there are likely always
mistakes in the process, mistakes which only centuries will
even partially rectify. This fact is the reason why the
various national churches of the world today are dependent
upon each other: they all are involved in some misunder-
standings—but not the same ones, and in symbiotic fellowship together their inadequacies tend to cancel each other out.

Furthermore, there seems to be neither a simple nor an
infallible way of determining whether a given utilization of
a pagan form has been proper or entirely successful. Here
we see the open endedness of the continuing need to evangelize and to re-express the faith. The adoration of the Virgin
as a case in point, which first gained momentum where the
cult of the virgin Diana was already prominent, may not have

been as helpful an employment of pre-existing ritual and be-lief as the comparatively harmless adoption of December 25th as the birthday of a Son in place of a celebration for the sun. Yet however safely removed Christmas now is from any original pagan connotations, it must be noted that we are still obligated to a constant and unrelenting attempt to obtain or maintain an authentically Christian meaning for the celebration. The Christian celebration of Christmas December 25th is probably neither harmed nor hindered by the fact that it was once another sort of festival. Even if it were once a totally new creation by Christians, its continu-ing Christian contribution would not thereby be guaranteed whatsoever by a supposedly "pure" origin.

In other words, suppose that 2,000 years ago the entire language and culture of the early Christians had been cut out of new cloth such that there were no possibility of tracing any word or form to any pre-existing language or culture. Today, two thousand years later, would we have a purer or safer form of God's revelation (truth) in our hands? Would such a faith be more durable? Would it necessarily be closer to the message which God is speaking to mankind? Would not even these brand new forms and words be susceptible to the loss of their Christian meaning? The answer must be yes. Therefore, we come full circle to the observation that pagan forms can as easily gain new Christian meaning as newly minted "Christian" forms could lose their originally pure meaning. It would appear that God is not in the business of replacing cultures but transforming them.

We discover something else by means of cross-cultural perspective: the Bible is providentially multicultured in-ternally. Suppose God had allowed a written revelation to be encapsulated in a single culture, whether Hebrew or Greek, would not that kind of monocultural revelation have been, 1) much more seriously subject to a mere mechanical external transmission, 2) less successfully interpreted as a universal faith, and indeed, 3) would not its internal meaning have been less reliably understandable than it is in the case of a Bible such as we have, which precisely portrays truth in cultural transition? It is not always possible to be sure of the reasons God has had in what He has done, but it is tantamount to a linguistic theorem that

if the same truth is propounded by two different men in two
different languages and cultures, as totally dissimilar say,
as Hebrew and Greek, that the result will inevitably be
more reliably interpretable 2,000 years later.

Anthropologically sophisticated missionaries today are
applauded in their straightforward attempts to allow people
to be culturally authentic in their expression of their Christian faith. Is it not then curious that we could be disturbed
to discover that a similar openness to various cultural forms
existed in the ancient world as the Christian movement took
upon itself Greek, Roman, and Celtic garments? Why is it
a good procedure for a careful missionary linguist today
to select key words from a primitive vocabulary in order
to express Christian faith, but it is not so easy to conceive of the New Testament epistles being written as
the result of such a process? Just because we believe this
process in the New Testament was carried on under unique
inspiration does not mean we are not to see it as an example
to us. Indeed, it is our conviction regarding its inspiration
that makes it so valuable an example!

Quite logically then, we may look on the experiences of the
early church as a divinely preserved, full-blown case study
of the missionary adaptation of the Christian message to
Greek linguistic and cultural forms. We misunderstand God's
intuition if we suppose that the precise words chosen in that
particular feat of communication were somehow better (in
their unmodified pagan usage) than other words that may be
chosen in a parallel way in other cultures. The inspiration
of the Bible thus does not lie in contemporary secular
meaning of the key words employed, but in the unique use
the Bible makes of those otherwise quite ordinary words.
Least of all must we feel that the procedure of dipping into
pagan vocabularies was illicit. We must confidently expect
that such borrowing was done, and for the same reason we
must confidently continue to recommunicate and to retool
contemporary words and forms as we meet new cultures
in other places around the world today. We must do the
same as we face new developments in our own culture
with the change of generations. The great value of the
Bible is therefore not merely that it constitutes the one
inspired case of truth transmitted cross-culturally. It is
of special strategic and missionary value as it stands as

an inspired example, not only of the gospel in two different cultures, but as an inspired example of the process whereby a cross-cultural bridge of communication may be built between two cultures.

Every book written on the subject of the New Testament —indeed every student of the New Testament—is forced to observe the clash of cultures in the period of the early church. Some expositors have tried to make Paul out to be the originator of a "new religion," by treating the changes as evidence of heresy. Others have treated the changes as the result of a new dispensation in which God himself takes a new approach in certain things. Some may agree that new forms were employed while effective communication of the same basic message took place. In the latter case, however, their discussions often focus more attention on the new formulations than they do on the nature (and limits) of the process whereby those formulations were achieved. That is, their emphasis does not seem to anticipate the necessity later on in the mission history of similar cross-cultural reformulations to take place, and therefore they deprive themselves of the great value of the Bible in casting light on those later reformulations.

Indeed our whole attitude subtly and profoundly changes toward what happened within the pages of the New Testament once we sense the essential repeatability—and the necessity for repetition—of the process whereby Paul bridged over to the Greek culture. In a parallel way Luther demanded that there be a bridge to the Germanic culture area, and helped to build that bridge. Just as Paul defended the Greek Christians against Roman formulations which, in effect, became legalistic in the Hellenistic situation, so Luther stoutly defended the Germans against the imperialism of a Roman formulation. Bultmann and Fletcher, in their demythologizing and "situation ethics" have groped ineffectively, but with the same problem, trying to achieve aspects of a new formulation for our generation. With greater clarity of purpose, I feel, Leslie Dewart has noted the distance the modern world has drifted away from Greek thought and has called for a massive "dehellenization" of the present-day Roman tradition, and so on. In a significant development, American scholars in the colonial period thrust away the tradition of studying the pagan classics in college and embraced Hebrew as the divine language, which they expected to be spoken in heaven; college presidents delivered commencement addresses in Hebrew. Specifically, this latter was a case of attempted restoration rather than reformulation. But in the process of rejecting Hellenistic molds, some real Americanization did take place under the guise of Hebraicization. Thus the process of cultural reformulation has gone on again and again down through history but has not always been clearly recognized as a necessary or wholesome process.

A Cross-Cultural Analysis of Christian History

Thus the early moments of the Christian movement exposit and sanction a cross-cultural perspective in which the diversity of cultural forms is not seen as an obstacle to the expansion of the faith or even a nuisance. We do well, therefore, not to consider human diversity a part of the problem of the Christian mission, but an essential feature in an exciting solution. This solution is for all mankind the wholesome fullness of God's redemption which ideally reaches man in all his diversity (without condemning the diversity itself), resolving the profound alienation between man and God which is the source of all man's sufferings and evil. The outward sweep of the Christian movement is therefore the story of a long succession of encounters between a universal faith and many particular contexts.

Rather than to try to condense or even list all such encounters in Christian history, in which the Christian mission has endeavored to cross cultural bridges, it may be well to explore the varied experiences of a single ethnic group outside of the Mediterranean world, one concerning which we have at least some continuous evidence.

While no one example is ideal, it should not be surprising that we would choose a society beyond the furthest reaches of the Roman legions, living in island isolation as well. Such might be the minimal conditions that would provide a laboratory of investigation concerning the possibility of local diversity being compatible with a universal faith. It has been said that:

> ... Ireland was the only head-taking, cattle-raiding culture to be converted to Christianity while retaining its tribal economic and social structure...(Scott, 1967:193).

This of course is a reference to the period of the early expansion of Christianity. There are many such societies which in the nineteenth and twentieth centuries have undergone similar experiences. Indeed, the relevance of this ancient example to modern times provides part of the impetus of our discussion.

The literature—the primary documentation alone—highlighting the whole Irish experience is voluminous. A brief treatment can only sketch the basic outlines of the encounter of this people with Christianity. It may also be noted that comparatively recently the subject itself has undergone the kind of objective scholarly study it has long merited. Anglo-Saxon scholarship, for reasons which may appear more clearly below, has to be superceded in these studies by French, German and Norwegian scholarship, the whole "Irish question" seemingly having postponed objective English investigation of the subject. Speaking of this tendency, Charles Thomas (1965:259) explains that—

> Nearly all general accounts of the period tend to be unevenly biased in favour of the Germanic-speaking invaders... The reasons for this are complex, but the main one is probably that, until the present century, almost no major historian of the period had any knowledge of, or indeed interest in, the story of the Celtic-speaking peoples of early Britain.

Indeed, with the renewed outbreak of hostilities in the north, feelings on the Emerald Island are running so high that it is not possible even now to speak of events that happened fifteen centuries ago without being enmeshed in arguments that have emotional overtones. Nevertheless, it is the worldwide experience of the emerging new nations that had brought into being so many parallels that many ancient questions long considered closed may be resurrected with new impetus and insight. Ours is pre-eminently the age in which the minority voice is going to be heard.

At this point, however, cross-cultural perspective may likely be considered a bias in favor of the Irish tradition. This may as well be confessed. We will certainly get nowhere if we do not recognize mechanisms of prejudice of one kind or another. In one sense cross-cultural perspective precisely consists of the ability to anticipate, to recognize and to tolerate prejudice between disparate cultures. The

Irish situation is rich with examples of prejudice.

Jerome may or may not have been reporting accurately when he recalled an encampment of Irish cannibals from his experience in Gaul (D'Alton, 1913: 36), nor can we credit him with objective charity when he referred to the famous Celtic scholar Pelagius as an "Irish dog." What is apparently incontrovertible is that some of the Irish became Christians at a fairly early date and that they were for a long time, mainly for geographic reasons, beyond the power of emperor or pope. These were the conditions that either fostered, or at least allowed, considerable indigeneity in their resulting Christianity. Harold Cook (1971: 46) quotes O'Donovan with approval, saying—

> Patrick engrafted Christianity on the pagan supersti-
> tions with so much skill that he won the people over to
> the Christian religion before they understood the exact
> difference between the two systems of belief and much
> of this half-pagan, half-Christian religion will be found
> not only in the Irish stories of the Middle Ages, but in
> the superstitions of the peasantry of the present day.

Cook goes on to summarize—

> This is what we should naturally expect. The remark-
> able thing is that this syncretistic tendency did not go
> further and pervert the basic Christian message.
> Perhaps it was the emphasis on the scriptures that
> provided the safeguard. It is certainly notable that in
> the last century after Patrick Ireland becomes a major
> center of Christian learning, even attracting students
> from the Continent. Moreover, it is beginning to send
> its own missionaries far and wide, even as far as Italy
> itself.

In the attempt to understand early insular Celtic Christianity and specifically Irish Christianity, our chief problem
is that the preservation of their story was, for one reason
or another, constantly left in the hands of non-Irish groups.

Pelagius is a case in point. What we know of his teachings remains today primarily in the writings of his opponents against words of his disciples. Looking back we
can recognize possible discrepancies in differing cultural
connotations of the same Latin words, with the result that
those of different backgrounds employed different explanations (theological formulations). If grace had a sinister

meaning for Pelagius (as for example in the Theodosian Code) implying favoritism (Hughes, 1966:20,21) we can almost assume the need for honest divergence between Celtic and Roman theologians.

Less significant theologically, perhaps, are the divergences between the Insular Celts and the Western tradition in the matter of tonsure and Easter date. In this case, the offending diversity was not homemade, but came simply from the opposite end of the Mediterranean. Yet beneath these two tangible symbols of independence from Western Roman customs was the much more important discrepancy that was probably based somehow on Irish tribal structure: the Celtic form of monasticism. This too derived from the east, but if it had not had some kind of resonance with indigenous social structure it may not have been so durably opposed to the implantation of the Roman diocesan system of territorial bishops.

Unlike those classical instances of Roman religion being planted by force in Saxony and in eastern Europe, in Ireland, Rome's physical power was all along totally inadequate to enforce any kind of uniformity. Bede's ostensibly pro-Roman account paints Augustine's mission to England in bold strokes, but clearly records that the only force available to his mission (as he tried to win over the Celtic Christians) was what could be called threats about the afterlife coupled with the assumed prestige of the see of Peter (as against John the Beloved on whose word the Celts relied).

Meanwhile Rome was handicapped profoundly by the centuries of confusion induced by the Barbarian invasions and subsequent see-sawing between Gothic and Eastern Roman military power. Irish scholars, for whom Latin was never a native tongue, were needed to teach Latin in the city of Rome. (This would be like black African Christians coming to the United States to teach English in the year 2030, following one-half century of Chinese occupation of North America). For similar reasons, it was Irish scholarship that allowed both Roman pagan and Christian scholarly traditions to be reinstated on the Continent—with the help (of course) of Anglo-Saxon scholars whose own scholarly formation, if not always their actual training, derived from Celtic centers of learning in Ireland or England.

Eventually the Danish invasions became a violent force inflicted against the Irish Christian tradition, but not a force conforming them to Roman Christianity except in the sense that their scholars fled to the Continent, taking with them manuscripts and learning in even greater abundance than had the steady stream of Irish missionaries. This exodus greatly enhanced the curious development whereby the Irish system of private confession became the "Roman" confessional, the Irish collar the "Roman" collar, and the Irish miniscule the "Carolingian" miniscule. Even Irish manuscript illumination became known for a time as "Anglo-Saxon" (Zimmer, 1891:16). In many other ways Irish Christian virility first saved the Roman tradition and then itself became labeled "Roman." If the Irish were generalized as savage in the fourth and fifth centuries, and as saints in the sixth, seventh, and eighth centuries, with the destruction wrought by the Vikings in the ninth and tenth centuries the shattered remains of Irish Christianity became looked upon as a much too rebellious deviation from the Roman tradition. This perhaps underlay the reasoning behind the pope's "gift" of Ireland to the Norman conquerors in 1164, which for the first time sent what could be called Roman force across the Irish sea. As a result, a drastically heightened antagonism between the Irish and the English (whether Anglo-Saxon or Norman) laid the basis for the final ironic twist at the time of the Reformation when the Irish, in order to maintain their distinctive identity from the "big brothers" on the larger island decided finally they would rather be Roman than Protestant.

The Irish people thus represent in a tragic and classical sense the plight of the people in a minority culture who at best can only choose between the dominant flavors of their environment, lying low as the major powers clash, choosing first one and now another of the foreign traditions, whichever seems best to favor their local free expression.

The tragedy is that the Christian tradition itself has not more clearly enunciated the principles inherent in cross-cultural perspective. The Irish, from early times, have never been a tightly knit society. The very existence of rival clans and tribes and perpetual feuding favored the development of a Christianity which was by no means perfectly uniform in Ireland itself. It was not the Irish who

were perplexed about achieving any kind of uniformity.
Pluralism would not have been hard for them to understand.
Kathleen Hughes (1966: 104) observes that—

> Celtic clerics seem to have been untroubled by the
> diversity of practice. Why should they be? The church
> had endured such problems for centuries, and the
> popes had made no clear official pronouncement. 'Let
> Gaul, I beg, contain us side by side, whom the kingdom
> of Heaven shall contain' writes Columbanus to the
> Gallican synod. To him, even in the midst of the Easter
> controversy, there were matters which seemed of far
> greater importance in the life of the church than
> liturgical diversity.

The greatest irony of all—looking now beyond the Irish
illustration to the experience of many other minorities
encountered by the advancing wave of Christianity—is the
fact that at about the time all of these questions seemed
resolved in the Western world, the whole profusion of
cultural diversity within the Christian church has burst
forth as the result of the missionary movement in the non-
Western world. The angriest problems in the world today
are not international imperialism but questions of conformity within national states—in a word, civil wars:
Korea, Vietnam, Nigeria, Sudan, and (here we are again)
Ireland. The question is how long the Amharas can dominate
the Gallas in Ethiopia, whether the Kikuyus shall forever
dominate the government in Kenya, whether a handful of
whites shall run the country in Rhodesia, etc. The reason
these problems are so nearly insoluble is the same: 700,000
Celtic people who speak Welsh do not feel that their potential
contribution to the larger world is ideally fulfilled in the
present political structure. There is not space to mention
the Basques, the Bretons, the Navajos, and other over-run
minorities still encapsulated in the Western world, whose
minority cultures are not treated with adequate cross-
cultural perspective by secular political powers.

The failure of secular rulers to view things with truly
Christian cross-cultural perspective is no excuse for
Christian strategists to ignore the heightened urgency of
the whole problem as the world Christian family struggles
to understand and accept both its unity and diversity.

The ecumenical movement will become a tyrannical

power if cross-cultural perspective does not prevent its projection of simplistic democracy as the only means for disparate Christian traditions to sit down in fellowship together. The Christian family is more complex than the small town in which a pure democracy has been made classical. Both union churches (single congregations) and united denominations can proceed with democratically correct procedures to trample on the minority culture. Homogeneous churches in one social stratum in India are not the most likely instruments of evangelism within other strata holding drastically different customs and traditions. Only monolithic concepts of unity can blind us to the healthy diversity God has intended among his people and his peoples.

There is no particular value in opening ancient wounds and re-arguing issues long thought to be settled. unless this holds promise for superior insight into the modern situation. Despite the recent outbreak of hostilities in Ireland and the continued existence of many unresolved problems of cultural diversity within the Christian tradition in the Western world today, it may still be possible that historical studies may be the only studies which offer any opportunity at all for the application of cross-cultural perspective at an objective distance. Who knows what specific tensions in overseas countries may be resolvable only if parallels can be intelligently drawn between them and conflicts long ago? It is at least with this hope that this chapter is offered.

BIBLIOGRAPHY:

Cook, Harold R.
    1971   "The Celtic Church of Ireland" from HISTORIC PAT-
             TERNS OF CHURCH GROWTH, Chicago, Moody
             Press
D'Alton, E. A.
    1913   HISTORY OF IRELAND, London, The Gresham
             Publishing Company
Hughes, Kathleen
    1966   THE CHURCH IN EARLY IRISH SOCIETY, London,
             Methuen & Co. Ltd.
Scott, William Henry
    1967   "Celtic Culture and the Conversion of Ireland," IN-
             TERNATIONAL REVIEW OF MISSION, Vol. LVI,
             no. 222
Thomas, Charles
    1966   "Celtic Britain and the Anglo-Saxons" in THE DAWN
             OF EUROPEAN CIVILIZATION, edited by David
             Talbot Rice, New York, McGraw-Hill Co.
Zimmer, H.
    1891   THE IRISH ELEMENT IN MEDIEVAL CULTURE,
             New York, G. P. Putnam's Sons

When churches multiply in a non-Christian population, they will bring God's purposes for His children to bear on the particular part of the social order which they can influence . . . The nation most of whose citizens become Christians will pass fair employment acts and fair housing laws—and enforce them. Not only will individual Christians take part in social action, but again and again whole congregations and denominations. . .

There should be no tension between mission and the advocates of social action. There is the most urgent need for both extension of the benefits of the Gospel . . . and . . . the application of Christian principles to all of life.

UNDERSTANDING CHURCH GROWTH
p. 258.

18

EVANGELICAL DYNAMIC
AND SOCIAL ACTION

J. Edwin Orr

The Good News of Jesus Christ was committed to the Apostles, but the dynamic was assigned to the Holy Spirit, the Lord of the harvest. The disciples were not left to their own devices in communicating the Gospel. The work of the Church began with the outpouring of the Holy Spirit of God at Pentecost, empowering the recruits for service.

There have been many such outpourings throughout the history of the Church, as at Herrnhut in which the Moravians were equipped for spectacular service. The effect of the outpourings of the Spirit is varied: to the company of believers it brings reviving; to those being discipled it brings awakening; to the communities of unindoctrinated people it brings a moving—the revival of the Church, the awakening of the community, and the instigation of folk movements: these are the work of the Spirit.

When the Church is thus revived, individual Christians are recruited for its ongoing work, that of preaching, of teaching and of social action. The Lord of the harvest has chosen to meet the needs of the awakened multitude or the unindoctrinated communities by evangelism, instruction in the faith, and by social ministry. The preaching and teaching constitute the Great Commission, to be engaged in always, to the ends of the earth and the end of the age. The concurrent ministry of the Church, commended but not commanded, is to follow the Divine example of service and promote the welfare of humanity in meeting their temporal needs, or, better still, in demonstrating to society how its needs may be regularly met. Christians initiated school systems at home and abroad, but they do not need for ever to bear the cost in time and treasure; to quote one of Britain's greatest social benefactors, Mrs. Tom Barnardo, with reference to a great social issue: "The State should do it, but does not: the Church of Christ must!" This truth has a corollary, that when the State satisfactorily deals with it, the obligation of the Church is largely fulfilled and its attention may be turned to other urgent forms of service.

Evangelism and Social Action

Donald McGavran has said that recognizing the efforts of a Wilberforce, a Kagawa, or a Martin Luther King as a "highly desirable Christian activity," provides no reason to confuse meaning and call their efforts evangelism. Such social action is important in its own right.

Any one of good will may join in ministering to the needs of humanity, and when Society accepts its obligations, the cause of God is advanced, for He cares for His creatures' material welfare as well as their spiritual need. No non-Christian, however, is able to fulfill the Great Commission, which pertains only to those regenerated by the Holy Spirit. To distinguish between legitimate evangelism and desirable social ministry, one may adopt a rule of thumb: if a kindly Buddhist can do it, it is not evangelism. I have seen social projects of great humanitarian value in Tashkent, in Central Asia. One could scarcely call such Communist projects an example of evangelism.

There was always some social concern shown in the Church, in Apostolic days, in patristic times, in medieval ages, in Reformation years; but the flowering of the social ministry came with the great outbursts of evangelistic activity following the Great Awakenings.

The sowing of the seed of social reform was aided by the eighteenth century Evangelical Awakenings. John Wesley denounced the greatest social evil of his days, slavery, and urged the reform of prisons, the education of the common people, and the like, as did other revivalists. It was in the extended nineteenth century—1776 to 1914—that a harvest of social reform was reaped in many a field of social concern.

The Great Awakenings

The First Great Awakening, 1725-1775, had raised up a number of American universities. A Second Great Awakening led to the founding of a monitorial school system for the common people of Britain and the founding of hundreds of colleges in the western United States. The same revival of Napoleon's day raised up Wilberforce and other engineers of the abolition of the slave trade, followed by the emancipation of the slaves in the British Empire (1834), in the United States as a war measure (1863). At the same time, Evangelicals such as Elizabeth Fry promoted successful prison reform, while Fliedner in Germany followed suit in building homes for ex-prisoners, hospitals for the sick, asylums for the insane, orphanages for children, founding the order of deaconesses to staff them, all on evangelical impulse. Florence Nightingale, trained at his school, became the mother of modern nursing.

The decades following 1830 in American life have been called the *Sentimental Years,* in which good works flourished as never before, the Revival producing societies to promote education, reform prisons, stop prostitution, recolonize Africa with freed slaves, advance the cause of peace, provide for sailors in port, promote temperance, and the like. The Awakening discouraged cruel sports, and produced societies everywhere for the prevention of cruelty to animals.

Great Britain was the first of the countries of the world to become industrialized, and its Industrial Revolution brought about a sorry exploitation of the toiling multitude, caught in a treadmill of competitive labor which kept them straining for sixteen hours a day in appalling conditions.

Anthony Ashley Cooper, the Seventh Earl of Shaftesbury, described himself as "an Evangelical of the Evangelicals," and harnessed the thrust of the Revival into a crusade for the betterment of humanity. He and his friends promoted legislation to cut the hours of labor in factories by half, to prohibit the use of women working in coal mines, of children in factories and farm gangs, to transform the lot of insane folk from abused prisoners to protected patients. He also promoted public parks, playing fields, gymnasia, garden allotments, working men's institutes, public libraries, night schools, debating and choral societies and other self-help.

The Tolpuddle Martyrs, transported to Australian penal colonies for refusing to work for less than a shilling a day, were evangelical lay preachers, except one who was later converted through their Christian behavior in convict camp. They gave a great impetus to the trade union movement in Britain. In later years, Keir Hardie, a convert of D. L. Moody, took up the cause of the working man, founded the Labor Party, and maintained until his death an evangelical Christian testimony shared with various other leaders of the Labor movement, which (quoting Lloyd George) found many of its officers among the converts of the Evangelical Revivals.

The Third Great Awakening, the 1858-59 Revival in the United States and Great Britain and around the world, raised up a corps of Christian philanthropists who went straight to the slums with a practical Samaritanism, yet cooperated in every wise legislative improvement. Numberless asylums, homes, refuges, and schools were founded in Britain. A good example would be Dr. Barnardo's Homes, founded by a convert of the Revival in Dublin. It became the world's largest private orphanage system. Out of the same Revival grew the Salvation Army, an extension in evangelism and social action of the Awakening in which William Booth was an ardent evangelist. The impact of the Revival was felt in the immediate reform of thousand of prostitutes, and it was carried on by Josephine Butler in a campaign against the state patronage of vice, as was Bramwell Booth and W.T. Stead's crusade against the white slave traffic. Henri Dunant, a student evangelist in Geneva, founded the Red Cross in 1865. The Y. M. C. A., established in London in 1844, was vastly expanded by the 1858-59 Revival, becoming a social fraternity, though for three quarters of a century it was ardently evangelistic.

Some have said that the 1858 American Awakening lacked social benefits. Within three years, the nation was involved in the bloodiest war of the century, its energies otherwise absorbed. However, when peace came, new enterprises were

transferred from Britain. In the pertinent words of Timothy
L. Smith:

> the rapid growth of concern with purely social issues
> such as poverty, working men's rights, the liquor traf-
> fic, slum housing, and racial bitterness is the chief
> feature distinguishing American religion after 1865. . .

Another worldwide Awakening about 1905, was not only
extraordinary in reviving the churches and evangelizing the
common people of the United States and elsewhere, but also
in social concern. The most numerous Protestant denomination, the Methodists, in reviewing the Awakening of 1905
as a "great twelvemonth," proclaimed "the signs of the revival of the public conscience . . . the firsx uits of a new
zeal for the living Christ as the Lord of all human activity
. . . social, industrial, commercial and political." Wash-
ington Gladden, "father of the social gospel," commended
the movement for "creating a moral revolution in the life
of the people." Many of the early advocates of the "social
gospel" were often the warmest supporters of historic
evangelism—the winning of individuals to Jesus Christ—
because of its social outworking.

The great social reforms in the homelands were seldom
spontaneous. Wilberforce did not wait for the support of the
Convocations of Canterbury and York, nor did Shaftesbury
seek the approval of the Methodist Conference. They went
straight to the seat of power with the heart of the matter,
and spoke as enlightened churchmen possessing the privilege and responsibility of Christian citizens. The forum of
the Church is not the fulcrum of reform; in parliament or
palace great decisions are made; conscientious Christians
have taken opposite sides in many social issues.

It seems clear in Scripture that violence is forbidden the
servant of God, though there seems to be no denial of the use
of force against evil-doing by legitimate civil authority.
Thus the Christian social witness is mainly a matter of
persuasion.

The improvement of social conditions in the homelands,
the leavening of the lump, resulting in the development of
a social conscience by society itself, enabled the missionary forces to apply their strength overseas where the social
conscience was often feeble, but where their hosts accepted
their evangelism along with their social ministry.

The Social Ministry Overseas

Already the missionaries—from William Carey on—had secured the abolition of widow-burning and of child sacrifices; they had taken the lead in the education of the people of India; they had helped found the vernacular press; they had introduced western medical practice.

In Africa, they fought the slave trade, opposed trial by ordeal, challenged exploitation by unscrupulous traders, built schools and hospitals, and helped prepare the Africans for self-government—while sharing with rulers and traders the responsibility for cultural havoc, but this is the short-coming of western man as a whole rather than the missionary. In 1875, for example, there were in Malawi "no schools, no teachers, no pupils, nobody could read." Within thirty years Scottish missionaries operated more than 200 schools with 20,000 pupils. In a single generation, the C.M.S. taught 200,000 to read in East Africa.

Following the 1858-59 Revival, medical missions spread in India, medical missionaries multiplying twentyfold in less than forty years. A survey in World War II showed that 90% of all nurses in India were Christians, four-fifths of them trained at mission hospitals. Missionaries have built Asia's biggest hospitals for leprosy, tuberculosis and the like; and Christian medical colleges pioneered in many countries of the world.

A convert of the 1859 Revival, Timothy Richard, may be regarded as the founder of China's great universities. The educational system of Korea owed its beginnings to pioneer missionaries. A mission school became Japan's Imperial University, while a convert founded Doshisha University as an all-Japanese institution. Mission schools profoundly influenced the development of Brazilian education, and a team of teachers, largely impressed by the 1858 Revival, gave a teacher training system to Sarmiento's Argentina. And 70% of African students in American colleges are graduates from mission primary schools, 50% from secondary. Frequently the language in which they did their elementary studies had been reduced to writing by missionaries.

Evangelical missionaries have been the products of centuries of limited knowledge of other cultures, and have made many mistakes. They have much to be proud of, indeed.

The Post-War Witness

The years following World War II saw an extraordinary expansion of the evangelical missionary forces throughout the world, due in part to the reviving of the work of God at the mid-century. Their evangelism was matched by social concern, as seen in the worldwide ministry of World Vision International (begun in the 1950s), which promoted pastors' conferences on evangelism overseas as well as maintaining a many-sided service program in situations of great emergency. Converts of the first Billy Graham Crusade of national importance, Los Angeles 1949, engaged in worthwhile social ministry—Jim Vaus in the gangland of New York and Louis Zamperini in the correctional farms of California, for example. While the significant civil rights campaign began without clearly Evangelical initiative, it could be said that the mid-century awakening had conditioned Evangelicals to set their eyes on a nobler standard of social justice, and all but the obscurantists supported the drive for rights, though many rejected the extreme and violent methods employed to obtain them. Many of the discussion groups and service projects of American Evangelicals seem to indicate they have been re-asserting the social conscience of the nineteenth century and of historic British Evangelicalism.

At the same time Evangelicals protested the attempts of theological radicals to equate legitimate social action with evangelism, a classification resulting in abandonment of personal, group and community evangelism entirely. Social action, though certainly desirable, is no substitue for proclamation of the Good News of Jesus Christ. The solution of the race problem, the question of social and economic justice, and the problem of war, would place the American community in the same position as contemporary Scandinavia, with its equally great need of the Gospel. The secular state—by revolution in the Soviet Union—has preempted all social service and prohibited Christians from engaging in such as Christians. The secular state—by evolution in the democracies—has taken over, more and more, the social work of the Churches and voluntary societies. Christians, though not prohibited, are being displaced as Christians from such service. The time may come when only the preach-

ing of the Good News will be left to them. Yet even should
the state take over all organized social work, we could never
have redeemed men who were not in some way also serving
men. Thus we return to McGavran's point: the two ministries
should not be confused. Social service is important in its
own right; but it is the complement of, not a substitute for,
evangelism. The history of the Awakenings shows that very
many of the greatest social reforms arose in Revival.

The documentation for this chapter may be found in the
more detailed volume by the writer, CAMPUS AFLAME,
Evangelical Awakenings in Collegiate Communities, 1972,
a U.C.L.A. doctor of education dissertation; and in earlier
volumes, such as THE LIGHT OF THE NATIONS, 1965.

Letters from the field are an excellent source of under-standing—an original source, very close to the actual hap-pening. . . .

Mission minutes are readily available and furnish an impeccable source of information concerning policies and men which have affected church growth. . . .

Budget distributions should be scrutinized. They reveal true long-range goals and indicate where the actual empha-sis of the mission lies. . . .

UNDERSTANDING CHURCH GROWTH
pp. 134, 135

19

DIGGING FOR THE FACTS
(Latin America)

J.B.A. Kessler

Two of the most fascinating periods of church history occur in the first two and the last two centuries of this era. These periods are so special because they were characterized by great efforts to 'translate' the Gospel into new cultures. The challenge faced by the church in the first two centuries was to express the Gospel, which had been nurtured in Jewish soil, in terms which could be understood by those brought up in Greek culture. The challenge in the nineteenth and twentieth centuries is to transpose western culture so as to make it understandable, not only to the cultures of the third world, but also to the new secular societies growing up out of traditional western civilization.

The great danger in such 'translations' of the Gospel is that vital elements are left out, and at the same time unessential elements are kept in, which create unnecessary barriers to the acceptance of Jesus Christ as Lord and Savior. In order to sail between Scylla and Charybdis in this region it is necessary to keep immersing oneself in the Gospel in its original form and habitat. That is why careful and devoted Bible study is a 'must' in these times, both for the church corporately and for its individual members. There is also another important aid in determining a right course. A comparison of the various attempts made to translate the Gospel into new cultures will help us to distinguish those vital elements which must be retained and how they can best be transposed.

In the nineteenth and the early part of the twentieth century a flood of new information became available about the first two centuries and many important books were written about this period. However, this flood is drying up. The archives of the old monasteries have been ransacked and the chance of digging up new and exciting papyri from the Egyptian sands is steadily being reduced.

Quite the reverse is true about modern attempts to 'translate' the Gospel. In most cases a spade is not needed, merely a notebook and pencil. The amount of material lying around to be collected is quite staggering. The writer has the impression that only in something like seven or eight of the hundred or more mission fields has anything like a systematic attempt been made to gather up the relevant facts. At the moment important church growth is going on in eastern Europe, but as far as the writer knows, almost nothing is being done in this field. As for records about the attempts to 'translate' the Gospel for modern western secular society more is being done by the World Council of Churches than by movements of an Evangelical or Pentecostal persuasion.

Making Notes

The urgent need is to collect and systematize material before the evidence is lost. The department of history in Aberdeen University and the Institute of Church Growth in Pasadena under the leadership of Donald McGavran seem to be the only Evangelical institutes which are systematically addressing themselves to this task.

Firstly, the unhistorical attitude prevalent among many Evangelicals must be overcome. This was not always so. In 1846, when 800 delegates from fifty denominations met in London to establish the Evangelical Alliance, the full and careful way they recorded the whole development shows that many of them possessed a keen historical sense. The

controversies about evolution and higher criticism of the
Bible caused most Evangelicals to retreat into their shell
and it is noticeable that the historical records of a movement such as the Evangelical Alliance deteriorated in
quality from about 1860 onwards.

It is necessary in this connection to distinguish between
academic training and a historical sense. When the
writer went to Peru as a missionary in 1949, the need of
understanding Peruvian culture was impressed upon him,
but no one pointed out the need for understanding the
development of the young church into which he was coming.
This task fell to a humble Indian preacher of the high
Andes called Juan de Dios Guerrero. He had only had two
weeks of formal schooling, but he had accompanied the
early missionaries on their travels and had listened to their
conversations. Many of Juan de Dios' stories were amusing
human anecdotes but in the course of his long life, the
main issues facing the young church had become plain to
him and the moments of crisis had been indelibly stamped
on his memory. During an evangelistic trip in 1953 the
writer took a notebook and pencil with him and wrote up
his reminiscences. These reminiscences were a first
start to a thesis which was produced fourteen years later.

Therefore, it should be impressed on young missionaries
and Christian workers gathering up these facts by listening
carefully to veterans who have grown up in the situation
and noting down what they feel is part of their task. In
making these notes it is important to indicate accurately
the name of the speaker, something about his age and
background and the date of his remarks. Not only will
such notes be invaluable for later studies, but they will
warn the young worker of present pitfalls and give him an
insight into the development of the work he is entering.
The God and Father of our Lord Jesus Christ is the God
of history, and therefore those who wish to serve Him
must be trained to have an eye for history. Furthermore
such notes will help him avoid the mistake often made of
writing the history of a certain field on the basis of presuppositions derived from experience in an entirely different culture and period. The writer has found that at
moments of conflict and division people are forced to take
sides and in doing so are no longer able to cover up the

real problem. Tactful enquiries by a young worker about these moments of stress can give him a unique insight into the main issues that have dominated the development.

In the case of Peru, the writer came to the conclusion that the basic issues of the Protestant church there were those of division, nationalism and the establishment of a native ministry. These themes were noted in his diary and when the time came to gather the facts for his thesis, the quotations written down were all related to these subjects. The material in the thesis was also grouped around these three strands. Concentration on the main issues is vital for a proper selection of the vast mass of materials available and also for the final product to have the necessary coherence. Naturally each country has its own main issues. If the writer had started with Protestantism in Chile, he would have chosen church division, the indigenous expression of the Gospel and the training of a lay ministry as his main themes.

Experience in the field is usually essential if the main issues are to be singled out correctly, but once this has been done the gathering of the facts can begin. Some general literature on the subject should be read. This can be found at a local library. The names of those who have played a part in the development must be noted down and anything directly related to one of the basic themes must be copied out verbatim in a notebook with an accurate indication of the name of the book or magazine from which the quotation is made, the name of the author, the place and date of publication and the page number from which the quotation has been taken.

Once the general literature has been combed, a final decision must be made on the limits of the study to be undertaken. In general these limits are never narrow enough, with the result that either the study becomes too voluminous, and has to be done in a slip-shod way, or at the last moment much material gathered at great effort has to be dumped, or worse still that half way through the wrong kind of limitations have to be imposed. The most sensible limitations are those of a geographical or cultural nature. In other words it is usually more rewarding to study all the missionary work that has been done in one tribe or ethnic group, rather than follow up the work of one

mission or Church throughout a whole continent. Furthermore it is not wise to make limitations in time unless these
limitations correspond to definite breaks in the development.
For instance it is unsatisfactory to deal with Protestantism
in Latin America during the nineteenth century because the
development up to 1900 proved to be only the start of the
growth during this century. The longer the time span, the
more clearly can the development be followed, and the
better can temporary changes be distinguished from vital
ones.

It is also unsatisfactory to limit the study to one aspect
of the church development. Many missionary magazines
stress the work of the missionaries and describe the
development of the mission, without placing adequate
emphasis on the development of the national church. The
object of these missions is to establish churches and only
by carefully following the development of these churches is
it possible to understand the significance of the work the
missions are doing. Equally it is rather meaningless to
study church growth only on the basis of numbers. The
significance of such growth can only be seen when it is
set against its cultural, economic and general historical
background. Even this is not enough. Church growth is not
only affected by external factors such as the cultural or
economic background, but by inner-church factors such
as the way the Gospel is presented and the congregation is
structured. Such inner-church factors can only be appreciated by means of a study of the historical development of
the church itself and therefore the writer would like to
make a plea that a careful study of the history of the church
in question be an integral part of any study on church
growth.

It is clear from the above that church growth is such
a complex phenomenon that any study of it must not be
undertaken lightly. Until the ground has been covered
by adequate case studies in depth no attempt should be
made to make surveys on a wider scale. It can be helpful
for a writer to deal with a field beside the one of which he
has personal knowledge, but this adds considerably to his
task and in view of the need for limitation he may well decide
against this. Certainly he should do so if something has
already been published about a related field. Much time

may be needed before the main themes and the limitations
of the study can be established, but these things are basic
to all that follow. Once this ground work has been laid the
researcher can proceed to an examination of the specialized
libraries and archives.

Researchers in the United States are fortunate that many
of the denominations have excellent libraries in the building at 475 Riverside Drive, New York. Next door is also the
Missionary Research Library. The collection available at
the Missionary Research Library, except for recent
material, is perhaps the greatest in the world, but the
topical index tends to be unsatisfactory. This means that if
one asks for books related to a certain area one does not
get a true impression of all the material that is available.
However, every book is catalogued under the name of the
writer. A researcher should start as soon as possible to
build up an alphabetical list of all those who have been
connected with the field under study and who may have
published something about it. Other important sources of
information are the magazines published by churches.
Usually these magazines have been produced for promotional reasons and avoid delving too deeply into developments, but they are invaluable as an aid to establishing
the date on which a certain event occurred, and for providing such statistics as are available. Dates are important
for establishing the correct historical sequence, and in
turn this often gives an indication as to what caused a
certain happening to take place.

In addition to the magazines of the individual churches
or missions there are magazines covering a wider field.
The magazine of the *Evangelical Alliance* which was published under the title *Evangelical Christendom* included up
to 1892 an excellent survey of international Christian events.
A complete set of this magazine is available at the headquarters in 19 Draycott Place, London, S. W. 3, but quite
a few copies are also available at the Fuller Theological
Library in Pasadena, California. The *International Review
of Missions,* started in 1912, contains a mine of information together with an index for rapid access. Then there
is the *Evangelical Missions Quarterly* as well as several
other magazines of a more general character, such as
Christian Century and *Christianity Today.* The records of

both the British and Foreign Bible Society and American Bible Society are well worth consulting. The magazine *Practical Anthropology* often provides articles which help to a better understanding of the cultural backgrounds. Finally, magazines such as the *Missionary Herald* the *Missionary Monthly* and the *Missionary Review of the World* which have been discontinued should also be consulted.

After the material on the home front has been combed, and after interviews have been arranged with retired missionaries, the stage is then set for an investigation on the spot. The sources of information are fourfold. There is firstly the local magazine of the church movement. Often these records have been kept very untidily and a visit to the archives of churches in several cities is needed to gain anything like a complete insight. There are then newspaper reports available at the national library. This kind of research is only fruitful if the exact dates of events have been noted down during the investigations on the home front. Thirdly, there are the accounts of the missionaries and other workers on the spot. These accounts can be very valuable, but their writers can also be sincerely mistaken. Only someone who has first done a thorough job of research on the home front will be able to distinguish quickly the true from the false. Fourthly, there are the accounts of the nationals. Great importance must be attached to them as they so often provide a healthy corrective to the views advanced by the foreigners. On the other hand, nationals too can be mistaken. It is important to note down everyone's views even if one has strong suspicions that they are mistaken.

The research worker then returns to his base heavily laden with notebooks and with the feeling that his work is more than half-finished. In this he is mistaken because it usually takes longer to prepare the materials for publication than to gather them. His first task is to number all the pages of his notebooks. Secondly, he must make a subject index of all his materials noting down the number of the page in the note-book, the name of the writer, and the date of the writing. Thirdly, he must reduce all his statistics to graphs.

Evaluating

The task of evaluating and sifting the various sources can then begin. There will often be duplicate or triplicate accounts of the same events. If one account is a repetition or a summary of an earlier account and adds nothing new, then the later account can be crossed off the list. If the later account is more complete then its extra source of information needs to be ascertained. If this extra source of information can be identified as a document and if this writing can be found then the fuller account can be crossed off the index. If this extra source of information consists of personal recollections either of the later writer himself, or of some acquaintance of his, then the question needs to be asked why the later writer wished to present a fuller account. If there are no contradictions between the two accounts and there is no indication that the later writer wished to correct an earlier impression, but only to expand it, then the earlier account may be crossed off the index. It may be, however, that the two or more accounts are in some way contradictory. If it is a matter of dates then a consultation of the relevant magazines often provides the answer. One cannot assume that the earlier account is necessarily the more accurate in these matters. The research worker can then justify his choice of dates in a footnote to his final paper. If the contradictions touch on matters of importance then the research worker must try to marshal all the evidence and if necessary write extra letters to people concerned in an attempt to clear up the difficulty.

In his final document he must clearly set out the various contradictions and explain why he has chosen to believe one source or why he has in the end not dared to make any choice. These contradictions are important because they reflect the conflicts which helped form the development being studied. There are no fixed rules for deciding who to believe. In some cases the later development makes it clear who was right. In other cases the documentary evidence on one side is clearly superior and more consistent. Often they are not available or are still treated as classified material, but the minutes of properly conducted board meetings usually give the most objective view of happenings and conflicts. In many cases a mission executive is prepared to check classified board minutes for an answer to a specific question. There are times, however, when missionaries have consciously or unconsciously, witheld vital information and even the board minutes of a mission do not present a true picture. Therefore it is necessary to compare the official mission view with the view gained from talks with the national workers and a study of local newspaper and magazine reports.

The research worker is now ready to prepare separate draft accounts of the main happenings in the development he is following. Every statement must be justified by a reference to one or more sources and after completing the writing of each draft the researcher must check that all the relevant sources have been referred to in each draft. The research worker must then compare the drafts he has made with his graphs of church growth. It is customary in some circles to decry the importance of church statistics. The writer of this article would like to disagree. The statistics may well be faulty in an absolute sense, but provided that they have been gathered in the same way in each succeeding year the shape of the curve given is explained by the happenings described in the drafts. Some sharp changes in the graphs may be due to a change in the way statistics have been collected and careful attention needs to be given to this point, but the experience of the writer of this article is that all other changes in the rate of growth are related to important developments and happenings. This is one of the acid tests of the quality on the research done up to this point. If a change in the curves cannot be properly explained it may be necessary for the researcher to start digging for new facts and he may even have to come to the conclusions that the facts he has been collecting are not the significant ones.

Writing

If the researcher has no time to start digging for new facts, he must write up all that he has gathered in a coherent account, complete with documentation and in his conclusions He must point to the evidence indicating that the facts he has gathered are not adequate to explain the development.

Not only is it impossible to decide in advance with surety what facts are going to be significant, but such apparently unsuccessful research papers present a magnificent opportunity to later researchers.

If the researcher has harmonized his draft accounts with the shape of his curves, he must then arrange the whole into a coherent account. He will need to start with a brief introduction giving the geographical, ethnic, social and economic background. For this he will need to consult several secular and sociological works. It is important to keep the introduction brief. If, in order to point to the significance of some development, the research worker wants to make a special reference to the geopraphical, ethnic, social or economic background, this should not be done in the introduction but at the relevant place in the account itself. As the account is built up by tying the separate drafts together and relating them to the graphs and other materials the researcher must make a start at building up his conclusions. These can all be put at the end but the writer of this article prefers to start building up the conclusions at the relevant places as the account proceeds. The conclusions in their final form are then given at the end. When this final draft has been completed the researcher needs to revise the whole work in the light of his final conclusions. He must ask himself at each stage whether the facts he has presented really support his final conclusions. If they do not he must either change his conclusions or at this late stage start digging for more facts. He must also ask himself whether each fact presented is really significant to the development as he has described it.

One of the great failings of many research documents is that they are cluttered with facts that are not really relevant. Such papers are difficult to read and do not hold the reader's interest. Therefore the researcher must dare to cut out every detail that is not really significant. It will be painful to drop much interesting material but it needs to be done. The experience of the writer of this article is that about two thirds of the original facts have in the end to be dropped. These materials must be kept in their draft form as they can be useful for later articles or books of a more popular nature. The researcher should then dare to extrapolate some of the developments he has been following and make prophecies about the chances of future progress or failure. This constitutes another acid test of his work. If his prognoses are later corroborated this will be solid proof that he did indeed isolate the elements of real significance. If his prognoses fail then later researchers can ask themselves why the prophecies failed and have a ready made base from which to start new investigations.

The time has come to choose a title for the research paper which exactly covers the contents. This is a difficult undertaking usually best solved by giving first a general title and then a sub-title. A table of contents must then be prepared to the chapters with the sub-divisions of each chapter. It is also important at the beginning of the paper to present a complete list of all abbreviations used. This must include in particular a complete explanation of the abbreviations used in the footnotes. To avoid confusion the number of abbreviations used must be strictly limited. It is helpful to add a list of the addresses of the movements, missions and churches to which reference is made in the paper.

It is cheaper when producing a printed book to include the footnotes at the end but there is no doubt in the mind of the writer of this article that the right place for footnotes is at the bottom of the page concerned. First the name of the writer in full, then the full title of the book or article printed in italics. In the case of an article there follows the title of the magazine, the place and date of publication, and the page number, or numbers. If a statement is based on someone's recollection or letter, then the footnote should read as follows :— "John Smiths' letter to the author dated . . . and written from . . . ".

At the end of the paper there should be a complete bibliography of all materials used which should be divided into a leading section for books and printed brochures, a second section for magazine articles and newspaper reports, a third section for mission reports and minutes, a fourth for microfilms, a fifth for mimeographed papers, a sixth for typewritten papers and a seventh for handwritten documents. In each section the name of the writer comes first arranged in alphabetical order according to the surname, then the title of the book or paper, followed by the place and date of publication exactly as in the case of the footnotes. Except in the cases of widely published books, it is helpful to add in abbreviated form an indication of places where these sources can be found. An explanation of these abbreviations must then be included at the beginning of the bibliography.

In most cases an alphabetical index is necessary of all the people, places and subjects mentioned in the paper. In the case of a long book it will be wise to separate this index into three sections, personal names, geographical and subject. During the final revision the research worker must note down all the names and clearly defined topics that are mentioned. He then brings this list or these lists into alphabetical order and then it is a comparatively simple matter during the reading of the galley proofs or of the final revision to add page numbers behind each name or topic.

The experience of the Dutch missionary societies working in Indonesia has been that such case studies have been of invaluable help both in determining policy on the field and at the home end. Only when one such paper was translated into the language of the field concerned, were the indigenous Christians activated into writing about their own history. This paper gave them an example of how the work should be done and at the same time gave them something they could react against from their own point of view. The missionary cycle was thus completed. First the people were given the Gospel. They they were helped in the development of a national church and finally they were given the example and the stimulus to reflect on their own development.

History and ethnography describe the matrix in which Churches grow. They inform the reader about culture, customs, racial characteristics, and governments which condition those to whom the Gospel is presented. . . .

They (books on history and ethnography) contribute to understanding of church growth if we read them asking, "What do these books mean for the propagating of the Gospel?" The growth of the Church is closely conditioned by both history and anthropology.

UNDERSTANDING CHURCH GROWTH
pp. 131, 132

20

ETHNOHISTORICAL RESEARCH IN WEST CAMEROON

Lloyd Kwast

In 1971 the Prime Minister of West Cameroon appealed to the Baptists of his country to produce an authoritative history of their Church. Now it happened that I was engaged on such a project at the time (Kwast: 1971). I was discovering what a complex process the growth of the Church really is and in this article I propose setting forth some of the problems I encountered and the principles and techniques that I used to deal with them.

I did not want a mere record of chronological events. The missionary historiography towards which church growth writing has been gravitating over the last decade or so is as much anthropological reconstruction. I am trying to describe the development of Cameroon Christianity in the light of the character of local life and culture; namely, the cultural and environmental *Sitz im Leben*, in which the church has emerged (Scherer, 1971: 132).

To research the many complex processes by which the church in West Cameroon has developed historically has been no easy task. Vast amounts of information had to be gathered, documents examined, translations made, interviews recorded, questionnaires tabulated, data interpreted, questions asked, graphs tested, comparisons made and conclusions cautiously drawn.

To accomplish this task, the various techniques and methods of anthropology, sociology, psychology and theology were employed. Most significant were the tools and techniques of the historical method. The theoretical framework of Gottschalk (1945), Barzun and Graff (1962), Renier (1965), and other historians has been a guiding element throughout this study.

Historical Method

Broadly considered, the historical method involves four basic functions: (1) Gathering records and survivals of past events. (2) Critical examination of those records and survivals. (3) Imagining what the past was like. (4) Presenting the results in ways that are consistent with the records of history and sound scientific procedure (Gottschalk 1945:8). Specifically, the written reconstruction of past events is called historiography, and the critical examination of historical records is called historical method. Both processes, however, are often referred to simply as historical method.

Of primary concern to the purpose of this research was gathering much relevant data from as many sources as possible. This led inevitably to the familiar research activities of interviews, correspondence, field observations, and archival and library research.

The information of greatest value is usually found in primary sources, recorded by eyewitnesses who actually experienced the events of history being studied. Many of these documents were written in the ordinary business of life and not intended for posterity.

Great treasuries of church growth facts are often locked up in the fading memories of old, retired missionaries, or aging lay Christians; or in long, monotonous lists of cramped statistical figures; or in half-forgotten records, musty notebooks, termite-eaten bundles of letters, stacks of dusty mission minutes and budgets, magazine and newspaper articles yellowed with age, faded missionary diaries, books buried deep in the stacks of libraries, or in endless bundles of brittle papers neatly packed in forgotten archives.

Secondary sources, recorded by people who were not

present at the events described, were also used in my research, mostly for reference purposes. Some of these containted primary particulars, such as quotations from personal letters, probably no longer extant. In several cases I was aided by bibliographical listings and thus was led to primary sources of which I had not known. Gwei (1966) and Ardener (1968) especially helped me in this respect.

But mostly I depended on written documents, which I had been collecting and studying for nine years. Many of these were found in the Cameroons in the categories of forgotten records I have listed above. Their discovery was a truly exciting experience.

Anthropological Method

My exciting experiences were not confined to the discovery of old documents. As anthropological dimensions depend more on establishing rapport with informants, I also made a few very good friends, who were able to answer my questions from the distant past. One of these Cameroonian informants was almost a hundred years of age.

As I felt I could not write a cross-cultural history without researching the anthropological dimension I had to extend myself beyond the normal range of historical method. I gathered my data through field study, interviewing, participant observation and the documentary studies of anthropologists according to the well-known methods (R. A. I. G. B. 1929; Bennett, 1948; Nadel, 1951; Malinowski, 1944, 1945, &c.) and kept my own note books. In many of the early historical documents I found valuable ethnological material. It is possible to reconstruct a picture of culture change to set beside the historical record.

The study of early Cameroon ethnological documents in conjunction with the writer's field notes proved invaluable in reconstructing the ethnological and cultural context of nineteenth century Cameroon for reasons given by Tippett: (In ethnohistorical research) "documentary studies . . . help (1) To recapture lost contexts from the sub-recent past; (2) To provide cultural data for comparison with present facts; (3) To observe and record the changes over time; and (4) To seek out the reasons for those changes (1968: 16-17).

Problems of Documentary Interpretation

Not all sources, even primary sources, are of equal value or reliability. One has to be continually on his guard. He needs to approach his documents with an adequate chronology and biography so that in projecting himself into the past he does not also assume knowledge of the present on the part of his sources. He needs to remember that all sources have their biases and become more valuable when the bias is understood. Here we have entered the problem of historical interpretation.

A number of problems of documentary interpretation were met in my research. These might be designated problems of (1) authenticity, (2) reliability, (3) textual inconsistency, (4) meaning and (5) personal bias. Let me cite some examples.

(1) The problem of document authenticity is encountered —where a document was intentionally or unintentionally in error (Renier, 1965:108-110). I found that the documents by Innes (1862:1895) were obvious attempts to misrepresent the personality and true character of Alfred Saker and falsify the actual events of history.

(2) The problem of reliability was troublesome in a number of my missionary documents, especially those written for promoting a particular missionary cause. Often the information given, though not intentionally false, presented a distorted picture of the over-all situation. To help determine degrees of reliability in his documents, the writer used the rules established by Gottschalk, (1945:16) in giving some documents precedence over others for reliability: (a) The closer a document is to the event it describes, the more reliable it is likely to be. Generally, reliability is inversely proportional to the time-lapse between the historical event and its documented recollection. (b) The author's intended purpose for producing the document is important in judging its reliability. Personal documents intended purely as personal, confidential records or aids to one's own memory are usually more reliable than apologia or propaganda, for example. (c) The size of audience for which the document was written may influence reliability. In general, the fewer the people it addresses the more intimate and open it is likely to be. (d) Documents

produced by trained and experienced field observers are usually superior to those of casual arm-chair reporters, board secretaries or missionary promoters.

In evaluating secondary sources especially, the problems of purpose and perspective were encountered repeatedly. Not only was it important to determine specifically the purpose for which a document was written, but also to know generally the vantage point in time and philosophy from which it was written. This was often difficult to determine. But in no case did I permit secondary sources to speak uncritically for the historical period they attempted to interpret.

The problem of interpolations was encountered in at least two secondary sources (Metch, 1967; Tita, 1965), where because of "recasting" history, changing the historical perspective or "filling-in" the blank spaces of history, a distorted picture appears to have resulted.

(3) Textual inconsistencies in sources referring to the same original document were confronted in several instances. One is dealt with at length under the head of the Niger Expedition of 1841 and the differing accounts of Cox (1844) and Crowther (1859). Another is the mistaken identity of Missionary John Diboll as a black Jamaican given in several sources (Victoria 1958, Southern Cameroons 1958), when in fact he was a white Englishman (Ardener, 1968:54).

(4) Of all the problems faced in working with written documents, the most difficult and complex was the task of determining what the author of the document intended to say—or the problem of meaning. The problem relates to semantics, psychology and cultural difference. The meaning of words and their use has changed much since the nineteenth century. Complicating the problem even more for me is the fact that many of my primary sources are in nineteenth century German and French, which have experienced great semantic changes also.

The problem of meaning becomes most acute for students conducting cross-cultural historical research. As a general rule the greater the span of time and culture difference separating the document and the researcher, the more difficult it is to arrive at precise meaning. Only those with the widest range of experience and knowledge can ever hope to succeed. It was at this point that I found my years of experience in Cameroon, my knowledge of the land and people and my limited ability to work in German and French invaluable in dealing with cross-cultural documents.

From the anthropological point of view also, in dealing with informants, the problem of meaning can be obstructive, even to a person who speaks the language well. Tippett (1968:273-275) has enumerated several factors which obscure meaning in cross-cultural communication. The obscuring factor may be in the cultural values or in the person being interviewed, or in the researcher himself. In dealing with informants or documents it is never easy to make allowances for oneself.

Finally, each document was subjected to the following interrogation: (1) Who is its author or creator? (2) What information does it establish? (3) What is the relation in time and space between the author and the statement, overt or implied? (4) How does this source compare with other statements on the same subject or event? and (5) What can I know independently about the author and his credit-ibility? (Barzun, 1962:134).

Arrangement of Materials

Probably the most difficult task before the church growth writer is the selection of relevant material from the plethora of documents and field notes and the arrangement of this into an orderly manuscript. Whether he determines to give it a topical or chronological entity both possibilities have to be considered, as also the balance of historical and ethnological weightage. A glance at the titles of the theses in missiology done at the School of World Mission will suffice to indicate the wide range of possibilities one has for the arrangement of his data. As this matter of arrangement and presentation is the researcher's more original contribution to the study it is here that his subjective biases are more likely to show through. This calls for some discussion.

The Problem of Subjectivity

While there are some who believe that full objectivity is possible in historical interpretation (Beard, 1934:219-231), this writer has found subjective interpretation absolutely necessary in his historical methodology, and agrees with the statements that "an objective judgment is one made by testing in all ways possible one's subjective impressions, so as to arrive at a knowledge of objects" (Barzum, 1962: 146); and "good guesses as to the major trends of history lay the basis for the best ordering of the facts" (Wilson, 1940: 101-115).

Good historical methodology recognizes the need of sound, disciplined and informed subjective judgments in the writing of history. At some point in his study, the historian must usually resort to the techniques of psychological method, such as empathy, projection, intuition and imagination, to aid him in his task (Barzun, 1962:60). Only in so doing is he equipped to "feel" what the past must have been like, and thus attempt an "imaginative reconstruction of history," but does so only by remaining scrupulously faithful to the historical records and canons of scientific investigation.

(1) This writer found the psychological quality most needed at points of this study was historical-mindedness— the mental act of stepping out of one's own cultural and historical context and casting oneself into the place of other people at other times. Gottschalk points out that—

> historical-mindedness requires the investigator to shed his own personality and to take on, as far as possible, that of his subject in the effort to understand the language, ideas, ideals, interests, attitudes, habits, motives, drives and traits of the subject (1945: 33).

The quality of historical-mindedness is especially needful for the student conducting cross-cultural historical research.

(2) Another essential ingredient for sound subjective judgment is the widest range of personal experience, knowledge, talent and inspiration. The student of cross-cultural research is often called on to view historical events in strange, foreign surroundings through the eyes, thoughts, standards, values, beliefs, sympathies and personalities of a people culturally different from himself. Admittedly, the task borders on the impossible. Only those with field experience and knowledge of the culture and language can hope to succeed.

> No platitude tells how to acquire a wide range of
> experience, wisdom and knowledge and how to transfer
> those qualities to an understanding of the past. For
> they are not accumulated alone by precept or example,
> industry or prayer, though all of these may help. And so
> historiography, the writing of history books, is not
> easily made the subject of nomothetic study. Some
> room must be left for native talent and inspiration
> (Gottschalk, 1945: 9).

The experience of living in West Cameroon since 1963
was my most valuable asset in producing this study. I
lived and worked only a few miles from where Joseph
Merrick established the first outpost of Christianity in
Cameroon in 1843. I stood and viewed the historic sites
and their surrounding environment spoken of in this study.
I have learned to know and love the people and their language.
I have gained an appreciation for their culture and thought
habits. To be sure, evaluations on personal experience are
not ipso facto trustworthy; yet no amount of library research
can be an adequate substitute in this type of investigation
for intimate, day-by-day living with the people; although
it is admittedly impossible to share their culture fully,
personal confrontation affords a kind of understanding and
insight which can be achieved in no other way.

Historiography furthermore often makes use of subjective imagination. Good historical imagination attempts
to "picture" the setting of past events. Documentary study
alone is not adequate for a cross-cultural imaginative
reconstruction of history. The student should also possess
first-hand knowledge of local geographical settings, such
as terrain, climate, vegetation and travel access, as well
as traditional and contemporary ethnological settings.
Knowledge of contemporary language, demography, material
culture, agriculture, social institutions and religious
beliefs provide invaluable stimulus for good historical
imagination.

Historical method often ascertains truth by much the same
way as most people use for daily life—the process of subjective common sense and the rule of probability (Renier,
1965: 142-146). Common sense discriminates between truth
and conjecture by exercising personal judgment based on
broad general knowledge, personal and vicarious experience,

knowledge of previous history and a critical evaluation of all the evidence at hand. Someone has rightly observed that "good judgment is the historian's form of genius, and he is judged by the amount of it he can muster." The rule of probability simply states that "truth rests not on possibility nor on plausibility but on probability" (Barzun, 1962: 138). The author confesses that at several points in his study he was required to resort to his own common sense judgments and the rule of probability.

Another problem arising from the subjective interpretation of historical data is the problem of influence. At certain points, as with most historians, I attempted to determine subjectively the relative influence of antecedent persons or events upon subsequent historical development. Although historical method provides no scientific means for measuring such an influence (Gottschalk, 1945: 58-60), nevertheless I tried to estimate the influence of an individual, a document, a policy, an idea, a movement or an episode upon succeeding developments.

One is well aware of the danger in this and church growth historians can err here if caution is not taken. In writing up my research I consciously avoided assigning various kinds of influence to events that were not really comparable. One has to be alert at this point. Similarly, in estimating causes, effort must be made to distinguish between immediate and obvious causes and remote or underlying ones. Furthermore, I continuallly had to resist the temptation to argue too strongly from historical antecedence and sequence to casual relationships.

The International Factor

Historical reconstruction of missions in the one-time European colonies frequently have to allow for a change of rule either during or after the war. If one's mission passed through a German or Japanese phase, one's research will probably assume still another linguistic dimension. Researchers at the School of World Mission have sometimes had to use documents in French, Spanish, German, Portuguese and Dutch. I had to use both French and German. In contrast to the easy availability of many primary documents relating to the period of British Baptist activity in Cameroon, documents covering the era of German Kamerun are very scarce indeed.

In extensive correspondence with friends in Germany and with the University of Hamburg and the Prediger Semiar in Hamburg, I found that the valuable archives of die Mission der deutschen Baptisten that were stored in the Hamburg Prediger Semiar were completely destroyed in a bombing raid during the Second World War.

Fortunately, I was able to find some material in the Cameroon, and in particular a box of old forgotten letters, journals and station minutes found in 1968. I am fortunate in having collected through the years a number of important primary and secondary sources in German. among the most valuable of these are primary sources by Morgan (1893), Suvern (n.d.), Scheve (1901), Lewis (n.d.), Bender (1921, 1926), and Hofmeister (1921).

Also important are interviews with informants who remember the German era, and some of whom still speak a fluent German. Secondary documents by Rudin (1938), Ardener (1968), Hallden (1968) and Keller (1969) proved especially valuable in helping to fill in some of the historical gaps left through the loss of German archives and the fading memories of old Kamerun nationals and retired German missionaries.

The editor of this Festschrift asked me for a personal account of how I tackled what I take to be an ethnohistorical analysis. A church growth history is not a general history. I suppose one should call it topical. This means a further dimension in the complexity of the task. One uses historical and anthropological methods but one's mind is focused all the time on a theme. Did the Church grow or not? When did it grow? How? Why? One is using the interrogative hypothesis of historical method. The questions themselves are non-committal. They cannot be answered unless one is anthropologically equipped to be led away from national generalization into specifics of homogeneous units. Of course all the criteria of critical method must be applied, but nevertheless one is gathering mainly "those facts which are needed to understand the thrusts of growth and recession" (McGavran, 1970:98).

As an interdisciplinary research methodology I believe the techniques and values of the church growth historical study form a valuable contribution to ethnohistory in general, quite apart from the equally valuable information they provide for the science of missiology.

BIBLIOGRAPHY:

Ardener, Shirley G.
1968   EYE-WITNESSES TO THE ANNEXATION OF CAMEROON, 1883-1887, Buea, West Cameroon, Government Press
Barzun, Jacques and Henry F. Graff
1962   THE MODERN RESEARCHER, New York, Harcourt, Brace and World, Inc.
Beard, C. A.
1934   "Written History as an Act of Faith," AMERICAN HISTORICAL REVIEW 39:219-231
Bender, Carl Jacob
1921   DER WELTKRIEG UND DIE CHRISTLICHEN MISSIONEN IN KAMERUN, Kassel, J. G. Oncken
1926   TWENTY YEARS AMONG AFRICAN NEGROES Girard, Kansas, Haldemen-Julius
Bennett, John W.
1948   "The Study of Cultures: A Survey of Technique and Methodology in Field Work," AMERICAN SOCIOLOGICAL REVIEW, 13:672-689
Cox, F. A.
1844   HISTORY OF THE ENGLISH MISSIONARY SOCIETY FROM 1792 to 1842, Boston, Isaac Tompkins
Crowther, Samuel and John C. Taylor
1859   THE GOSPEL ON THE BANKS OF THE NIGER: NIGER EXPEDITION OF 1857-1859, London, Dawsons of Pall Mall
Gottschalk, Louis
1945   "The Historian and the Historical Document," In Gottschalk, Kluckhohn and Angell (eds.), THE USE OF PERSONAL DOCUMENTS IN HISTORY, ANTHROPOLOGY AND SOCIOLOGY, 3-75, New York, Social Science Research Council, Bulletin 53
Gwei, Solomon Nfor
1966   "History of the British Baptist Mission in Cameroon, With Beginnings in Fernando Po, 1841-1886," An Unpublished B. D. thesis, Baptist Theological Seminary, Rüschlikon-Zürich, Switzerland
Hallden, Erik
1968   THE CULTURE POLICY OF THE BASEL MISSION IN THE CAMEROONS 1886-1905, Uppsala, Sweden, Berlingska Boktryckeriet for Studia Ethnographica Upsaliensia

BIBLIOGRAPHY (cont.)

Hofmeister, J.
    1921   ERLEBNISSE IM MISSIONSDIENST IN KAMERUN
              Neuruppin, Deutschland, Selbst-Verlag (Erster Band)
Innes, A.
    1862   CRUELTIES COMMITTED ON THE WEST COAST
              OF AFRICA BY AN AGENT OF THE BAPTIST
              MISSION AND OTHERS London, J. Cooper MORE
              LIGHT: THE ONLY TRUE BIOGRAPHY OF AL-
              FRED SAKER AND HIS CRUELTIES BY EYE-
              WITNESSES, England, Birkenhead
Keller, Werner
    1969   THE HISTORY OF THE PRESBYTERIAN CHURCH
              IN WEST CAMEROON, Victoria, West Cameroon,
              Presbook
Kwast, Lloyd E.
    1971   THE DISCIPLING OF WEST CAMEROON: A STUDY
              OF BAPTIST GROWTH, Grand Rapids, Eerdmans
Lewis, Thomas
    n/d   THESE SEVENTY YEARS: AN AUTOBIOGRAPHY
              London, The Carey Press (second edition, London
              1931).
Malinowski, Bronislaw
    1944   A SCIENTIFIC THEORY OF CULTURE AND
              OTHER ESSAYS, Chapel Hill, University of North
              Carolina Press
    1945   THE DYNAMICS OF CULTURE CHANGE: AN
              INQUIRY INTO RACE RELATIONS IN AFRICA
              New Haven, Yale University Press
McGavran, Donald A.
    1970   UNDERSTANDING CHURCH GROWTH, Grand
              Rapids, Eerdmans
Metch, P. L.
    1967   A SHORT HISTORY OF CAMEROON, Onitsha,
              Nigeria. Providence Printing Press
Morgen, Curt
    1893   DURCH KAMERUN VON SUD NACH NORD:
              REISEN UND FORSCHUNGEN IM HINTERLANDE,
              1889 bis 1891 Leipzig, F. U. Brockhaus
Nadel, S. F.
    1951   THE FOUNDATIONS OF SOCIAL ANTHROPOLOGY
              London, Cohen and West
Renier, G. J.
    1965   HISTORY, ITS PURPOSE AND METHOD, New
              York, Harper & Row, Publishers
Royal Anthropological Institute of Great Britain and Ireland
    1929   NOTES AND QUERIES ON ANTHROPOLOGY
              London, Routledge and Kegan Paul
Rudin, Harry R.
    1938   GERMANS IN THE CAMEROONS 1884-1914, New
              Haven, Yale University Press

BIBLIOGRAPHY (cont.)

Scherer, James A.
1971   "The Life and Growth of Churches in Mission," IN-
        TERNATIONAL REVIEW OF MISSION, LX, 237:
        125-135
Scheve, E.
1901   DIE MISSION DER DEUTSCHEN BAPTISTEN IN
        KAMERUN WEST-AFRICA VON 1884 bis 1901
        Berlin, Missionsbuchhandlung Missionsgesellschaft
        der deutschen Baptisten
Southern Cameroons, Government of
1958   INTRODUCING THE SOUTHERN CAMEROONS
        Lagos, Nigeria, Federal Government Printer
Süvern, E. R.
n/d   UNSERE MISSIONSREISE INS HINTERLAND
        KAMERUNS, Kassel, Druck von J. G. Oncken
Tippett, Alan R.
1968   FIJIAN MATERIAL CULTURE: A STUDY OF CUL-
        TURAL CONTEXT, FUNCTION, AND CHANGE
        Honolulu, Hawaii, Bishop Museum Press
Tita, S. N.
1965   HISTORY FOR CAMEROONS, Bamenda, Cameroon,
        Nooremac Press
Victoria Centenary Committee
1958   VICTORIA, SOUTHERN CAMEROONS, 1858-1958
        Victoria, Basel Mission Book Depot
Wilson, Louis, (ed.)
1940   THE PRACTICE BOOK SELECTION, PAPERS
        PRESENTED BEFORE THE LIBRARY INSTITUTE
        OF THE UNIVERSITY OF CHICAGO, Chicago,
        University Press

Part V

God and Man
in
Field Situations

GOD AND MAN IN FIELD SITUATIONS

In the final analysis theology, theory and historical reconstructions have value only when they relate to real life situations, and indicate why churches grow or do not grow, or how they might be expected to grow. McGavran was always a man for case studies. After he left India, where he had himself done numerous case studies, he visited the Philippines, Taiwan, Mexico, some parts of Africa and some North American Indians. He demanded some kind of a case study from all who studied under him. It seems appropriate to assign the papers for this section of the Festschrift to field missionaries, rather than to his colleagues and friends. As McGavran himself would say: these articles come out of the battle. Dr. Yamamori's article on Japan, which is included in the research section because of its methodology, and Stan Shewmaker's application of church growth theory to the Tonga (Zambia) could have been in this section as they also are case studies. The five men represented here have all taken their master's degree in missiology and represent a fair sample of McGavran's men. The topics on which they write were assigned to them.

Any Festschrift honoring McGavran would be incomplete without a people movement study of some kind. Ed Murphy describes one in Colombia. This is written up from the point of view of the key personality behind the movement. We have long needed such an article devoted to this particular aspect. It keeps recurring in people movement studies, but is usually dismissed in a paragraph or a page. Murphy's account is more than a narrative: he pin-points church growth insights all along the way. It is a typical movement he describes. This is one way the Church is growing in our day.

In the SWM—ICG the course in "Culture and Personality" explores ethnopsychology, decision-making and problem-solving, in as much as they relate to church planting and to internal qualitative growth. McGavran touches on this at many points, but as far as I know he never identified it as a field of study in its own rights. Yet many of his emphases on obstructions to church growth fall into this area, as for example, the problem of individuals extracted from family groups to become mission station employees. James Sauder takes up this problem area for his article. He identifies some themes calling for deeper research, gives them names, and suggests directions for field exploration so that church growth may draw from the resources of psychology.

Erwin Spruth is a pioneer missionary among the Enga in the New Guinea Highlands. He is involved with the problems confronting a pioneer as he approaches a new ethnic group. What kind of researching has to be done before a meaningful gospel may be presented to such a people? He gives us the positive and negative aspects, the factors that lead to acceptance and rejection.

Gunnar Kjaerland is a Norwegian. English is his fourth language, but his heart burns for the nomad and the illiterate. Without any anthropological training he penetrated deep into an understanding of one the most complex of all social systems and found that it explained many of his church planting problems. In this volume he writes on the need to bring the Gospel to the illiterate nomads, and puts forward a number of practical approaches he is now trying to develop himself among the Borana of Southern Ethiopia.

Somewhere in this volume someone had to deal with Latin American syncretism, one of the major obstructions to qualitative growth—perfecting, as McGavran calls it. The editor had a feeling this ought to be dealt with from the inside rather than by an American missionary. Joel Romero builds his study on a base of his observations in Argentina. The article has a non-American ring about it. Romero differentiates between feeling and reasoning and has much to say about the curandero. He recognizes the need for symbolism, yet puts his finger on the dangers of syncretism. He recognizes that something must be changed yet something must be preserved if the new religion is to be meaningful, and he believes the evangelist succeeds or fails at the point of his follow-up program after conversion.

Not only is this team of writers a typical representation of McGavran's graduates, but they write of a typical set of field situation problems. In some way or other they all show that McGavran's insights and influence reach out a long way from his Institute in Pasadena.

A characteristic of static mission stations is that they have án institutional life many times greater than is needed for the little congregation and quite impossible of support by it. The congregation is made up quite largely of the employees of the big mission institutions. . . . The institutionalized mission station is like an inverted pyramid, with huge accumulation of service organizations dominating the little congregation. This inevitably creates the idea that to be a Christian is to receive aid from institutions. . . The mission station . . . should be considered the temporary encampment of an army . . . Houses and institutions . . . should be considered expendable. But the psychology of the Mission Station Approach is never this. It is almost impossible for one who is immersed in the Mission Station Approach to avoid the conviction that his primary duty is to serve the station . . . instead of a means to the discipling of peoples.

BRIDGES OF GOD,
p. 59.

21

PSYCHOLOGICAL DIMENSIONS
OF CHURCH GROWTH (Honduras)

James Sauder

Much has been written on how theology and anthropology relate to the growth of the church, but the study of how psychology does so has barely begun. This may be due to the fact that missionaries have given little attention to the psychological aspect of the task. Most psychological studies focus on the individual in western culture. This paper recognizes the need for cross-cultural psychological studies and is a tentative or exploratory approach.

The easiest approach would be to select a theory and test it on the field. But no theory of the psychology of church growth has been enunciated. The on-the-field experience needs to become the basis for articulating a theory of this kind. Eight years ago, as I began my missionary work, the series of experiences I encountered did not seem to fit into any logical pattern. Only after several years of

---

*The names of persons referred to in this paper are withheld in order to maintain confidence and because some of the observations are tentative pending further research.

field exposure did any patterns become evident. In this paper I will use my participation in the growth of the Honduras Mennonite Church as case study material in an attempt to formulate a tentative concept of the psychology of church growth. The starting point for such a study involves me in some introspection and participant observation. These processes will help identify certain problems and themes which will be related to what others have written about these problems.

Identifying the Themes

(1) When a new missionary arrives on the field, he must think about relating to the national people. The first thing which deeply impressed me was my apparent affluence over against their poverty. Some came to me looking for work. For the first time in my life, I was expected to be an employer. As time progressed, I found myself operating from a postiton of wealth within a culture of poverty. Young men who came to me wanted to depend on me. I discovered later they were boys who were not living under the influence of their fathers. They wanted me to be their "substitute father" with all the economic and social benefits that would imply. But my role as missionary, supervised by a mission board and budget, did not permit me to fulfill their expectations. As a result, a certain ambivalence developed between the boys and myself. I met some of their needs but I had to neglect others.

When a missionary from a richer nation goes to a people of a poorer nation a dominant-dependent relationship can develop between the missionary and national. In the long run, a sort of ambivalent reaction can set in. Therefore *the dominant-dependent relationship* is a theme for psychological analysis.

(2) Shortly afterwards I developed a relationship with a head man of a large family. After he listened to several open-air services we conducted under a pine tree, he invited us to his house. His living conditions were even poorer than those of the boys. But this father invited people to his home to hear the Gospel. In time he participated very actively in the services himself. At present he is the congregational leader in his town.

Since this family man was a recognized leader in his community, he saw me as a guest whom he sponsored. This leader-guest relationship was quite compatible with my missionary role. Our relationship served as a basis for encouragement. The same man has related well to other church workers in the area. One missionary almost spoiled him with generous gifts but a national pastor was able to help him snap out of his dependence on the missionary. The Gospel has penetrated throughout the extended family of which this man is a head.

(3) In the same community I was introduced to the tensions that the individual experiences in society. The most visible form of tension was the political campaign that was gathering momentum. The young boys happened to be from families who were sympathetic to the opposition party. On repeated occasions these boys were discriminated against by being drafted into public service while other young men were untouched. Since they wanted to be dependent upon me, they expected me to speak in their favor to the authorities in power. However, the day arrived when a military coup upset the whole political campaign. Suddenly the young boys found their party in power. They received a new status. It was not long until they stopped depending on the missionary. On the other hand, the family man in the same military coup lost his position in the town hall. The violent, abrupt political change is only one evidence of the tension that the individual can experience in the setting of the social structure.

For purposes of study, this political phenomena can be described as a build-up of tension that leads to an abrupt release of tension. What happens in the political realm often happens in a lesser degree in many of the human relations in family, church and community. This process of tension build-up and release produces a marked shift in the personality of the individuals involved. Young men who were once overly dependent become bold and fearless. On the other hand, some men who were once powerful began to demonstrate a submissive attitude. For some persons the personality shift is too great. As a result, they move to another community and try to make a fresh start. These migrating people are often open to receive the Gospel if it is presented to them properly.

(4) In another community, I observed the problems of the mission employer and mission employees on a different level. In the former case, the young boys were occasionally employed for various small jobs. But in this community the national was employed as a church worker. Through the years the pattern emerged. The church worker would be asked to serve. He would request a level of support. After several months he would report that his support was inadequate. Sometimes a minor adjustment was made that did not fulfill the expectations of the worker. Gradually the worker started to take more and more of his church employed time to work in his own material pursuits. In time the tension built up to a breaking point and the worker would withdraw from active service, sometimes to be critical of the church.

This pattern was repeated three times. This reaction pattern whereby a former leader becomes a disgruntled observer is not the most conducive to church growth. I call this the company mentality. The company mentality suggests that the national worker sees the Mission as an employment agency and himself as an employee with a disposition to bargain for better conditions.

(5) Fortunately not all the national pastors have gone through this cycle. Recently another pattern is developing. A pastor who has served well for several years in various places also finds the employee status uncomfortable. (Since the Church's budget is subsidized with mission funds, the company mentality relates to both the Mission and the Church). Just lately this pastor has started several projects which contribute to his self-support. He thereby relinquished a part of his church support for other worthy projects. These steps suggest a pattern of increasing responsibility.

(6) There is yet another pattern that presents great hope for church growth. Several Christian merchants dedicate time to witnessing in their business contacts and in the organized church services. These men think of receiving pay from neither the Mission nor the Church. Rather they give freely to the cause of evangelism and church building. Some of them have become congregational leaders, but they need training to enable them to serve better. Nevertheless these fully responsible men are most effective communicators of the Gospel. The Gospel they

communicate is an indigenous message without being
identified with foreign control. We might call them independent lay leaders.

(7) While the role of leaders in the Church is important,
church growth research must also investigate the interpersonal relationships within the church group. A questionnaire completed by the church leaders of the Honduras
Mennonite Church indicated the most common hindrances
to church growth. The majority of the responses fall into
two categories: (i) disharmony among church members,
and (ii) reversion to the former life. At one time I thought
the church growth studies investigated only the entrance of
people into the church; but I learned that church growth
studies also include what happens to members within the
Church and also why some people leave the Church. In a
sense, the tensions within the church group relate to
people leaving the Church. If there is disharmony it is not
surprising that some people leave. But why is disharmony
so common in the Church?

The Church is intended to be characterized by worship
to God and fellowship with other Christians. Ideally, tension
should not exist in the Body of Christ. But in reality, the
Church which is made up of human beings, reflects some
of the tensions of the prevailing society. At one stage in
my investigation, I assumed that tensions within the Church
resulted from what happened in the public services. But I
found that this accounted for only a small number of problems. Then I searched to see if what happens in the social
environment is the clue to the disharmony within the Church.
In this area I found a wealth of evidence.

Many of the tensions within the Church arise from the
social pressures upon the individuals. In the scope of this
paper I can only list some of the kinds of social problems
that impinge upon the church's fellowship: unsettled land
rights; political party animosities; problems between cre-
ditors and debtors; between producers and buyers, between
traditionalists and innovators; and problems relating to
leadership roles and personalities. Many of these problems
relate to such mundane factors as economics and politics.
As I continued my investigation, I was increasingly impressed with the prevailing disharmony in the society. In
fact, the tensions within the churches were a miniature

reflection of the far greater conflicts in the context of society, and I became thankful that the Christian field had reduced the discord to the extent it had.

(8) In addition to the theme of tension, it is necessary to consider the matter of basic needs. When the young men needed to earn money at the mission compound, they attended church regularly. After the political situation changed, their contact with the Church became more infrequent. Church leaders report that when a certain national leader struggled to establish himself in a new community, he was faithful in church attendance. After he established a prosperous business, church leaders report that his dedication to the Church has lessened. I also observed a group who migrated into a community. During the first months they showed great interest in the Christian life. In time many of them scattered and they lost interest. These cases seem to indicate that people in great need are more open to the Gospel than when they consider their needs supplied. At least this is a hypothesis we might well set out to investigate.

This brief sketch of case histories reveals a few themes: the dependency patterns, the tension patterns and the basic need patterns. This tentative list is not exhaustive but does provide a starting point for the analysis of the problem involved.

Analyzing the Problems

(1) The psychological trait of dependence has been described in the setting of the family. A young child is very dependent upon his parents. If he develops properly he will become more self-reliant. However, if a child becomes overly-dependent, he will not mature in a healthy manner. Even as an adult he will want to lean upon someone for security. He will be afraid to venture out. Too much dependence either hinders maturation or even leads to illness (Ruesch, 1959:128). However, child dependence is slightly different from cultural dependence. A child has a biological development that should equip him for eventual autonomy. But if people of one culture depend upon a missionary from another culture, the implications can be quite enduring. The young men were able to overcome their

dependency when the political situation changed. But the employed church worker found himself "in a bind." He wanted the benefits of dependence but in time the relationship became unbearable. He tried to work his way out. Then he set up a sort of ambivalent pattern by getting in and withdrawing several times. When finally a missionary told him that he will no longer receive support, even his ambivalent pattern was threatened. His pattern then became one of detached withdrawal.

A study made of the Negroes in the United States shows some patterns of dealing with dependency that throw light on the reactions of national church workers (Powdermaker, 1959:597-608). The Negro slave's reaction to dependency could take several directions: (i) There is direct aggression against the true object. Only occasionally has the Negro slave attacked his white overseer. (ii) There is substituted aggression against a more vulnerable person. He is too inhibited to attack the real originator of the problem. So he takes it out on someone else. (iii) There is a retreat from the situation. For the slave this was not always possible. (iv) There was indentification with the prestige of the white master. (v) There is the diversion of aggression into wit. (vi) There is the pattern of deference to the white man but an assumed superiority over the white man. In a Christian setting this took the direction of suffering-greatly-now to be rewarded-greatly-in-heaven. To make this pattern work the Negro kept his real thoughts from the white man. The slave forced into a dependent role would be meek and humble to the white man but an energetic and influential person in his own group.

The relations of missionaries and national church workers provide some interesting parallels. Direct aggression is seldom used unless the missionary takes a less domineering position. Substituted aggression is quite common. If an administration team, made up of a missionary and a national, displeases the group, it is quite common for the national to receive the blame. It is only when the missionary involved manifests that he is willing to be vulnerable that the missionary gets his rightful share of the blame. The retreat pattern is quite common. National church leaders are not slaves and therefore the withdrawal door is open to them. Withdrawal may save the person from greater frustration but it does not contribute to the growth of the Church. An unhappy ex-church worker is the worst advertisement a church can have. Identification with the prestige of the missionary is common. Some missionaries openly foster it while some nationals are happy to follow it. However, Samuel Ramos' exposition of this will be given later. Diverting the aggression into wit is frequent. Maybe not all missionaries are aware of this. But if a missionary is alert enough to detect it, he will be wise to join in laughing about himself and the missionary image. The pattern of deference to missionaries with the accompanying assumed superiority of national ways, has been the prevailing pattern. A foreign newcomer will usually get the answers the nationals think he wants. Only after a long confidential conversation does the real picture begin to emerge. National leaders have stated on various occasions that much church business takes place on a fictitious level out of deference to those that are present. This can become a source of tension.

(2) The management of tension is another problem requiring analysis. The reduction and generation of tension are recognized processes in psychological adjustment (Murry and Kluckholn, 1959: 35-37). The generation of tension is a normal process. A hungry man will put forth effort to get a satisfying meal. The dramatic quality of Latin culture reflects how tension helps to make life tick. The mainspring of a watch needs a certain amount of tension for the watch to run. However, sometimes the tension becomes quite strong. The tension between the suitor and the girl's father can become intense. The tension between a legal wife and her husband's occasional mistress can become dangerous. This state of affairs is summed up in a common word, *celos.* A wife becomes terribly *celoso* when she thinks her man is unfaithful. Sometimes violent aggression results. In politics the "election" campaigns are times when increasing tension sometimes breaks out in violence. The economic difficulties between the "haves" and the "have nots" sometimes build up terrific tensions. Problems of agrarian reform have led to threats and violence. The pistol under the belt is a symbol that serves as a reminder of the latent tension that is present.

The tension factor is evidenced in Latin American literature. The stories of the Spanish conquest, the struggles of revolutionary leaders and the frequent emergence of de facto governments are tension themes that are expressed repeatedly. Samuel Ramos, a Mexican writer with great clarity, uses psychoanalytic categories to deliniate the real self from the ficticious self. The Mexican, as Ramos sees him, is frustrated because he is trying to be what he is not (Ramos, 1962). Nida highlights the dualistic character of Latin American society (Nida, 1969). I have no space to list the many other writers who express similar ideas.

If tension generation is so prevalent, then what are the mechanisms of tension reduction? In politics, the *golpe de estado* (military seizure of government) is an effective way of releasing tension. It is probably only a short term solution. In love, a reluctant father gives in if his daughter runs off with her lover. Sometimes the celos leads to the actual use of the pistol. But there are milder forms of releasing tension. A complaint to the civil authorities may be effective, depending on one's social position. The more common folk resort to gossip. For some persons, alcohol seems to release them from their anxieties (Horton, 1959:680–690). However, as one can readily detect, these mechanisms may reduce tensions for a short time, but often contribute to the creation of still greater tension. I know of one case where attempts at tension reduction led to a series of vengeance murders between two rival families. So apparently some people at best can work off a frustration, knowing full well that it may lead to greater problems.

Some people, however, can manage the tension quite well. Even though psychological studies tend to focus on the abnormal features, a psychology of the church growth needs to see the motivations that can lead toward constructive, healthy activity. The family man, who was mentioned earlier, had been involved in many quarrels, went to visit his former enemies, and told them of the Gospel. The folks in his community marvel at the genuine change that he has experienced. The Christian merchant also received his share of knocks. Some "friends" took advantage of his goodwill, borrowed money and then disappeared. On a few occasions his store was robbed. After the initial frustration was over, he decided that diligent work and efficient management would soon make up for his losses. He resolved his tension by being really industrious in his business and the Lord has prospered him.

(3) The basic needs patterns also relate to church planting. In the case histories referred to, people who were in need became responsive to the Gospel. Unfortunately, some of those same people became indifferent as they became prosperous. Traditionally the Mennonite Mission has been concerned about the physical and material needs of people. The Mennonite Central Committee has served to relieve the sufferers of famine, hurricane damage and war. The Voluntary Service program channels the conscientious objectors to war into agricultural projects in Honduras. Mennonites believe that Christian love seeks to meet not only spiritual but physical need as well.

The crucial problem to consider is how the alleviation of basic needs relates to the growth of the Church. Why do people who were responsive become indifferent? The most tangible human needs are food, medicine and clothing. The Mission has tried to help meet these needs. In some cases the people respond to the Gospel while they are being helped. But the services of Christian love, it is alleged, should not be used as bait to attract rice Christians. So much of the service program is given as benevolence. The decision to accept Christ needs to be a voluntary matter. What is the result?

As has been demonstrated, people tend to be less interested in the Gospel after their needs are met. This phenomenon is expressed in two forms: (i) those who did not accept the Gospel while they were being helped are often less inclined to do so in the future and (ii) those who do accept Christ while they are being helped in some cases become indifferent as their needs are met. What is the solution? Should we disregard the basic needs? Is there a more complete approach?

Psychological studies indicate that human needs involve more than food, clothing and medicine. Maslow's book *Motivation and Personality* indicates five need levels: (i) physiological, (ii) safety, (iii) love and belongingness, (iv) self-eteem and (v) self-actualization (Maslow, 1945 and Arnoff, 1967). When a person supplies his physiological needs, then he is able to devote more attention to his safety needs. When his sense of belongingness is satisfied, then he can work on his need for self-esteem and self-actualization. This analysis of human need has many church growth implications.

Since the physiological needs are visible, Christian Love responds by trying to meet them. Mennonites, with agricultural background, are especially equipped to tackle problems at that level. But when the physiological needs of a person are met, he thereby moves outside the range of our service ministries and becomes indifferent. In fact, from his improved standing he is able to look down upon the ministries that only serve physiological needs. But what about his safety needs, love needs, self-esteem needs. By and large the Mission has neglected these higher needs. In some cases the service program involving a great proportion of North American personnel and the use of technological methods, may even threaten to some extent the national's need for self-esteem and self-actualization. If and when this is true, the Mission has succeeded in innoculating the community with a small dose of the Gospel, which effectively immunizes them to the whole Gospel.

These psychological factors of dependence, tension and basic needs relate to each other. Ramos has provided a lucid analysis of the Mexican personality. According to him, the Mexican in poverty suffers from an inferiority complex. As he observes the foreigner, he manifests his dependence by trying to imitate him. This is essentially similar to the dependency trait of trying to identify with the prestigious white man mentioned by Powdermaker. After the Mexicans exert great effort to mimic the foreigner, he discovers that he cannot really bridge the gap between what he is and what he wants to be. Therefore he becomes even more frustrated, thereby intensifying the tension between his real and fictitious self. Ramos suggests that the Mexican should be willing to be a Mexican (Ramos, 1962).

Searching for Solutions

After analyzing the problems it is necessary to search for solutions. The solutions can be found through careful research. Let me briefly outline some of the areas of investigation that can lead toward solutions that will foster church growth:

(i) Research should discover the processes of church growth that are authentic in each segment of the Honduras population. In the tightly knit communities the "homogeneous unit" approach probably is significant. But in some areas the heterogeneity seems more predominant than the homogeneity. In such settings how is the Church to grow? Should the Church use tension-reduction methods as evangelistic tools?

(ii) Further research should identify how the personality of the Honduran people relates to church planting. Which theme is most useful—tension, dependence or basic needs? Or are there other themes that have not been identified? How do the Latin American themes relate to the themes of Anglo-America? What are the similarities and differences? What orientation should all Anglo-American personnel have before attempting service in Honduras?

(iv) How can the administrative structures of Mission and Church be modified to reduce the Anglo-Latin tension? What structures fit the Honduras needs?

(v) How can the tensions within the Church be reduced? What tension reducing resources are found in the Gospel? What is the role of the Holy Spirit in integrating the personality?

(vi) How can the service ministry be modified to meet the full spectrum of human need? How can the program work toward the goal of the self-actualization of Christians? What new psychological, anthropological orientation will service personnel need? How can all the mission personnel be trained in church growth studies?

This paper could have been called "Toward a Psychology of Church Growth." The implication is that the understanding of church growth, especially those aspects termed perfecting by McGavran (1955, 15-16) and qualitative by Tippett (1966) could be greatly deepened in the next decade by exploring the dimensions of ethnopsychology.

BIBLIOGRAPHY:

Aronoff, Joel
    1967   PSYCHOLOGICAL NEEDS AND CULTURAL SYS-
            TEMS, Princeton, New Jersey, D. Van Nostrand Co.
Horton, Donald
    1954   "The Functions of Alcohol in Primitive Societies" in
            Kluckhohn and Murray (eds.).
Kluckhohn, Clyde and Henry A. Murray (eds.)
    1954   PERSONALITY IN NATURE, SOCIETY AND CUL-
            TURE, New York, Alfred A. Knopf
Maslow, A. H.
    1954   MOTIVATION AND PERSONALITY, New York,
            Harper Brothers
McGavran, D. A.
    1955   THE BRIDGES OF GOD, London, World Dominion
            Press
Murray, Henry A. and Clyde Kluckhohn
    1954   "Outline of a Conception of Personality" in Kluckhohn
            and Murray (eds.)
Nida, Eugene
    1969   COMMUNICATING THE GOSPEL IN LATIN
            AMERICA, Cuernavaca, Mexico, CIDOC
Powdermaker, Hortense
    1954   "The Channeling of Negro Aggression by the Cultural
            Process" in Kluckhohn and Murray (eds.)
Ramos, Samuel
    1962   PROFILE OF MAN AND CULTURE IN MEXICO,
            New York, McGraw Hill Book Co.
Reusch, Jurgen
    1954   "Social Technique, Social Status and Social Change in
            Illness" in Kluckhohn and Murray (eds.)
Tippett, A. R.
    1966   "Church Growth or Else!" WORLD VISION MAGA-
            ZINE, February

People-movement churches are led by their own natural leaders, are out away from mission stations and Western-educated nationals, run on their own power, and are not assisted much by the missionary or educated national, are thrown back on their own resources, and are free to be led by the Holy Spirit. Consequently they look, sound and smell indigenous.

UNDERSTANDING CHURCH GROWTH,
p. 352.

22

THE KEY PERSONALITY
IN A PEOPLE MOVEMENT
(Colombia)

Ed Murphy

Dr. McGavran has made a great contribution to missiology by bringing to light key principles which are discoverable in the movements of people to Christ. Certain factors occur over and over again. McGavran helps us to penetrate the fog, and come to the heart of the question as to why people come to Christ in one situation and not in another. He has shown us that spiritual factors are not the only causes operative in such a situation. He has seen that cultural, sociological, and strategical factors also play a decisive role. One of the principles upon which McGavran has laid great stress is the role of the key personality in a movement of a people to Christ. The story I am about to relate illustrates this principle in action in a people movement to Christ which is now taking place in rural Colombia.

Perhaps the most remarkable people movement to Christ in the history of the Church of Colombia, South America has taken place in the thinly populated northwestern interior of that country. Charles Bennett, writing in the Church Growth Bulletin, described this spiritual stirring as, "the spontaneous Cauca River Movement (related to the

Latin American Mission) which, on a thoroughly indigenous basis, has started eighty-two congregations in a little more than a decade" (Bennett, 1970: 85).

Bennett's article describes the impact of this movement on the Presbyterian churches located in bordering areas. He states, "Contacts with the Cauca River Movement have provided most of the impetus for church planting evangelism and charistmatic manifestations" found in the nearby Presbyterian churches (86). My own experience based on seven years of evangelistic and Bible teaching ministry in Colombia, confirms and even expands Bennett's praise of this movement. The stimulation it is giving to both discipling and perfecting in the entire north-western part of Colombia is remarkable. In November of 1969, I was part of a group of missionaries and national leaders ministering in the extreme north-western jungle-agricultural tip of the State of Choco. Sandwiched between the Darien Mountains of Panama and the Caribbean gulf of Uraba on the Colombian side, this area had been opened by the government for homesteading. We found at least two almost entirely evangelical villages, colonized by converts of the Cauca River Movement. Several other communities had strong evangelical churches also founded by migrating believers of this people movement. Colombian laymen touched by this movement were "going everywhere preaching the Word."

Bennett's description of this movement as the "Cauca River Movement" is justified by the fact that it has spread through villages bordering on or close to the Cauca River. The latter is an important river in Colombia, coming second only to the mighty Magdalena. Yet one could object that this movement could better be called the San Jorge-Cauca River Movement, the former being the main tributary of the Cauca in this part of Colombia. It was in the small villages bordering this river that the movement first began. Its strength now lies in the settlement between the two rivers.

Some other observers (including myself) refer to this movement as the "Landero People Movement." This is juyified for two reasons. First, it is characterized by a continued series of "multi-individual and mutually interdependent decisions for Christ," which is McGavran's definition of a people movement (McGavran, 1970: 302-305). As such it has spread through nuclear family, extended family and friendship conversion patterns. Second, it is the Landero People Movement for the key personality in this turning to Christ since the beginning has been Victor Landero. The story of the San Jorge-Cauca River Movement is thus basically the story of the power of God operating in one life—Victor Landero. He is the key personality, to use McGavran's definition, in this work of God's Spirit.

When I first met Victor at a Colombian pastor's conference in 1963, I was not immediately impressed. He did not seem to possess the charismatic personality usually attributed to such aggressive spiritual leaders. He was shy, very quiet and somewhat retiring. He was humbly dressed, looking like a typical "campesino" (country dweller) one would run into anywhere in the interior of this country.

Such first impressions could never have been more deceiving. When it was time for him to speak about the Lord or His work, words of grace flowed from his lips. He possessed an insight into the work of the Spirit in winning men to Christ, forming them into New Testament indigenous churches and leading new believers into the reception of the gifts of the Spirit needed for the full growth of the churches, like few other men I have ever known. Before his conversion to Christ, Victor lived up river in the interior of the State of Cordoba. His home village, Nueva Estacion, is a tiny port on the San Jorge River. Victor had lived anything but a moral life. For years he ran a "cantina," a bar, as well as a house of prostitution. For some time he lived simultaneously with three different women. Furthermore, he was completely illiterate (Strachan, 1970:34).

In the city of Monteria, the capitol of the State most affected by the Landero Movement, the state of Colodobi, lived one of Colombia's outstanding evangelist-pastors, Rev. Pedro Gutierrez. Pedro is a rugged, forceful, dynamic, country-style evangelist. He has probably led more men to Christ who in turn have gone into the full-time ministry than any living man in Colombia.

Pedro was pastoring the Iglesia Evangelica in Monteria. It was 1949, and *La Violencia,* (The Violence) had just hit Colombia. It was dangerous to go outside of the largest cities to evangelize, but this did not detain Pedro. He was burdened for a small village called Provedencia, in the interior of the State. Provedencia was a "city of refuge," a pueblo known to be the hideout of thieves, murderers and others who lived outside the law. Setting off on one of his frequent evangelistic journeys, Pedro finally reached the village. He preached alone in the plaza, offering Bibles for sale. No one showed the slightest interest in purchasing a copy. Soon, several men began to argue with him. It wasn't long before he found himself engaged in a heated discussion. Before he was aware of it, the sun was beginning to set. Pedro had not planned on spending the night in the dangerous village. Yet, it would be even more dangerous alone on the trails at night; so finding a small room, he locked himself in and began a long, sleepless night.

About 2:00 a.m. he was startled by a loud knocking on the door. A voice on the other side shouted, "Are you the man who was selling Bibles in the plaza?" Pedro answered that he was. "Well, I want to buy one right now," came the voice. Hesitatingly, Pedro opened the door and in stepped a very young man who identified himself as Victor Landero. He bought the Bible and went his way. The next day Pedro returned to Monteria (Gutierrez, 1963).

David M. Howard, formerly the Director of the Latin American Mission in Colombia and one of Victor's most intimate friends, continues the story in a personal letter to Dr. Paul S. Rees of World Vision International.

> Victor's purpose in buying it (the Bible) was simply out of curiosity because someone told him that this book would show him how God made the world. He did not know how to read at the time, so put the Bible away in a box. . . About eight years later, having learned a little bit how to read, he dug the book out of a trunk for the first time and began to look it over. A friend walked by his house and saw him reading the Bible and asked him about it.

> Three days later, a graduate of our Bible Institute in Sincelejo (Centro Biblico Del Carribe) named Eliezer Benavidez went into the village where Victor Landero then lived. (Nueva Estacion). Asked if any evangelical lived there or if anyone had a Bible, Victor's friend, who had seen him a few days previously with a Bible, directed Eliezer to Victor's house. Eliezer arrived to

find Victor reading a tract that someone had given him. He began to talk about the Bible.

For a period of several weeks, Eliezer visited Victor on several occasions. The Holy Spirit began to speak, and primarily through the reading of Scripture plus the witness of Eliezer, Victor gave his heart to the Lord (Howard, 1963:1-2).

The story of Eliezer's faithfulness in ministering the Word of God to Victor is described for us in David Howard's recent book, "Hammered as Gold." It is exciting reading, for it details the inner struggle in Victor's heart in coming into full assurance of his faith and then allowing the Spirit of God to purge his life (Howard, 1969:103-139).

The violence ended about 1959. David had been hearing rumors of the existence of believers in the interior of Cordoba state. Since it was now safer to make the journey, he decided to make a survey trip through this jungle and mountainous area. He told me the following story:

> I began to speak to people in different homes that I visited along the trail. I would take out the Word of God and present the Gospel to them. Invariably their response would be, 'Oh, we are already believers.' On inquiring how they had come to Christ and who told them about the Lord, their answer was invariably the same, 'Victor Landero led us to a knowledge of the Lord Jesus Christ.' This same thing happened everywhere that my journey took me. I soon found groups of believers meeting in homes, through the entire region. Always, on inquiring who had taught them to organize themselves into churches, the answer was the same: 'Victor Landero taught us.' I estimated that there must have been about 1,000 believers in the area gathering together in some 20 or 25 different groups. And this was supposed to be an unevangelized area! (Howard, 1963b).

Victor told David that immediately after his conversion the Holy Spirit filled him with a hunger for the Word of God. The more he meditated in the Scriptures the more he felt himself a debtor to share its message with all men.

He began with his own family. It was not long before his common-law wife, his ten brothers and sisters and his parents were safe in the Lord. Next he reached out to relatives, friends and acquaintances. Many of them came to

Christ. Soon he began to take evangelistic journeys, winning families to Christ along the rivers and trails.

In 1957 he became burdened for an area along the San Pedro River some distance from his home. He sold his farm to his brothers and bought a plot of land there. As far as he knew there was not a single believer in this vast stretch of farm and grazing land. Soon his converts covered the area for miles in every direction. Dave Howard later writes:

> Today it is impossible to calculate exactly the total number of believers, as they are scattered all over a vast area, some of which is dense jungle, and other which is farm lands. There are congregations scattered all over, along the rivers and back into the deep woods. A conservative estimate which we tried to make recently with Victor's help . . . would put the figure at 2,000 believers as the very lowest with the probability of its being closer to 3,000. All of these are either a direct or indirect result of Victor's personal witness (Howard, 1963a).

When Victor moved to the San Pedro River, he did not know exactly how to go about his new evangelistic work. It seems that one night he dreamed a dream. He saw himself walking through the forest in the area where he lived. Soon he came upon a house in a grove of trees. He saw himself preaching the Gospel to a group of people in that house. When he awakened, he was certain that God had spoken to him and was telling him to go to that place to preach the Gospel. The problem was he had no idea where that particular farm was located. Soon, however, the impression became unbearable that he should strike out through the woods and find that area he had seen in his dream. The late Dr. Kenneth Strachan, one of Victor's most intimate friends, spoke of this experience in Victor's life:

> For two days he traveled back and forth through the woods until finally, suddenly, he came to a spot in the forest where, before his eyes, he saw the house that he had seen in his dreams. He went to the door and knocked. A woman came to the door and he asked her, 'Would you give me permission to hold an evangelical meeting in your home tonight?' The lady looked at him with astonishment in her eyes and said, 'Yes you may.' And that was all.

> That night, some 37 people gathered together in the house;
> that night, 37 people accepted the Lord Jesus Christ as
> their Saviour. The next day the lady said to Victor, 'The
> night before last, I dreamed a dream; in my dream I saw
> my house filled with people, and I saw a man preaching
> from a Book to all of the people.' (She had never seen
> a Bible before in her life.) 'When you came to the
> door last night and asked me for permission to preach
> the Gospel in my house, I was so astonished that I was
> afraid to tell you of my dream of the night before.' . . .
> On that spot today is a congregation of believers.
> (Strachan, 1963:34-35) (Translated from the original
> Spanish by the author).

Thus began the ministry of a man that I have called elsewhere, "Victor Landero, a Colombian Apostle"(Murphy,
1971: 68-80). If we consider a modern-day apostle as a "sent
one" who moves into an area where Christ has not been
named, proclaims the truth of the Gospel with such overwhelming power that soon a group of believers is gathered
together, taught, trained, organized into a local church and
then repeats the process over and over again until a group
of indigenous churches is established, then Victor Landero
is a true modern apostle. As Dr. J.D. Pentecost has written:

> I believe that this, in a sense, is a permanent gift,
> (the gift of apostle). When one goes into an area where
> Christ has never been named and brings a message of
> the Gospel so that a few of those in darkness believe,
> and then teaches them, instructs them, and organizes
> them into an indigenous assembly, that man is doing
> the work of an apostle (Pentecost, 1963: 172).

Some of the undeniable evidence of Victor's apostleship
in the above sense will be seen as I further describe his
church-planning strategy.

First, Victor is not interested in just winning a few
isolated converts. He seeks to win families to Christ and
form these believers into New Testament churches, which
is good church growth technique.

David Howard relates some information which reveals
the apostolic gift and faith possessed by Victor.

> He told me that he had an unwritten principle on which
> he worked, namely, that he ought to be able to visit an
> area five times, and in that time have a congregation

> established which he would no longer have to help. I asked him how this has worked out and he said, 'So far it has never failed once.'
>
> I know many of his congregations scattered all through the back woods and they are thriving, active groups who are reaching out in effective witness to their area (Howard, 1963a).

Secondly, in true apostolic fashion, Victor refuses to pastor any one particular church.

Following the Biblical principle of training by example, he takes some key people from among the new converts with him on his missionary journeys. With this type of on-the-job training, plus the atmosphere of prayer, Bible study and faith that characterizes the life of the church in this area, laymen soon discover their spiritual gifts and become immediately involved in the Christian ministry. This has led to a spontaneous multiplication of churches governed by members raised up from within their own ranks. These key laymen, trained by Victor, in turn train others. Soon small teams go about evangelizing or visiting newer churches, encouraging them in the faith.

Such a ministry takes time. How could a busy farmer ever engage in church-planning and shepherding ministry? Strachan gives us our answer:

> When the Lord called him to preach the Gospel . . . he promised Him to separate three days out of every week to work full-time in the Lord's harvest, and he would use the remaining four days to cultivate his land and take care of his family. The result was that he soon discovered that in three days he could take care of his farm so effectively that he decided he would give four days to the Lord. At the present (1963) he is dedicating five days a week full-time to the Lord and in two days he is able to take care of his small farm (Strachan: 1970) (Translated by the author from the original Spanish. EM)

Victor's affirmation that he expects to leave an indigenous church in an area after no more than five visits, introduces us to the strategy of church-planning that the Holy Spirit has given to him.

First, it is a strategy based on local culture.

The growth of Christ's churches is rooted both in

sociology and theology. They grow among men in society and the society can either encourage or hinder their growth. If the church planter recognizes the major features of the culture of the people among whom he is working, and tries to work in harmony with those cultural components, churches can take immediate root among a responsive people and spontaneously multiply. This is what is happening in Cordoba and Bolivar. Victor and his co-workers have not conscientiously set out to work along this line. They are, without a doubt, totally unaware that they are following sound anthropological procedure as they engage in their church-planning ministry; but in reality this is what they are doing.

In the blessing of God it is fortunate they have not had to work under foreign control. By foreign control I mean not only foreign missionaries, but also Colombians from other parts of the country who would be ignorant of local culture. Thus, from the beginning, Victor has set out in his church-planning labors doing what would be natural for a man from his cultural background. Some of the aspects of his strategy follow well-known principles of church growth.

The churches continue to meet right where they begin, in the converts' homes or yards. This is where Colombians naturally meet for socializing in these rural areas. Thus there is nothing foreign about the way the churches meet for fellowship.

When the churches grow so large that the homes cannot contain the people any longer, they do not hesitate to build special buildings. It must be borne in mind, however, that the buildings are identical to the other homes or buildings in the area. They are rustic, made of branches and of mud, just as simple as the homes of the believers who make up the churches. It has never occurred to them to seek for money from a foreign mission to build their places of worship.

The Gospel naturally flows along the webs of intimate relationships. It usually spreads first through the nuclear families, then into the extended families and finally through friendship ties. These are tiny parts of a people movement, each being multi-individual and mutually-interdependent decisions for Christ. Soon, entire settlements and villages become evangelical. As a result of such group movements, the converts experience little or no social dislocation. They come to Christ in the comforting companionship of their fellows.

Second, it is a strategy based upon New Testament principles.

The Church is recognized to be the people of God in a given community. Where the Church worships, its form is secondary. The spiritual life of the people making up that church is primary.

The churches have been indigenous from the very beginning. They have no foreign overtones. Furthermore, it has never occurred to them to expect outside leadership or financial help in order to carry on their ministry. This is their responsibility and they have never doubted it. They expect the Holy Spirit to give spiritual gifts to His people to serve the Body.

The question of charismatic endowments has caused great controversy among many believers in America. It would be very instructive to the reader to study chapters 12 and 13 of Howard's book, Hammered as Gold. There the author discusses both the positive and negative aspects of the gifts as they appear among these believers. Suffice it to say, God has given to Victor, among his many other gifts, the gift of discernment of spirits. He is usually able to determine the source of the spirit operating in the believers. When counterfeit gifts are manifest, it is his practice to gather the elders and pastors together for fasting and prayer. They are forceful in reprimanding false spirits. This has produced a church in which the gifts of the Spirit are freely manifested, and false or extreme emotional manifestations are in held in check. Furthermore, the emphasis upon the gifts of the Spirit has been true to the Bible in that the stress is on gifts given for the edification of the Body and for the extension of the Gospel, not for personal aggrandizement.

In obedience to Scriptural principles, Victor has expected God to raise up men possessing the supporting, ministerial gifts, (Ephesians 4: 11-12). It has never occurred to these churches to import pastors from other areas of the country. They have expected God to raise up from among themselves "apostles, prophets, evangelists, and pastor-teachers."

Anyone who is personally familiar with this movement cannot deny that God has done just that.

A remarkable system of training members of the church in the exercise of their spiritual gifts has been instituted. Such believers are trained in at least three different ways—

(1) Training programs are held within the local churches themselves. The pastors and elders are expected to train their believers. They are given constant help by the leaders who travel in a circuit from church to church. Thus, the local leadership training program is not allowed to bog down.

(2) These include both on the job training and training by example. Victor and the other gifted leaders continually teach the new believers by taking them with them on their missionary journeys. In this way, their 'Timothys' learn what it means to go outside of their own community to testify for Christ and engage in aggressive church-planning.

(3) Special training programs are held. Some believers are able to go into a nearby Bible institute for short periods of training. Others are trained through extension programs which make training available for the believers without their having to leave their families and means of livelihood. Still others are trained in evening Bible institutes and by the periodic week-long spiritual retreats and training seminars held throughout the entire region.

The strength for the great ministry these believers carry on seems to come from three sources: (1) their insatiable hunger for the study of the Word of God; (2) their complete obedience to the work of the Holy Spirit; and (3) their intensive prayer life. Their morning devotions may start at 5 a.m. and continue to 6 or 7 a.m. This time is spent in intense Bible study; dialogue among themselves on the portion of the Word of God read; fervent, audible prayer, praise, worship, praise, worship; and, when it is necessary because of the great amount of sickness in the area, the laying on of hands for healing.

The new converts are immediately involved in outreach with the Gospel. This serves not only to help them discover their spiritual gifts but also to recognize that to be a Christian means one must serve the Lord.

Most of these new believers are either illiterate, or at the most, semi-literate farmers or herdsmen. They know little about the intricacies of theological debate. There is one thing they do know, however. The love of God within them compels them to witness everywhere of their faith in Christ. David Howard has written—

> It was late at night and the small oil lamp in the thatch house was flickering low. Nevertheless, the young man kept plying the three missionaries with questions about the Bible. He had been saved for seven months, but this was his first contact with missionaries . . . having been led to the Lord by other laymen, he himself was now enthusiastically witnessing to his friends, using what little knowledge of the Scriptures he had been able to pick up on his own. When asked about how many believers there are in this area, he thought a moment, and finally counted 30 or 35 who loved the Lord and would meet around His word . . . that was two and a half years ago (1958). This year (1961) at the annual convention . . . the statistical report of about 860 believers (Howard, 1961).

David recounted to me his experience when he visited a group of these believers some years later. He asked them how many of them had been led to Christ either by a missionary or by a full-time pastor. Not a single one raised his hand. He then asked how many of them had been led to Christ by one of his family members or one of his neighbors. All of them raised their hands, some 100 adults (Howard, 1965).

Victor Landero's story is remarkable yet it is just one of the many movements of the Spirit of God which have come about through the life and ministry of one man, the key personality. So often when we read the stories of such men we are reading about what happened in the past, many years ago. One of the exciting facts of the Landero People Movement is that it is taking place right now. Even as you read these words, Victor Landero and his fellow believers are busy about the Lord's business, spreading the Gospel throughout the northwestern part of Colombia.

What does all this have to say to missionaries and missionary strategists? While there are many lessons to be learned here, let me reiterate again that God works through key men. If we can locate the key personality in a given situation, or by the grace of God that person is brought

to Christ, and if we have the faith to allow the Spirit of
God to use that person according to His sovereign will
regardless of whether or not he be an educated man, that
key man can open up an entire area to the Gospel of Christ.
This is what is happening in Colombia through Victor
Landero. May such incidents become the rule instead of the
exception, as missionaries and church leaders seek to
cooperate with the Spirit of God both in discipling the lost
and equipping the saints "for the work of the ministry."

BIBLIOGRAPHY:

Bennett, Charles
    1970   "Notable Church Multiplication in Colombia." CHURCH
           GROWTH BULLETIN
Gutierrez, Pedro
    1963   Personal Interview.
Howard, David M.
    1961   "The Latin American Mission Moves Ahead in Colom-
           bia." LATIN AMERICAN EVANGELIST
    1963a   Letter to Dr. Paul S. Rees, June 11.
    1963b   Personal Interview.
    1965   Personal Interview.
    1969   HAMMERED AS GOLD, New York, Harper & Row.
Murphy, Edward F.
    1971   CHURCH GROWTH AND THE GIFTS OF THE
           SPIRIT, M.A. Thesis, Fuller Theological Seminary,
           Pasadena
McGavran, D. A.
    1970   UNDERSTANDING CHURCH GROWTH, Grand
           Rapids, William B. Eerdmans Co.
Pentecost, J. D.
    1963   THE DIVINE COMFORTER, Westwood, New Jersey,
           F. H. Revell Co.
Strachan, Kenneth
    1970   DESAFIO A LA EVANGELIZACION, Buenos Aires,
           Editorial Logos.

The more we know about how men organize their lives, make innovations, shift to new cultures, and graft new ideas into their intellectual rootstock, the better we can help them to make the transition to the Christian faith. By themselves these sciences are neutral. They neither favor nor oppose the expansion of the Christian religion. They are bodies of knowledge about how men behave. We believe this knowledge can be used to the glory of God and the expansion of His Church. We yoke these sciences to the missionary passion and use them in the service of the Great Commission.

CHURCH GROWTH AND CHRISTIAN MISSION
p. 239

23

TAKING STOCK
OF AN ETHNIC UNIT
FOR CHURCH PLANTING
(New Guinea)

Erwin Spruth

Although church growth is always the result of the Spirit
of God working in the hearts and lives of His people, for God
alone gives the increase, yet I am convinced that the method
of planting makes a big difference in the size and quality of
the harvest. It is not only necessary for someone to preach,
but people must be able to hear and understand the message
if it is to change their lives. God wants a Gospel more than
a foreign proclamation. He demands more than a silent
Christian presence or a mere dialogue that leads nowhere.
God wants people who are made new, freed by Jesus Christ,
living in forgiveness. He wants entire peoples brought into
a living relationship with Himself so that they may reach
their full potential as redeemed men. God wants and expects
church growth. As His people, chosen to carry out His will
in the world, it is our task to work for this, to plant in such
a way that growth is possible. I am well aware that I am
speaking in the language of Donald McGavran, who has
repeatedly stressed the necessity and the possibility of
church growth in these terms.

His studies into the various factors, which have aided or retarded church growth, have given a new direction to the mission outreach of the church in our day. Other church growth writers have followed his lead and have added to our knowledge of the many varied factors which effect church growth. Some of their studies have shown that churches stopped growing or failed to grow because the planters were unable to communicate the Gospel. Planting was done without adequate preparation; without a thorough knowledge of the people and their needs and ways (Tippett, 1967; Olsen, 1969; Read, 1965). Churches have remained small. Countless individuals have been lost and have never come face to face with the Lord Jesus Christ, because the Christian mission often assumed that all peoples are the same and that Western culture is the way to God. The mission task in our day must make full use of insights gained through church growth research—listening before we speak, knowing before we teach, understanding before we advocate change, and preparing before we plant.

McGavran closes his book, *Understanding Church Growth,* with a chapter on planning for growth (1970: 354-69). He points out the need to have each plan fit the population at which it is aimed. Now I shall develop this idea of planning and preparation.

No adequate plan can be devised until the missionary knows the people and their sociological and cultural background. Patterns of kinship, land ownership, marriage, and self-image do make a difference in how one approaches a given group of people with the Gospel (183-193). A missionary has to understand the fears, needs, and drives of a people in order to share Christ in a way that has meaning for them (Tippett, 1968). The local pattern of leadership may well determine the best form of ministry and shape of the church among a given people. Therefore we must become familiar with the culture and life style of those to whom we bring Christ. Where we are not an integral part of an ethnic group, many of our efforts at church planting will be in danger of being without knowledge and empathy that can be gained only through a thorough study of the groups. Fully recognizing the fact that it is always God who acts to bring His Church into being, I am convinced that planting which leads to great growth usually takes

place when missionaries are fully aware of and considerate
for the structure and beliefs of the society.

Collecting Data

Even if a missionary is not a trained anthropologist he
should be familiar with the methods of anthropological
research and make use of them in attempting to understand
the people among whom he is working. All available written
materials concerning the group should be studied and
evaluated. This includes not only formal ethnographic
studies, but reports of government officers, and other
travelers. All details concerning the social institutions and
patterns of relationships must be noted and checked. Where
a missionary anthropologist is available, the sending organization would be foolish not to make use of his services.

Regardless of who does the research, the only effective
way to learn to know any group of people is to live and work
among them. However, I would urge that missionaries first
go as learners and observers, until such time as they know
the people and their ways. It is almost axiomatic that the
learning of the local language is a sine qua non for collecting adequate data and for communicating with the people.
Many missions, including the one under which I serve, have
made mistakes in evaluation and procedure because they
were unwilling to take the time to understand before they
began to speak and teach. Let me illustrate the need for
an adequate "stock taking" for the planting of the church
from the life and growth of the Wabag Lutheran Church
among the Enga peoples of the Western Highlands of New
Guinea. Knowledge and understanding aided in planting
this church, but misunderstanding and ignorance of certain
dimensions of the culture have raised problems which are
only now being met (Arndt, 1970; Brennan, 1970; Spruth,
1970; Wagner, 1970).

Social Structure

The social structure of any group of people should
determine both the method of planting and the form of the
church. A missionary coming from the highly individualized
society of the West often worked with the individual without

considering the group. If he follows this inclination, he often only succeeds in pulling several marginal or dissident people out of their social group and effectively blocks any church planting among the rest of the people. We plant the church within the society rather than impose a foreign church that destroys the social structure. It is important whether a given group of people think of themselves as a unit or whether they consider themselves as individuals. A missionary must know how people are related to each other and the importance they place on that relationship. He must also be aware of what unites the group and how the individual receives his identity from the group. Without this knowledge, it is almost inevitable that the missionary will approach the group with the Gospel in a way that becomes a threat to its existence. Such an approach will only hinder church planting. On the other hand, where the missionary is aware of the social structure and how it functions and respects it, he will be able to present the Gospel in a way that does not threaten the group and thus ensure a fairer hearing.

The Enga people of the Western Highlands of New Guinea have a rather tight social structure based on patrilineal descent and residence. Land and its use and division seem to have determined the structure of Enga society. Clans, sub-clans, and patrilineages are tied together not only by their putative blood relationship, but by the land they hold in common over against other groups. The Enga individual is part of the group and receives his identity only as part of the group. Thus a man makes all the major decisions in his life in consultation with the group.

The Lutheran Mission working among the Enga people recognized this unity of the group and made no conscious attempt to break down the natural group. Preaching places were always opened with group approval and individuals were rarely, if ever, enrolled in membership classes without group approval. This approval made it possible to plant the church among many Enga groups and allowed interested individuals to become Christians without breaking into their social ties. I believe this is one of the factors which led to the growth of the Wabag Lutheran Church which now has a baptized membership of approximately 40,000.

Nevertheless, this respectable growth could have been better. The Lutheran Mission was not fully aware of the

strong group consciousness of the Enga people. It should
have been possible to plant the church in such a way that
the entire social unit was won to Christ. Large groups were
reached, but the total clan structure was never won to
Christ. Thus "the congregation became a rival for the
loyalty of the clan rather than an expression of the unity
of the entire people in Christ" (Spruth, 1970: 291). A
more thorough study of the Enga people could have changed
the approach of the Mission and reduced the number of
divided social units. This belated knowledge is now helping
the Mission and the Wabag Lutheran Church to consider
ways of winning the whole social unit to Christ. Only knowledge of the structure of the society will enable missionaries
to bring people to Christ without disrupting the social unit.

World View

Without a knowledge of the world view of a people, much
communication of the Gospel will miss the mark. Missionaries with a scientific world view will tend to dismiss talk
about spirits and try to prove that they do not exist, rather
than showing Christ's power over the spirits. Thus the
struggle is set up between the world view of the people and
world view of Western civilization. Even should the Western
view prevail, it does nothing to bring people closer to
Jesus Christ. On the other hand, it is possible to express
the truth of God's love for men in Christ Jesus in the terms
of differing world views. St. Paul did this in his letter to
Colossae.

The Enga view their world as a three level structure in
which there is a relationship between the living, the dead,
and the sky people. Some missionaries have attempted
to change this world view and prove to Enga people that
there are no such things as ghosts of the dead and spirits.
They have only succeeded in having Enga people give their
own concepts new names drawn from the Christian message,
and certainly have not dispelled their fear and fatalism.
Thus the ancestral ghosts now become a Satan who functions
in the same way as they did. How much better it would
have been to say with Paul, 'Christ has authority over all
of them, He defeated each and everyone,' (cf. Colossians
I: 15-20, II: 10b, II: 15). Such a declaration cannot be made,

however, until the missionary knows what the people believe about the world in which they live.

Religion

No one attempting to understand the people of another
culture can afford to ignore their religion. Missionaries
have seen the need to know the pre-Christian religion of
the people they are working among, if only to be able to
help them rise above it. This, however, must not be the
only aim in studying the religion of any people. Particularly
when dealing with a tribal group, religion often gives the
key to understanding the operational organization and thought
forces of the people. Even though religion seems to be only
a small part of Western thought and action today, it plays
an important integrative role in most societies.

Thus as missionaries we are not only interested in the
culture activity of religion, but in the role it plays in the
life, vocabulary and thought of the people. No real planting
of the Gospel among a given people can take place if the
message does not answer the needs supposedly met by
the traditional religion. Cultic practices and forms may be
changed by a strong advocate, but only where the Gospel
of Jesus replaces the old religion in meeting felt needs, and
becomes the intergrating force for the life of the individual
and the group, has an indigenous church been planted in the
soil. It is here where most missions have failed in their
church planting. Thus one sees caricatures of Western
churches among peoples of many other cultures. Churches
which have been transplanted as exotic species rather than
planted to become indigenous.

The problem of a transplanted religion which has grown
up beside the old, rather than replacing it, can be seen
sometimes in the Enga church. Missionaries not fully
understanding the function of certain socio-religious practices, such as funerary and initiation rites, both urged and
supported their condemnation by the Wabag Lutheran Church.
Yet practices have not died. No functional substitutes were
offered and the society could not successfully function
without them. The Christian finds himself taking part in
death rituals against his conscience and the heathen sees
the church as saying one thing and doing another.

Better understanding of Enga religion would have shown the missionaries that with re-interpretation some of these practices ought to be winnable for Christ; that often the form itself is not in conflict with the Gospel, and the precise problem is itself a biblical issue. Intensive studies now, some fifteen years after the first group of Enga believers was baptized, are showing both missionaries and church leaders that certain changes must be made in order that the Enga church become genuinely indigenous. The failure of the first advocates of the Christian Gospel to understand and empathize with the religious concepts of the people, has blunted the message and garbled the communication.

A further example from the Enga church will illustrate the point. The message of Christ is one of peace, forgiveness, salvation, and freedom; freedom also from the fear of ghosts and spiritual powers. Missionaries of the Lutheran Mission never mastered the Enga beliefs in ghosts and spirits. In dealing with Enga fears, they usually attacked the idea of existence of ghosts, often resorting to the still unproven scientific viewpoint of Western culture. Many Engas were persuaded to admit that ghosts are non-existent. If you ask most Enga Christians if there are temongoes (ghosts of the dead) they will say no. The evidence of their daily life, however, shows that they still very much fear ghosts and spirits (Wagner: 1970). When a large gathering of Christians flees in every direction from a grave site at a Christian funeral simply because someone said that a rustling in the grass was the other temongoes coming to welcome the person being buried, you get a small idea of the fear that still remains in Enga life. A sympathetic understanding of Enga belief is necessary if the Gospel is to be presented as an instrument of freedom and peace in their life. A missionary cannot plant the Church of Jesus Christ in the hearts and lives of a people he does not know. The meaning he intends to communicate will not come through.

Relationships and Leadership

The patterns of relationships between individuals and groups and the practice of leadership are two additional facets of a culture with which the church planting missionary must be thoroughly familiar. McGavran pointed out the great value of using the lines of relationship to spread the Gospel in *The Bridges of God* (1955). To make use of these "bridges" one has to know what they are or how they are formed. The kinship system of the group must be understood, including the level which various types of decisions are made. Answers must be found for the how, when, and why relationships outside the consanguineal group are made. What is important in relationships, blood, reciprocal trade, occupation, age? With answers to these questions the missionary will know the place to plant, the group or individuals to approach first, and the possibility of a people movement. Among a group of people where decisions on important social and religious matters are made on a sub-clan level, a people movement would not develop nor would the church be likely to be indigenous if a missionary extracted either individuals or families in his attempt to plant the church. Furthermore, church planting which ignores the leadership of the group and attempts to establish a new pattern of leadership at odds with the natural pattern will stifle growth and maybe divide the group. Often a failure to incorporate the traditional leadership into the church will cause the Christians to find themselves facing a divided loyalty. The social structure and its patterns of leadership and relationship are thus frozen out of the Christian community, and Christianity itself is guilty of causing social disequilibrium.

The patterns of relationship in Enga society were used somewhat in the planting of the church among them. Individuals were encouraged to bring their families and families were encouraged to reach out for the whole group. Much of the growth of the Wabag Lutheran Church followed just such bridges of relationship. The Gospel moved from one area to another through the relationships established by marriage and trade. People were eager to have their relatives and trading partners hold the faith they had found. Thus missionaries received invitations from community after community to bring them the Gospel.

On the other hand, the fact that the Gospel did not spread to the entire group in a greater people movement can be attributed to the inhibiting factors introduced by the missionaries as they attacked certain socio-religious customs and practices and were willing to receive individuals and families who were in conflict with their group. Western prohibitions at the planting stage may set up extra barriers and tend to keep people from coming to see Christ. Where a conflict develops between Christians and their heathen neighbors concerning these customs, the relationship breaks down, the spread of the Gospel is stopped, and a state of factionalism becomes the norm. Soon people come to accept a pluralistic society and no longer feel the need to bring their neighbors and relatives to Christ. This has been the experience of the Enga church where, at the present time, there is a conflict between the clan group and the congregation. This conflict has not, for the most part, been caused by the offense of the cross, but rather by the various prohibitions of the Wabag Lutheran Church concerning certain important social customs including plural marriage.

A re-study of the more precise functions of the proscribed customs and their relationship to the Word may free the Enga church from its legalism and open the door to further planting and growth. Had such a study been made before death payments, youth initiations and the pig exchange festival were forbidden, the relationship between Christian and non-Christian Enga may have remained intact, leading to a further growth of this church.

Population Distribution and Movement

A church planting missionary needs to know the demographic as well as the cultural features of the area in which he plans to work. If possible, he should consult the local government statistics on population. Where not available, he should survey the area himself to determine the centers of population, and seek out information about the movement of both people and ideas between the various groups. It may be that one group is recognized as the leader. To by-pass that group could hinder the development of the church. News, innovations, and the Gospel may pass more rapidly either from larger centers of population to smaller centers or from the higher status communities to the lesser. The missionary on the spot, however, must base his decisions on his knowledge of the people and their social structure and customs and the receptivity of the group, not on population alone.

The work of the Lutheran Mission among the Enga people began in the heavily populated Lai Valley. This proved to be a valid approach as the church continues to spread further and further to the fringes of the Enga population and beyond to related language groups. In some individual areas, however, growth has been hindered by establishing the main center among either a weak or a non-receptive group. In at least one instance, the placement of the mission center among one group had a schismatic effect and caused two others to seek a rival mission. Thus the action hindered the development of a united body of believers and increased factionalism. Had the missionary been aware of all of the social relationships a more satisfactory program could have been worked out. As it happened, the Christian community in the Upper Lakaip Valley is now divided between the Roman Catholic and Lutheran Churches.

Homogeneity

In addition to determining the centers of population, the church planting missionary should be aware of the homogeneity, or lack of it, among the various groups of people in the area. It will make a difference in the approach and in the way the church develops if the entire population is part of a homogeneous group; centers of population alone may determine the best place to start. On the other hand, where the population is split between many differing subgroups, the missionary must determine whether or not it is possible to combine work among them all; or whether there must be separate approaches to each group including work in different languages.

The Enga people among whom I have worked are not a homogeneous, monolithic group. There are five major divisions of culture and dialect which are obvious to the people themselves as well as to outside observers. While the similarity in culture between these various groups made it possible to use the same approach to all of them, it was necessary to establish mission outreach centers among each major group. There is a certain amount of tension and mistrust between the groups and an under-

standable pride in the local dialect. By working with each
group separately and bringing them together in the church
as Christian brothers, much of the animosity has disappeared. Pastors, teachers, and evangelists are readily
exchanged between areas and there is a feeling of unity. I
doubt very much if this would have been possible had the
Mission attempted to put 'unity' as one of the requirements
of the Faith. This problem of trying to make unity a prerequisite for becoming a Christian rather than an outgrowth
of the life in Christ has long retarded the movement of
Hindu people into the church. B. V. Subbamma has pointed
out the need for presenting the Gospel to an accepting
homogeneous caste group in India (1970). "Men like to
become Christians without crossing racial, linguistic, or
class barriers" (McGavran, 1970:198). The church planter
must be aware of the barriers so that he does not give
people the idea that becoming a Christian means leaving
"my people," and joining another social group.

A Call for Taking Stock

Above I have discussed some of the important factors
which a church planting missionary should know about the
people to whom he is sent. There are many others: land
tenure, marriage patterns, economics, rate of cultural
change, rites of passage, sickness and healing, etc. The
church planter should become as familiar with the culture
of the group as is possible for one not born into it. He will
never have all the answers or be its saviour. He is an
ambassador of Christ, who has come to make known His
Lord to a people whom He loves, and for whom He died. His
task is to plant the Church among these people so that it
becomes a part of their life and culture, allowing the Lord
of the Church to bring about changes through the working
of the Spirit. Only one who is sympathetically aware of the
customs, thinking, hopes, and fears of the people can be
this sort of planter.

The missionary enterprize must not be ashamed of
making use of the tools of anthropology and sociology.
All things are to serve our Lord. Church planting may have
very little to do with agriculture as such, but there are
certain principles which apply to both. In agriculture the

preparation of the field and the method of planting the seed make a big difference in the size of the crop. In like manner, the preparation one makes and the way the seed is planted among a non-Christian people shows up in the indigenous nature, the size, and the quality of the church that grows in their midst. We, who with McGavran, see the need for church growth among the receptive peoples of the world, have no choice but to truly know the people among whom we work. Anything less weakens our witness and closes off communication.

This kind of intelligent empathy with the life style of the people should continue in places where the church has been planted but the mission task is still to be completed. Research of the missionary staff serving with the Wabag Lutheran Church and the attempts at a fuller understanding of the Enga both as an individual and as a group are helping in the re-formation of this church along more indigenous lines. Without this "stock taking," and evaluation, nothing ever would have changed. The Wabag Lutheran Church would have continued to become and remain a Western oriented church trying to survive in the rapidly changing New Guinea Highlands.

Finally then, this article is a plea to other church bodies to take the time to study and to understand the people of their respective areas.

> A congregation which is for people or for the world must wisely work with the basic laws governing the structure of society in the area of its service, giving adequate consideration to the genius (sic.) of peoples, the social values unique to them, and the direction given to the church by the Holy Spirit as He speaks to the church in such circumstances (Meinzen 1966: 37).

Whether you are working among a pre-literate tribal people or a sophisticated sub-culture of a modern industrial society, taking stock of the things that make the people who and what they are cannot but help in communicating the Gospel, in stimulating effective church planting and checking up on its growth patterns.

"And every day the Lord added to their group those who were being saved" (Acts 2: 47b TEV).

BIBLIOGRAPHY:

Arndt, Gerald
    1970   "Cultural Implications of the Enga Indigenous Church"
            EXPLORING ENGA CULTURE: STUDIES IN MIS-
            SIONARY ANTHROPOLOGY, Paul W. Brennan, ed.,
            Wabag, New Guinea, New Guinea Lutheran Mission.
Brennan, Paul W., (editor)
    1970   EXPLORING ENGA CULTURE: STUDIES IN MIS-
            SIONARY ANTHROPOLOGY, Wabag, New Guinea,
            New Guinea Lutheran Mission.
Meinzen, Luther W.
    1966   PRINCIPLES, PATTERNS, AND PROPOSALS FOR
            CHURCH GROWTH, Valliyoor, Tamilnadu, India
            (Unpublished manuscript).
McGavran, Donald Anderson
    1955   THE BRIDGES OF GOD, New York, Friendship
            Press.
    1970   UNDERSTANDING CHURCH GROWTH, Grand
            Rapids, Eerdmans.
Olson, Gilbert R.
    1969   CHURCH GROWTH IN SIERRA LEONE, Grand
            Rapids, Eerdmans.
Read, William R.
    1965   NEW PATTERNS OF CHURCH GROWTH IN
            BRAZIL, Grand Rapids, Eerdmans.
Spruth, Erwin L.
    1970   THE MISSION OF GOD IN THE WABAG AREA
            OF NEW GUINEA, An unpublished M. A. Thesis,
            School of World Mission, Fuller Theological Seminary,
            Pasadena.
Subbamma, B. V.
    1970   NEW PATTERNS FOR DISCIPLING HINDUS, So.
            Pasadena, William Carey Library.
Tippett, A. R.
    1967   SOLOMON ISLANDS CHRISTIANITY, London, the
            Lutterworth Press.
    1968   "The Missionary Problem of Meaning" CHURCH
            GROWTH BULLETIN, Vols. I-V. So. Pasadena,
            William Carey Library, pp. 273-5.
Wagner, M.
    1970   "The Enga Concept of Fear" EXPLORING ENGA
            CULTURE: STUDIES IN MISSIONARY ANTHRO-
            POLOGY, P. W. Brennan (editor), Wabag, New
            Guinea Lutheran Mission.

O Holy Ghost, we lift up for Thee the poor on earth, the masses of mankind, the rural multitudes whose backs are bent with toil . . . The illiterates, the oppressed, the disinherited, the fishermen and the carpenters, the landless laborer, the unskilled—the poor, Lord, the poor for whom Thou didst shed Thy precious blood and on whom Thou didst look with compassion, that we too may see the great masses of mankind as Thy lost children, and like Thee spend ourselves for them. In Thy blessed name. . .

UNDERSTANDING CHURCH GROWTH,
p. 247.

24

COMMUNICATING THE GOSPEL TO ILLITERATE NOMADS
(Ethiopia)

Gunnar Kjaerland

Is there any way and any expectation of evangelizing the nomads of the world? Can there ever be a satisfactory pattern for a church—either the congregation or the place of worship—for a nomadic people? How can the leadership for such a congregation be trained for this kind of situation: especially when we remember that the people are probably illiterate?

My observations among the nomadic Borana indicate that we can expect a response from the nomads only when we have people who can move with them and sit down with them to present the Gospel in the same manner as they pass on their tribal tales. Nomads have the time to talk and listen and they love to do so. Each hamlet can be a church, each evening fire a meeting-place, each family a fellowship group, each father a performer of rituals—and thus may worship spread over the plains.

I believe we can expect devoted Christian people of all ages—illiterates, who listen, worship and obey—to be formed into congregations; but they will have to be reached through a plan which assures them of both contiguity and continuity within their desert world.

Even the desert world is undergoing change. Slowly the nomads are tending to become semi-nomads, often settling (at least for part of the year) near the water-wells or seasonal rivers. Nevertheless we cannot expect them to turn to Christianity until we ourselves have more time and concern to concentrate on them and identify. And identification is far more than a matter of physical geography.

My study of the Borana, though concentrated on Southwest Ethiopia, opened my eyes to the great numbers of nomads in the world at large. Not only was I confronted with millions of people, but millions in dire need. I envisaged Asian herdsmen living in tents, hunting tribes of the trackless forests, Eskimos of the Arctic, semi-nomads of the transhumance peoples, closely-knit tribal units living by plunder on the settled peoples along the fringes of their territory. I asked myself what common denominator they have apart from the nomadic life. The answer came back: they are almost entirely illiterate.

Recently UNESCO conducted a research project which showed that there are millions of people unable to read. This is true in Ethiopia, where the percentage of adult illiterates runs between 95 and 99, as it does also in Afghanistan, Nepal, Saudi Arabia, Yemen, Mozambique and Angola. Twenty other countries were listed as more than 80% illiterate.

A few years ago I was discussing illiterates with a certain mission executive. He told me that in his entire organization, which worked among hundreds of peoples, they had only one expert for illiterates. He was operating in South America at the time—his efforts confined to one continent. From coast to coast in Asia and Africa, though they sent many resources to these regions, no conscious effort was being made to reach the illiterate.

Three of us at Fuller, 1970-1971, gave a good deal of attention to planning work among the nomads. We wanted a plan with a penetrating thrust where only very few of the people had much chance of learning to read. The purpose of this article is to enumerate the points of such a plan, but before doing this there is a question to be asked and answered. Is it possible at all for a western missionary to minister to the nomads; and if it is, then under what circumstances?

Presuppositions

My experiences among the Borana would lead me to believe that an effective ministry, and especially an evangelistic thrust, is certainly possible, if we recognize the following pre-suppositions:

1. One must concentrate on the nature of the problem; the life style of the nomads, so different from our own. If the nomads we desire to win have to make the great religious adjustment; the majority of cultural adjustments should be made by the missionary—he should use the language of the people, use as many of their forms as possible, and engage in dialogue in the tribal manner at the tribal fireside, or the meeting of the ways.
2. One has to realize that a sedentary missionary will never win a nomadic people. One has to be itinerant. At least, one has to go out to them. One cannot expect them to come in to a station.
3. One has to collect data about the people he wants to win. He has to get to know them and he had better be systematic about this. One learns more of a tribal language in a day with the people than in a month with a dictionary—if there is a dictionary.
4. One has to expect that any church he is able to plant will reflect the structures of the nomadic people, and may be the diametric opposite of his home denominational patterns.
5. One has to be ready to remain in the background as much as possible. The indigenous convert, despite the inadequacy of his training, is a better witness than the foreign missionary. New believers should be brought into participant roles as soon as possible.

Given these anthropological insights and presuppositions, I see no reason why fellowships or churches should not be planted among people like the Borana. However, some kind of a strategy or program is needed. One feels that the Bible should lend itself to some kind of curriculum for nomadic illiterates. God who guided Abraham and Jacob; who led the Children of Israel first from Egypt and later from Babylon back to Israel; can surely speak also to the Borana—either with or without printed books.

There ought to be systematic research in each country to establish how the gospel could be presented to illiterates. "A Bible Curriculum for Illiterates" could doubtless bring help for many national workers and missionaries if it were made available.

The picture method has just been introduced in Ethiopia on a large scale and the results seem promising. There is yet much to do in order to provide better material, but what has been done up to now shows response that leads to steady growth in class members. Flexibility is necessary in order to meet the needs of the different people, for some may be more easily reached by using symbols, songs, dances or drama for expression or communication.

In his study upon 'Communication of the Gospel to Illiterates,' H. R. Weber writes of how a journey among the illiterates made him aware of the fact that little had been done to help them understand the Gospel. He began a systematic work among them and had Bible Courses. Besides well-planned instruction they had time for discussion and also for study in smaller groups. In the afternoons they spoke of community life, applying the Christian life to daily situations. He wrote that the climax of the course was on the last evening. They had called the people from the whole village and put on some plays which had been well rehearsed. The parables were first mimed and then presented. The audience was asked to guess which one was being presented, after which the same parable was done again but with the text being read with an explanatory introduction. They gave a final challenge. "The whole became an impressive missionary sermon" (Weber, 1957: 17).

For years there has been a songbook (Evangelical English songs translated in Kenya into the Galla language). The melodies are also imported and the Borana Christians participate in meetings. Again it is amazing how easily they learn these songs. They learn the verses thus having the content of the song whereby they gain further instruction. An accurate observation is made by Weber:

> Wherever we read about illiterates we can detect a certain helplessness. While they are illiterate nobody seems to know what to do with them. There appears to be an undisputed axiom that you have to be literate for proper Bible study (36).

But in point of fact this is not so. A great many people who received the Gospel in the days of the early Church could not have been literate. In any case the scriptures were not circulated in written form at the very beginning. Yet there was a proclamation of the Word and there was singing. We are blessed in our day in having the Word in written form, and some of our national helpers will be able to understand and use it, but much of their communication will have to be through music, story, picture, drama and so forth. Bearing this in mind I now propose a "Bible Curriculum for Illiterates," and of course I have the Borana people more particularly in mind.

A Bible Curriculum For Illiterates

A.   The Need

Much of the world's population is still illiterate. Is salvation only for the literate? No, but a non-written or illustrative method of teaching illiterates is needed. Follow-up instruction of new believers is necessary. Is Bible training for literate believers only? No, but a curriculum for illiterates is needed.

B.   The Plan

1. Large pictures of Bible stories and doctrines— historically true and simple.*
2. Smaller pictures—duplicates of the larger one
    a) to be given to all who attend the lesson—two to each person so when one is given to a friend the lesson can be repeated.
    b) attractive enough to be put on the wall as a continual reminder of the lesson as well as a conversation piece for visitors.
    c) written memory verse and reference at the bottom.

---

*Mr. Kjærland and his associates corresponded with a great number of publishers of biblical pictures, selecting those which seemed most ethnically accurate.

3. Lesson outline booklet
    a) written simply enough for a poorly educated person to read.
    b) Scripture reference of the story or truth—not printed out in the booklet because the Bible should be used in the telling of the story.
    c) list of main points to be covered in the lesson.
    d) memory passage printed out.
4. Cassette recordings in the tribal language of the lesson and memory passage.
    a) will help standardize the instruction and avoid extraneous teaching.
    b) should assist less qualified teachers in presenting the main points.
5. Teachers read and study the lesson in the written language but teach it in tribal or local dialect—all memorization done in local language.
6. Radio broadcast
    a) in national language to help teachers in preparing the lessons.

C. Uses of curriculum

1. Adults who have little hope of learning to read can be taught Bible truth.
2. Children in Sunday School program should have a full coverage of the Bible pictures handed out in class and this will reach parents.
3. Evangelists and pastors will have a good tool and lesson guide.
4. Bible schools and courses could use materials and train evangelists and teachers to use them also; they could be used also for review of basic doctrines for pastors.
5. Age group clubs and schools could use pictures in regular classes or meetings.

D. Other Possibilities

1. Distribution of pictures through traders if there is enough profit in sale to encourage this.

2. Cooperation with existing churches—for distribution and use.
3. Pictures should increase use of the Bible—scripture reference printed on each one.
4. Should encourage literacy once people hear how interesting the Bible really is.
5. Memorization of Bible verses, songs and creed should be stressed each time.

E. Advantages of picture curriculum

1. Easy to use—anyone hearing or reading the story likely repeat it.
2. Picture symbol is worth more than 10,000 words to illiterates—easily remembered.
3. Economical—easily mass-produced and distributed, may be saleable.
4. People are attracted by a taped message in their own language—often considered more true than spoken word of a teacher.
5. Wide usage possible—in many language areas, across age groups, in schools, churches or open-air meetings.
6. Long lasting reminder of the lesson when mounted on house wall—pictures must be treated to retard any insect damage.
7. Non-controversial—Biblical material without narrow bias should draw little opposition and allow many varied church groups to use it.

F. Basis for selection of stories and truths to be taught.

1. Basic Bible doctrines—creation, sin, salvation, etc.
2. Illustrative stories reveal important truths in human situations. Example: Abraham's sacrifice of Isaac replaced by Christ's sacrifice for all.
3. Narrative Bible stories—narrative is often an indigenous means of imparting truth among non-Western peoples.
4. Culturally relevant—group oriented people should

    see how God dealt with family and communal groups
    in the Bible.
5. Use of local calendar as much as possible—planting
   and harvesting cycle, local and national holidays.
6. Visualization of all memorized passages should aid
   retention.

A curriculum is of little value without people approved
and qualified to put it into effect. Two things strike me as
I see the Church growing among my Borana friends. First,
the local leaders who are so useful, have very little opportunity to receive adequate training. They, at least must be
literate to some extent. They have to be introduced to the
Bible as a book. Usually they were the first to respond to
the missionary message, and had the courage to break with
the old customs and walk in the New Way. Many of their
children are now receiving some education.

Second, it is so difficult for these older folk to fit into
learning programs. They need to understand the Bible, but
how can they learn when they are tied to the family and the
herd? It is here that I believe Dr. Winter's pattern, known
as "Theological Education by Extension" speaks to our
situation, because it trains the natural leader at whatever
level he proves to be.

But once again the missionary must be mobile and he
must be proficient in the vernacular—I do not mean able to
read something in that language, I mean that he must be able
to engage in spontaneous dialogue. While it is true that the
educational program for the children will speak to the next
generation twenty years hence, the battle of the moment is
clearly the winning of the adults—the leaders, the decision-
makers, the heads of families—and they are mostly illiterate.

The plan for the use of pictures for approaching illiterates,
or any other scheme for communicating biblical truth, such
as drama, for example, would need to be fitted in to the
structure of the Christian Year. This in turn would have to
speak to the seasonal cycles of tribal life. One would hope
that as the tribes become Christian they would establish
Christian festivals as functional substitutes. Immediately
then, the festival becomes the occasion for using the pictures, cassettes and the dramas. Undoubtedly some kind of
Christian liturgy would accompany the occasion. Special
instruction for the heads of households could also be given

at this time. The Church which is being planted has an indigenous and festival base, geared for an illiterate community.

I offer this as some preliminary thinking on a subject very much calling for attention. Winning the present-day illiterate for Christ is a challenge to Christian mission. I believe it stands beforc us as both an opportunity and a responsibility.

BIBLIOGRAPHY:

UNICEF
  1967   "A Statistical Survey of Illiterates." New York, in
          ENCYCLOPEDIA AMERICANA (International edition)
Weber, H. R.
  1957   THE COMMUNICATION OF THE GOSPEL TO
          ILLITERATES, London, S. C. M. Press.
Winter, Ralph D.
  1970   THEOLOGICAL EDUCATION BY EXTENSION, South
          Pasadena, William Carey Library.

In the countrysides are the superstitious barrio people who may go once a year to mass and more frequently do not. Plenty of them believe that Joseph is God the Father. Few of them ever pray to God, confining their prayers to the saints, angels or Mary. They are unvisited by the priests, uninstructed in their Faith, totally unaware of the moral power available in Christ and the moral demands made by Him.

MULTIPLYING CHURCHES IN THE PHILIPPINES,
p. 41

25

SYMBOLISM AND SYNCRETISM
(Argentina)

Joel Romero

Symbolism

Symbolism is associated with the communication of meaning. Language, for example, as conveyed by the average person to a mixed group, may be variously interpreted, because each person will receive the message through a personalized filter of experience. This is especially so if the group is multi-cultural. Every time a message is transmitted there is some kind of change. It may be a positive or negative response. Symbols, including language, have rhythm. They are aesthetic ways of feeling a message. All disciplines of life have their symbols. Man cannot live without some kind of symbolism.

In this study we shall be concerned with the use of symbols in communication and sharing of religious meaning and experience. As Lessa & Vogt (1965:203) say:

> The human mind comprehends ideas better when they are expressed in visual and auditory symbols, and responds more quickly to such symbols as stimuli . . .

When the Spaniards came to America they found Indians using many symbols in their religious rituals that were similar to their own. Both had holy day observances, temples, rites, fasting and so forth. The Spaniards found it relatively easy to incorporate these new world peoples, partly because of "the manifest impotence of the Indian deities" to protect their devotees from the white man (Fagg 1963: 244), and partly because they accepted Catholic symbolism and gave it their own meaning.

> Because Indians in most areas did not understand the Christian doctrine as it was taught in Rome, they developed variations of their own ... If such communities (Indian villages) had a local deity, a protector whose stone statue stood in the temple and was guarded by the medicine man, it was easy for church teachers to persuade the people to adopt a patron saint instead (Bailey & Nasatir, 1968: 182).

In Argentina many of the mestizos and white men have confused the symbol for the reality. Only a few of the elite and the educated understand that they are not supposed to worship the material objects of their religion. Even non-Catholics tend to fear and reverance the religious statues of stone, silver, and wax. Many who are careless about church attendance worship at private shrines within their homes. One must agree with Nida when he says—

> Even as idols have been hidden behind crosses, so real religious beliefs have often been masked by outward focus . . . Behind the facade of Christian cathedrals, the symbol of the cross, and the days of the saints, there still remained the ancient worship of the spirits enshrined in the mountains (1954: 143).

One is hard-pressed to understand how the intelligensia of Argentina can still believe in the myths, fetishes and still animistic practices. Is it a case of choice between symbolic thinking and reason, and if so is this a rejection of a God-given gift? Do the childhood experiences and the fear that the church has instilled in these people overrule their capacity to think positively? Are they deifying a symbol and forgetting the reality it is supposed to represent? Or are they merely accepting more recent symbols for their ancient gods?

Feeling or Reasoning

I used to witness to an Argentine lawyer the regular rational way, but I could not convince him. One day, after some informal sharing, this lawyer said, "Today you have not tried to convince me. You have hit me from the emotional side. If you go on with this you will win a convert." This convinced me that the Gospel could be presented by feeling—by appealing to the emotional nature of Latin personality. Thereafter the results of my private and public evangelism improved. Without discarding my theological and philosophical reasoning, the Gospel nevertheless was brought to the people where they were. I think I came nearer to understanding the value of symbolism and feeling.

Animistic Practitioners

Dwelling on the place of feeling in the lives of the people of northern Argentina I saw animism as a real factor in their lives. Many who came to our Evangelical meetings were seeking release from fear and suffering. They had physical, psychological and spiritual problems. This is why many Argentines visit the *Curandero,* or curer. This person serves an important function in the community. He meets certain felt needs. The Church needs a similar role on a higher spiritual level.

Many of the elite have confused the curandero with the sorcerer and the brujo or specialist in witchcraft. These are different persons with distinct functions. Nida has classified animistic practitioners in the following way:

> (1) those who engage in black magic (witches or sorcerers), (2) those who foretell the future (clair-voyants, diviners, seers), (3) those who heal or protect by magic means, detect witches and sorcerers, or reconcile offended spirits or gods (medicine men, witch doctors, shaman), (4) those who represent the people in conducting religious rituals (priests), (5) those who speak to the people on behalf of the supernatural power (prophets) (1954: 160).

Sometimes a single person may perform more than one role, but at this point I am concerned with the shaman or curandero, whose role is a benificent one. He is a herbalist, chiropractor, psychologist and a professional counselor. People go to him to counteract some wickedness or malady they believe has been inflicted on them through the ill-will of some unknown person. Or they may have some sickness. He meets deep felt needs in the community.

Sometimes the people come to us, imagining that we are curanderos or professional curers. At least, this indicates a good feeling towards us. It also demonstrates the reality of the felt need. It shows why they still believe in the curandero, even after conversion.

The outlying areas of our mission field are inhabited by folk communities of the cattle country. These areas have many symbolic customs and associated fears. One custom is to spit out the first mouthful of food, or to throw out food before eating, as an offering to the earth goddess, Pachamama. I believe this custom was borrowed from the Quechua. The curandero often combines the priestly role with his own and performs a ritual for the productivity of the land. If the cattle are sick he prescribes some rite or sacrifice to propitiate the goddess who has caused the sickness.

In some Christian sects the preacher may take over the function of the curandero priest and lay his hands on sick cows and pray for them This would appear to be a good functional substitute, but can well become just another form of animism. It could be merely a rite of symbolic or magical purification in folk thinking. On the other hand, with proper teaching perhaps the cult leader may be reaching the country people with the message of his church, that the Lord who created animal life in the first place can surely be prayed to for their well-being. However such a preacher is certainly obligated to make clear his teaching, that this is prayer and not magic. Because of the possible confusion the matter calls for careful consideration and adequate instruction. Arnold van Gennep described a similar case "among the Votyak, when a shaman or ustotuno is called for cases of illness or animal epidemics" (1960: 37). Once again we see how religious practices are related to unsolved problems or communal felt needs.

The people of northern Argentine frequently visit the cemetery to place food on the graves. Especially on the Day of the Dead, or All Saints Day, the observer will recognize many similarities to ancestor worship. If a person is afraid of the cemetery the curandero is consulted to cure the susto or fright. He may prescribe some medicine and also perform a ritual of some kind to drive away the evil spirits. It may be a ritual of reconciliation if the offender has neglected the departed souls of his ancestors. A similar case is presented by Taylor in *The Primal Vision* (1963: 41) where the ritual is performed by an African rainmaker: "The whole process had been a ritual of reconciliation, dependent upon 'speaking out' the offence, the resulting malevolence and the fear."

The animism of the old-lying districts and rural communities of northern Argentina is deep-seated. On the surface the tourist or casual observer may imagine that these rituals are merely the supposed manipulation of magic to control the material world. This is far from the truth. These are spiritual practices. They have spiritual implications that can affect church growth on the level of perfecting the members because they are spiritual and religious exercises, which Christianity seeks to replace. To do this Christianity has to meet the same felt needs and solve the practical problems and curandero claims to do at present.

The curandero is a power to be reckoned with in any pueblo, village or city. Because of the relatively low economic status of the people and reasonable fees, he is a popular person. Usually he has some considerable insight into the fears and ills of the people. Much of the sickness is psychosomatic, and the majority of the cases are cured, giving him great prestige.

Often the curandero will prescribe the carrying of an amulet. When such a person is converted to Christ, whose power is above all power, he discards the amulet. A power encounter has resulted and he proves his change of faith by casting away the charm. This applies also to the converted curandero who must discard his paraphernalia to demonstrate the genuineness of his conversion. In a different part of the world, Tippett (1967: 109) documents a case of a shaman who failed to do this and was plagued by people who came to him for curing and would not take his Christianity for granted until he disposed of his magical artifacts. In the same way a certain curandero of my missionfield was converted. He was a town man and cut himself off from the old routine and declared his new life in Christ. His declaration for the new power in Christ as greater than all he had in the past influenced a number of others to become Christian.

Since the curandero is, as Keesing puts it, a "practitioner in things spiritual" he is a key man in the community. The evangelist, missionary or national, must take him into account. He may, if won, become a powerful ally. On the other hand, if offended or despised, he may become a major obstruction to evangelization.

Syncretism

In Latin America the traditions and associations of the church, the formal and informal contacts and experiences of the people, have been oriented toward animistic symbolism. We have seen that even the intellectual community tends to use the curandero. For the Evangelical missionary the question is how to approach these people, who seem to crave for some symbolic ritual, with an adequate functional substitute that is something higher than formalized magic. The evangelist believes in the power of the Holy Spirit, which he has experienced in his own life and continually seeks through prayer. He believes that only in this power can the demonic powers of animism be dealt with. It is a religious encounter. Somehow the right power has to be transmitted or transformed. As Tippett has said "It is a tragic experience to find oneself with the right kind of power, but the wrong voltage." Symbolism, meaningful to these people, somehow has to be won for Christ.

Is there any light to be found in the symbolism of myths? Many myths are associated with religious beliefs. These are not merely childish explanations: they are part of the sacred tradition. They often control and regulate the moral, social and religious behavior. Of a people very different from those of northern Argentina, Malinowski once wrote that their myth "is not an idle rhapsody, not an aimless outpouring of vain imaginings, but a hard-working extremely important cultural force." The manner in which Christian traditions have been interwoven into Indian myths indicates to me, not that this form of narrative transmission should be discarded, but rather that it should be studied, with the idea of better teaching Christian truth through a somewhat symbolical narrative form rather than our western theological approaches.

Symbols are directly related to church growth and evangelism. The wrong use of symbols will result in syncretism and become a formidable obstruction to discipling the peoples of my area. Or the failure to use any symbolism may also lead to syncretism as people try to meet the voids created by the loss. Syncretism, as I know it, is the fusion of Christian and pagan beliefs and forms.

We are not opposed to indigenous structures, indeed we desire to operate through them. The transmission of our Faith requires forms with which the people will be comfortable. However, some 'Christian' Churches have virtually embraced pagan practices. South of the border from Mexico to Argentina the incorporation of pagan symbols, practices and meanings have resulted in what is often called Christopaganism. Nida (1960: 210) has evaluated this as follows:

> . . . there is very little left of the Christian message. God may be feared because He sends pestilence, famine and earthquake, but He is not the One to whom a person prays. In fact He is not the only god, for He shares his domain with a female deity, the Virgin, the 'Mother of God' and source of life. Furthermore the saints and all the deities are dependent on the people for sacrifice and offerings.

Often the approved symbolism has nothing to do with the cardinal tenets of our Faith. If our ministry is to be held responsible to God for the teaching of the true Gospel the worship forms (symbolism) must be meaningful in a Christian way.

The Roman Catholic Church cannot be blamed entirely for the syncretism which plagues them. They covered too vast a region with too limited a missionary personnel. But they also used foreign words and forms that never became meaningful to the people. Yet one of the best analyses of the problem of Christopaganism comes from a Roman Catholic scholar, Louis Luzbetak, who saw it as "a problem as complex as culture itself." He saw the possibilities of solving the problem only in the following terms: (1) making an exact historical analysis (research), (2) recognizing it as the result of undirected selection, (3) and of undirected reinterpretation, (4) realizing that even a good innovation (functional substitute) does not meet all the functional aspects of its traditional counterpart, (5) recognizing that the acceptance of Christianity is uneven and this encourages syncretism, and finally (6) realising that Christopaganism is generally the result of inadequate or unsound catechetical instruction (Luzbetak 1970: 244-8).

We have no space to develop these valid points and must be satisfied with pointing out that they are all crucial and that they speak to the missionary responsibility, when he sets out to bring about religious change in a society. The old animist society has to be changed. It should be a transformation rather than a destruction. And the new religion has to be meaningful if there is to be a new life.

I cannot help but feel that there is another matter, not mentioned by Luzbetak, which is essential in making our symbolism meaningful but not syncretistic. I speak of the place of the Word of God, the Bible. This implies literacy— at least for the preacher, teacher and pastor. The Bible has value as a book for study, for both moral and spiritual guidance, but it has to be used as a book, not as a mere sacred object for the priest. It is easy to make a fetish out of the Bible, but if we regard it as a gift of God for study our people may learn to know something of the nature of divine guidance. Thus it may be serviceable as a substitute for the divination of the curandero, but it will be used intelligently not in any magical way. A working faith based on Bible study could be added to Luzbetak's final point. I think we are both saying that you cannot make true Christians out of animists without a follow-up program to their conversion, and without incorporating them into the fellowship of believers.

BIBLIOGRAPHY:

Bailey, M. H. and A. P. Nasatir
  1968   LATIN AMERICA: THE DEVELOPMENT OF ITS
           CIVILIZATION, New Jersey, Prentice-Hall.
Fagg, John E.
  1963   LATIN AMERICA, New York, The Macmillan Co.
Lessa, W. A. and E. Z. Vogt
  1965   READER IN COMPARATIVE RELIGION, New York,
           Harper & Row, Publishers
Luzbetak, Louis
  1970   THE CHURCH AND CULTURES, Techny, Illinois,
           Divine Word Publishers
Nida, Eugene A.
  1954   CUSTOMS AND CULTURES, New York, Harper &
           Row, Publishers
  1960   MESSAGE AND MISSION, New York, Harper & Row,
           Publishers
Taylor, John V.
  1963   THE PRIMAL VISION, London, S. C. M. Press
Tippett, A. R.
  1967   SOLOMON ISLANDS CHRISTIANITY, London, the
           Lutterworth Press
Van Gennep, Arnold
  1960   THE RITES OF PASSAGE, Chicago, University of
           Chicago Press (Trans. from French by Vizedom &
           Caffee)

Part VI

Research Techniques
for the
Work of God

RESEARCH TECHNIQUES FOR THE WORK OF GOD

From the beginnings of the Institute of Church Growth at Eugene McGavran sought to bring together experienced missionaries for concentrated research of the fields they knew. Churches were to be studied in their contexts, and those with a common context were to be compared—graph against graph—and written up. His own doctoral work was in education, and he believed in correcting ignorance (the 'fog' he called it) by publishing these comparative studies. The first studies were published in India but many American publishers now have church growth studies in their lists. Certainly these studies have not been of equal value, partly because the researchers were themselves unequal and partly because the time they had for research was unequal; but on the whole McGavran's policy of "getting the facts into print for the Christian public" has paid good dividends, and scores of men who came discouraged went away enthusiasts, and returned to their fields to a far more effective ministry. A decade ago McGavran wrote in his Jamaican study—

The Church grows differently in each population and needs accurate assessment. Church growth is a many-sided process. No formula for it exists. The task therefore is to describe the precise Church which God has built in each specific population, and the ploughing, sowing, weeding, and reaping, which have brought these particular sheeves into the Master's storehouse. Since each Church has its own individuality, founding mission and heilgeschichte, this means hundreds of careful descriptions. These writings on church growth should be done by many . . . they should all bind themselves to a single task—describing the physical increase of the Church (1962: iii-iv).

The articles in this section are, at best, only a sample of the dimensions of church growth research. Several of McGavran's colleagues are exploring new areas. They apply to church growth but have not grown out of seeds scattered by McGavran, in that his colleagues are applying tools from other disciplines. We have not included these in this book.

Dr. Tet Yamamori's study on Japan is based on McGavran's use of the comparative method for studying church growth across a region. Many (but by no means all) of the research projects at the School of World Mission use this model. Yamamori deals with the church as a sociological reality and discusses the question of what is being compared in a church growth study. He bases his findings on the analysis of specific churches from his own field research in Japan and suggests some further aspects of church growth in Japan calling for sociological analysis.

Dr. Barrett deals with statistics of the broader sweep of Africa. As a statistician he is concerned with trends and projections, but he starts with McGavran's dream of discipling

Africa in a generation, and his concepts of discipling and perfecting. He uses material McGavran never had when he articulated his dream; and he explores the whole situation from different perspectives. This is an important article, which no mission executive with an African program can afford to miss. The meeting of McGavran and Barrett is one of the significant events for church growth history.

Ed Dayton was trained as an aerospace engineer. He now heads up the Missions Advanced Research and Communications Center (MARC). We call on his special qualifications at many points and make use of his computer service. He lectures on disciplined planning and data retrieval. McGavran as one of the "Men of MARC" is involved in the MARC program. In this volume, Dayton (as a disciplined planner) takes a hard look at Christian missions, and asks some pertinent questions about the kind of information mission planners need to gather, and how they ought to be using it. He is impressed with the great potential of his field of specialization for the services of Christian mission.

Representing those missionary agencies which Dr. Winter now calls sodalities is Charles Bennett of the Missionary Aviation Fellowship. Few of these organizations have studied church growth as has the M. A. F. A church growth library is maintained at their headquarters, and their members attend our seminars in great numbers. Bennett discusses "Aviation and Mission" and shows McGavran's influence on their program. He indicates the flexibility of aviation for church planting and as a research tool. The selection of the M. A. F. for inclusion in this Festschrift should be regarded as representative of this type of horizontal missionary structure, which might have been (say) broadcasting or Scripture translation.

McGavran himself has always been a man to demonstrate his convictions. He always insisted that research had a legitimate claim on time and funds of people if the Lord's time and funds were to be wisely administered by those He called to ministry and mission. To this end, the S. W. M.—I. C. G. exists as a research institute, not just for the sake of the research itself, but for the sympathetic exposure and correction of human error in our world ministry, so that, by more responsible stewardship of all our gifts, the Lord's Name may be praised and glorified. Thus he wrote for a promotional brochure:

A successful manufacturer constantly evaluates his results and makes plans for the future. He puts aside 5% of his budget for such research. Without this he could not expect his business to grow. Just 5% of your missionary or benevolence giving channeled to the School of World Mission, the world's largest mission research institution, could make a tremendous contribution to the effectiveness in evangelism of the other 95% you spend around the world.

In these days, study of growth of other Churches than our own is not merely possible but highly desirable. No one can afford to neglect the comparative study of church growth. It uncovers a rich vein of knowledge concerning how Churches grow, and increases understanding of God's purposes for His Church and the methods He is blessing to their increase.

The basic methodology for study of other Churches is the same as that used in studying one's own. Secure accurate figures for communicant membership and other pertinent data across the years. Refine the data to eliminate statistical errors and redefinitions. Make sure all the figures are for the same geographical unit. Draw accurate graphs portraying growth histories. Dig out from histories, biographies, interviews, and report the reasons for growth or decline shown in each graph of each denomination. Check all thinking about church growth against the graphs.

UNDERSTANDING CHURCH GROWTH
p. 155.

26

APPLYING
THE COMPARATIVE METHOD
TO CHURCH GROWTH STUDIES
(Japan)

Tetsunao Yamamori

The comparative method is a useful tool of research and is often utilized in church growth case studies. The writer applied this method to his research on the growth and non-growth of Japanese churches (Yamamori, 1970). This article discusses its methodological procedure, summarizes its findings, and suggests further research. The emphasis is placed on methodology.

The purpose of the study was to describe and analyze the growth and development of eight Protestant denominations[1] founded in Japan before 1900 by identifying the factors which made for the growth, or non-growth, for the period between 1859 and 1939. It was historical in its approach and sociological in its use of material and its analysis.

As the implementation of the purpose largely depended upon the method utilized to achieve the desired goal, the methodology[2] must be stated accurately and in detail. The methodological procedure had two major steps.

1. Measuring church growth. The capacity to measure something is predicated on the assumption that the subject of measurement will yield to the principle of measurement;

something to be measured must be objectively measureable. This may sound too simplistic, but when the principle is applied to the matter of church growth, the picture suddenly changes; it is not at all clear. Whether the growth of the church should or should not be measured is to be debated elsewhere. Here we are concerned with the question of whether or not it can be measured. The writer judges that it can be.

First, the terms "church" and "growth" must be defined. The term "church" is variously defined for different purposes. The definition ranges from the strict theological interpretation to the sociological. Theologically, the meaning of "church" is used "in no less than six different senses."[3] Sociologically, the church may be defined as "a man-made institution" in the sense that it is "a set of human relationships organized to facilitate adaption to the Unknown" (Ballard, 1936: 441). While the church, as a divine society, draws its inner courage from the grace of God revealed in Christ and constantly made available by the Holy Spirit, it nevertheless exists in time and space and is composed of men and women vulnerable to human influences and environment. In other words, the church, among other things, is a sociological entity subject to analysis by the principles used in the study of all other human institutions. Only by defining the church as being made up of concrete individuals taking part in the society at large, the study of church growth becomes possible.

The term "growth" indicates an increase of membership constituency composed of men and women who can be counted. Admittedly, this is not the only way in which the church is commonly known to grow. For one example, the church like any special group grows in its creedal and organizational aspects which are pursued primarily by the theologians and historians of the church. While these aspects received our attention in so far as they influenced the physical expansion of the church, they did not serve our purpose of becoming the objective criterion by which the growth of the church was measured. They inevitably involve theological and ecclesiastical value judgments which would cause never-ending arguments centering on the nature of the church and the norms of the Christian faith. For another, the church—its membership—is said to grow qualitatively in patience, humility, kindness, obedience, faithfulness, hope and love. These are the qualities which are measured only by God and not by men. These no doubt influence the kinds of numerical growth obtained, but they themselves cannot be the criteria by which church growth is measured.

Having specified the meaning of "growth," we are confronted with a further difficulty: who among the members should be counted? Nida states the problem succinctly when he writes:

> Even if we restrict ourselves to so-called statistical growth, we really do not know how to count, for in the opinion of some persons one must count only baptized believers (that is, adults), while other church leaders insist that if one is to obtain an accurate view of the significance of the Christian witness it is not only legitimate but necessary to count the total number of persons in the Christian community (1965: 57).

The problem will be intensified when we realize that there are, within the church, members who, according to their religious participation, might be grouped as "nuclear" (most active) at one extreme pole of the scale and as "marginal" (least active) at the other (Fichter, 1954).

Are we justified in counting only the baptized adults and not their dependents? Or should the criterion of comparing the growth of one church with that of another be based on the size of only the nuclear members who constitute the very core of any church? What category of membership (in the face of this obvious confusion) must we use as the standard of measurement? Fortunately, there is a category of membership which has a long and honorable history as the best single measure of the size of a denomination. "Communicants" is the word and category used by missionary statisticians who compiled *World Atlas of Christian Missions* (1911), *World Missionary Atlas* (1925), and *Interpretative Statistical Survey of the World Mission* (1938). In these three books, "communicants" is a technical term meaning "baptized members in good standing." This category does not include catechumens, inquirers, sympathizers, church attenders who are not baptized believers, or infants who have been baptized. The "communicants" of the paedo-baptist denominations and the "members" of the baptist denominations are roughly comparable. The writer uses this word in this meaning.

The problem put forth by Nida may be more clearly elucidated when we distinguish between community and communicants. Any denomination consists of the communicants plus their intimate dependents. Communicants have babies who are Christian, not Buddhist or Shintoist babies. Communicants sometimes grow cold, quit coming to church, or never contribute to the church. Yet when asked if they are Buddhist, Shintoist, or Christian, they identify themselves as Christian. Communicants have aged parents, widowed daughters, and sometimes servants or other dependents who attend church and count themselves as Christians but are not full members. Some denominations seek out and baptize infants and dependents, and keep their names on the roll even if they are inactive for a long period. These denominations say that they report only the baptized, but they baptize very many infants. Other denominations baptize only after much instruction. Whatever they do, both kinds of denominations have intimate dependents who count themselves in some way as Christians. The communicants plus intimate dependents make up the Christian community.

The Episcopal Church in Japan, for example, has for forty years recorded membership under four headings:[5] (1) Active Communicants—adult members only, who commune at least once a year; (2) Total Communicants—adult members only, who are entitled to commune if they choose to; (3) Active Members—members, infant or adult, who have been baptized and take some part in the life of the church; and (4) Total Members—total registered members including baptized infants and adult members, active or inactive, known or unknown.

Let us look at the record for 1938:

Active Communicants	Total Communicants	Active Members	Total Members
11,605	18,192	28,606	47,244

The figure which missionary statisticians through the years have used and are using today (Bingle, 1957), is Total Communicants—18,192 in this case. This category would include, in Fichter's terminology, "nuclear," "modal," and to a certain degree, "marginal" members (communicants) within the church. (Factors like keeping inactives on the

list affect all churches alike). This entity comprising the
category of Total Communicants is the best available set of
figures which will form the basis of comparative analysis
of church growth. But it must be added that a community
of 47,244 (about 2.5 times as large as 18,192) is also an
important figure.[6]

What is meant by "church growth" has been this far
explicated. It is made clear that the growth of the church
can be measured on the basis of numerical increase of
communicants. In order to measure church growth or to
pinpoint specific periods of growth or decline among the
eight churches, the writer constructed Figure 1 (p.385) as
a measuring device. The vertical scale indicates communicants and the horizontal base shows the chronology in
decades. The graph vividly portrays how these churches
grew in Japan.

The accuracy of Figure I in painting the growth picture
depends upon the reliability of the figures. Utmost care has
been taken in compiling the facts; getting them was a long,
complex process.[7] Archives in Japan, America and Canada
have been combed. The writer presents these figures as
the best available. But the question must still be asked:
are the lines of growth shown on the graph reliable? The
answer is affirmative. The official figure for a given year
may be in minor error, for any one of a number of causes.
But the general trend of growth is highly reliable. The
succession of figures cannot be in error; a mistake made
in one year will be corrected in the next.

Once in a while, however, the written material proves
the graph "wrong." The graph may be "wrong" in that the
figure reported is a statistical redefinition. It may be
"wrong" in that the figure reported is a typographical error.
Furthermore, it may be "wrong" in that the figure reported
shows a split or a merger. By cross-examining the written
material, the figures must be refined and correctly interpreted.

In the main, Figure 1 portrays a fair picture of the
trends of growth of eight churches. Whatever the margin of
error, it is far better to discuss the dynamics of church
growth in Japan against the graph than against subjective
factors.

(2) Testing the causes against the graph. The primary

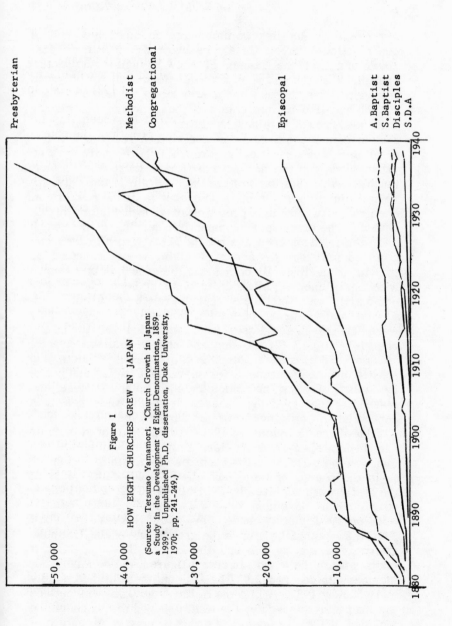

Figure 1

HOW EIGHT CHURCHES GREW IN JAPAN

(Source: Tetsunao Yamamori, "Church Growth in Japan: a Study in the Development of Eight Denominations, 1859–1939." Unpublished Ph.D. dissertation, Duke University, 1970; pp. 241–249.)

Presbyterian

Methodist
Congregational

Episcopal

A.Baptist
S.Baptist
Disciples
S.D.A

1880   1890   1900   1910   1920   1930   1940

50,000

40,000

30,000

20,000

10,000

purpose of compiling communicant membership and of
constructing Figure 1 as a measuring device was to discover and test the causes of growth against the actual
growth. With the graph of growth before him, not only can
the writer see the ups and downs within the history of one
church but also he can compare the growth of that church
with the growth obtained by other churches. Figure 1 is
rich in comparison. Mission and church records are full
of alleged reasons for the growth (where there was no
growth) and for the non-growth (where there was, in fact,
much growth). Failure to have the accurate graph of growth
before him leaves the mission executive or church official
open to the wrong interpretation of growth history of his
church. The practice of constantly referring to the graph
and testing the causes against the actual growth saves one
from committing the error of giving wrong reasons for
growth or decline. By comparing the growth of one church
with that of another, alleged reasons may be further eliminated and a truer picture of church growth procured.

The main sources of information utilized in the study
were: (1) theses and dissertations which had bearing on the
church in Japan; (2) mission and church publications; (3)
'secular publications' comprised of census reports and
studies by the Japanese government and articles and books
by anthropologists and sociologists, both Japanese and
Western; and (4) data gathered from the field research
conducted in Japan by the writer during 1968-69.

Elsewhere (Yamamori, 1970) the findings of this study
are discussed in detail. Here only brief comments are
made on the patterns and structures of growth in Japan.

In the course of the study, the writer became aware of
the fast growth achieved by the Holiness Church (an indigenous church movement originally known as the Oriental
Missionary Society founded by Jyuji Nakada in 1905).
Figure 2 graphically shows the growth line of the Holiness
Church soaring up through the others like a spacecraft
taking off for the moon. In actual figures, the communicant
membership reached 2,987 by 1924 and then climbed rapidly
to 19,523 by 1932. While the Holiness advance was outside
the scope of this study, the writer judged that it should be
included in the discussion in order to clarify the nature of
growth which the eight churches had experienced. Two

distinct patterns of growth, then emerged—one, the pattern of the eight churches, the other that of the Holiness Church. The former is called the school approach pattern, and has been defined as the intellectual and individualistic response to the Christian faith. The latter is labeled as the conversion approach pattern, and has been defined as the experiential and group-oriented way into the church.

The school approach pattern—the most common way into the church in Japan—gathered its members largely from urban middle class intellectuals and their successors. The eight churches concentrated their efforts on the student population either through their mission schools or the government institutions. In fact, those who flocked to these churches were mainly students and white-collar workers (the post-school population). These individuals entered the church one by one while attending schools or shortly after graduation but before their marriage.

The study shows that this pattern of growth contained within it the structure of slow growth in contrast to the conversion approach pattern of the Holiness Church which early adopted a definite policy not to run schools except to train its own preachers and evangelists.

What are the basic elements of this slow growth structure?

The individualistic way into the church is one such retarding element. The converts entered the church one by one, completely isolated from their familial ties. The eight churches rarely experienced entrance into the church of persons in families and groups.

A second element was the way Christianity was understood as a learning. The convert joined the church after a long period of study. Many inquirers, who showed interest in mass evangelistic meetings, or lost the original zeal in the process, were lost to the church.

A third element was its monolithic leadership structure. The task of propagation was largely left to the professional clergy. Historically, this is not difficult to understand. The laity has always been a passive recipient in Buddhist and Shinto worship services. Psychologically, the Japanese Christian could not divorce himself from the sensei-seito (master-disciple) relationship due to the heavy premium placed on learning. Sociologically, the unique character of the white-collar workers influenced the behavioral pattern

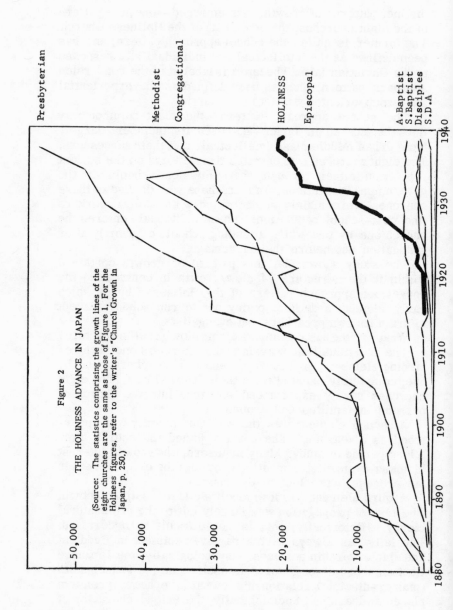

Figure 2

THE HOLINESS ADVANCE IN JAPAN

(Source: The statistics comprising the growth lines of the eight churches are the same as those of Figure 1. For the Holiness figures, refer to the writer's "Church Growth in Japan," p. 250.)

Presbyterian

Methodist

Congregational

HOLINESS

Episcopal

A.Baptist
S.Baptist
Disciples
S.D.A

50,000

40,000

30,000

20,000

10,000

1880 1890 1900 1910 1920 1930 1940

in their religion. The white-collar workers including their successors (students) internalized their faith and became less altruistic towards evangelism than their predecessors. Also, they were most keen on the principle of the division of labor. As far as they were concerned, missionaries and pastors were trained specialists on Christianity. Thus, the doctrine of the priesthood of all believers was hardly practiced among them.

A fourth element was its vulnerability to membership leakage. The members who came into the church one by one through the school approach lacked moral support through web relations.

On the other hand, the Holiness Church countered these retarding elements through various emphases. (1) The Holiness Church utilized the existing social structure advantageously by emphasizing the conversion of the whole family as a unit. One of the advantages to this approach is that the new converts had little danger of social dislocation leading to membership loss. Furthermore, families of Christians would be more open (or hostile) to Christianity by their prior acquaintance with at least one Christian. Finally, being joined by other members of his family, the existing member received the spiritual and emotional support he needed to keep his faith alive and lively. (2) Stress on immediate conversion was the hammer that broke the common pattern of the eight churches. The original zeal of the person who responded to the gospel was not lost due to "months of intellectual training before one can really be said to have entered the Christian life" (Iglehart, 1932: 75). The new convert was quickly taught the fundamentals of Christian faith and was in turn communicating the newly found faith to others. (3) Revivals deepened the spiritual life of the whole church and heightened its evangelistic zeal. (4) The Holiness Church zealously evangelized the remote regions of the empire, but when faced with the solid wall of unresponsiveness, it shifted its emphasis to the more receptive population in the city. (5) The Holiness Church had a multiple leadership structure. It was successful in mobilizing its entire lay membership. (6) The Holiness Church was most equipped to reach the masses and actually received its strongest support from them. In sharp contrast to the eight churches, it gathered within its membership the blue-collar workers, employers and employees of small business concerns, and their dependents. Church leadership came from among themselves. (7) Nakada through his charismatic leadership challenged the entire constituency with the high goals of attainment.

The Holiness Church thus countered the intellectual and individualistic way of the eight churches with the experiential and group-oriented way. It replaced the monolithic leadership structure of the eight churches with a multiple leadership structure. By seeking the whole family as a unit, it increased the web relationship among the church members which contributed towards the lessening of membership leakage. And its emphasis on immediate conversion and subsequent indoctrination helped conserve those persons who would have been lost through the prolonged intellectual training of the eight churches.

It may be concluded therefore, that the church in Japan generally grows when it: (1) takes advantage of the prevailing social structure for growth: (2) overcomes the notion of Christianity as a learning by the program of immediate conversion followed by careful Christian nurture; (3) possesses fervent faith in the saving God and an impassioned zeal for evangelism; (4) concentrates on the responsive population which it is uniquely equipped to reach; (5) develops a multiple leadership structure which mobilizes its entire lay membership; (6) acknowledges the various homogeneous units within the society and creates a multi-dimensional leadership structure which best suits the various social units; (7) follows a definite, comprehensive strategy of evangelism with a high goal of reaching many people; and (8) devises a way to prevent membership leakage by a conscientious attempt to build Christian families.

In concluding, the writer wishes to suggest some areas for further research.

First, a more complete picture of the structure of growth in Japan may be obtained by elucidating the conversion approach pattern. This may be accomplished by contrasting the pattern of the Holiness Church with that of the Kirishitan communities in Nagasaki, with that of the Spirit of Jesus Church soon after World War II, or with that of the Soka Gakkai after 1950.

Second, studies should be made of the cases with notable church growth in the postwar period to see if their patterns differ from the ones described above.

NOTES:

1. The eight selected churches were as follows: (1) The Nippon Seikokai (Episcopal); (2) The Nippon Kirisuto Kyokai (Presbyterian); (3) The American Baptist Church; (4) The Kumiai Kyokai (Congregational); (5) The Nippon Mesodesuto Kyokai (Methodist); (6) The Christian Churches (Disciples of Christ); (7) The Southern Baptist Church; and (8) The Seventh Day Adventist Church.

2. The principle behind the methodology used here is no monopoly of this writer. What is commonly known as 'church growth literature' adheres to it, whether it is explicitly stated or implied. A few notable examples are: Donald Anderson McGavran, HOW CHURCHES GROW (London: World Dominion Press, 1959), chapter XIX; Keith E. Hamilton, CHURCH GROWTH IN THE HIGH ANDES (Lucknow, U. P., India: The Lucknow Publishing House, 1962); Roy E. Shearer, WILDFIRE, CHURCH GROWTH IN KOREA (Grand Rapids, Mich.: W. B. Eerdmans, 1966); John B. Grimley and Gordon E. Robinson, CHURCH GROWTH IN CENTRAL AND SOUTHERN NIGERIA (Grand Rapids, Mich.: W. B. Eerdmans, 1966); Alan R. Tippett, SOLOMON ISLANDS CHRISTIANITY: A STUDY IN GROWTH AND OBSTRUCTION (London: Lutterworth Press, 1967).

3. Stephen Neill, THE CHRISTIAN SOCIETY (London: Nisbet & Co., Ltd., 1952), pp. 296-298. The word "Church" is used to: (1) connote its "mystical sense" in which it is interpreted "as the body of Christ, the Bride, not having spot or wrinkle or any such thing, the Church as Christ intended it to be"; (2) "express the fellowship of all those who now or at any time are or have been of the company of the redeemed in Christ"; (3) "mean all those who at any one time in the world's history are within God's covenant of grace"; (4) "describe the group of Christians worshipping in a single place, and bound together by a common loyalty and an experience in common of the presence of Christ in worship"; (5) refer, beyond the local basis, to the Church of England, the Church of Sweden, and so forth; or (6) signify a denomination.

4. Joseph H. Fichter, SOCIAL RELATIONS IN THE URBAN PARISH (Chicago: The University of Chicago Press, 1954). The entire book is an illuminating discussion of the typology of religious participation on the basis of research conducted in urban Catholic parishes in the United States. He uses such categories as nuclear, modal, marginal and dormant depicting the degrees of participation in the parish life.

5. The Reverend Itaro Matsudaira's letter (March 6, 1962) to the writer containing figures under these four headings 1913-1960.

6. The category "community" is an elastic one, because different denominations define their own "communities" in different ways because the community itself fluctuates. In time of persecution, community will shrink much more than communicants. But while elastic, the category must be used for two reasons.

   First, since the total population consists not of adults, but of adults and minors, parents and infants, therefore the only figures for Christians which can truly be compared with total population is community. If in a population of 1000, there are 100 communicants, it is grossly misleading to say that Christians comprise one tenth of the population. The 100 communicants have at least another hundred dependents, so Christians comprise at least two tenths of the total population. In the case of Japan, it may be necessary to multiply the communicants by 2.3 in order to come up with the community figure. The reason for using the figure 2.3 is the following. The protestant Episcopal Church in Japan has kept careful membership records under four headings for many years (as mentioned earlier): (1) Active Communicants; (2) Total Communicants; (3) Active Members; and (4) Total Members. The average "Total Members" for the last forty years is 2.3 times the average "Total Communicants." There is every reason to believe that the "Christian Communities" of the other major churches in Japan are very similar to the "Christian Community" (listed under Total Members) of the Seikokai; and that the ratio of their communicants or full members to their "Christian Communities" would be somewhat the same.

   Second, since some denominations report only community (for example, the Baptists) when figures are compared, one must either transform communicants into community by multiplying by a carefully determined factor, or he must reduce community to communicants by dividing by that same factor. To report 17,000 members (communicants) for one denomination and 38,000 members (community) for another and let readers infer that denomination two is twice as large as denomination one is extremely careless. Granting that transforming communicants into community involves error, it is minor error compared with the major untruth of comparing incomparables.

7. The writer began by consulting inter-church sources such as ENCYCLOPEDIA OF MISSIONS (1891), WORLD ATLAS OF CHRISTIAN MISSIONS (1911), WORLD MISSIONARY ATLAS (1925), and INTERPRETATIVE STATISTICAL SURVEY OF THE WORLD MISSION (1938). Many histories of Christian mission in Japan were carefully examined. The complete files of THE JAPAN CHRISTIAN YEAR BOOKS (1903-1940) and of THE INTERNATIONAL REVIEW OF MISSIONS from 1912 on were tapped. Membership records were obtained from all eight denominations. Church historians, both Japanese and American, were consulted. Government statistics on church membership were inspected.

World-wide missionary sources and government statistics were found less reliable than denominational. Confusion has been caused by some compilers of world-wide missionary statistics who have taken communicant figures for one survey and community figures for another. Episcopalian communicants given by world-wide sources, for example, should be compared with those given to the writer by the official historian, the Reverend Itaro Matsudaira. (See McGavran, ed., CHURCH GROWTH AND CHRISTIAN MISSION, pp. 165, 166). Government statistics before World War II, on the other hand, were compiled by the Department of Home Affairs mainly for the purpose of religious and political control and showed, as a rule, much less than the figures claimed by various churches and other statistical sources, though there was no real consistency.

The figures given in THE JAPAN CHRISTIAN YEAR BOOKS are generally regarded as more reliable and the denominational figures used in this study closely correspond to them. The trends of growth by both sources resemble each other. Since the communicant figures before 1903 (when THE JAPAN CHRISTIAN YEAR BOOK began) were needed in constructing the graph, the writer used the figures of membership obtained at the denominational mission archives or supplied by their own church historians.

The graph thus constructed, the reader needs to keep in mind, shows the strength of the church which merged within its denominational family such as Presbyterian (1877), Episcopal (1887), and Methodist (1907) on the single line graph collectively as though forming one church even before its merger. This is done partly to reveal the continuity of the particular church throughout the period of this study and partly to permit comparison of the growth of eight churches.

BIBLIOGRAPHY:

Ballard, Lloyd Vernor,
    1936   SOCIAL INSTITUTIONS   New York, D. Appleton-Century Company.

Beach, Harlan P. and Charles H. Fahs (eds.)
    1925   WORLD MISSIONARY ATLAS, New York, Institute of Social and Religious Research.

Bingle, E. J. (editor)
    1957   WORLD CHRISTIAN HANDBOOK, London, World Dominion Press.

Dennis, James S., Harlan P. Beach and Charles H. Fahs (eds.)
    1911   WORLD ATLAS OF CHRISTIAN MISSIONS, New York, Student Volunteer Movement for Foreign Missions.

Fichter, Joseph H.
    1954   SOCIAL RELATIONS IN THE URBAN PARISH, Chicago, The University of Chicago Press.

Iglehart, Charles W.
    1932   "The Churches in 1931," THE JAPAN CHRISTIAN
            YEAR BOOK.
McGavran, D. A.
    1965   CHURCH GROWTH AND CHRISTIAN MISSION, New
            York, Harper & Row.
Neill, Stephen
    1952   THE CHRISTIAN SOCIETY, London, Nisbet & Co.
Nida, Eugene
    1965   "Idealogical Conflicts," in CHURCH GROWTH AND
            CHRISTIAN MISSION, edited by Donald McGavran,
            New York, Harper & Row.
Parker, Joseph I. (editor.)
    1938   INTERPRETIVE STATISTICAL SURVEY OF THE
            WORLD MISSION OF THE CHRISTIAN CHURCH,
            New York, International Missionary Council.
Yamamori, Tetsunao
    1970   "Church Growth in Japan: A Study in the Develop-
            ment of Eight Denominations," Ph.D. dissertation, in
            Duke University.

We have long thought of Africa as "a mission field" in which, against great odds of health and climate, church work was being carried on and missionaries were bravely proclaiming the Gospel. Let us now think of Africa as a continent which God wants discipled in this generation . . . that by the year 2000 all Africa south of the Sahara will be as completely discipled as any country in the West.

HOW CHURCHES GROW,
p. 6.

27

THE DISCIPLING OF AFRICA
IN THIS GENERATION

David B. Barrett

For one hundred years now, the most massive influx into the churches in history has been taking place on the African continent. By 1970, as Table I indicates, 130 million persons called themselves Christians, and were recognized as such by governments; but of these only 100 million had come into touch with the churches or were recognized by them. Thus in present-day Africa, what we may call the largest nominal fringe in history has sprung up on the periphery of the churches—30 million persons who claim to have begun the move into the Christian religion, who have in effect asked to be discipled, but whom the churches have so far been unable to contact or to in any sense disciple. This fringe, which is growing in size at a rate of 4 per cent per year, is usually interpreted by Western observers to be composed of persons who call themselves Christians without any basis in reality; nominal Christians, non-practicing professing Christians, backsliders, and pagans or agnostics trying to ingratiate themselves with Christian politicians, or otherwise seeking the material benefits of Christian profession. This explanation is imported direct from the

TABLE I: THE EXPANSION OF CHRISTIANITY
IN AFRICA, A.D. 1900-2000

	1900	1955	1960	1970	2000
Christians (in millions):					
(a) affiliated to churches	9	52	66	100	300
(b) nominal (not affiliated)	1	15	20	30	95
(c) total (a) plus (b)	10	67	86	130	395
Christians as percentage					
of Africa	7.5	28.0	32.0	32.0	48.3

Notes. The statistics in (a) are derived from returns of
total Christian community known to the churches, including
catechumens, children, fringe members, and adherents.
Those in (c) are derived from government censuses of
religious profession, which are conducted on average
every ten years in about half the countries of Africa.
Those in (b) are derived by subtracting (a) from (c), and
are interpreted in this essay as persons who have requested discipling but whom the churches have so far been
unable to contact. The projections for the year 2000 are
taken from the author's detailed analysis, THE FUTURE
OF CHRISTIANITY IN AFRICA; they are based on the
trends existing over the previous seventy years.

contemporary post-Christian West, and may be relevant to
a declining Christianity among numerically static churches
in Europe and North America; but it has little validity in
lands of rapid Christian expansion and phenomenal numerical increase. Neither does it take into account the sincerity
of the African desire and genius for religion. We must
therefore reject the usual interpretation. A more correct
explanation is that this is one of the problems of outstanding
success in mission. The fringe has arisen because of the
inadequacy of the churches' present mechanisms of Christian initiation, and because of legalism and perfectionism on
the part of many churches. It exists because of a failure in
'statistical compassion' (concern for the fate of the whole
population as opposed to that of a favored minority); and it
continues on indefinitely as a result of an almost total
absence of future-oriented planning in, or between, the
churches.

On all of these subjects, Professor Donald McGavran of
the Institute of Church Growth, Pasadena, has taught, written
and warned for over twenty years with prophetic insight.
The lot of the prophet has been his, too, in that the majority

of his audiences have comprehended neither the immensity
of the situation in Africa nor the urgency of planning to
meet its realities. This essay therefore attempts to describe the plight of the more than 30 million persons caught
in this dilemma, to assess the value of McGavran's contribution, and to examine the prospects for the discipling of
Africa in the coming generation.

The Strategy of Discipling

McGavran's basic philosophy at this point was set out first
in *The Bridges of God: a Study in the Strategy of Missions,*
published in 1955. One of his fundamental themes was that
the intricate webs of human relationship already existing
in extended families formed the most fruitful bridges across
which Christian witness and Christian faith could move to
reach the non-Christian masses of the Third World, in
which Africa presented the greatest opportunity. A second
basic theme was the need for the churches to distinguish
between two stages in the conversion of a people—the
stages of discipling, and of perfecting. By discipling is
meant the bringing of people to the hearing of the Christian
message, to the response of faith, to some kind of commitment or conversion, and to baptism and initiation into the
Christian community. In Africa, this essay holds, an almost unprecedented opportunity has arisen in that some
30 million people are not only ready for such discipling
but have gone on record in government censuses as, in
effect, requesting it. By perfecting is meant the bringing
about of ethical change in the life of the newly baptized or
initiated converts, the achievement of a Christian tradition.
McGavran saw that, with the limited resources available
to the younger churches and their missionary collaborators,
there was a real danger of concentrating on persons in the
second stage to the neglect of persons who wanted to enter
the first stage (1955: 15-16). The present essay will demonstrate that, regrettable though it is, this is precisely what
has happened across Africa.

During the same year, 1955, McGavran also distributed
a mimeographed confidential appeal to missionary societies,
originally delivered orally the previous year, entitled 'The
Discipling of Africa in This Generation,' in which he applied

this philosophy directly to the African situation (McGavran, 1971:126–129). In it he gave seven reasons why it now appeared possible to win the whole of non-Muslim Africa to the Christian faith within a generation, if the churches could be persuaded to initiate a strategy of massive ingathering. Mindful of the closing of doors to evangelism in parts of Asia, he closed with an appeal for immediate action, using the Apostle Paul's call: 'Now is the acceptable time . . .' Despite the cogency and passion of this appeal, however, it aroused no interest at all, no surveys were commissioned, and no new initiatives taken.

With the benefit of hindsight, we can now look back over eighteen years and assess this remarkable document as a tract ahead of its times. Not enough statistical groundwork and analysis had at that time been done by the churches to assess or document the veracity of the basic phenomenon itself.

Before the attainment of territorial independence in Black Africa during the decade 1955–65, it had been fashionable to regard Christianity in Africa as having been over-Westernized by foreign missionaries to the point where it would be increasingly rejected by African peoples after political independence, as the religion of the discredited white races. With that premise, McGavran saw, it was imperative to exhort churches and missions to spare no effort to seize the opportunity before it was too late. What has subsequently happened, however, was foreseen by hardly anyone else. Since independence, Black Africans have poured into the churches in ever-increasing numbers. It is now clear that the era of colonialism with its accompanying missionary paternalism was, far from stimulating the expansion of Christianity, in fact hindering its full flowering. The basic reason why Africa has in the last ten years embraced Christianity and is making of it a genuinely African religion is not the efforts of the vast army of church and mission workers, but the rediscovery of African culture, history, and the African identity and personality, and the parallel discovery that these together with African traditional religion have in fact acted all along as praeparatio evangelica, an indigenous preparing of the way for the gospel of Christ, whose effectiveness had been hitherto completely misunderstood.

The statistical groundwork not available to McGavran in 1955 has now been attempted, and it justifies his appeal in a remarkable fashion. Whilst he was writing, there were, as Table I has indicated, some 15 million Africans in the nominal fringe awaiting discipling by the churches; by 1970, the situation had worsened in that this number had doubled to 30 million. In order to analyse where this massive growth is coming from, Table II therefore presents another aspect of the phenomenon, namely the basic statistics of population increase, both for Africa's total population and for the entire Christian community, over the last seventy years, with estimates for the next thirty years.

The first thing to be noted from Table II is the startling magnitude of the annual increases in the Christian population, which itself goes a long way towards explaining the churches' inability to cope with the dilemma of the nominal fringe. In 1970, there were 6.1 million births into the Christian community in Africa, together with around 1.7 million conversions (from pagan affiliation to Christian profession). This means that, in that one year alone, some 7.8 million persons came to the point where the churches could have, or should have, discipled them—the point of Christian initiation. So far as present statistics indicate, the churches only managed to initiate most of the 6.1 million increase already within the Christian community, together with about half of the 1.7 million conversions; the other million or so persons remained undiscipled and so increased the size of the nominal fringe still further. By the year 2000, these projections suggest, the problem will have become so enormous that the churches will be faced with a nominal fringe of 95 million, and 17 million new persons every year requiring, asking for, or even demanding, Christian discipling and Christian initiation. McGavran's whole argument is that no church or mission can hope to meet a problem of this magnitude without initiating a deliberate and determined policy of discipling, if necessary at the expense of the perfecting of the existing Christian community, and certainly at the expense of the multifold internal activities that take up the churches' time and energy.

To understand in greater depth the dilemma facing those awaiting this discipling, let us now examine the identity of the nominal fringe in Africa which by 1972 had become 32,000,000.

The Christian Fringe in Black Africa

Since the nominal fringe that we are investigating is found entirely south of the Sahara, our analysis from this point describes the situation in Black Africa. Who these millions are, and the depth of their predicament, will become apparent as we examine their identity from a variety of seven different standpoints or perspectives. First we will enquire into their social background.

1. The sociological perspective

Who are these masses, sociologically speaking? The perspective of sociology is concerned to describe people's social origins, social background, and socio-economic characteristics. First, let us describe the whole of sub-Saharan Africa from this point of view. Black Africa's population in 1970 was 265 million, made up as follows: 16 per cent rural-dwellers, and 84 per cent urban-dwellers; 80 per cent illiterate, and 20 per cent literate; earning an average per capita income equivalent to U. S. $70 each year; 45 per cent aged under 15, and 55 per cent 15 years and over. The constituency recognized by the churches is above average on most of these characteristics—more urban, richer, more literate, more educated, more adult in age. By contrast, the nominal fringe around the churches is definitely below average on most of these characteristics. They are largely peasants, agriculturalists, rural-dwellers, more rural in fact than average; poorer than average; less literate and with less formal education than average; and younger than average. Coming from the deep countryside, they are more rooted in and aware of traditional values, tribal culture and customs, and traditional religion. Large numbers are from polygamous families, and traditional marriage patterns are more entrenched.

These facts tend to explain why they are invisible, and therefore uncounted and unplanned-for, so far as the churches are concerned. Christians are relatively easy to find and observe in cities, and statistics are relatively easy to gather there. Public opinion poles with religious questions have in fact been taken in Dakar, Abidjan, Accra, Ibadan, Lagos, Kampala, Nairobi, Dar es Salaam, Pretoria,

TABLE II: ANNUAL GROWTH OF CHRISTIANITY
IN AFRICA, AD 1900-2000

	1900	1960	1970	2000
1. Population of Africa in millions	133	270	344	818
Annual births in millions	5.3	12.7	16.2	31.1
Birthrate per cent per annum	4.0	4.7	4.7	3.8
Annual deaths in millions	4.3	6.8	6.9	8.2
Deathrate per cent per annum	3.2	2.5	2.0	1.0
Annual increase in millions	1.0	5.9	9.3	22.9
2. Christians in millions	10	86	130	395
Percentage of African population	7.5	32.0	37.8	48.3
Annual additions:				
(a) Births in millions	0.4	4.0	6.1	15.0
per cent per annum	4.0	4.7	4.7	3.8
(b) Conversions in millions	0.3	2.2	1.7	2.0
per cent per annum	3.0	2.5	1.3	0.5
(c) Total additions in millions	0.7	6.2	7.8	17.0
per cent per annum	7.0	7.2	6.0	4.3
Annual losses:				
(d) Deaths in millions	0.3	2.1	2.6	4.0
per cent per annum	3.2	2.5	2.0	1.0
Annual natural increase	0.1	1.9	3.5	11.0
per cent per annum	0.8	2.2	2.7	2.8
Total annual increase in millions	0.4	4.1	5.2	13.0
per cent per annum	3.8	4.7	4.0	3.3

NOTES:

1. Population totals, rates, and projections for AD 2000,
   are taken from United Nations publications, 1966-71.
   The annual increase of a population is found by subtracting annual deaths from annual births. Increases
   due to migration are, by comparison, negligible in Africa.
2. Northern and sub-Saharan Africa, including Madagascar
   and the African islands (i.e. the continent of Africa
   according to U.N. definitions).
3. Government census statistics of Christian profession.
4. Birth, death and increase rates of the Christian community are here assumed to be the same as for the
   whole population.
5. These rates are taken from graphs of the total Christians
   over the years.
6. In order that totals in millions in this table should add
   up correctly, rounding of the decimal place has not
   always been carried out.

and scores of other cities across the continent. But the countryside is far more difficult to enumerate. Again, illiterates and persons of low formal education are less articulate and make their presence and opinions felt less. They have little or no leisure to dedicate to the demands of the new religion. They have less money and opportunity for travel to church centers in order to seek instruction.

Over half of the nominal fringe, also, are children under 15 years old, a large proportion of whom are schoolchildren. Although Roman Catholic statistics of baptized persons include children and infants, Protestant statistics concentrate more on adults. In addition, no churches count fringe children who are not yet on the rolls either because they have not yet been baptized, or are not in instructional classes, or because they have non-Christian parents.

2. The religious perspective

Next, we should enquire into the question of what religion persons in the nominal fringe actually adhere to. As we have seen, governments call them Christians in a census; the churches call them pagans. One explanation of this paradox is that both census enumerators and church statisticians are wrong in formulating the question as a set of mutually exclusive alternatives, so that the respondent has to say he is either a Muslim, or a Christian, or a pagan. In some parts of the world, millions adhere formally to two, or even three, religions at the same time. It is well known that in Japan 40 per cent of the population are both Buddhists and Shintoists at once. In a similar manner, the nominal fringe in Africa largely adheres to two religions at once—African traditional religion, and Christianity. Few would be able to articulate their position, but those who could would say they were pagans in one set of circumstances and Christians in another. Multitudes in fact practice a dual religious life in this way. At certain times they engage in Christian activity, even to the extent of Sunday church attendance; but under the pressures of sickness, unemployment, bereavement, perplexity, or other strains, they visit traditional healers or practice traditional ritual. This is true of individuals and families, it is also true of whole tribes.

Double allegiance of this kind is fairly widespread. If this is so, then one can see that both governments and churches are describing the nominal fringe correctly, given their own differing standpoints. To be accurate, however, we would have to elaborate their statements and to explain that the fringe adheres in fact to two religious systems, and is both Christian and pagan at the same time.

It is important to recall at this point that 'pagan' and 'traditional religion' describe the traditional way of life that is essentially African, and out of which no African can opt at his own volition. McGavran drew attention to the disastrous legalism in many churches which refused to disciple or initiate believers who still adhered to traditional elements of functional importance in society, such as polygamy, drumming, or the drinking of native beer or palm wine. As mentioned earlier, African theologians and others are now interpreting this pagan or traditional way of life as essentially a *praeparatio evangelica*. Those in the nominal fringe who practice elements of the two religions are not therefore so inconsistent as the churches once thought.

3. The psychological perspective

We can take this line of interpretation further by considering the subject from the psychological standpoint. Psychology is the study of people's minds, of what they think and why they think it. We have just seen that in the nominal fringe people adhere to two religions at once. It is important to realise that they see little contradiction in their position; in pluralistic ceremonies, participants have no feeling of betraying either one religious tradition or the other.

Traditional religion and culture still constitute a powerful psychological background force on the minds of Africans. Most tribes have long and strong traditional rites and beliefs concerned with the strengthening of the corporate existence of the tribe, the avoidance of misfortune due to wrong social behavior, and the mitigation of the results of natural calamities. In some tribes this complex has religious connotations, and may be termed traditional religion; in others, as with the Acholi of northern Uganda, there are no religious connotations, and the complex may be termed clan ritual. A century of Christian missions and Western education has had little effect on this situation; the African weltanschauung, world-view, remains almost untouched by the scientific world-view. It is still the world-view of those in the nominal fringe; and even if individuals attempted to break with it, they would find it virtually impossible.

A second psychological background factor in sub-Saharan Africa has been religious toleration, and the acceptability of conversion to Christianity. In 1955, McGavran pointed out that many governments in Africa were friendly to the idea of the discipling of Africa; and most of the new governments in tropical Africa since independence have made it clear that, although religious toleration is the norm, they value the Christian faith and ethic highly and want to see them adopted. In such a psychologically favorable and tolerant climate, huge nominal fringes arise composed of people moving into the Christian religion.

There is no doubt that, so far as motivation is concerned, multitudes in Black Africa today are determined to become Christians; this is a further interpretation of the nominal fringe. According to censuses, they are 'professing' Christians; but we would do their efforts considerably more justice if we called them intending Christians, attempting Christians, seeking Christians, even struggling Christians. Millions too, have regrettably to be termed 'failed' Christians—persons who have failed to enter or to pass the catechumenate, due to insistence on literacy or the attainment of perfectionist ethical standards, or insistence on immediate abandonment of all traditional ritual and weltanschauung. The sad fate of many such sincere efforts to become Christian disciples is a major challenge to the Christian mission in Africa.

Then there is the question as to where the psychological turning-point is for these masses in the nominal fringe. At what point in their progression from traditional religion to Christianity do they reach their crisis, their kairos, their day of decision, their moment of choice, after which they become more Christians than pagans? It is usually assumed by the churches that the crucial point is at the time of the catechumenate culminating in baptism, and that those in the

normal fringe have not yet come to that point and therefore
cannot yet be called Christians. The evidence from all parts
of the continent indicates that the crucial point is not
baptism, but a point very considerably earlier in time, and
that those in the nominal fringe have already passed that
point. From their point of view, they have already made
the decision to leave the pagan religious community and to
join the Christian community. They have passed the point
of crisis; psychologically, they are now Christians. One
evidence of this is that they answer 'Christian' when questioned by the government census enumerator. Further, it
has often been said that African Christians, by contrast
with those of the Western world, have a very low view of
the Christian sacraments, and of baptism in particular.
One of the major reasons for this has recently become
clear. Baptism has been allowed by the churches to be so
distant in time from the actual point of decision that it has
become, for persons in the fringe, merely a remote phase
in their future Christian life, a distant goal, and in no
sense the point of Christian beginning, conversion or
initiation.

It is therefore clearer now why the churches do not
include the fringe in their statistics. By its very nature, the
crucial point for most individuals and families is personal,
private, and invisible outside the local or village level.
Officials of the organized churches are very likely to know
nothing about such decisions until months later when the
first tentative approaches are made to them.

4. The ecclesiological perspective

The nominal fringe is comparatively easy to interpret
from the standpoint of Christian ecclesiology, which is the
study of church order and structure. From this point of
view, the nominal fringe consists of people outside the
churches' terminology of membership, and outside their
statistical machinery of quantification; they are persons
whom the churches have no means of contacting, seeing,
enumerating or labelling.

Catechumens, strangely enough, fall on both sides of the
fence. In the Roman Catholic Church, they are never counted
as Catholics, a term applied exclusively to baptized persons

only, but statistics of active catechumens are almost always kept. In some Protestant denominations, catechumens are not counted at all; and in most other Protestant bodies, only those catechumens are counted who are active and regular attenders at classes. But it is often difficult, sometimes impossible, for a peasant in an agricultural area, or for a laborer subject to seasonal variations in the urban labor market, to remain a regular catechumen for the required two to three-year period. Hence a certain proportion of the nominal fringe are catechumens who for reasons of sickness, migration, the demands of their work, or other insurmountable barriers, cannot at present be regular.

Then there is a paradoxical category, recorded by a handful of churches, known as "church-going non-Christians," "worshipping pagans," or "attending unbelievers" — persons who are not church members, nor catechumens, and who in most cases never can be, but who are nevertheless regular attenders at Sunday worship. Although most churches in Africa experience this phenomenon, only one body in Africa has kept and analysed accurate statistics of this category—the Tiv Church in Northern Nigeria. Of its regular Sunday attendance of 199,000 persons over 7 years old in 1,400 places of worship in 1968, 14,400 were communicant members, 10,000 were catechumens, a large number were children over 7, and a large number were described as 'interested pagans'—of whom about 50,000 were polygamists and therefore ineligible for any category of church affiliation. Almost all other churches ignore, in their counting and activities alike, these latter two groups, who thus are forced to remain indefinitely as part of the nominal fringe. We therefore have the remarkable state of affairs that, whereas a proportion of full church members in Africa do not attend church regularly, a proportion of the nominal fringe are regular attenders, despite the knowledge that the churches will never accept them as members. If it came to a choice, presumably, all of our churches would prefer to have attending non-members rather than non-attending members.

Next, there is a very large group of persons, at least 15 million in number, who have in the past been catechumens, or baptized members, or even communicants, in the major churches in Africa; but who are now excommunicated, or self-excommunicated, for the rest of their lives. The reason is found in the centuries-old clash between African marriage patterns and the churches' ideal of monogamous marriage. Most larger churches in Africa have developed complicated codes regulating the marriages of Christians; and any family or couple unable or unwilling to comply with these codes thus knows its marriage is irregular in church eyes, and that its members are therefore ineligible to participate in communion services. Thus in the Roman Catholic Church almost all baptized persons under marriageable age are in communion; but upon marriage, at least a third of all Catholics in Africa become excommunicate, either for contracting a tribal marriage, or for not marrying in church, or for marrying a Protestant or other non-Catholic partner, or for assisting in arranging marriages of these types. In the Anglican and larger Protestant churches, the percentage of excommunicated persons approaches 80 per cent in some areas. Formal excommunication by the church or bishop in such cases is rare; the vast majority know they cannot keep church law, and therefore excommunicate themselves. A number continue as regular church-goers; whereas most feel they are outlawed and not wanted, and gradually become inactive. The majority of the excommunicated Catholics continue to be counted in that church's statistics; but a vast number of the Anglicans and Protestants unchurch themselves completely, are removed from the rolls and statistics, and so become a permanent part of the nominal fringe until the day of their death.

These three classes of unfortunates—inactive catechumens, attending pagans barred from membership, and excommunicated families—are all persons trying to become Christians, who, for reasons beyond their immediate control, get stuck somewhere along the tortuous path of Christian initiation into adult discipleship. But numbers of other classes of person get similarly enmeshed, for different reasons. In fact, a large proportion of the nominal fringe consists of persons who started out well but who then got stuck somewhere along the way. This tragic state of affairs must now be examined in greater detail.

5. The missiological perspective

We now come to our most important interpretation concerning the nominal fringe. Such a fringe is a direct product of successful and ongoing Christian mission. It does not arise in countries where that mission has already won the allegiance of the majority, nor where that mission has become static, nor where it is failing to make converts. Consequently the fringe in Africa requires, ultimately, an interpretation from the standpoint of missiology, the science of the study of mission.

In studies of the remarkable numerical success of Christian missions in Africa, it has been largely forgotten that mission is a dynamic process. It is a process continually in motion, one which is never completed, and one involving a continuous procession of individuals and communities participating in a continuous procession of events. In Africa, mission has usually involved the following stages; an initial request by the populace for an evangelist or catechist; the sending of personnel, their reception by the people, recognition of their credentials; their proclamation of the Word of God, the testimony of Christian living; a long period of the sowing of the seed; protracted discussion and explanation, lengthy examination of the men and their message by the people; and, eventually, the response of enquiring, hearing, seeking, believing, and decision; then, a formal approach to church authorities, with a request for baptism; classes, the catechumenate; and finally, the day of baptism itself. It has also seldom been realized what lengthy periods of time all this involves. The last phase, for example— from the request for baptism to the actual day of baptism, averages five years in present-day tropical Africa.

Thus when a historian of mission reports that 'by 1970 Roman Catholics in Africa numbered 35 million,' or 'by 1970 there were 2 million Baptists in Black Africa,' he is enumerating only those who have reached the end of the above process and are now baptized; the millions who are still moving through the earlier stages are not taken into account, or even mentioned. It is they who form the majority of the nominal fringe.

The nominal fringe is, in fact, the direct product of a rapidly-expanding church in cultures whose psychology of conversion differs radically from the churches' understanding of Christian initiation. When a church is expanding rapidly by conversion among a pagan population, a widespread atmosphere of excitement and expectancy is generated. People seem to sense some imminent parousia or appearing of Christ, and to hear his words; 'The time is fulfilled, and the Kingdom of God is at hand' (Mark 1.15, RSV); and, 'When you see all these things, you know that he is near, at the very gates' (Matthew 24.33). This atmosphere of expectancy results in increasingly large numbers attending church activities, calling themselves Christians, deciding to apply for church membership, and eventually embarking on the lengthy process towards baptism. In Latin American countries, these attending non-members are called simpatizantes, and in the French-speaking world simpatisants—sympathisers. In Africa, the nominal fringe consists to a large extent of such sympathisers—pagans (on the churchs' definition) who are fascinated by the Christian Gospel, the person of Christ, and the church, who admire the churches' ethical position and sympathise with its members' witness, and who earnestly wish to join themselves, although this may not be practicable for several months or even years to come.

The effect of this enormous fringe of simpatisants surrounding the churches is to produce a massive bottleneck effect in which it becomes physically impossible for more than a fraction to enter the churches each year. The churches' machinery of Christian initiation is ponderous and somewhat inflexible at the best of times. When to this is added the physical difficulties of the African milieu, the result is an entrance far too small to cater for the multitudes pressing in from outside.

We arrive then, at our central interpretation of the nominal fringe. In consists of millions of people, young and old, who are crowding outside the doors of the churches seeking their turn to enter. Despite determined and sometimes desperate efforts, only a fraction each year manage to push their way to the front and get in. Meanwhile the millions waiting outside get larger in number, and the waiting periods correspondingly longer. For a church which proclaims 'Now is the acceptable time; now is the day of salvation' (2 Corinthians 6.2), this is an intolerable

situation. It calls for a total overhauling and speeding-up
of the entire machinery of Christian initiation.

6. The evangelistic perspective

We close this analysis with two final evaluations of the
nominal fringe. Evangelism, which is the church's primary
task, has been defined as 'one beggar telling another where
to find bread'—the passing on to other people of the Good
News in Christ. A more formal definition comes from the
Church of England, as follows:

> To evangelize is so to present Christ Jesus in the power
> of the Holy Spirit, that men shall come to put their
> trust in God through Him, to accept Him as their Saviour,
> and to serve Him as their King in the fellowship of His
> Church (Archbishops' Enquiry, 1918).

From this standpoint, how are we to describe the nominal
fringe in Africa? The answer surely must be that it represents an unprecedented phenomenon in the history of
Christian mission. The fringe consists of 32 million simpatisants, persons who are receptive to the Christian presentation, who have a high regard for the Christian faith,
for the person of Christ, for the churches and their members, who want to find the Bread of Life, who have already
passed the point of decision and now call themselves Christians, who know that this is only the beginning of the Christian pilgrimage, who want to be discipled and to put their
trust in God through Jesus Christ, who therefore want to
enter the fellowship of the church to serve Him as their
King as soon as possible, and who are prepared to go to
considerable lengths for a certain period of time in order
to achieve that end. Numerically, at least, this must be one
of the greatest opportunities placed before the Church of
Christ in the two thousand years of its history.

7. The theological perspective

The final evaluation of this phenomenon must be left to
theology, the systematic study and interpretation of the
Christian faith, based on the revelation in Christ, assisted
by insights gained from all other perspectives. From the
theological standpoint, can the millions in the nominal

fringe justifiably be called Christians, and if so in what sense? A clear answer can be given. In New Testament days, the criteria for being a Christian were few and simple: confession with the lips, usually in the words Iesous Kyrios (Jesus is Lord), belief in the heart, and some signs of active discipleship. Baptism would then follow as the norm, but it was certainly not indispensable to the name of Christian; indeed, in the Early Church a pronounced tendency arose to postpone baptism until years of Christian maturity. Augustine of North Africa became a catechumen when a child, and asked for baptism during a boyhood illness; but his devout mother deferred it when death no longer threatened, and he was 33 at his baptism. The great preacher Chrysostom was baptized at 25, the theologian Gregory Nazianzen at 28. Ambrose had not been baptized at all when he was chosen Bishop of Milan, nor Nectarius when he was elected Bishop of Constantinople. At this point the churches in contemporary Africa have become more legalistic than at many other periods in the history of the expansion of Christianity.

Further, this essay has demonstrated that there is very considerable Christian activity and Christian enquiry going on in the nominal fringe. Many parts of the fringe are decidedly more active than many church members themselves, as we have seen in connection with Sunday attendance. In fact, we can now see that the fringe is far from being merely nominal at all.

By the criteria of the New Testament and of subsequent church history, we conclude that the millions in the nominal fringe in Africa can properly be called Christians. The African insight which places the crucial time of decision at a point invisible to the churches, months or even years before the churches are approached, has thus resulted in a positive re-evaluation of one of the most puzzling phenomena in African Christianity.

Conclusion

We can sum up this analysis of the discipling of Africa by describing further what is perhaps the most remarkable case of rapid mass discipling on the continent, namely that of the Tiv tribe of Northern Nigeria. The statistical picture is outlined in Figure I. At the time when Donald McGavran delivered his appeal in 1954, there were some 100,000 Tiv who professed to be Christians; by 1972 the figure had risen to almost one million—a ninefold increase. Vast numbers—around 330,000—attend each week the Sunday services of the two churches, the Tiv Protestant Church and the Roman Catholic diocese of Makurdi. Yet by 1972 the churches had only managed to baptize some 30,000 Protestants (adults only) and 100,000 Roman Catholics (adults and children). In other words, the churches' machinery of initiation has fallen far short of the requirements of discipling a willing people. This case is even more significant when one realizes first that, by any standards, the Christian mission among the Tiv is one of the most enlightened and successful in Africa; and second, that the pastors and missionaries in the Tiv Protestant Church have put into practice McGavran's philosophy and methodology more than the churches in, probably, any other African people on the continent. Despite these advantages, the problems of success—the existence of a massive nominal fringe—are as large here as anywhere else.

So then, the question of the discipling of Africa within the next generation has taken on a somewhat different aspect. It requires not a response by Africa to any supposed invitation extended by Christian churches and missions; rather, it requires a response—a far clearer, more decisive and more relevant response than hitherto—by those same churches and missions to the demand from Africa that adequate means of discipling and Christian initiation be extended to her sons and daughters, and in adequate time. Such a response calls for immediate detailed, interdenominational and ecumenical joint planning by the churches and missions; for the acknowledgement of the churches' responsibility in discipling; and for the clear establishing of priorities. If this is done, the Church of AD 2000 in Africa may well become the most effective missionary church of any continent or era.

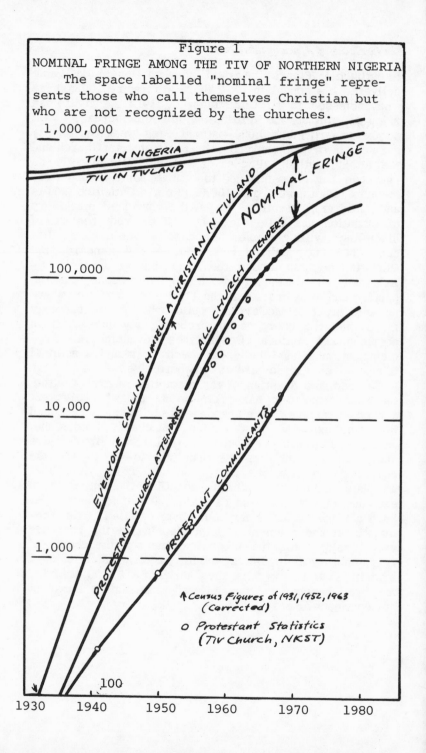

Figure 1
NOMINAL FRINGE AMONG THE TIV OF NORTHERN NIGERIA
    The space labelled "nominal fringe" repre-
sents those who call themselves Christian but
who are not recognized by the churches.

1,000,000

TIV IN NIGERIA
TIV IN TIVLAND

NOMINAL FRINGE

EVERYONE CALLING HIMSELF A CHRISTIAN IN TIVLAND

ALL CHURCH ATTENDERS

100,000

10,000

PROTESTANT CHURCH ATTENDERS

PROTESTANT COMMUNICANTS

1,000

↑ Census Figures of 1931, 1952, 1963
   (Corrected)

o Protestant Statistics
   (Tiv Church, NKST)

100

1930   1940   1950   1960   1970   1980

BIBLIOGRAPHY:

Archbishops' Enquiry on Evangelistic Work, 1918

McGavran, D. A.
    1955   THE   BRIDGES   OF   GOD,   New York, Friendship
            Press
    1971   "Do You Believe the Sixteen-Year-Old Document
            Below?" Published in CHURCH GROWTH BULLETIN,
            VII, 4 (March) pp. 126-129

The computer enables tremendous amounts of information to be stored and recovered instantaneously. When fed the right kind of information, it 'keeps account' of the current state of any enterprise and reports it back to the management when desired.

Such technology, potentially extremely important, has yet to be understood and used by missions, which too frequently do not see the task as a whole and are concerned only about a very small segment of it. Research and information centres will help missions plan their enterprises in the light of the whole and keep them aware of current developments and priority ratings are a variety of technology which Christian mission will undoubtedly use in the years immediately ahead to its very great benefit.

"Technology & Mission" in
CONCISE DICTIONARY OF
CHRISTIAN WORLD MISSION

28

DISCIPLINED PLANNING

AND DATA RETRIEVAL

Edward R. Dayton

In the spring of 1966, Dr. McGavran, Dr. Tippett, and three working missionaries at the School of World Mission, and the author used some aerospace planning methods in an attempt to develop the necessary elements needed to evangelize the world. This ten-weeks' seminar led to the following six points:

1. In order to make progress toward world evangelism, we need a goal for world evangelism. But we do not have a quantitative Biblical description of what it means to evangelize the world. But before we could proceed further we had to pragmatically set forth what appeared to be a reasonable goal for world evangelism. To be useful such a goal must be measurable. We therefore selected as a working goal for our experimental investigation that, "There should be ten witnessing Christians in every town of more than 500 people in the world." Our assumption was that if this goal were met, this would be strong indication that the world had heard the preaching of the Gospel.

2. What would have to happen to reach such a goal? Before this could come about, it would mean that the Gospel would have to be communicated in such a manner that

people would have a valid opportunity to either accept or reject Jesus Christ. Definition centered around the phrase "valid opportunity." So much of what passes for "witnessing" is not witnessing, nor is it giving valid opportunity. A valid opportunity is only given when actual communication of the Gospel takes place. Telling what God has done for me in a foreign language is not communication. Speaking in a vocabulary unfamiliar to the hearer is not communication. Giving someone a tract is not communication (unless it is read and understood). Communication is a two-way function. Information is given, and it meets the need of the receiver, who in turn, responds. It is response that we are seeking—acceptance (which, of course, includes the possibility of of a knowledgeable rejection).

3. With the tremendous diversities of culture and language in the world, it is evident that before such communication can take place, much more research must be done. Research here can be thought of as an act of supplying missing experience. A great deal of such experience-gathering has been done by thousands of Christian men and women who have sought to cross language and cultural barriers to share what Jesus Christ has done in their lives. But with the rapid growth of population of the world, and by the very nature of their success, currently adequate information about what is happening and has happened in the world is not available.

4. However, before a great deal of research can be undertaken, there is a need for more information about what the Church has done and is doing in the world. There is a need to put to work the technology of the world and build, if you will, a more effective communication network within the Body.

5. At the same time there is a need to analyze the resources available. The total investment of all Protestant North Americans in overseas missions in 1969 was less than four hundred million dollars. This was expended by some thirty-five thousand missionaries (plus some estimated five thousand people in the home offices in the United States and Canada). With such limitations the resources available must be a major factor in our planning.

6. Lastly, we saw the tremendous need to undergird all of this with disciplined planning, to seek out God's strategy for the Church in this day. One of the tools that we had already begun to see as valuable, was the planning tool called PERT (Program Evaluation and Review Technique). Dr. McGavran pointed out in an article in World Vision Magazine, October, 1966, "The PERT approach forces those who use it to answer the crucial question: what is the goal?"

In the discussion that follows I would like to cover two of these six elements: planning and information gathering. This discussion is carried out in the context of great change and great opportunity.

We are rapidly moving into a new age for the Church and a new age for missions. The Church now finds herself in every nation state of the world, and faced with a wide variety of situations. These are great extremes of culture, wealth, material prosperity, and possibilities for service. In some places the Body is strong, in other places it is weak. In some places it is shrinking. In other places it is growing rapidly. In the words of Teilhard de Chardin, the world is being compressed ever tighter by a growing web of humanity.

In the midst of this tremendous stress of human striving and tension, new forms of communication are raising both hopes and frustrations within the peoples of the world. At the same time these new forms of communication are rapidly changing the forms of organizational structures as we have known them. Because of rapid communication, many formal structures are no longer needed. Rapidly changing means of communication have also affected church structure. Whereas, in the past, a newly formed church was completely dependent upon communication to the founding church to even understand its role in its country, today the communication media provide input from many different sources.

The Bible assumes the oneness of the Body of Christ. Each member is seen as part of this Body, with a special role to play. And yet, though we are one in Christ, we are separated by cultural, language and national barriers. Our ability to evangelize the world is limited to a degree by these same barriers.

The situation can perhaps be best portrayed by seeing

the world as covered by Christian circles of influence. In some nation states the circles are large and expanding. In other nation states the circles are small, perhaps ineffectual. In many places the circles overlap. The space between all of these circles is the area of "mission." These are the "unevangelized fields" for which the entire Church is responsible. These circles of influence represent the local church's capability to share Jesus Christ with the rest of the world. This capability will vary greatly from church to church, dependent upon their own spiritual maturity and growth, the resources God has put in their hands, and the gifts with which He has ordained them.

One might have imagined that improved world communication would have tended to break down national barriers, instead, world communications seem to have raised the expectation levels of people all over the world. One of the things that they see in the "have" nations is a strong sense of national unity and national purpose. They see such nationalism as a key to their own welfare. This nationalism is a deterrent to church growth because it promotes a view which seems to say, "we are the ABC Church in this country. No work should be done here in the name of the ABC Church without consulting us." Such a view can easily result in a situation such that within national boundaries there may be millions of people who will never hear of Jesus Christ, because the newly planted church within those boundaries will not be capable for years to come (perhaps never!) of reaching them. Although no part of the Body has the right to say to another part of the Body, "you must not evangelize this field because it lies within my political boundary," such unity of the Body should also mean that no part of the Body has a right to move into the sphere of influence (or even the perceived sphere of influence) of another part of the Body without taking them into account. No matter how high the walls of separation another church may build around itself, if the idea of unity of the Body says anything, it says that if we believe that these are those who are brothers in Christ, we must include their goals and their presence in our thinking.

If this assessment of the form and mode of operation of the Church is correct, then one of the greatest needs the Church has today is to become aware of herself and her various parts all over the world, and to become aware of the voids (area of mission) that exist between her circles of ministry. There is a need for primary information about where the Church is, how strong the Church is, and what the Church is doing. This information is needed on a world wide basis. Such information is basic to our understanding of the forms that Christianity has taken and the cultural molds into which it has poured itself.

There are great differences between local bodies of Christ in different parts of the world. The mission methodology that may be appropriate for one people may be quite inappropriate for another. How men and women in one country of the world may act out their Christianity may be in direct contrast to the local mores in another country. The "Bridges of God," for which Dr. McGavran has pleaded, need to be firmly founded at both ends on adequate understanding of our differences as well as our similarities.

Planning

Planning is an attempt to write a history of the future— to us planning 'under God.' In one sense the "present" never exists; it is just the dividing line between what has happened in the past and what is yet to happen in the future. When we go through the process of planning, we try to think through the circumstances that lie ahead based upon the history that lies behind. We do this 1) so that we will encounter fewer surprises, 2) so that we can be effective stewards of the gift that God has given us, and 3) so that we can measure our progress against objectives.

The first assumption of all planning, therefore, is that we do have an objective. If we attempt to talk about strategies or plans that are not related to objectives, then we are talking in immeasureable quantities. Few of us realize how much communication is hindered by unqualified sentences and phrases. One has only to look through the various mission promotional material to discover that adjectives such as "forceful," "dynamic," and "aggressive" when applied to a mission program may mean everything from a one-man effort to a hundred-man field force. We need to quantify our terms by qualifying them.

And so it is with goals and objectives. We set them, not

because we are confident that we have complete wisdom that this is God's specific goal, but rather as milestones against which we can measure progress. We expect them to change, and we are not surprised when they do, but they permit us to talk to one another about our progress, and that greatly enhances communication.

Setting objectives and making plans to meet them are not new to the mission enterprise. The eleven points of William Carey's Serampore Covenant stand out in bold relief to some of the fuzzy thinking that has cropped up from time to time in subsequent years.

In planning strategies the Christian has a special advantage. If we believe that God has a plan for the world, then we must also believe that He has a strategy. We may not be able to comprehend with our finite minds God's mode of operation. We certainly should not conceive of His strategy as being limited by time or by our "mistakes." In one sense God's strategy is new every day. He is taking all of the events of history and working them together for good for the future of His Church. The advantage that we have as Christains is that we can believe that God will always make available to us that information we need to make us effectively part of His plan. And we have the assurance (and therefore should not be surprised) that whether we are in Bangkok or Montreal, Rio de Janeiro, Nairobi, Brussels or Perth, if we are seeking to understand God's plan, we are going to discover one day that each one of us was taking part in one total and overall plan.

This means that as each one of us sets his goals and objectives he is responsible to ask where these goals fit in the larger picture. If we truthfully believe that another mission or another church working within the same political boundary within which we are working is also doing the will of God, then we need to do our best to understand their goals and objectives and to work out our own in light of theirs.

During the past 20 years we have learned a great many new methods of planning. Planning techniques such as PERT, which in the late 1950s were considered to be the esoteric tools of the aerospace industry, have now been demonstrated to be extremely useful to such diverse groups as pastors in Korea and black Christian leaders in the

United States. At the same time, we are moving from a once widely held view that planning might be "trying to do the work of the Holy Spirit" to seeing that planning is a liberating function which helps us to understand better who we are, where we are going, and why we are going there. As one black Christian leader said after a management conference in 1970, "All my life I felt like I was in a box. Now I think maybe somebody has shown me the door."

As we urge mission and church leaders to use modern planning methods, it is important to recognize what planning is and what it is not. Planning is not deciding in advance each step we are going to take and then faithfully following these predetermined steps. Planning is not trying to decide for God what He is going to do. Planning is not the imposition of one person's ideas upon another's.

Good planning can be conceived of as an arrow. It attempts to point the direction in which we should go. As we do our best to ascertain in what direction we should move, planning seeks to keep us from moving in the wrong direction. If we believe we should be heading North, it is much better to discover that instead of the final goal being due North, that it was somewhere Northeast, than to discover that all the time it was South. Good planning assumes measurement of progress. Good planning assumes that we take the first step and then re-plan. Good planning brings together all of the people involved and uses the plan as a vehicle around which they can discuss their common goals and objectives and their progress towards those goals.

Planning is most effective when the entire Christian enterprise is led by men who are committed to managing by objectives. The purpose of an organization is to meet a goal outside itself. Men are brought together in organizational relationships for such goals. Effective organizations are effective because they have been able to motivate men towards these goals in a way which permits each person to see his progress toward the overall objective. How great is the impact of one well-educated, dedicated man who has thought through his strategy and yet remains flexible and open to new ideas.

There is a close relationship between planning, decision-making and problem-solving. The success of all three is based upon good information.

Information

We all make plans, decisions and solve problems on the basis of this thing we call "experience." Either ours or someone elses. This is why we view research or information gathering as supplying missing experience. We will never have enough information, and there is a constant need to assess what kind of information we need and why we need it. The important question is not how well we know something but what difference does it make. The type and amount of information that we need is directly related to the objectives that we are trying to reach. If our goal is to evangelize a given people in a given country, we probably do not need information about the economic systems of countries which are entirely different. On the other hand, if we are thinking about a total world strategy and trying to understand the role of our organization in that total world strategy, we need information of a much broader and comparative nature.

There are a number of ways of viewing the type of information we need. First, we need to get information about our own operations. There is a need to build a feedback system into our organization which will permit us to gather that data which will assess our own performance (management by objectives). Second, there is a need for information about the people or country within which we intend to operate. This may or may not include the third category of information about what others are doing in the same area. This leads us to the fourth category of information which is information about the larger system of which we are a part. All of this information could be described as current history. It is situational.

Another type of information which we need to fill up our bank of missing experience is information about methodology. By definition a method is something which has been worked out and tried to the extent that its characteristics are identified and its results can, hopefully, be anticipated.

Information about methods immediately leads to information about problems that others have encountered. A good idea of what we mean by this kind of information can be had by scanning the table of contents of McGavran's Understanding Church Growth (Eerdmans, 1970). We see such section titles as "Discovering the Why of It, Sources to Search for Causes of Church Growth, Helps and Hindrances to Understanding, The Masses, The Classes and Church Growth, Halting Due to Redemption and Lift, Discipling Urban Populations."

Information gathering has been going on all over the world ever since men found ways to record history, but improvements in communication of such information over the years came slowly until the 1900s. We are presently in the midst of a communications revolution which has been triggered by the explosion of the population and technology. At a time in which the Church is finding herself witnessing in every nation state, God has put in our hands tools which match the need. We not only have a capability of rapidly transmitting information to large numbers of people through the media of radio and television, but through computer and microfilm technology we have a capacity of storing and retrieving vast amounts of information. However, by its very nature, this technology faces us with new challenges. We can become so inundated with information that we will end up worse than we were before. We are beginning to talk about "information overload." Slowly we are recognizing that it is a long, hard task to get the right information at the right time.

If the Church is to share within the various parts of the Body that information which will permit her to get on with her God-ordained task of world mission, there are a number of elements which must be included in the Church's information system.

First, there is a need for comparative data. This implies both an agreement on what data are being collected and a data collection system which permits the comparative data to be collected within a reasonable time frame. Data about the same subject that is collected in different places ten years apart is no better than ill-defined data. Information must always have an associated date of collection. This is a basic part of the information.

In many areas we have made a good start in this type of comparative data collection. *The North American Protestant Overseas Directory* edition for 1968 and 1970 gave us a new level of breadth in comparative statistics. The forthcoming edition of the *World Christian Handbook* will include data that has been collected for over a brief period of time from churches and Christian organizations all over the world against a common definition of terms and a common understanding of church growth statistics. The World Christian Handbook will also include an extensive directory of Christian organization.

Second, there is a need to identify the Church to the Church. It is estimated that there are at least 10,000 Christian organizations in the United States alone. The directory section of the forthcoming World Christian Handbook will list approximately 15,000 churches (denominations) and major Christian organizations. The groupings within the Body have a wide range of objectives and capabilities to meet those objectives. They are experiencing a great variety of results as they work toward their objectives.

These groups represent a huge amount of experience. This experience needs to be made available to others who are facing similar opportunities and difficulties. Within each country there needs to be at least a directory of names, addresses, and a description of objectives and capabilities. This basic information needs to be further expanded to include a description of the people being reached, and the growth of the Church.

Ideally, such information should be brought together in one or more places within the country, a place where those working in the country could have easy access to it. A good illustration of what can be done with limited resources is the Missionary Information Bureau in Sao Paulo, Brazil. MIB carries information on travel, purchasing, government relations, and church growth statistics for the mission community. The existence of this information needs to be communicated and the means for making it available must be found.

Another example is the growing number of highly qualified men and women engaged in mission oriented research. Daystar Communications grew out of the concern of men whose lives had been greatly touched by Dr. McGavran's teaching. The results of this organization's research in both the U. S. and Africa need to be made available. The same is true of research being carried out in hundreds of locations around the globe.

One way of expediting the transfer of information is to

create known information centers, places where one can go for information about information. The Mission Advanced Research and Communication Center (MARC) is an example. This center grew out of discussions between the School of World Mission and World Vision International in 1966. In 1967, MARC became a division of World Vision. Today it is located eight miles from the School of World Mission. It processes over 3,000 requests for information each year. Many of these are passed on to other organizations who have demonstrated knowledge or interest in the area in question. Information about sources of information—individuals, documents, and organizations—is computer-stored and assembled.

Centers such as MARC are needed all over the world. Some may tend to specialize in types of information (literature, literacy, etc.). Others will cover areas such as the Asia-South Pacific. The office operated by the Korean Evangelistic Inter-Mission Alliance in Seoul is an example. But men must be trained for such roles. Men who have already had field experience make apt students and should be encouraged to seek additional training in the social and information sciences.

Fourth, there must be continuing discussion on the type of information to be stored in various data banks. This is an on-going task that cannot be ignored. The problem is somewhat analoguous to the question of standards for electrical power. All the world may use electricity, but unfortunately, there are great differences in voltage and frequency. A 115-volt American washing machine does not work well on 220-volt electricity. We need to agree on the broad major categories within which we will gather data, and then move on to finer classifications. Emphasis should be put on the user. Again, the question is not, "How well do you know it?" but rather, "What difference does it make?"

Fortunately, there is a good amount of secular systems analysis that can be brought to bear on the problem.

Conclusion

We are living in an age in which, for the first time in history, it is technically possible to give every person in the world an opportunity to know the good news that he can be reconciled to God through Jesus Christ. In order to realize such a goal we need clear-cut objectives supported by good planning that results from the right information at the right time. The use of newly developed tools and the establishment of a Churchwide information system are key elements of meeting the challenge.

Will not the methods for the new age, sensing the centrality of church growth now so abundantly possible in the responsive peoples, test all mission activities and apparatus for the degree of church growth which they actually attain? Must not all the paraphernalia of mission work—the technical gadgets, the modern machines, which require so much upkeep and do such wonderful things—be constantly tested against actual achievement in church growth?

"New Methods for a New Age in Missions"

29

AVIATION AND MISSION

Charles Bennett

The surge of creativity and new awareness of foreign cultures which World War II brought to North America spawned numerous new mission agencies, among them the Missionary Aviation Fellowship. Missions had used airplanes before—the Bolivian Indian Mission, the Christian and Missionary Alliance in Borneo, the Evangelical Covenant Church in Alaska and Roman Catholics in South Africa and North China. During 1944 a group of Christian military pilots met on Long Island to talk about post war prospects for mission aviation. George Fisk, who had flown for the C. & M. A. in Borneo before the war, encouraged them to form an interdenominational, inter-mission service agency. Before the end of 1945 they had incorporated as the Christian Airmen's Missionary Fellowship with an office in Los Angeles (by the courtesy of the Navigators) and a membership of 325 airmen, many of them still in military service.

Funds to buy airplanes and pilots overseas came slowly. By the end of 1946 they had only one field aircraft. CAMF pilots also helped at least two mission agencies establish their own flight departments. Similar aviation service missions sprang up in Britain and Australia, using the name "Missionary Aviation Fellowship" which the American organization also adopted. By 1955 the three MAFs together had eleven aircraft, in six countries. Other missions and individual missionaries were operating about twice that number.

Since 1955 mission aviation services have proliferated. Today about 190 airplanes serve Protestant missions and Churches in the Third World. Three MAFs combined operate seventy and account for more than half of all hours flown. Four other missions with professional flight departments operate a total of fifty more. They are the Sudan Interior Mission, Africa Evangelical Fellowship, American Lutheran Church and—by far the largest of the four—Wycliffe Bible Translators. Most of the remaining seventy aircraft are flown by individual missionaries, with varying levels of technical competence and administrative supervision.

The Missionary Aviation Fellowship pilots today work shoulder to shoulder with missionaries and national church leaders of more than sixty-five different denominations and organizations in twenty-four countries and territories on every continent except Europe. Thus a group of technicians, admitted novices in ecclesiastical matters, has become perhaps the example par excellence of grass roots ecumenism in many parts of the Third World.

The Role of the Airplane in Christian Mission

To most people "mission aviation" conjures an image of a tiny airplane carrying a Bible translator or pioneer church planter and his supplies into a remote jungle station. It may also suggest a mission doctor being flown out to conduct a clinic or a seriously ill national being airlifted to the hospital. While these are among its common uses, the mission aircraft today is a highly flexible tool which is used every day in many ways to aid missionaries and church leaders in the planning, planting and developing stages of church growth.

Planning for Church Expansion:

In *Peoples of Southwest Ethiopia* Tippett has pointed out how the airplane can be used as an effective tool for anthropological research (1970: 1-7). In New Guinea, the Amazon jungles and elsewhere, MAF planes have located in a few hours, scattered tribal peoples who would not have been found in months or even years of surface travel. Not only can such isolated peoples be located from the air but a trained observer can estimate their numbers, identify their tribal or cultural affiliation and tell much about their social structure.

Nor are exploration and research flights limited to locating small, hitherto unknown tribes. During a recent study conducted for the Presbyterian Church in Yucatan Peninsula of Mexico we were told that many new settlers were moving into a certain jungle area of about 100 miles diameter. Such recently uprooted people are usually receptive to innovation and thus would be a prime target for a planned evangelistic thrust. But we had no idea of their numbers. In a one-hour flight we were able to look at every village in the region. We could tell whether the village was old or new, Catholic or Protestant, how prosperous, how much contact it had with the government, whether it had a school, whether the men farmed nearby or at a distance and where their supplies and communications came from. Among other things we determined that the number of new settlers had been greatly exaggerated and we modified our strategy accordingly.

Planting the Church:

Missionaries established their first bridgehead in the hard-to-reach Baliem Valley of New Guinea in 1954 by landing an amphibian on a winding river. To this day virtually every move that missionaries (and government officials) make in that area depends upon MAF airplanes.

Also in the mid 1950s MAF pilot Nate Saint lowered gifts on a long cord from his circling airplane in the much-publicized first contacts with the Auca Indians of Ecuador. More recently, Wycliffe Jungle Aviation and Radio Service pilots have talked to other Auca groups by means of a simple radio transceiver which they parachuted to them.

Not all MAF airplanes serve North American and European missionaries nor, for that matter, even highly trained national church leaders. In northwest Colombia one pilot

flies in the interests of a rapidly expanding rural lay movement. There the volunteer evangelists have already reached
out as far as they can travel by land, since they can only
take a few days at a time from their farming. Now they
'leap-frog' out to more distant points where new congregations are already beginning to spring up.

I served as pilot for a similar rural people movement
in southeast Mexico—an area which had an average of
twenty-six congregations for each ordained minister. Probably less than 20% of the 15,000 flights I made there
carried Mexican ministers. Expatriate missionary passen-
gers were even more rare, about one or two per month.
Most flights carried volunteer lay teachers and evangelists.

MAF planes in Brazil and elsewhere fly seminary
students for weekend evangelistic trips to outlying villages.
In Rhodesia a medical evangelistic team of missionaries
and Africans uses the airplane to cover an area of rapid
resettlement in a carefully planned program of church
planting, with specific goals for the number of congregations
to be planted and for eventual missionary phaseout.

Serving Developing Churches:

A decade or more ago MAF leaders talked of the airplane
as a tool to help missionaries supervise larger numbers
of national churches, which they had turned over to the
care of marginally trained local leaders. Today "missionary supervisors" are now pretty much a memory. But
airplanes are still performing vital roles in some countries
by allowing a few highly trained national leaders to supervise large numbers of churches which are scattered over
vast areas where road travel is either impossible or so
slow as to be impractical.

Bishop John Wesley Shungu of the Methodist Church in
Congo, as one example, has almost single-handedly kept
his Church from splintering along tribal lines during the
difficult post-independence days. Because his churches are
located in two widely separated geographic areas, only the
MAF airplanes have enabled him to keep in constant personal
contact with local leaders.

Most Lutheran missionaries to the Philippines have
turned over their jobs to local men recently; but the MAF

airplane has stayed on, now flying Filipino church leaders and medical personnel.

In Brazil the faculties of two different extension seminaries (Baptist and Presbyterian) reach some of their study centers by MAF airplane. In Bolivia the Andes Evangelical Mission operates its own airplane in a similar program. As theological education by extension continues to expand, the mobility of the airplane will undoubtedly be used to advantage in many other regions.

In some areas, when the missionaries leave, the need for mission aviation will virtually cease to exist. This fact of itself may be a criticism of past mission methodology. Many present mission aviation programs—MAF and others —are dependent upon the relative affluence of the expatriate missionary and geared to his (not always necessary) desire for mobility and western standards of living. Other areas, which can make effective use of the airplane for church planting and development after the missionary leaves, will be dependent on outside financing if the air program is to continue.

The Role of the Airplane Pilot

The founders of MAF were strongly influenced by the faith approach to missions and the examples of Hudson Taylor and Andrew Murray. Like the men chosen by the Early Church to administer the distribution of food, they considered themselves servants. The modern day counterparts of the Apostles were, of course, the missionaries— meaning North Americans and Europeans. Saving them time and energy would automatically result in more people reached and converted, on the basis of Acts, chapter 6. True, the missionary occasionally seemed a bit demanding and his goals sometimes not too clearly defined. But what could technicians understand of such matters? The missionary was the expert in things cultural and spiritual. It would have been presumptuous to question his methods.

As the number of MAF pilots increased and they 'hopped' freely between mission outposts, they observed literally thousands of missionaries of every 'stripe' at their work. Try as they might to suppress them, questions kept popping up.

What about the jungle missionary who had been highly effective back in the trail-slogging days, but once we had given him air transport had saddled himself down with a huge compound filled with machines and equipment of all kinds which were completely impractical for that situation?

What about the mission that requested an airplane to fly medical and evangelistic teams but actually used it mostly for shopping trips to the capital?

What about the plane loads of cowrie shells we flew into central New Guinea to pay for airstrip construction and which, like printing press money, devalued the local shells and played havoc with tribal economy?

And what about the missionary who was so insensitive to the feelings of the people he had ostensibly gone to serve that he would scream insults and throw stones to chase them off the airstrip? Or those who use the airplane for "hit and run" evangelism rather than spending enough time to identify with the people in each place?

Perhaps as one pilot wrote home, "Our equipment may not fit our goals. Can we use or modify our use of technology to encourage, aid and develop a grass roots outreach—not tie the local fellowships to the distant overseer, but unite the believers in one general area. To share and grow together" (Johanson, 1969).

The typical MAF pilot is in an excellent position to observe both mission and church, and to make comparisons between different denominations, cultures and geographic areas. Few mission administrators have the opportunity to observe such a broad range of methodology. Whether the pilot grapples with his questions or tries to suppress them, he knows the tension between his deep-felt desire to carry the Good News to those who have not yet understood and his role of an unquestioning servant, which his organization has assigned him and which the low status of the technician in his home culture confirms.

To add to his quandary, he often finds that the local people assume he has higher status than any of the other missionaries. Does he not have the power to make even doctors and government officials wait? Does not the government often have to ask to use his radio for official business? Does he not carry large sums of money from place to place. Does he not collect more for a single flight than the mission doctor does for an operation? Obviously he must wield great power in the mysterious workings of the mission (Gordon, 1971).

In point of fact, some MAF pilots do wield considerable influence in setting mission policy and strategy. This is particularly true in remote and rugged regions where the missionary is totally dependent on air service to survive. Seldom has the pilot used his position to demand a voice in the affairs of the missions he serves. More often than not he has been welcomed into the local or denominational missionary community—as a member of the team. So much so that MAF pilots generally take on the customs and biases of the local missionary sub-culture. However, the pilot is occasionally seen as a threat and kept at arm's length by missionaries. In one or two unfortunate instances he has been treated almost contemptuously——as a mere employee.

On the other hand, in more than one situation, where a number of exclusivistic missions work in the same area, the pilot has been the key to inter-mission cooperation. Because he does not represent a church planting agency he is not suspect as a potential "sheep stealer" and may be the only person who can gain the confidence of all the different groups and draw them together for discussion and fellowship. On a more individual level, sometimes a pilot —with real or feigned naivete—has placed two feuding missionaries or national church leaders together in the back seat of his airplane. Forced into conversation and close proximity, they seldom emerge with the same hostilities.

Obviously the missionary, the national leader and the pilot have much to learn from each other, and when they have treated each other as persons and shared their observations and concerns the life of the Church or Mission has always been invigorated.

McGavran's Influence on MAF Policy

As MAF leaders have struggled to redefine the roles
and priorities of their organization in recent years, McGavran's writings and personal counsel have been invaluable.
I personally first met him ten years ago in Central America.
At the time, I was confused by the conflict between what my
original professors and fellow missionaries had taught me
to expect of Christian mission and the patterns I was actually
observing as I worked with a fast-growing rural lay movement. As I heard McGavran lecture I found myself saying,
"That's it! That's what I have seen." But how could he know
about those things when he has never even heard of the place
where I had been working? It was the beginning of a relationship which transformed my outlook and ministry.

In Bridges of God, McGavran wrote of the all too typical static mission stations which "have an institutional life
many times greater than is needed" by the little local
churches.

> The institutionalized mission station is like an inverted
> pyramid, with a huge accumulation of service organi-
> zations dominating the little congregation. This inevit-
> ably creates the idea that to be a Christian is to receive
> aid from institutions rather than to live a Spirit-filled
> life (McGavran, 1955: 59).

Not only has MAF air service contributed to building up
such top heavy compounds but a mission aviation program
itself qualifies functionally as an "institution," amazingly
similar in its effect to a school, hospital or orphanage.
Like other institutions, it may either contribute to the
growth of the Church or stifle it, depending on how it is
used. It requires specialized personnel and extensive funds.
It can easily contribute to the isolation of the missionary
from the local people, both by encouraging him to accumulate
the symbols of affluence and by literally flying him over
their heads. And, like other institutions, a mission air
service may harm the local economy and disrupt social
patterns if not used wisely.

Similarly aviation programs have a habit of collecting
vested interests that make them difficult to discontinue when
they are no longer needed. Fortunately, it is easier to sell
an airplane or move it elsewhere than is true of a mission

compound. Due in part to McGavran's influence, MAF now periodically evaluates each overseas operation and has already phased out five separate aviation programs that were no longer meeting his criteria.

No longer is a new aviation program started simply because a mission or group of missionaries requests it and has the money to pay for flights. Today a study is made to find out who and where the responsive people are, what the mission and/or national church is actually accomplishing, and whether the air service is likely to make an appreciable contribution to the growth and maturation of the Church. The emphasis is on concentrating resources where they are likely to have the greatest effect, sometimes with the phase-out date determined before the operation even begins.

All new MAF pilots and those on furlough are exposed to the church growth philosophy, as well as orientation into cross-cultural adaptation and communication.

Questions About the Future

The Missionary Aviation Fellowship has no organizational ties with any denomination, either in the homeland or overseas. Yet it is in constant contact with many churches, and profits from their experiences. Because its members come from many denominational backgrounds and are predominantly laymen, they have perhaps less ecclesiastical hangups than the average, They are free to experiment and in an enviable position to innovate. In the past they have seldom taken advantage of this freedom. It remains to be seen whether they will do so in the future.

The organization is presently wrestling with a number of serious questions and studies are already under way to seek practical solutions:

1. Will the overseas churches need air service after the missionaries move on? Even if they have a valid need in some places, how will they pay for flights? Should there be subsidy from abroad, part-time commercial operations or some other method of finance?

2. How does a highly specialized organization with its personnel spread thinly around the world go about nationalization? It is not always practical to turn

things over to a national administration as we have done in Mexico and Brazil because the total operation in some countries consists of only one pilot and his airplane. Is a truly international staff the answer? Will Third World countries allow foreign pilots to operate within their borders indefinitely— even if this is desirable?
3. Does God want MAF to limit itself to aviation and radio services? The need for such services will soon begin to decrease. Should the organization begin to phase-out or are there other valid ministries which its particular contacts and experience have qualified it to perform?

In brief, where is God working in our world today and what place does he have for a small, heretofore highly specialized group of laymen who sincerely desire to serve Him and contribute in any way they can toward the discipling of the peoples of the world?

BIBLIOGRAPHY:

Gordon, Robert
    1971   "What to do with a Pilot" Unpublished paper, (Spring)
Johansen, Robert
    1969   Letter to MAF Goals Committee (May)
McGavran, Donald A.
    1955   THE BRIDGES OF GOD, London, World Dominion Press
Tippett, Alan R.
    1970   PEOPLES OF SOUTHWEST ETHIOPIA, South Pasadena, William Carey Library

CONCLUSION:

WHERE DO WE GO FROM HERE?

The Editor

In the "Greeting" at the beginning of this Festschrift the nature of the volume was stated to be a representative collection of contributions, perhaps of uneven academic merit, not a textbook or manual, but a memory of a typical working day of McGavran's personal contacts, for a man, who, at 75 years of age, is justified in looking back for a moment at the people he has influenced in some way or other.

However, for most who read this book the look will be a forward rather than a backward one, as McGavran himself has continually spoken of "a new era of missions" even under the analogy of the geological shifts of the earth. The question has to be asked then—"Where do we go from here?" Or where are McGavran's colleagues and men going?

God's Purpose and Man's Responsibility

In the field of theology the five contributors demonstrate a certain solidarity and confidence in the authority of Scripture, and its relevant word for the new era in spite of

the social and religious changes going on about us. Each
writer shows an awareness of current debate and the problems of semantics which confuse it, and none are disposed
to have such highly significant terms as mission and evangelism, for example, merely redefined to suit the present
mood! This does not mean they are unwilling to face change.
It merely means they do not intend to accommodate with
respect to the basic belief structure of Christian mission.

This would seem to say that any hope for winning the
world to Christ has to be found in a biblically based theology.
These church growth theologians see no hope for a missionary philosophy hanging on a few isolated "proof texts" and
word studies without context. On the other hand it has to be
a contact not an arm-chair theology. It must possess the
capacity for winning men to Christ in the existential situation: the Spirit of God changing men through the world mission; God speaking to men through men—His stewards.
Thus the two loci of church growth theology are seen to be
the purpose of God and the responsibility of men under God.
It is an activist theology because the God of action calls His
servants to action.

A significant link between the theology of the purpose of
God in mission and the responsibility of his missionaries is
found in Dr. Kraft's article on Ethnotheology. This is an
exploratory dimension and it may be only a foretaste of
things to come. This article recognizes something which
is valid to communicators across both the generation gap
and the cross-cultural gap. Somehow our own ethnocentricity has to be strained out of our theology if it is to be
meaningfully communicated. The new era of mission demands this. I think we will hear much more from the
"cultural and the supracultural."

God's Work in Human Structures

Application of theology requires a theoretical bridge or
structure of some kind for application. The dangers of bad
missionary method comes from two directions, 1) action
based on theoretical or philosophical rationalizations to
fit situations, (economic, for example, or political) with
disregard for, or distortion of, the norms of Scripture, or
2) action based on Scripture but in total disregard to the

contexts where this Scripture has to be applied, and where the Gospel has to find this embodiment. Most bad mission programming can be put down to either departure from Scriptural norms, or failure to allow for anthropological requirements.

The section of the *Festschrift* entitled "God's Work in Human Structures," shows many ways in which church growth writers are reaching out for better strategy in mission. Several of these are what we have come to call "interdisciplinary." In the last decade church growth has demonstrated its capacity for theoretical and methodological cross-fertilization. Here we have evidence of it—Shearer with Psychology, Read with Sociology, Tippett with Anthropology and Kraft with Linguistics. I am convinced this is only a beginning. The old static missiology has suddenly become dynamic. The roots of this movement go back to the Eugene days, when McGavran brought together three of us who have contributed to this section. *Wildfire: The Growth of the Church in Korea, New Patterns of Church Growth in Brazil.*, and (published later) *People Movements of Southern Polynesia* came out of that interaction. It was also at this point that Homer Barnett, the anthropologist, gave us his ideas on innovation, which more than anything else turned us in this theoretical direction. His terminology of advocacy, acceptance and rejection has been taken over by church growth theory.

Ethnolinguistics, which were taught at SWM-ICG for a while in Anthropology II has now been given the status of a full course; likewise Culture and Personality. Both of these areas are rich with 'down to earth' possibilities for missionary application, and each year someone at the SWM-ICG becomes caught up with this potential for new applications in Christian mission. McGavran always said that these sciences were neutral but could be applied for the propagation of the Gospel. He speaks of "harnessed anthropology" (1966). Any harnessed science, of course, requires an accompanying ethic; but the most unethical approach to mission is for the missionary to proceed without any anthropological training at all when this is accessible in any university. With three professional anthropologists on the faculty at SWM-ICG, the theme of God's work in human structures is not likely to be neglected. Thus as we look

forward into tomorrow, as McGavran says "into the sunrise, not the sunset of missions," we see the two ends of the
process: the purpose in the heart of God and the application
in the human situation.

God in Human History

Since the time of Christ the Christian mission has been
an ongoing concern. When William Carey became excited
about the discoveries of Captain Cook and other reports of
hitherto unknown lands, people, customs and languages,
his immediate question was—what does the Great Commission now say to us in our day and generation, with our new
knowledge of navigation which the apostles did not have?
We recall the duration of the Christian mission as specified
by Christ himself "until the end of the age" (Matt. 28:20)
or as Vatican II put it, "the time for missionary activity
extends between the first coming of the Lord and the second"
(1966: 595).

Church Growth studies, especially those which are based
on McGavran's model, are diachronic. This involves us in
the search for records and statistics, and the study of all
kinds of documents. The current tendency of church growth
research is rather toward ethno-history, which is as much
anthropology as history. Church growth ethno-historians
(Tippett, 1968: 15) would probably agree that the values
and methods of historiography have to be employed and set
over against the cultural values and patterns of the people
being researched. The primary sources thus have a double
danger for the untrained and a double potential for the
competent researcher.

This is brought out philosophically by Dr. Winter and
methodologically by Dr. Kwast. One of McGavran's methods
is to reconstruct and verify a statistical picture over a
period of history, if possible in a line graph, and to use
this as a measuring tool, probing the historical records to
explain the behavior of the graph. More and more we are
discovering the need for deeper anthropological analysis at
different points of history. More and more I believe that
our research method will become ethnohistorical rather
than historical. This will require more time than a missionary furlough; but as some men complete the master's

degree in missiology and return to the field with the expectation of putting the following furlough into the doctoral
program, I anticipate some good ethnohistorical studies
will be produced. Some of the earlier church growth case
studies could well be worked over again.

Any theory, to be valid, needs an historical data base.
As long as there is a theory of church growth, historical
studies will be needed. There are two ways of dealing with
this. A historian may be presented with a theoretical
generalization and asked to investigate it. Thus, for instance, Dr. Orr took a look at the evangelism and social
action issue in this book. On the other hand, we live in a
period of history characterized by a sudden increased
availability of primary sources. These are exciting for
their own sake. Many of them have viewpoints which differ
from the standard histories, and have their own evidential
value. I predict that a good deal of mission history will be
rewritten and may-be many of the historical problems of
growth and non-growth will be explained. This in turn will
indicate principles of value in missions today. History is
never entirely in the past. It always has something to say
to us today, as Dr. Winter has pointed out in his article.

God and Man in Field Situations

In this Festschrift we have presented case studies from
Honduras, Colombia, New Guinea, Ethiopia, Argentina,
Zambia and Japan. With the exception of Dr. Yamamori
(Japan) the writers of all these articles are field missionaries or fraternal workers. Each man was asked to deal
with some specific dimension of church growth analysis.
They demonstrate something of what church growth men are
doing in the way of research and recording—new methods
of communication, church planting and leadership training.

In the last analysis church growth theology, theory and
case studies are of little value unless the national leader
and his front line missionary colleague make some practical use of them in their field situations. These studies
bring out numerous points worth deeper consideration, as
for example, problem-solving, decision-making and cross-
cultural confrontations. Most of them have a forward look
and suggest directions for further thought, experiment and

action. Through men like these, McGavran's insights will
certainly go on. These field situation studies show the day
of Christian mission is far from spent.

Some of these studies also emphasize the need for drawing more and more from the resources and methodologies
of the social sciences, and thus they tie in with other parts
of this Festschrift which also call for further research.

Research Techniques for the Work of God

From the very beginning McGavran wanted his program
to include a research institute for data collecting, evaluating
and publishing. The final section of this book covers the
use of such things as the comparative method, statistical
projections, disciplined planning, data retrieval, and technology in church growth analysis. This might have been a
much larger section had space permitted. We had considered an article on interviewing and data collection.
Another on a schema for urban church growth studies fell
by failing to meet the deadline. We are sorry about these
gaps, but Research Method is taught as a subject at the
SWM-ICG.

McGavran's contention has been that without solid research tragic mistakes are made. To the supporting boards
and churches, he has always said that at least 5% of the
budget should be spent in research in order to know how
best to utilize the other 95% (1966). It is a good principle.

Even though we can speak of the continuity of the Gospel
message, the new era of mission certainly calls for new
methods of communication and better understanding of
cross-cultural situations. We live in a day of unprecedented
opportunity, but the situations need researching, for ours
is also a day of deplorable waste of the Lord's money, and
many of his servants are stationed in tragically static
situations. Now then, we ask in conclusion, may we answer
the question: Where do we go from here?

Theologically, the Christian mission stands firm as our
Lord commissioned it until His return. There can be no
talk of the day of mission "being dead." Cross-cultural,
and cross-generation communication certainly demand new
forms of expression and worship, but "He is the same
Lord," and the Gospel is still relevant. God's purpose

stands. He continues to call men to mission and holds them responsible. The world in which we witness and serve is full of opportunities, but it behoves us to husband our stewardship in ripe fields. To be more efficient stewards we are bound to research our opportunities, and to seek to understand the people who are open for the gospel. This means ethno-historical, linguistic and anthropological research within the missiological frame of reference.

There is no longer room for mere academics or for the old static missiology. Missiology as a study must have a dynamic, interacting, interdisciplinary structure. It has to penetrate into the total human situation. The theory of mission has to relate to cultural groups and be validated in the dynamics of real life, not in mere humanization, but in bringing men and groups to Christ according to the redemptive purpose of God, planting fellowships (churches) of men made new in Christ. Their forms need to be culturally appropriate. Their activities need to be indigenously operated. Their self-image needs to be that they see themselves as the Body of Christ, ministering the mind, love and word of Christ in their respective localities. Missions have to get beyond the idea of decision-making mission boards and paternal individuals, to local communities — witnessing, nurturing, serving. The process is already underway but it has much further to go. If Christian missions are to count for anything in the next 20 years the battle has to be won in cities, suburbs and thousands of villages by the planting and revitalization of local congregations.

BIBLIOGRAPHY:

Abbott, W. M. (ed.)
    1966   THE DOCUMENTS OF VATICAN II, New York, Guild Press
McGavran, D. A.
    1966   "The Church Growth Point of View and Christian Mission" Reprint from THE JOURNAL OF THE CHRISTIAN BRETHREN RESEARCH FELLOWSHIP, No. 13
Tippett, A. R.
    1968   "Ethnohistory" in FIJI MATERIAL CULTURE, Honolulu, Bishop Museum Press, pp. 14-18.

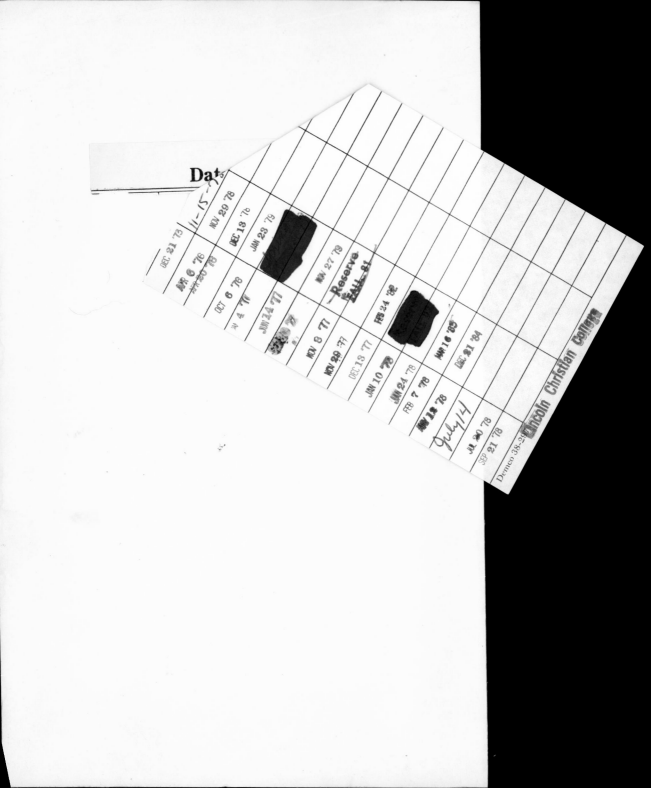